SITES OF EUROPEAN ANTISEMITISM IN THE AGE OF MASS POLITICS, 1880–1918

*Robert Nemes and Daniel Unowsky, editors
Sites of European Antisemitism in the Age of Mass Politics, 1880–1918

Sven-Erik Rose
Jewish Philosophical Politics in Germany, 1789–1848

ChaeRan Y. Freeze and Jay M. Harris, editors
Everyday Jewish Life in Imperial Russia: Select Documents, 1772–1914

David N. Myers and Alexander Kaye, editors
The Faith of Fallen Jews: Yosef Hayim Yerushalmi and the Writing of Jewish History

Federica K. Clementi
Holocaust Mothers and Daughters: Family, History, and Trauma

*Ulrich Sieg
Germany's Prophet: Paul de Lagarde and the Origins of Modern Antisemitism

David G. Roskies and Naomi Diamant
Holocaust Literature: A History and Guide

*Mordechai Altshuler
Religion and Jewish Identity in the Soviet Union, 1941–1964

Robert Liberles
Jews Welcome Coffee: Tradition and Innovation in Early Modern Germany

*A Sarnat Library Book

SITES OF EUROPEAN ANTISEMITISM IN THE AGE OF MASS POLITICS, 1880–1918

ROBERT NEMES & DANIEL UNOWSKY editors

AFTERWORD BY HILLEL J. KIEVAL

A Sarnat Library Book

BRANDEIS UNIVERSITY PRESS
Waltham, Massachusetts

Published by
UNIVERSITY PRESS OF NEW ENGLAND
Hanover and London

BRANDEIS UNIVERSITY PRESS

An imprint of University Press of New England

www.upne.com

© 2014 Brandeis University

Manufactured in the United States of America

Designed by Richard Hendel

Typeset in Huronia and Giza by Tseng Information Systems, Inc.

University Press of New England is a member of the Green Press Initiative.
The paper used in this book meets their minimum requirement for recycled paper.

For permission to reproduce any of the material in this book, contact Permissions,
University Press of New England, One Court Street, Suite 250, Lebanon NH 03766;
or visit www.upne.com

This publication was made possible through the generous support of
Brandeis University's Bernard G. and Rhoda G. Sarnat Center for the
Study of Anti-Jewishness, which aims to promote a deeper understanding
of anti-Jewish prejudice, as well as Jewish and non-Jewish responses to this
phenomenon, from both a historical and contemporary perspective.

Library of Congress Cataloguing-in-Publication Data

Sites of European antisemitism in the age of mass politics, 1880–1918 /
Robert Nemes and Daniel Unowsky, editors; afterword by Hillel J. Kieval.
    pages cm.—(Tauber institute series for the study of European Jewry)
A Sarnat library book
ISBN 978-1-61168-581-7 (cloth: alk. paper)—ISBN 978-1-61168-582-4 (pbk.: alk. paper)—
ISBN 978-1-61168-583-1 (ebook)
1. Antisemitism—Europe—History—19th century. 2. Antisemitism—Europe—History—
20th century. 3. Europe—Politics and government—1848–1871. 4. Europe—Politics
and government—1871–1918. 5. Europe—Ethnic relations. I. Nemes, Robert, editor.
II. Unowsky, Daniel L., 1966–, editor.
DS146.E85S58 2014
305.892'4009409034—dc23

                                                                2014003200

5 4 3 2 1

CONTENTS

ACKNOWLEDGMENTS

It is a great pleasure to thank the institutions that supported us in various ways and the people who offered advice and assistance during the long process of bringing this book to publication. We are fortunate to have enjoyed generous travel and research support from the departments of history at Colgate University and the University of Memphis. We are grateful that both universities continue to place great value on the advance of knowledge in the humanities and social sciences. The editors and contributors benefited from the opportunity to participate in and organize panels related to this volume at conferences hosted by the Association for the Study of Nationalities, the American Historical Association, and the Association for Jewish Studies. We also want to thank Werner Bergmann, Ulrich Wyrwa, Tim Buchen, and the Center for Research on Antisemitism at the Technical University of Berlin for inviting Daniel Unowsky to speak about his work and the project represented in this volume. Several contributors are affiliated with the Center or recently have completed doctorates there. Their scholarship is a testament to the success of this institution.

We were humbled by the contributors' dedication, commitment, and willingness to work with us as we shaped the volume into a coherent whole. We thank Hillel Kieval for his close reading of all the chapters and for his generosity and patience. In addition to his inspired Afterword, he shared numerous insights from his own work with us. Many other colleagues offered suggestions for improvements after listening to conference papers or reading part or all of the manuscript. We are especially grateful to Marsha Rozenblit, Jonathan Sarna, Helmut Walser Smith, Harald Binder, Ted Weeks, and Rebekah Klein-Pejšová. The authors would like to thank Noah Dauber for putting them on the track of "Dreyfus in Kasrilevka."

It has been a wonderful experience to work with the editors and staff at Brandeis University Press, and we are thrilled to have this volume appear in the Tauber Institute Series for the Study of European Jewry. Our thanks go to Phyllis Deutsch, Susan Abel, and Elizabeth Forsaith for shepherding the manuscript through the review process and beyond.

We cannot let this opportunity pass without acknowledging the debt we owe to our teacher István Deák. His magnificent scholarship, meticulous attention to detail, willingness to challenge conventional interpretations, and *Menschlichkeit* remain a model for us and so many others.

SITES OF EUROPEAN ANTISEMITISM IN THE AGE OF MASS POLITICS, 1880–1918

pay attention to what happens in France (and vice-versa)? How do residents of small towns and villages explain the breakdown of their social order? Finally, how do state and local authorities respond when minorities are persecuted?

These questions drive this book. *Sites of European Antisemitism in the Age of Mass Politics* examines the unexpected upsurge of antisemitism that shook Europe in the decades around 1900. Following in the footsteps of Sholem Aleichem, the book ventures into Europe's small towns and villages, it looks at episodes of violence and discrimination, and it listens carefully to the locals' stories.[4] The result is a series of case studies of antisemitism from different parts of Europe. Together they reveal the many factors that produced modern antisemitism and illustrate the many forms it took. By stretching from Great Britain to the Russian Empire, the book looks for elements common to antisemitic activity across the continent, including rumors, riots, and religiosity. The essays collected here take seriously Sholem Aleichem's suggestion that events such as France's Dreyfus affair could reverberate in places as far removed as Russia's villages. This book thus follows the threads, however thin, that tied seemingly spontaneous and local antisemitic behavior in one part of Europe with another. What happened on the ground—in taverns, streets, churches, and meeting halls—we contend, can help unravel the knotty problem of violence and exclusion in modern mass politics, both in the East and in the West, in cities and in villages.

■ Much has been written about European antisemitism, and with good reason. Antisemitism runs through the history of modern Europe. Careful study of nineteenth-century antisemitism can help us map the twisted road that led to Auschwitz and the Holocaust.[5] It helps explain the emigration of millions of East European Jews in the decades around 1900; it helps us understand the political choices made by Jews who remained, many of whom turned for answers to socialism and Zionism.[6] Antisemitism flowed into the political mainstream, coursing through new, illiberal political parties (nationalist, Christian Social, populist, and conservative) and murmuring in the "cultural code" of the era's Christian elites.[7] The history of antisemitism also can clarify important topics in social and economic history, including relations between city and countryside, the role of states in the lives of their citizens, and the place of religion in modern societies.[8]

The upswell of antisemitism around 1900 nonetheless remains puzzling. As historian Helmut Walser Smith has asked, "How do we understand prejudice, hatred, and violence in the context of modern societies, like our own, among people much like ourselves, among men and women who lived, not in dark times, but in an era when the balance of opinion was against the all-too-open expression of hatred?"[9] Many contemporaries (and some historians) looked to the past, seeing in nineteenth-century blood libels and pogroms the remnants of older, enduring religious hatreds that the Enlightenment and education had as yet failed to eradicate. More material-minded observers claimed that antisemitism's causes lay in unsolved social problems, from the impoverishment of the countryside to the downward mobility of craftsmen and shopkeepers. Looking up the social ladder, other commentators pointed their fingers at Christian intellectuals and politicians, for whom antisemitism offered an ostensibly modern, scientific blueprint for the reconstruction of tottering states, societies, and nations. None of these explanations excluded others: all emphasized the power of fear, prejudice, protest, and scapegoating.

The historiography of modern European antisemitism is rich and dense. In recent decades, scholars have looked anew at its origins, development, and consequences. Synthetic works on the "long nineteenth century" have revealed a clear set of landmarks: the French Revolution, Jewish emancipation, the Russian pogroms, the Dreyfus affair, the election of Karl Lueger as mayor of Vienna, and the First World War.[10] This scholarship has illuminated the genesis and spread of antisemitism as an ideology, helping us recognize the influence of texts such as *The Protocols of the Elders of Zion*, thinkers such as Wilhelm Marr (who coined the term "antisemitism"), and organizations such as Charles Maurras's Action Française. With an eye on the twentieth century, scholars also have shown how antisemitic movements, largely marginal before 1914, moved into the mainstream in the interwar period, with deadly consequences for European Jewry during the Second World War.

This book owes much to this scholarship. But it also looks to recent works that have complicated the history of modern antisemitism by shifting attention away from its intellectual history, away from capital cities, and away from well-known incidents.[11] At the heart of this work has been an impetus to *disaggregate*: to look for multiple causes, forms, outcomes, and meanings of antisemitic behavior and episodes.[12] Such approaches emphasize particular and contingent factors; they accept the proposition that multiple perspectives are needed to bring small details into focus, even if this sometimes blurs the bigger picture. Writing about Imperial Germany, historian Oded Heilbronner has concluded that "there was no such thing . . . as national antisemitism in Germany. This does not mean that hatred of Jews did not exist, but it was local, lasted for relatively short periods of time, and served the interest of particular social groups."[13] This newer scholarship on antisemitism has influenced this book in three important ways, leading us to emphasize local studies, search for transnational links, and insist on the multiple meanings of antisemitic violence.

Sites of European Antisemitism in the Age of Mass Politics looks at antisemitism "from below." It gives primacy to local contexts and to local actors. It is no accident that many of the studies presented here explore small towns and villages. But the term "sites" also encompasses other settings, including the neighborhoods and editorial offices of larger cities. The historical actors who appear here are no less diverse, ranging from village preachers and publicans to urban politicians and pamphleteers. What unites the studies is the contention that local conditions *mattered*: they help explain why antisemitism emerged, what forms it took, how Jews and their Christian neighbors responded, and what consequences it had. In the studies that follow, then, "sites" are not merely backdrops to violent episodes, but are themselves crucial to understanding the nature and significance of antisemitic behavior. By studying them closely, we hope to grasp what anthropologist Clifford Geertz once called the "webs of significance" that give meaning to social action.[14] What happened in villages and neighborhoods cannot be viewed in isolation: transformations on the regional, state, and European levels also affected what happened on the ground. In this book, we attempt to strike a balance between a "thick description" of local conditions and analysis of how these "sites" in turn reveal broader changes remaking states and societies in the years around 1900.

This brings us to the second theme of this book: its attempt to situate local cases of antisemitism within a wider European framework. Scholars have long been aware of the transnational nature of modern antisemitism. Like socialism, liberalism, and other modern political ideologies, antisemitism slipped easily across state boundaries, language frontiers, and class lines. The wide circulation of *The Protocols of the Elders of Zion*, with its Franco-Russian parentage and polylinguistic progeny, is a well-known example.[15] Scholars have also recorded the many aftershocks of both the Russian pogroms and the Dreyfus affair.[16] This book too attempts to find common patterns, mutual influences, and surprising links among places and events far removed from one another. But the essays in this volume extend existing scholarship in two meaningful ways. First, they look for less well-known (but no less significant) transnational touchstones and landmarks. The influence of Karl Lueger far beyond Vienna looms large here, as do the Catholic press, boycott campaigns, and Jewish refugees. Second, this book dusts for transnational fingerprints in places one might not expect to find them, including villages in Lithuania and islands in the Aegean Sea. Our findings here may be more suggestive than systematic. With few exceptions, the chapters that follow do not examine transnational organizations, media, or actors as such. For example, neither the antisemitic congresses of the 1880s nor international human rights organizations play a role here. Still, when taken together, these case studies confirm that even when seen "from below," local displays of antisemitism often bore the marks of wider European influences. Sholem Aleichem's fictional villagers have many real-life counterparts here.

The search for multiple meanings in episodes of antisemitism and anti-Jewish violence is the third theme of this book. Crucially, it treats antisemitism as a distinctly modern phenomenon, inseparable from the emergence of mass politics across the continent. Here we part ways with commentators, then and now, who emphasized the traditional, irrational, and exceptional nature of antisemitic politics. Instead we situate antisemitism within a rapidly changing Europe, a continent being remade by the forces of urbanization, industrialization, rising literacy, and capitalist agriculture, as well as by new forms of governance, transportation, communication, and electoral politics. Seen in this light, antisemitism was not simply a neo-Romantic rejection of the modern world and its challenges to traditional life, but as Brian Porter has written in regard to the Russian Polish lands, antisemitism and anti-Jewish violence can be understood as part of "an aggressive war against . . . foes *within* the context of the modern world."[17] This book extends this analysis by looking for the multiple meanings of this struggle to its participants. In other words, what functions did antisemitism serve for those who adopted and acted on it? What role did newer print media (newspapers, pamphlets, and books) play in the construction of meaning, and how did print interact with an older oral culture of rumors, gossip, sermons, and speeches? The answers given here follow recent scholarship in seeing in antisemitic violence patterns of exclusion, protest, and political mobilization.[18]

The chapters that follow offer what might be called a "micropolitical" approach to antisemitism. Describing this approach, political scientist Charles King has analyzed the growing concern among scholars "with uncovering the precise mechanisms by which individuals and groups go about trading in the benefits of stability for the inherently risky behavior associated with violence — and how, as Thucydides knew, they often do it at the expense of people whom they previously called friends and neighbors."[19] In King's reading, microlevel studies of violence can reveal its unpredictability, social meanings, life cycle, and impact, as it creates group solidarity and begets more violence. He confirms the value of disaggregation, both for adding new case studies and for adding "nuance to our understanding of the diversity of violent outcomes within the dominant unit of analysis, the nation-state."[20] These goals underlie this book as well. By adding new chapters to the history of antisemitism, we hope to demonstrate the great value of local studies, the surprising pull of transnational forces, and the many meanings that hide beneath the term "antisemitism."

■ The chronology and geography of this book deserve explanation. The book examines the period from around 1880 through the First World War. By the late nineteenth century, many European states had emancipated Jews, expanded suffrage, raised literacy rates, and begun to industrialize, urbanize, and colonize the globe. Yet the early 1880s also brought pogroms in Russia, a sensational blood libel case in Hungary, an Antisemitic League in Germany, and growing Jewish emigration to western Europe and beyond. The uneasy coexistence in Europe of a liberal modernity with antisemitic agitation would last through the First World War, which, to many observers, brought the liberal era to a close and opened the door to unprecedented levels of anti-Jewish violence and discrimination.

This is a book about European antisemitism, but it does not cover all of Europe. Important regions, including Scandinavia, Iberia, and the Low Countries, are not addressed here. Nor does Germany have a chapter, in part because the historiography on antisemitism in Imperial Germany is so rich. Readers familiar with German scholarship will see its influence on this book in many areas, not least in our emphasis on local studies, attention to the ritual dimensions of violence, and insistence that study of the nineteenth century can provide insight into the violence of the twentieth century.[21] With this volume, we have tried to bring together essays on places less often featured in surveys of European antisemitism. We also have tried to span the continent. By including essays ranging from Great Britain to Greece and from France to Lithuania, this book makes clear that antisemitism and anti-Jewish violence did not distinguish the "backward" regions of Europe. The authors read antisemitism and anti-Jewish violence as evidence that modern mass politics arrived in rural eastern Europe with little if any time lag compared to the more "advanced" central and western European states.

We have chosen not to organize the book's essays by geographic region or to follow a west-east gradient, as is often the case in volumes on European history. Rather, we have grouped the essays around common themes and questions, although, as the reader will recognize, the chapters are often in conversation with each other across these section divisions. The aim is to suggest connections, both historical and historiographical, between regions rarely viewed alongside one another.

Catholicism and modern politics link the first three essays, which cover Habsburg Galicia, France, and Italy. Daniel Unowsky's close study of the 1898 anti-Jewish riots in Galicia shows that antisemitism ran deep in the new mass politics in the Polish-speaking countryside. Catholic institutions, journalists, and politicians posited anti-Jewish action as the key to modernizing the rural economy. The monarchy's commitment to political reform and press freedom also contributed to the outbreak, course, and legacy of the 1898 events. Still, as Unowsky argues, local contexts and the mixed motivations of participants on the ground shaped the 1898 violence, which contributed to the increased isolation of Jews in Galician society. The events in Galicia were influenced by Catholic antisemitic activity in other regions of Europe. As chapters by Vicki Caron and Ulrich Wyrwa reveal, French and Italian Catholic publicists played a key role in legitimizing a wide range of antisemitic arguments and antisemitic politics. Through newspapers, pamphlets, essay contests, and books, Catholic activists made antisemitism the centerpiece of the case they built against liberal regimes, which they blamed for the emancipation of Jews, rampant secularism, and deadening materialism. How this new Catholic antisemitism related to the era's racial theories of antisemitism is a matter of some dispute. But the importance of Catholic writers to the development and dissemination of antisemitic rhetoric, images, and arguments is not. In all three case studies, the authors expose deep anxieties held by many Catholic thinkers and activists about modern politics and society.

In late nineteenth-century Europe, anti-Jewish violence (and efforts to understand that violence) was deeply intertwined with questions of national belonging and nationalist politics. The second set of essays usefully reminds us that local episodes of anti-Jewish violence took place within the framework of nation-states and multinational empires. Both political structures posed risks and rewards for Jews, and they also influenced how antisemitism functioned. In culturally cohesive states such as Romania—or France or Italy—where one ethnoreligious group dominated public life, Jews were often seen as "foreigners," no matter what level of integration they had attained. This emerges clearly from Iulia Onac's study of anti-Jewish violence in Romania. Peasants and parliamentarians agreed that Jews (even if native born) were foreigners who did not deserve human rights; indeed, expulsion was the frequent consequence of this antisemitic logic. Things were more complicated in the Habsburg Monarchy. Throughout central and eastern Europe, Jews often found themselves caught between competing national movements. Michal Frankl demonstrates that Czech activists in Moravia stirred antisemitism into the cauldron of national tensions. Here Jews were increasingly seen as an "internal" enemy,

PART 1

CATHOLICISM, ANTISEMITISM, AND ANTI-JEWISH VIOLENCE

LOCAL VIOLENCE, REGIONAL POLITICS, AND STATE CRISIS
THE 1898 ANTI-JEWISH RIOTS IN HABSBURG GALICIA

Hurrah! Hurrah Get the Jews!... You have shed the blood of our savior and you have shed our blood. You have degraded our country, you rob our people, and you grow rich from our work. You are everywhere. Go back already to Palestine; there your Messiah awaits you.... We hate you as God hates you. As long as we can see you, we will never stop beating and burning you.... Hurrah brothers, Hurrah get the Jews, Hurrah! The Holy Father has granted complete indulgence to those who drive the Jews out from among Catholics. Gather together, you already know when, and do not forget about the marketplace. Hurrah! Hurrah! Hurrah!

— Handwritten flyer posted on houses in the village of Szczurowa in late June 1898.

In the spring and early summer of 1898, anti-Jewish violence swept across the western and central districts of Habsburg Galicia. Bands of peasants broke into shops and taprooms administered by Jews on the outskirts of small villages, bashing in windows and knocking in doors with scythes, hatchets, canes, metal spikes, and rocks. They drank vodka and beer, shattered glasses, destroyed furniture, ransacked chests of drawers, and broke holes in walls searching for mythic piles of Jewish money. Attackers beat Jews with canes, hit them with rocks, and assaulted mothers in front of cowering children. In towns such as Kalwaria, Frysztak, Nowy Sącz, and Stary Sącz, hundreds of peasants, artisans, shopkeepers, and members of town councils looted Jewish-owned businesses. Participants loaded flour, vodka, clothes, kitchen utensils, mattresses, and pillows onto carts driven in for this purpose.

From mid-March until the end of June, when Galician viceroy Count Leon Piniński announced a state of emergency, anti-Jewish violence erupted in over four hundred communities. The army and gendarmes shot down more than a dozen rioters; scores of Jews were injured. The authorities charged some 5,170

The Unrest in Galicia, in *Die Wiener Bilder*, July 10, 1898.
Courtesy of the Austrian National Library.
Upper left: "Rescue of a Jew by the gendarmes."
Upper right: "Plundering of a Jewish tavern in Nowy Sącz."

people: peasants, day laborers, miners, and railroad construction workers; city council members, village leaders, teachers, and shopkeepers; men in their late teens, but also fathers in their forties, village elders in their sixties and seventies, and women of all ages. Of these, at least 3,816 were tried and 2,328 sentenced to prison terms lasting from a few days to more than a year.[1]

Scholars studying "ethnic violence" face many challenges if they seek to do more than document drunken disturbances.[2] One approach is to focus on the social, economic, and ideological background of the period and then assume that the combustible situation described needed only a spark to set it off. This approach, however, relates none of the local texture of time and place and also risks what Rogers Brubaker has denounced as "groupism": the assumption that groups of people think and act uniformly for reasons defined by organizations and institutions claiming to speak on their behalf. Such an approach inevitably will smooth over jumbled and chaotic events, diverse motivations, and choices made that cannot be so neatly accounted for in the coherent narratives constructed by interested partisans.[3]

Anti-Jewish violence and antisemitic politics were far from rare in the decades around 1900. The treason accusation, trials, public debates, and violence of the Dreyfus affair in France remind us that the 1898 Galician riots should not be understood as leftovers from the medieval world that continued to plague backward eastern Europe while the progressive West had moved past such ancient hatreds. Yet merely acknowledging this broad European context does not provide satisfying answers to this question: What transformed confrontations between Catholics and Jews in western Galicia—the kind of local incidents that took place regularly before and after the spring and summer of 1898— into a wave of mass violence, coded as ethnic and spreading from town square to village tavern while drawing in ever greater numbers of people as both participants and objects? In an effort to approach this question I will begin—but not end—with a brief overview of the local, regional, and European contexts. The second section will focus on the actors and actions at the sites of violence. Finally, I will consider the political contest to interpret this wave of riots.

The 1898 riots were among the most extensive and sustained anti-Jewish attacks in the Habsburg state in the post-1867 constitutional era. Yet until recently, scholars have paid little attention to these events.[4] The 1898 anti-Jewish riots should not be viewed merely as a series of obscure moments of violence in a "backward" region of Europe or as another example of toxic "ethnic relations" in the late-Habsburg Monarchy. Antisemitic and anti-Jewish violence in Galicia reflected a European-wide trend toward mass political mobilization.

According the 1900 Habsburg census, of the 7,315,939 inhabitants of Galicia, 3,350,512 were Roman Catholics, 3,104,103 were Greek Catholics, and 811,371 were Jews.[5] The social and economic profile of the Jewish population contrasted sharply with that of their Christian neighbors. Jews constituted less than 8 percent of the population of western Galicia; however, in 1910, Jews made up more than 70 percent of the 1,506 residents of Frysztak, the small market town that was site of the bloodiest single moment of the 1898 riots. Between 20 and 30 percent of the inhabitants of Kalwaria Zebrzydowska, Jasło, Limanowa, and Nowy Sącz and Stary Sącz, other centers of violence in 1898, were Jews. In all of these places, Jews owned at least 75 percent of the taverns, restaurants, bakeries, artisan shops, and dry goods, clothing, furniture, and shoe stores.[6] Jews also were prominent among the merchants buying and selling in the temporary stalls lining central squares on market days.

In 1900, about 35 percent of west Galician Jews lived in rural areas, many in small enclaves on the edge of or in between villages. Thousands lived in cramped rooms adjoining the small shops, inns, and taprooms they administered. The *szlachta* (Polish nobility) still enjoyed a monopoly on the production and sale of alcohol (*propinacja*) and often leased these rights to Jews.[7] Such taverns were popular destinations for peasants traveling to and from towns for Sunday church services and to sell agricultural products and purchase manufactured goods. There they spent their earnings and purchased spirits, tobacco, and other items on credit.[8] The economic crises of the 1890s sharpened the divide between Catholics and Jews. Overpopulation, division of land into increasingly smaller plots, and rural bankruptcies gave rise to a growing number of landless peasants. Many pushed off the land became seasonal laborers on railway expansion and river regulation projects or sought more permanent positions in the oil industry in central Galicia.[9] Jews were among those purchasing the land of bankrupt peasants and nobles.[10]

Social and economic divisions between Catholics and Jews corresponded to an equally visible cultural divide. As was the case in the other partitions, growing numbers of Polish-speaking Jews lived in Galicia's major cities. In smaller towns and villages, there were also signs of acculturation; however, dress and language, as much as occupation, still clearly distinguished Jews from Christians. Most Jews spoke Yiddish. Traditional forms of Jewish practice prevailed. In Nowy Sącz, among the largest towns of the region, many Jews were followers of the powerful Sandz Hasidic dynasty.[11]

This marked otherness of language, social status, and economic role, as historian Hillel Kieval has argued, did not translate inevitably into conflict between Jews and Catholics.[12] Some Galician Jews would remember this period as one characterized by close and friendly relations between peasants and Jews, if interrupted by occasional conflicts.[13] Still, a sense of essential difference was not an import from the big cities or from abroad.[14] At the same time, Catholic organizations and peasant-oriented political parties did transfer "knowledge" of Jewish danger from other regions of Europe into the Galician countryside.

In the last decades of the nineteenth century, elements within the Catholic Church imagined an organic society unified in its struggle against the forces of liberalism, capitalism, and socialism undermining Christian values—forces in which the "Christ killers" were deemed central. In Habsburg Galicia this vision, propagated by the Jesuit press in Rome among other sources, found a positive reception. Pope Leo XII's 1891 encyclical addressing Catholicism, politics, economic development, and modernity inspired Catholics in Galicia to found workers' associations, a Christian Social movement in contact with Karl Lueger's in Vienna, and publications such as the popular Cracow daily *Głos Narodu* (The People's Voice) and *Prawda* (Truth), aimed at the Catholic peasantry and produced under the protection of the Roman Catholic hierarchy in Cracow. These new institutions promoted boycotts of Jewish businesses. They agitated for the separation of Jewish and Christian pupils in public schools, and more broadly, for the reversal of Jewish emancipation.

Jewish Secrets, penned by Cracow priest and catechist Mateusz Jeż, is a particularly striking example of the transnational influence of Catholic antisemitism on public opinion in Galicia in the period of the 1898 riots.[15] This pamphlet originally appeared as a series of articles in *Prawda* that called on its readers to recognize the nefarious nature of Jewish power in Galicia and beyond. Jeż drew from the publications of Polish priests, the Russian-Jewish apostate Jacob Brafman, German "scholars" of Jewish practice, French texts from the early nineteenth century, and the Austrian priest Josef Deckert's *The Eternal Jew*. To prove the truth of the blood libel, Jeż cited passages in the Talmud and Prague professor August Rohling, the "expert" witness in several ritual murder trials in the Habsburg lands whose theories had been soundly and repeatedly debunked.[16] The pamphlet charged that the Jews, in only the latest example of their age-old tactic, paid off Émile Zola and other French citizens to call for the release of Captain Dreyfus, the French Jewish officer accused of passing military secrets to the Germans. In the Jews' essential nature, Jeż found the origin of the corrupting nature of the Jewish tavern, Jewish usury, and Jewish control over politics and the economy of Galicia, the monarchy, and Europe as a whole. The twisted character of the Jews was "evidenced" by their eternal responsibility for the death of Christ, their scheming brains, and their supposedly inherent and repulsive physical characteristics (including a special Jewish smell that could not be washed away by baptism). According to Jeż, "It is either the Jews or us." Thousands of copies of this pamphlet were distributed in the regions where the 1898 violence took place. The perceived effects of this pamphlet on peasant attitudes led the Galician authorities to ban its dissemination.[17]

The arrival of mass politics in the Galician countryside created possibilities for the articulation of agendas that highlighted Catholic-Jewish division. In the 1880s new peasant political organizations vied for the few seats to the Galician Diet (Sejm) that could be wrested from the grip of the conservative alliance, which controlled the majority and—aided by the distribution of beer and sausages—manipulated elections. The 1896 suffrage law in the Austrian half of the monarchy created a fifth universal male suffrage curia for elections to the Vienna parliament. This reform eliminated wealth as a prerequisite for voting (the curia remained weighted, and only the 1906 election laws created a truly universal male suffrage system) and sparked a wave of political activism.

Several new political parties maneuvered to take advantage of the changing structure of Galician politics. The Galician branch of Social Democracy, with its stronghold in Cracow, sought to expand its constituency into smaller towns and regions with a visible working class (the salt mines of Wieliczka and the petroleum fields of central Galicia). The electoral success of the Social Democrats in March 1897 shocked the Catholic establishment.

Three new peasant parties competed with the Social Democrats for the votes of the newly enfranchised. Jan and Stanisław Potoczek founded the Peasant Party Union in Nowy Sącz in 1893. This regional party represented wealthy farmers and townspeople, maintained close ties to the Catholic hierarchy, and was virulently antisemitic.[18] Every edition of its newspaper called on its readers to boycott the Jews. The geographically more widespread People's Party, founded in 1895, was allied closely with the democratic movement in the provincial capital of Lemberg. The People's Party was far more secular and Polish-nationalist in orientation.[19]

The last of the three, the Christian People's Party, was established in 1896 by Father Stanisław Stojałowski.[20] In the 1870s Stojałowski had organized mass pilgrimages and peasant participation in national celebrations. In the 1880s Stojałowski and others had founded Agricultural Circles, rural cooperatives, stores, and reading rooms. More than two thousand Agricultural Circles dotted the Galician countryside by 1900. The Agricultural Circles were promoted not simply as a means of securing better economic livelihoods for rural people, but as a way of minimizing Jewish influence as well.[21] Stojałowski also edited popular newspapers aimed at the Roman Catholic peasantry. Stojałowski's party, which cooperated briefly with the Social Democrats, was the most successful of the peasant parties in the March 1897 elections. The Catholic Church pronounced a ban on Stojałowski in response to his radical social vision and his incessant attacks on the Polish nobility and the princes of the church. The ban only succeeded in enhancing his popularity and was lifted in the late fall of 1897. Stojałowski then turned against the Social Democrats, and his Christian People's Party became the main vehicle for promoting an anti-Jewish agenda in the countryside.[22]

The peasant parties viewed elections in the first half of 1898 to replace two deceased representatives to parliament as battles for the political souls of Catholic voters. The first election was for a fourth curia (rural commune) seat in the district of Łancut-Nisko and took place in February. The peasant parties and the Social Democrats held scores of political meetings. On more than one occasion, followers of Stojałowski attacked and harassed leaders and supporters of rival political movements.[23] Stojałowski himself won an overwhelming majority.

The second election was for a fifth curia (universal male suffrage) seat representing seven political districts that sprawled across the western and central region of the province. Włodzimierz Lewicki, a lawyer and the candidate from the Stojałowski party, and Jan Stapiński, an energetic peasant journalist and a leader of the People's Party, competed for the favor of the Roman Catholic peasantry. Father Kałużniacki, a Greek Catholic priest, tried to gain the support of Greek Catholic Ruthenian speakers. Stojałowski's party distributed *Jewish Secrets* and Stojałowski's publications. He and his allies denounced Peasant Party politicians as serfs of their "friends with *pejas.*" They railed against the alleged Jewish corruption of Christian morality through liquor and capitalism. Stojałowski urged peasants to defend themselves against the Jewish "leeches" who "suck the blood" of the Christian people.[24] The election took place on June 23. No candidate captured the absolute majority of the votes cast by the election delegates, and a runoff was held between Stapiński and Kałużniacki. Stojałowski's party called on its supporters to back the Greek Catholic priest in the second round; however, despite this effort, Stapiński received the most votes and claimed victory.[25] Stojałowski's party paper asserted that the Jews had purchased the votes of the Ruthenians with beer and cigars.[26]

The 1898 violence in Galicia took place in a society experiencing wrenching economic, social, and political transformations. New Catholic institutions and peasant-oriented political parties did not respond to change with a rejection of the modern world. They instead called for a modernization that worked for the benefit of Catholics and not for the despised Jewish alien.[27] Before and during the wave of violence, they disseminated this anti-Jewish message to the towns and villages of western and central Galicia.

■   EVENTS ON THE GROUND

In *Ethnicity without Groups*, Rogers Brubaker warns scholars against reinforcing the coherent narratives about communal violence created by partisans and self-styled ethnic spokespeople that integrate such moments into larger stories of "ethnic conflict." In Galicia in 1898, the multiple motivations, actions, and choices made by actors on the ground belie any such effort at neat interpretations. Only by looking at Catholic action, Jewish reaction, and the role of government in preserving order can we come close to understanding how the riots themselves were experienced.

The violent events took place in specific settings. Major incidents most often commenced in towns flooded with visitors from surrounding areas during market days, Corpus Christi and other holidays, regular Sunday worship services, or newly invented Polish "national" festivities. After being forced to disperse by the military or gendarmes, the rioters fanned out into the countryside. Groups then made their way homeward, ransacking village homes, taverns, and stores owned by Jews and spreading news and rumors about anti-Jewish violence. Other incidents commenced in relatively isolated village taprooms. Here peasants demanded free drink and food. They cited nearby or well-publicized violent incidents and tales of alleged imperial permission and then proceeded to break bottles and glasses, steal alcohol and other items, and assault the Jewish tavern keepers and their families.

Who participated in the violence and why did they join in the riots? Some of the most active riot leaders and organizers came from the more educated strata, had ties or connections with political movements, and were regular readers of the partisan and antisemitic Catholic press. These people transmitted calls for anti-Jewish action to better the lives of the peasantry to the villages and small towns of western Galicia. In Kalwaria Zebrzydowska, an important Catholic pilgrimage site and location of the first major urban riot on May 26, a thirty-year-old employee of the local criminal court egged on the crowds to loot Jewish-owned property and to attack the gendarmes who protected them. The day after the Kalwaria riot, Johann Pieróg, a clerk in the bank of nearby Maków, printed and distributed notices that echoed the language used by Stojałowski: "The Jews have drunk enough of our blood, it is time to make an end to them."[28] Michał Miczkowski, who owned a mill near Jasło, was known to be a supporter of the Christian People's Party and a reader of Stojałowski's newspapers — something noteworthy in a region in which, despite advances in education, more than 50 percent of the population was functionally illiterate in 1890. Miczkowski read aloud from one of Stojałowski's rural papers, *Pszczółka* (The Bee), which in turn quoted a speech made by the Christian Social politician Josef Gregorig in the Vienna parliament, claiming that the inflated price of grain would fall if only three thousand stock exchange Jews were hanged.[29] His illiterate listeners told others that Stojałowski's newspaper had confirmed that official permission had been given. On 24 June sixty-eight-year-old Thomas Olchawa, a peasant father of six, along with two companions read aloud anti-Jewish charges from *Jewish Secrets*. They claimed that it was permitted to assault and rob Jews; however, no one was allowed to beat Jews to death. Then, brandishing his cane, Olchawa yelled "Hurrah, beat the Jews!" and led many villagers in a rampage. They broke into homes and stores in and around his home village of Iwkowa. The attackers grabbed a Torah from a private prayer room, stomped on it, and threw it into water.[30]

Agitators, organizers, and promoters of local violent incidents were often people known and respected by those whom they persuaded to join the plundering. Many were fathers between thirty and fifty, who had traveled with others from their home villages to larger towns for various occasions. In Frysztak, for example, forty-five-year-old Jan Miras, the *wójt*, or village headman, of Huta Gogołowska, was the most prominent identifiable riot leader. In Löw's tavern, Miras assured his fellow drinkers — many of whom came from his and nearby villages — that "we have it on paper that it is permitted to rob the Jews." Miras's leadership was one of the factors that transformed a drunken tavern disturbance into a large-scale riot suppressed only when the local gendarmes fired on the crowd, killing twelve and wounding dozens.[31] In Lutcza, site of another mass riot, the participation of Mateusz Urban, a thirty-year-old father of one, community policeman, and successful peasant farmer from Domaradz, was cited as proof that peasants from his town had official approval for anti-Jewish violence.[32]

While for some of those noted above, anti-Jewish hatred and political agitation clearly were motivating factors, this does not appear to have been central for other riot leaders. Many of those tried for leading the bands that had attacked isolated Jewish enclaves near Limanowa in late June had records for assault and battery and other violent crimes.[33] These offenders simply may have taken advantage of the breakdown in law and order to pursue an agenda of alcohol, violence, and theft. Some of the most serious incidents were inspired by the desire for personal revenge. In Dzierżaniny, for example, Abe Platner tried to padlock the door of his farmhouse when he saw a crowd rushing toward his property. After breaking in, Jan Dziedzic beat Platner bloody with a cane and yelled: "Beat this dragon, because he has money." How did he know? Recently, Platner had bought the farm from the bankrupt Dziedzic, and the fog of the riots provided the perfect cover for Dziedzic to avenge his humiliation.[34]

Such promoters of violence—the educated, police, clerks, criminals, and those seeking to settle personal scores—would not have achieved the critical mass to transform isolated incidents into a wave of anti-Jewish assaults without another central reality: rumors of official permission. Those who heeded the calls of riot leaders and joined the crowds moving along the roads from market towns to village taverns almost universally justified their actions by citing widespread rumors that the violence against Jews had received permission from the highest authorities.

This was clear from the first incident. In early March in Wieliczka, the location of Galicia's famous salt mines, rumors spread that Jews were preparing to attack the local priest, Andrzej Szponder. Szponder was a member of the Stojałowski party, a representative to the Reichsrat, and a charismatic speaker known for his antisemitic sermons. According to the story, the Jews, angered by Szponder's distribution of *Jewish Secrets*, planned to murder him when he returned from Vienna.[35] This was only one of several rumors about Jewish crimes against Catholics spread in the early days of the riots; according to others, the Jews had poisoned wells, sold rotten baked goods that resulted in deaths, killed a priest, and so on. In response to these (nonexistent) attacks, the Pope allegedly issued a call for his flock to beat the Jews.

The most persistent rumors concerned imperial permission. In Kalwaria, physical evidence seemed to confirm that Emperor Franz Joseph had authorized attacks against Jews. In the days before the outbreak of violence there, Leo Kąkol, a Kalwaria merchant, received flyers from the Baumann firm touting a new product to remove ink stains from clothes. Kąkol passed out the leaflets. In this semiliterate society, ads about removing ink stains—the word for ink stain (żyd) is also Polish for "Jew"—quickly transformed in the imaginations of many into official documents providing the bearer with immunity from prosecution for assaulting and robbing Jews.[36] Rioters in Kalwaria also cited the red posters advertising festivities in honor of the great romantic Polish poet Adam Mickiewicz. This celebration had been the occasion for the influx of peasants into town on the day of the riot. The witnesses claimed never to have heard of Mickiewicz and, therefore, had interpreted the red posters displayed in surrounding villages as a call from the good emperor to take revenge on the Jews.[37]

The rumors of imperial permission became more fantastic in the weeks following the Kalwaria riot. According to one rumor originating near Jasło, the

Vienna court barber had been bribed by the Jews to slit Franz Joseph's throat. When the moment came to do the deed, however, the imperial hair stylist broke down and confessed to the plot. The emperor, enraged, ordered the Jews beaten for thirty days. The saintly Empress Elisabeth, however, prevailed on him to show mercy, and so he reduced the sentence to two weeks.[38] Other stories declared Rudolf, Franz Joseph's son who had committed suicide in 1889, to be alive in Asia (or America or Canada). Rudolf now called on his loyal peasants to strike out for three days (or two weeks, or a month, or on market days) against the Jews, who were keeping him from resuming his rightful place beside his father.[39]

In the towns and villages around Cracow and Jasło, followers of the Christian People's Party claimed that Stojałowski had brought back imperial permission from Vienna after a meeting with Emperor Franz Joseph. In the Nowy Sącz region, stronghold of the Peasant Party Union, the rumor credited one of the Potoczek brothers as an intermediary. In both cases, imperial permission was alleged to have been communicated from Vienna to the smallest Galician hamlet (of course, it was claimed, the Jews tried to use their financial resources to keep the local authorities from acting on this information).

Such official permission in this particular region at this time appeared plausible. Many believed — or chose to believe — these outlandish rumors even when confronted by gendarmes, mayors, military forces, priests, and other figures of local authority. At the same time, the rural press disseminated news about ritual murder trials in Tiszaeszlár and elsewhere, the Dreyfus affair in France, and the electoral success of the Christian Social Party in Vienna, thereby bearing witness to the "fact" that the Jewish problem was one faced by people beyond Galicia. In the months before and during the riots, the constant campaigning of the new political parties carried the transnational Catholic antisemitic message to the towns and villages of Galicia in hundreds of political gatherings attended by tens of thousands. The politicians seeking to represent the peasantry, those with the closest connection to rural life, defined the Jew as the cause of all misery and laid out a political agenda of "self-defense" against the crafty enemy. The Catholic press and Sunday sermons linked the supposed eternal evils of the Jew to present-day economic and social crises while quoting from the "objective" scholarly work of Brafman, Rohling, Jeż, and others. When newspapers reported on the rumors, participants cited those papers as additional "evidence" that such rumors were in fact true.

The light gendarme and military presence seemed to be yet another confirmation of official approval (Galician officials had long complained that the military and police presence was not strong enough to deal with serious threats to public order and had pressed, to no avail, for larger budgets to support larger police forces). With jails soon full, most of those arrested were released immediately and bore witness to the supposed support from official circles for robbing and attacking Jews.

Western Galicia's rural population heard these rumors of imperial permission and news of events elsewhere. Many were tipped off about upcoming riots while on the way to or from an Agricultural Circle or local political meeting. Single men and women as well as married couples with children saw cane-wielding crowds yelling about Jews, often led by prominent local figures, elders, or criminals, and chose to follow them in order to find out what was going to happen. In Limanowa, for example, stories about upcoming anti-Jewish violence supposedly to be perpetrated by "socialists in uniforms" attracted a large crowd of peasants who had never seen a socialist before. They themselves then constituted the aggressive crowd and participated in the violence they had come to observe.[40]

The issue of imperial permission was not new. Similar rumors were spread during the 1881–82 pogroms in the Russian Empire and, earlier, in Galicia itself during the 1846 peasant massacre of noble landowners. The region of the 1846 riots largely overlapped with the areas that experienced the most violence in 1898. The fiftieth anniversary celebrations of Franz Joseph's accession to the throne, promoted from pulpit, town hall, and newspaper pages and present in the form of an endless series of jubilee souvenirs and pamphlets sold everywhere, brought to life again the myth of the good emperor who had freed the peasants from serfdom decades before.[41]

A few people defended Jews and their property at great risk to themselves. In Barcice, a small community just south of Stary Sącz, a band of more than a hundred would-be plunderers gathered near midnight on June 24 to break into David Weinberger's tavern. They found the tavern protected by a group of armed men led by Leopold Jenschke, a forester, Michał Garwol, the newly elected *wójt* of Barcice, and his father, Franciszek, the former *wójt*. Despite mocking charges that they were "Jewish" foresters and "Jewish" wójts and, therefore, enemies of the Catholic people, the defenders guarded the inn until dawn.[42]

Not all of those who opposed the violence were opponents of antisemitism. After the riots, the town council of Nowy Sącz granted the Peasant Party Union newspaper *Związek Chłopski* (Peasant Association) a subvention for its efforts to convince the peasants to reject violence.[43] The editors of this publication could hardly have been accused of philosemitism. Before, during, and after the riots, the paper's editors insisted that the most effective way to push Jews out of the economy and out of the countryside was through systematic disciplined action: cooperative movements, self-help, and the election of political parties dedicated to this goal.[44]

In some towns, citizens' guards, often including Jews, patrolled the streets. In Jasło on June 12, for example, police, gendarmes, the volunteer firemen, and a hastily organized citizens' guard blocked the bridge over the Jasiołka river that divided the town from the suburb of Ulaszowice. Across the river, a huge crowd of rioters looted and burned down a distillery and looted a small store.[45] Jasło's residents did not mount a rescue mission to protect the Jewish distillery owner from being beaten. More likely, as town dwellers, they simply hoped to preserve their homes from the barbarian peasant masses. Such mobs, after all, might just as easily burn down the entire town as surgically strike at the Jewish population.[46]

Many wójts, priests, and prominent members of local communities did try to calm the crowds. Yet they usually did not denounce violence against Jews as immoral. They tried to convince would-be rioters that such attacks were not condoned by the authorities and would lead to dangerous confrontations with the army and police. In mid-June, for example, Jan Madejczyk witnessed a meeting of the Wróblowa community council called by his father, the wójt. Most of the council believed the rumors, and since Jews were being robbed in all of the neighboring villages, they wanted to give the same treatment to the one Jewish resident in their hamlet. Jan Madejczyk interrupted: "I was already eighteen and understood that this supposed imperial 'authorization' had to be a fraud, that in a country like Austria, where order was observed, the issuing of such permits was not possible." He convinced the council to wait until written confirmation of such "permission" could be obtained.[47]

Jews were attacked where they regularly interacted with Christians: market squares, inns, village taprooms, and stores. What actions did Jews take when confronted by violence? With the first attacks in Wieliczka in mid-March, Jewish communities in the region contacted the Austrian-Israelite Union in Vienna, which immediately lobbied the Ministry of Justice and the Ministry of Religion to ban *Jewish Secrets*, viewed as the source of rising anti-Jewish sentiments. Jews pressed local and regional authorities to protect the Jewish population. The Sandz dynasty in Nowy Sącz demanded that the district captain investigate violent incidents.[48] Jewish leaders sent letters and approached officials requesting assistance. Some telegrammed from the sites of violence calling for immediate military protection, which invariably arrived too late. Jewish politicians led by Emil Byk, a representative from Galicia to the Vienna parliament, head of the Lemberg Jewish community, and president of Schomer Israel, the leading liberal Jewish association in the provincial capital, appealed to regional and state authorities and called on the Jews of the monarchy and beyond to donate money to compensate Galician Jews for lost property.[49] The Vienna Commercial Association, prompted by a letter about the attacks in Stary Sącz signed by Jewish businessmen in Cracow and Tarnów, appealed to the Vienna Ministry of the Interior to restore order. The Central Association of Industrialists of Austria, responding to "urgent pleas from a large series of the most reputable firms represented in Vienna," complained to the Vienna government that "business people were mishandled in barbaric ways . . . the security of life and property, which every state as such provides appears to be endangered in this highest degree."[50]

Individual Jews reacted in a variety of ways. Many who had advance warning fled vulnerable Jewish enclaves for larger towns; some of these were attacked and robbed en route to perceived safe havens.[51] Some padlocked the doors between shops or taverns and apartments. Other Jewish innkeepers satisfied demands for drink and, when the possibility arose, fled out windows to find police and gendarmes. Wives and children ran into fields or hid themselves in neighbors' attics.[52] Some Jews stood their ground, shaming those familiar to them among the looters. Others acted more aggressively.

Butchers were among the Jews who responded with a muscular self-defense. On March 13, a large crowd left church services in Wieliczka and attacked Jews and Jewish-owned houses in the town and nearby village of Klasno. There, butcher Mendel Kraus faced down a mob of stone throwers. Kraus charged out of his stall, knife in hand, and grabbed one of the leaders by the throat. He and the baker Hirsch Königsberger, who had returned fire by hurling stones back at the crowd, were themselves arrested and tried along with their attackers. When questioned as to why he had pulled a knife, Kraus responded: "So should I allow myself to be killed by rocks?" The defense attorney for the attackers pleaded for lenience, claiming that his clients had been involved only in innocent hazing, nothing dangerous, until the vicious armed Jew had rushed at them. This provocation, he claimed, had inflamed the crowd, which only then began to ransack Jewish property. This was apparently convincing to the court: Kraus was sentenced to two months at hard labor for public violence.[53] Jewish butchers in Nowy Sącz and Bursztyn—the latter a town in eastern Galicia—reacted to their attackers with violence and also became subject to a justice system that equated their efforts at self-defense with the assaults of their attackers.[54]

Perhaps the most widely publicized case of Jewish "provocation" was that of Jakób Hagel, a twenty-seven-year-old father of nine and caretaker of the old Jewish cemetery in Strzyżów, a small market town near Jasło. This region experienced the most serious anti-Jewish attacks in mid-June. On June 17, the day after the gendarmes had shot down twelve people during an anti-Jewish riot on market day in nearby Frysztak, a half-squadron of cavalry troops deployed to Strzyżów. A town official led the officers and their horses to the old Jewish cemetery situated in front of the synagogue. The cemetery was overgrown and no longer in use. It seemed to this local official to be an ideal location for the grazing of the military's horses. A furious Hagel insisted that the official "[l]ead the horses to your own church or to your own cemetery—it will be better there."[55] He was arrested for insulting a house of worship and inciting the peasants who stood within earshot to riot. Hagel was tried, convicted, and sentenced to one year in prison (this was later reduced to two months by the court of appeals in Vienna), much longer than most convicted of robbery and assault. *Głos Narodu* cheered that a "typical Jewish provocateur" had received justice.[56]

What roles did the various arms of the state play during the riots? Galician authorities and the Vienna ministries were slow to recognize the magnitude of the threat to domestic order. Antisemitic local officials discounted Jews' concerns about pending violence. For example, the district captain of Wadowice failed to act when delegations of Jews came to him on May 20 with information about rumors that anti-Jewish violence would take place on May 25 and 26 in Kalwaria: "Knowing, however, the cowardly nature of Jews and their inclinations to invent fairy tales," reported the district captain to the Galician governor, ". . . I did not believe them."[57] Not all bureaucrats responded in this way. Some, such as those in Sanok and Tłuste, incorporated Jews into self-defense units.[58] Whatever individual officials' views about Jews, the small number of gendarmes, army troops, and other forces available in Galicia's rural areas limited the effectiveness of any possible response.

As the riots persisted, the sense of crisis evident in the communications between the local bureaucracy and the Galician administration in Lemberg prompted vigorous government action. The recently appointed viceroy of Galicia Leon Piniński visited Frysztak after the bloodshed there. He ordered an immediate increase in the gendarmerie and called on the military command to move seven companies of foot soldiers into the area. The gendarmes and soldiers soon were patrolling every town square, train station, and public building.[59] Under pressure from oil and paraffin companies in nearby Gorlice, the police and military forces were bolstered there as well. Piniński also called on all wójts, district captains, and mayors to create citizens' guards. He urged local notables to convince the population that rumors of imperial permission were nothing but dangerous fantasies; that violence against Jews was against the law; and that offenders would be dealt with severely.[60] These actions, along with curfews and night patrols, suppressed the violence around Jasło.

Still, these measures were not able to halt the spread of violence. On June 24 and 25, thousands took part in massive urban riots in Nowy Sącz and Stary Sącz. In the region around Limanowa and Nowy Sącz, hundreds swept through the countryside assaulting and robbing Jews living in isolated communities and, in at least one instance, firing on troops. In the face of this complete breakdown of law and order, Piniński asked the Vienna ministry to issue a state of emergency in thirty-three counties in Galicia and to establish a special tribunal in Nowy Sącz and Limanowa. Freedom of assembly was curtailed. Socialist and antisemitic publications were subjected to censorship or shut down. The army redeployed thousands of troops.[61]

The first trials of those involved in the riots took place in the beginning of July. Jury trials were quickly suspended. Reliable judges were dispatched from Cracow to take over local courts that failed to mete out swift justice. For the next five months, the Galician and Viennese press reported in detail on court proceedings. Some trials were about little more than two or three drunks refusing to pay for vodka and breaking some glasses in a village taproom; others were mass trials of scores of people involved in large-scale urban riots. Thousands were sentenced, but sentences were often light. Defense attorneys' claims of extenuating circumstances apparently convinced many judges: their clients had been inebriated and remembered nothing; they were illiterate and had been misled by false rumors of imperial permission that were believed even by educated and prominent people; they merely had reacted to the provocative behavior of the Jews and had been acting on their justified hatred for Jewish exploitation.[62] This theme of Jewish provocation and exploitation was echoed in the reports from local officials to the Galician administration and between the Galician viceroy and the Vienna ministries as they sought to investigate the "real" causes of the violence and to uncover any conspiracies or secret networks of agitators assumed, for months, to be behind the events.[63]

On the ground, then, the evidence points to a chaotic situation, one in which the many people involved acted out of a variety of motivations: politics, personal revenge, search for loot, and curiosity. The rumors of permission bound the rioters together and separated them from the Jewish objects of their action. Galician authorities at first displayed little more than weakness and inaction inspired at least in part by antisemitism and sympathy with those who attacked Jews and their property. As the violence spread, the Galician administration, the Vienna government, the military, and the courts acted vigorously to restore the rule of law. However, for those who watched the accused marched to jail, who packed the courthouses, and who read the provincial press, the trials only confirmed that the provocative and arrogant Jews were the ultimate cause of the violence directed at them.

■   THE STRUGGLE TO CONTROL THE NARRATIVE

The contest to impose a coherent narrative onto these events began as soon as the violence commenced. The contest was predictable, as each of the partisan actors in western Galicia and beyond attempted to incorporate the riots into preexisting political frameworks. These public figures sought to justify specific political actions and garner support for their political allies.

Stanisław Tarnowski, among the most prominent of the Cracow conservatives, wrote a series of essays published in his monthly *Przegląd Polski* (Polish Review) and the Cracow daily *Czas* (Time) in mid-July. For Tarnowski and the landowning elites, the cause of the riots was clear: the expansion of the suffrage and the irresponsible and deceitful populism of the left and the right that threatened conservative domination. Demagogues agitated unceasingly among the ignorant rural people, convincing them that the rich were the enemy and that the *szlachta* (nobles) and the Jews were responsible for all of their suffering. Tarnowski supported the state of emergency and increased controls over electoral activity. According to Tarnowski, without more permanent policies along the same lines, the great progress secured for all Galicians by the Polish noble leadership in league with the emperor since the 1860s would be endangered.[64]

In newspaper articles in the Galician press in July and speeches in the Vienna parliament in November, the Social Democrat leader Ignacy Daszyński in turn denounced the hypocrisy of the Polish conservatives. He charged that they had supported Catholic antisemitic newspapers such as *Prawda* in order to gain popular support for their failed leadership. The conservatives had instituted the state of emergency not to oppose the antisemitic movement they had encouraged, but rather to attack the spreading social democratic organization in Galicia.[65]

In part, urban-based democratic-liberal politicians and journalists agreed with Daszyński. For these activists, the riots demonstrated the failures of conservative *szlachta* leadership to address the real problems that had led to the supposedly low level of morality of the Jews, their usury, and their encouragement of rural alcoholism, as well as to the stubbornly high rates of illiteracy of the backward local Catholic population. The democratic-liberal antidote was aggressive promotion of industry and education to combat stagnation and ignorance. The state of emergency and the measures taken against constitutional freedoms were, Polish democrats asserted, long sought by conservatives. The measures taken against the socialists, who had had nothing to do with antisemitic agitation prior to the riots, were proof that the conservatives had used this incident to bolster their once-dominant position in Galician politics and society.[66]

The new peasant parties also incorporated the violence into their existing agendas and rivalries. People's Party leaders directly implicated Stojałowski in the organization of the violence. They charged that he had used social and economic tensions in the countryside to rile up the peasantry for electoral purposes. In this interpretation of events, when Stojałowski had realized that his candidate would lose the June elections, he had turned to a last-ditch effort to keep voters from coming to the polls by instigating public violence. The People's Party thus rejected Stojałowski's overly simple solution (violence) to a complex social problem. Instead they called for an increase in discipline, self-help, anti-alcohol campaigns, government support for and expansion of rural credit, and Agricultural Circles. Only such a balanced and disciplined campaign would result in the achievement of the goal they shared with the Stojałowski party: the weakening of the stranglehold of the Jews in the countryside and the promotion of a healthy peasantry.[67]

On November 24, 1898, in the Vienna parliament, the Peasant Party Union's Jan Potoczek charged that the Jews had "reaped what they had sown" when peasants drunk on vodka purchased in Jewish-owned taverns destroyed Jewish property. Potoczek denounced the violence. After all, he noted, good Christians had to love their neighbors. Instead of violence, he called on the rural population to cease purchasing goods and alcohol from Jews. His long-term solution to the problem of Jewish rural power was a systematic program, including a reorganization of the school system to separate Christian and Jewish children, a government takeover of the alcohol monopoly, and more subsidies for Agricultural Circles.[68]

Stojałowski, his Christian People's Party, and his newspapers defended themselves from the charge of organizing the anti-Jewish violence. They blamed the violence and all the ills of the Galician countryside on Jewish arrogance and provocation, Jewish usury, and Jewish taverns. The resort to deadly force against the unarmed peasants by the gendarmes revealed, Stojałowski argued, the influence of the Jews in the highest levels of the Galician administration. Stojałowski reiterated his calls for the reversal of Jewish emancipation, restriction of Jewish property rights, boycotts of Jewish businesses, subsidies for Agricultural Circles, as well as government support for rural credit institutions, Christian shopkeepers, and Christian industry.[69] Editorials and peasant letters

Die Lage in Galizien.

Galizien

Nach der Natur aufgenommen.

This image, published in a "humorous" Viennese publication close to Karl Lueger's Christian Social Party, agrees with Stojałowski's interpretation of the Galician events (and also makes clear that not all of the "world press" was controlled by "the Jews"). *Kikeriki*, July 7, 1898, p. 2. Courtesy of the Austrian National Library.

to his newspapers asserted that the Jews had not only provoked the violence but also benefited from it. The Jewish-owned world press depicted the Polish peasants as brutish and animalistic. The innocent and trusting peasants had fallen prey to the Jews' plots yet again.

Jewish public figures and institutions also interpreted the riots in ways consistent with existing political frameworks. On the floor of the Vienna parliament, Emil Byk praised Piniński's efforts, denied the association of conservatives and antisemites, and blamed Stojałowski's party for the violence.[70] Rabbi Joseph Bloch, who resided in Vienna, represented a Galician district in parliament, edited the important Jewish weekly *Dr. Bloch's Österreichische Wochenschrift*, and had founded the Austrian-Israelite Union in 1886, was a vociferous critic of Byk. Bloch despised what he considered Byk's passive defense of Jews and humiliating ingratiation with the authorities. Bloch charged the conservatives Byk defended with attempting to overcome their isolation from the masses in an era of expanding suffrage by coming to terms with Stojałowski and harnessing antisemitism as a political weapon against social democracy.[71] Zionist organizations went further than Bloch. The Vienna academic Jewish Zionist society "Bar Kochba" lambasted Byk and his charity drive intended only for Jews who promised not to sue attackers for lost property. The Zionists interpreted the riots as the latest proof that Jews would never be accepted in Europe. They called on Jews everywhere to embrace Zionism, learn Hebrew, and prepare for a life elsewhere.[72]

While the riots were still ongoing and increasing in intensity, the Lemberg liberal daily *Słowo Polskie* (The Polish Word) sent a reporter to the Jasło and Nowy Sącz regions to discover what was happening on the ground. The resulting articles read like entries in an eighteenth-century journal kept by a western European traveler to the backward East.[73] The correspondent was surprised at how "intelligent" the peasants were and how much they knew about the province, the Habsburg Monarchy, and the world. The local people with whom he spoke in and around Jasło considered Stojałowski a prophet and rejected the more secular People's Party. The reporter was most impressed and repulsed by a visit to the church in Frysztak just days after twelve people had been killed there by the gendarmes. The church, he wrote, was packed with peasants from surrounding regions. They held prayer books and appeared to be reading and singing from them. They were respectful, quiet, and disciplined. But then, when the church service was over, the bulk of the worshippers went directly to taprooms (presumably administered by Jews), drank heavily, and became rowdy. Women sat at the tables with men, completely drunk, and told lewd stories over vodka, wine, and rum. "Overall, the people here have left me with mixed impressions of advantages and disadvantages, more of the latter than the former." This reporter, at least, had become skeptical that even the usual recipe of progress could have much impact on the backward people who populated the small towns and villages where the riots had taken place. He was not sure how or if such people could be integrated into a Polish national project without undermining the project itself.[74]

■   CONCLUSION

The vigorous Catholic press and the new political parties transferred "knowledge" of Jewish danger from other regions of Europe into the Galician countryside. They blamed all of the failures of modernization on the Jews, thereby confirming local knowledge of Catholic-Jewish difference and interpreting that difference as an immediate and mortal threat. The partisan press swiftly integrated the violence into preexisting politically oriented narratives that explained the past and the difficult present and offered a brighter future through action aimed at the Jewish enemy. An examination of events on the ground, however, makes it possible to see how such coherent narratives fail to capture the nature of the violence.[75] Despite the claims of the partisan press and similar evidence such as that provided by the flyer quoted at the beginning of this chapter, most participants did not understand the violence to be a means of permanently altering the structure of the countryside in ways that conformed to partisan visions.

The riots, on the whole, did not spark greater adherence to the various campaigns to boycott Jewish stores and to push Jews out of the rural economy. There were no notable gains in the success of the various temperance movements, which called on peasants to spurn the Jews' liquor, become more self-disciplined, and join the push to modernize and improve the countryside. Many of the violent incidents involved little more than drunk peasants demanding vodka and refusing to pay before breaking glasses and helping themselves to the tap. As the roving reporter from *Słowo Polskie* made clear, even in Frysztak the peasants and townspeople continued to follow up religious celebrations with a visit to the Jewish-administered tavern. The same paper that interpreted the violence as a misguided expression of a universal Catholic desire to be rid of the Jews pleaded with "My Brothers" that "[w]e have plenty of Catholic stores in nearly every village . . . but despite that we run to the Jew. Unfortunately, even members of the agricultural circles go to the Jew . . . Brothers!"[76]

While the various arms of the Habsburg state acted to suppress the violence, state actions did not send a clear message. Statements made and questions posed by judges and prosecutors in many of the trials of the rioters—and publicized in the press accounts of the trials to the broader readership of Galicia—blamed the Jews for provocations and considered drunkenness and Jewish exploitation as mitigating circumstances strong enough to reduce the sentences of violent offenders. Late in the year, Piniński, who had acted aggressively to halt the riots, publicly called on the district captains of Galicia to look more critically at applications to open taverns. Complaints by locals about the character of an applicant or court cases pending against said applicant would now lead to the rejection of requests to renew licenses to sell alcohol and tobacco. Piniński also pushed to phase out the *propinacja* altogether by 1910, even as he supported increased subsidies to Agricultural Circles organized by peasants and local clergy. These policies were looked on favorably by those eager to modernize the Galician countryside while cleansing it of Jews.

The evidence concerning Jewish reaction to the wave of violence is also ambiguous. While some prominent Jewish voices seemed, at least for a time, more favorable toward Zionism in reaction to the riots, the events did not cause a measurable spike in the already significant immigration of Jews from the region. That exodus had commenced in the early 1880s, and by 1910 more than two hundred thousand Jews had abandoned Galicia. Still, evidence suggests that at least some Jews living in isolated settlements on the edges of villages were not eager to return to these vulnerable locations or, when they did, found it difficult to remain there. In Żmiąca near Limanowa, to name one example, villagers did boycott the one Jewish-owned store. Young people broke the store windows and vandalized it, set their dogs on the owner, and effectively drove this isolated Jewish family out of town.[77]

The Austrian-Israelite Union in Vienna responded to the riots by sending a survey to Jewish and other politicians that aimed at discovering the causes of Jewish-Catholic tensions. What problems of economy or occupational distribution had contributed to the riots? What could be done to persuade Jews to become farmers? How nefarious was the hold of Hasidism in rural regions and how could this power be opposed? How did Jewish voting patterns affect antisemitism? The questions implied general agreement with the complaints and accusations against the Jews of Galicia, and the survey was greeted with cynical humor by the antisemitic press.[78]

Although the situation on the ground during the riots differed greatly from the coherent narratives forged by politicians and journalists, the riots and their aftermath promoted a sense of "groupness." By joining the riots—leading, spreading rumors about imperial permission, simply joining the crowd to see what was going on, and then taking Jewish-owned property because everyone else was doing it—Catholic peasants and small-town dwellers acted to create a community defined by violence against the Jewish "other." During the months of trials, newspapers reported on testimony as well as statements by the prosecution and defense that again and again told a story of Catholic victimhood and Jewish provocation.[79]

The struggle to interpret the violence pushed forward the institutionalization and politicization of this ever-deepening sense of difference.[80] By the turn of the century, most of the influential cultural and political institutions claiming to speak for and struggle on behalf of the Roman Catholic Polish-speaking peasants and townspeople of western Galicia shared this in common: with the partial exception of the Social Democrats, whose success in the countryside was limited, they interpreted these complex local acts of violence as part of simple and cohesive narratives that lifted the responsibility for anti-Jewish violence from the rioters and placed it on the Jews themselves. Who after all could criticize young farmers, workers, or day laborers kept ignorant, poor, and drunk by Jews for harboring a desire to get even? The pure hearts of the rioters were in the right place; however, their methods were counterproductive. If Catholic Polish-speaking inhabitants of western Galicia were going to enter the modern world and have that modernization work for "us" instead of for "them," the modern political movements informed their potential constituents, then the Jews must be pushed out of their positions in the countryside. Catholics could not become disciplined, sober, hard-working modern people until they shunned the Jews' taverns, alcohol, credit, and shops. This equation was most succinctly asserted by *Dziennik Polski*: "You may then claim not to be an anti-Semite, dear reader, and you may even snicker at that word, but know this: if that is truly the case, then you have no right to call yourself a good Catholic or even a good Pole."[81]

CATHOLICS AND THE RHETORIC OF ANTISEMITIC VIOLENCE IN FIN-DE-SIÈCLE FRANCE

In recent years historians have highlighted the inter-action between religion and the rise of modern antisemitism. In the German context, the Christian Social movement of Protestant court chaplain Adolph Stoecker in the 1880s has received considerable attention[1] and so too has Karl Lueger's Christian Social movement in the Habsburg Monarchy.[2] Moreover, many scholars have demonstrated the impact of the *Kulturkampf* in Germany on the rise of antisemitism there.[3] Although it has been argued that Catholic antisemitism in Germany had tapered off by the 1880s, commentators have convincingly shown that it remained strong and sometimes erupted in physical violence, despite the repudiation of antisemitism by the Catholic Center Party.[4] At the same time greater emphasis has been placed on the role of religion in the Nazi movement. Doris Bergen, Susannah Heschel, Richard Steigmann-Gall, and others have challenged the notion that a sharp break existed between the anti-Jewish attitudes expressed by the churches and Hitler's racial antisemitism.[5] Indeed, they have argued, without the support of most practicing Christians, Nazism never would have garnered such high levels of popular support.

Despite this trend, however, most scholars still suggest that religious varieties of antisemitism were significantly more moderate than their racial counterparts. In his classic study on Christians and Jews during the Kaiserreich, Uriel Tal pitted Christian antisemitism, which he identified with Stoecker's Berlin movement, against anti-Christian antisemitism, which he linked to racial antisemitism. Although Tal never minimized the radical nature of Stoecker's antisemitism, he depicted racial antisemitism, which severed Christianity from its Jewish roots, as far more virulent.[6] Similarly, John Boyer, in his work on the Christian Social movement in Vienna, has significantly downplayed the virulence of Lueger's antisemitism, especially in comparison to the racial antisemitism of Georg von Schönerer's Pan German League.[7] In France, too, Catholic antisemitism has been painted as considerably more benign than the racial antisemitism of Edouard Drumont. Catholic historians have frequently argued that the rhetorical violence of more secular antisemites such as Drumont or his lieutenant Jules Guérin "far outstripped" that of Catholic antisemites, such as Father Vincent de Paul Bailly, editor of the Catholic newspaper *La Croix*.[8] Secular historians have echoed this view as well. According to Frederick Busi, one of Drumont's biographers, Drumont differed from Catholic antisemites primarily in his rejection of the efficacy of conversion. Although Busi admits that Catholic spokesmen made "limited use of antisemitic themes," he nevertheless insists that they were more "ambivalent" about the Jewish question because of their recognition of the shared roots of Judaism and Christianity.[9]

In reality, however, there was far more ideological overlap between Catholic antisemitic spokesmen and Drumont than these scholars suggest. In order to examine this issue, I would like to focus on the responses of Catholic publicists to Drumont's writings in the years prior to the outbreak of the Dreyfus affair in late 1897. Here we will look briefly at Catholic responses to Drumont's antisemitic classic *La France juive* (Jewish France), which appeared in 1886 and experienced immense popularity. Within a year this book had sold over one hundred thousand copies, and by 1912 it had been translated into six languages and reprinted two hundred times.[10] But our principal focus will be on the love affair between Catholics and Drumont that persisted up until 1898. This period is of particular interest in that the Vatican and the French Church hierarchy were beginning to distance themselves from Drumont. Indeed, the Vatican even considered placing Drumont's book *Le Testament d'un antisémite* (Testament of an antisemite) (Paris: E. Dentu, 1891) on the papal index, not because of its antisemitism, but because it pilloried the French Church hierarchy and Catholic politicians like Albert de Mun for their obsequious stance toward the Third Republic.[11] By the mid-1890s a rift had opened between the Church hierarchy and Drumont when the latter challenged what he perceived as the hierarchy's excessively conciliatory stance toward the Ralliement, the papal policy that counseled French Catholics to accept the republic as a legitimate form of government.[12] Yet, as we shall see, the Ralliement did nothing to dampen Catholic antisemitism. Rather, it grew even more strident during these years, and many Catholic militants, including numerous priests and even a few bishops, called for an outright holy war against the Jewish-Masonic republic. Above all, attacks on the Talmud and charges of ritual murder became common fare. Although these themes are generally regarded as expressions of traditional religious anti-Judaism, in reality they expressed a distinctly modern form of Catholic antisemitism, which blended Christian theological views on Jews and Judaism with Drumont's racial and nationalistic antisemitism.

Before delving into the Catholic response to Drumont's publications, it is useful to examine why Drumont emerged as the preeminent champion of the Catholic cause. Although most scholars depict Drumont as the principal spokesman for a new brand of nationalist and racist antisemitism, which broke radically from traditional Christian brands of antisemitism, Drumont's Catholic credentials always occupied a central place in his ideology. Indeed, historian Zeev Sternhell, notwithstanding his designation of Drumont as the father of modern racial and nationalist antisemitism in France, nevertheless insists that Drumont's work "is that of a Catholic, and he proudly affirmed it."[13] Born into a republican, anticlerical family in Paris in 1844, Drumont was raised with little formal religious education, although he regularly attended Sunday mass. But by the late 1860s and early 1870s, he began to exhibit interest in Catholicism while working as a journalist. Although he wrote primarily for the secular and liberal newspaper La Liberté, owned by the Jewish entrepreneurs Isaac and Eugène Pereire, Drumont also began to contribute to Catholic periodicals, such as Le Contemporain and the Revue du monde catholique.

In the 1880s, just as the Third Republic was embarking on a virulent anti-clerical campaign, which included the secularization of schools and the im-plementation of divorce,[14] Drumont returned decisively to the Catholic fold. Most significantly, he forged a close relationship with Father Stanislas du Lac, head of the Jesuit order in France. Although Drumont's enemies maintained that he was merely a Jesuit stooge,[15] recent scholarship that draws on the ar-chives of the Jesuit order affirms Drumont's close ties with Father du Lac and the Jesuit order. Not only did Father du Lac review a draft of Drumont's 1,200-page manuscript to check for theological errors,[16] but the two men continued to maintain a close friendship, aside from a brief falling out in the mid-1890s when du Lac became frustrated with Drumont's attacks on moderate Catholic politi-cians.[17] Moreover, as historian Grégoire Kauffmann has recently shown, Father du Lac helped finance the publication of La France juive,[18] and the police had considerable evidence that the Jesuits had provided financial backing for Dru-mont's newspaper, the Libre Parole (Free Speech), created in 1892 at the height of the Panama scandal, when a number of deputies were found to have taken bribes from Jewish financiers to vote for government-backed bonds to shore up the troubled Panama Canal company.[19]

Although it is impossible to ascertain whether Father du Lac was behind "the initial idea for this agitation against the Jews," as the police suspected,[20] there can be no doubt that Drumont's turn to antisemitism coincided with the commencement of his relationship with Father du Lac. In 1884 Drumont pub-lished his first attack on Jews in the scholarly journal Le Livre. Here he declared that if the Jews "had not totally destroyed the Christian religion, this opinion-ated and insinuating people. . . . has nearly completely demolished the civilization founded on this religion. They have dissolved Christian society."[21] In an article published the next year Drumont charged that a Jewish-Masonic cabal had stolen the crown jewels on the eve of the French Revolution and used them to finance the Jacobin assault against the king and the Church.[22] Moreover, and perhaps most surprisingly, it may have been through Father du Lac and the Jesuits in Rome that Drumont came to embrace racism, since it was Father du Lac who had brought to Drumont's attention a series of venomously anti-Jewish articles published during the early 1880s in the *Civiltà cattolica*, the Jesuit periodical in Rome with close ties to the Vatican. These articles railed against Jews not as a religion but as an alien race and accused them of perpetrating ritual murder; indeed, Drumont cited them in *La France juive*.[23] As the Jesuit priest Father Giuseppe Oreglia had declared, Jews were an "enemy race, hostile to Christianity and to society in general."[24]

But it was the interweaving of racial and religious themes into his broader vision of history that highlighted the centrality of Christianity to Drumont's worldview. Although Drumont perceived history as an ongoing struggle between the aryan and semitic races, his racism was never scientific. Indeed, he spoke frequently of the "Christian race" or the "French race," and he used these terms interchangeably with "aryan." According to Drumont's vision, aryans were imbued with a sense of justice, honor, liberty, and beauty, and they alone engaged in productive work. By contrast, semites were cunning, greedy, parasitical, and devoid of any sense of honor or nobility. Physically, too, the two races were distinct: Jews, according to Drumont, had hooked noses, blinking eyes, protruding ears, flat feet, and "the fleshy and slimy hand of the hypocrite and traitor." Furthermore, he claimed that they bore "a stinking odor." Most significantly, they could never be French. Unlike aryans, whose roots were embedded in the soil and history of France, Jews were "perpetual nomads," incapable of becoming true patriots. Even the most highly assimilated Jews, including converts to Christianity, could never be integrated into the nation.[25]

But Jews posed a threat not only because of their alien nature. Rather, Drumont insisted, they had engaged in an ongoing battle against Christianity since the crucifixion of Christ. They had been commanded to hate Christians and Christianity by their central text, the Talmud, a codification and compilation of Jewish law and traditions written down by the rabbis in the academies of Jerusalem and Babylonia during the first centuries after Christ.[26] According to Drumont, the Talmud not only commanded Jews to cheat and betray Christians, but it also ordered them "to kill the best goyim." "Against the Christian, the gentile, the goy. . . . all means are legitimate," he declared. Above all, Drumont insisted, the Talmud commanded Jews to commit ritual murder. Medieval chroniclers had been unanimous "in recounting tales of assassinations of Christian children at the hands of the Jews." He insisted that the God of the Jews was not the God of Moses, but rather the Phoenician god Moloch, who demanded bloody human sacrifices, especially of virgins and young children.[27]

During the Middle Ages, Drumont alleged, this Jewish perfidy had been held in check by the anti-Jewish strictures of canon law, which had provided a rigid barrier between Christian and Jew. But since the emancipation of the Jews in 1791 during the French Revolution, these protective barriers had fallen away, and Jews again were free to pursue their nefarious anti-Christian acts. Most significantly, because Jews had received equal civil and political rights, they were no longer subservient to Christians. As a result of their cupidity and their ingrained mercantile skills, they had rapidly achieved financial mastery over Christians. As Drumont declared, "The sole beneficiary of the Revolution has been the Jew. Everything comes from the Jew; everything returns to the Jew."[28]

This Jewish infiltration, Drumont maintained, had become a "veritable conquest" in recent years.[29] After the republicans seized control of the government in the late 1870s, Jews had expanded their mastery over Christians. No longer was their domination limited to finance; they had achieved political domination as well by persuading their Masonic allies in power to appoint them to key political posts. From this vantage point, they were poised to wage a veritable crusade against their former Catholic masters. When the Opportunist, or moderate republican, politician Léon Gambetta had come to power in 1877, declaring, "Clericalism, that's the enemy," Jews had rejoiced as if a new era in world history were commencing. Indeed, Drumont insisted, these republicans, most of whom were Protestants, Freemasons, or Jews, were bent on a single goal: the annihilation of the Catholic Church. They intended to strip the Catholic congregations of their property and wealth, and they aspired to eliminate the Church's influence from the schools, "where children were taught to become good Christians and good Frenchmen."[30] Drumont also maintained that the anticlerical laws were a manifestation of a long-standing semitic conspiracy to replace the "glorious and beautiful" France of the ancien régime with a France dominated by "a handful of Hebrews from every country." This plan had been announced by the Jews' legendary chief rabbi, Sir John Readclif, in his famous speech published in Le Contemporain in 1881.[31] Indeed, Drumont predicted, once the Jews had expelled all the Christians, they would install a regime made up of their own coreligionists from Central and East Europe.[32]

Drumont concluded by calling on French Christians, by whom he meant Catholics, since Protestants too were excluded from his vision of the nation, to wake up and recognize that the republicans' anticlerical program was merely a Jewish plot aimed at ruining Christian France. Just as King Herod had massacred the innocents in ancient times and just as Jews had perpetrated ritual murder against Christian children throughout the Middle Ages, Jewish prefects and subprefects today were determined to humiliate Christ. As Drumont declared:

> Nothing has changed for them. They hate Christ in 1886, just as they hated him at the time of Tiberius Augustus, and they heap on him the same outrages. To flog the crucifix on Good Friday, to profane the hosts, to defile the holy images, this was the great joy of the Jew in the Middle Ages; this is his great joy today. Formerly he attacked the bodies of infants; today, it's their souls he's after with atheistic education; formerly he bled them; today he poisons them: which is preferable?[33]

Drumont then urged his compatriots to take up arms and crush "these beggars of yesterday who have become the tyrants of today."[34]

To be sure, Drumont's appeal was not limited to Catholics. His virulent antisemitism, which held Jews entirely responsible for the evils of capitalism, appealed to many on the left, who continued well into the 1890s to espouse a brand of socialism that conflated Jews and capitalism.[35] Nevertheless, the fact that Drumont championed the Catholic cause, and especially his exhortations to wage war against the Opportunistic republic's anticlerical campaign, won over many Catholics, despite his obvious racism, which undermined the Church's theological teachings regarding Jesus' Jewish origins and the continued validity of the Old Testament.

Drumont's enormous appeal to militant Catholics was already apparent in 1886 when nearly every organ of the Catholic press acclaimed *La France juive* as a groundbreaking publication. Baron A. de Claye, editor of the prestigious Catholic newspaper *Le Monde*, was delighted with the book's theme as well as its violent tone. As de Claye explained, Drumont had delivered "an enormous kick to the Jewish and Masonic gang that's in the process of invading everything, undermining everything, and defiling everything."[36] Oscar Havard, another publicist at *Le Monde*, similarly hailed Drumont as a "prophet, a Christian writer," who had finally sounded "that long awaited, desired and yearned for trumpet" that would awaken the French people to the danger they faced.[37] Although Havard harbored reservations regarding Drumont's racism and especially his criticism of the Old Testament, he nevertheless felt that the nation had suffered too long under the "*courbache* of the Jew." He therefore expressed the hope that this "good sergeant of Christ" would help bring about the "day of reparation and of justice."[38] Eugène Veuillot, editor of *L'Univers*, the principal

Catholic daily into the 1880s, similarly proclaimed that "the idea that inspires it [*La France juive*] remains just, since the danger against which the author wants to warn us—the *Jewish conquest*—undeniably exists."[39]

The vitriol level was ratcheted up another notch in the late 1880s and early 1890s. Although state-sponsored anticlericalism tapered off significantly after 1885 and the Vatican was beginning to move toward reconciliation with the Third Republic, these moderating forces had little impact on Catholic activists. Instead, inspired by the success of General Georges Boulanger's protest movement, which nearly toppled the government in 1889,[40] as well as the electoral victories of Christian Social movements in Germany and Austria,[41] Catholic activists believed that time was on their side.

This increasingly strident tone was evident in one of the major Catholic anti-Jewish works that appeared in 1889, *La Préponderance juive* [The Jewish Preponderance], by abbé Joseph Lémann, a convert from Judaism.[42] Published to coincide with the centennial of the French Revolution, this work complemented Lémann's earlier book, *L'Entrée des israélites dans la société française et les états chrétiens d'après des documents nouveaux* [The Entry of the Jews into French Society and the Christian States According to New Documents] (Paris: V. Lecoffre, 1886), which had appeared concurrently with *La France juive*. In this earlier work, Lémann had articulated many of the same arguments as Drumont. Still, he had placed much of the blame for the oppression of Jews during the Middle Ages on Christians, and he had held out hope for the Jews' eventual conversion.

In *La Préponderance juive*, Lémann retreated from these positions. Here he argued that due to the French Revolution, Jews had foolishly been allowed to enter French society. The unfortunate consequence, all too evident today, was that they had achieved mastery over Christians. Because of their profound hatred of Christianity, the secret societies, which had orchestrated the French Revolution, had emancipated the Jews. Jews and Masons had then banded together to betray France, just as the Jews had betrayed Jesus. Indeed, Lémann compared the Declaration of the Rights of Man and Citizen to "the head of a serpent," and he claimed that of all the segments of the serpent's body, the most "unexpected" and "terrifying" was "the vitality and preponderance of the Jews." Jews deserved toleration, but under no circumstances did they deserve equal rights, since the state needed to preserve its Christian character. Finally, Lémann abandoned any interest in converting Jews. Instead he asserted that the only way to reverse this "affront" to God was to reestablish the Christian state.[43]

Perhaps because he was a convert, Lémann did not allude to the most radical accusation against the Jews—ritual murder. In the late 1880s and early 1890s, a slew of books affirmed this charge. In 1889 two French translations of August Rohling's 1871 classic *The Talmud Jew* appeared: one edited and translated by a Belgian priest, abbé de Lemarque, and the other edited, translated, and augmented by a young disciple of Drumont's, Achille Plista, who wrote under the pseudonym "A. Pontigny."[44] The latter edition bore a preface by Drumont. Although most Christian publicists felt uncomfortable criticizing the Old Testament, since to do so negated the Jewish roots of Christianity and the continued validity of the Old Testament to Christianity, attacks on the Talmud were fair game. Such attacks had emerged as a major theme in Christian antisemitism in the twelfth and thirteenth centuries, and they continued to play a central role in antisemitic rhetoric well into the nineteenth century. Rohling's tract, whose publication had coincided with the onset of the *Kulturkampf,* was unequivocally the most successful exemplar of this propaganda. In the late 1870s and early 1880s, the St. Boniface Society in Münster distributed some thirty-eight thousand copies of the tract free of charge, and this work went through no fewer than seventeen editions, including many in foreign languages.[45]

Rohling's tract, which maintained that the Talmud was a book of immorality that commanded Jews to deceive, cheat, and even kill Christians, was already virulently antisemitic, but Drumont's preface and Pontigny's embellishments gave the French translation an especially violent edge.[46] Indeed, Drumont's preface was translated back into German and appended to all subsequent editions of the book.[47] Here Drumont affirmed that there could be no doubt regarding the authenticity of the texts cited by Rohling. What Jews thought about Christians was clear: "It's the hatred and contempt for the goy, the conviction that all means are legitimate against the goy . . . the 'offspring of cattle.'" Drumont further declared that the crisis engulfing the entire world could be summed up by a single phrase: "the revenge of the Talmud on the Gospels." Due to their role in finance and the press, "the Jew" had achieved complete mastery over non-Jews. Although Jews spoke incessantly about equality of rights, Drumont charged that they had no qualms about trampling on the rights of Catholics, as evidenced by their prominent role in championing the Third Republic's anticlerical legislation. As he stated, they "perpetually outrage everything that's worthy of respect, everything that represents faith, ideals, devotion: Christ, the Pope, the priests, the Sisters of Charity." Drumont admitted that most Western Jews at the end of the nineteenth century were no longer familiar with the Talmud. He nevertheless proclaimed: "What need do Jews today have to study the Talmud? It's imprinted on their brains by the law of heredity."[48]

Pontigny's introduction and his embellishments to Rohling's text continued in this vein. In the introduction, Pontigny claimed that "Israel" had endeavored to block the distribution of Rohling's book, just as it had blocked the distribution of earlier works that had advanced the ritual murder charge.[49] The truth, however, could not be suppressed. To be sure, "Israel" always disguised its true nature. But thanks to Rohling's work, the Talmud has been shown to be "the book *par excellence* of exclusivism, of separatism, of . . . hatred . . . against the entire human family." Pontigny also maintained that "Talmudism" was no less vibrant today than in the past. Indeed, he declared, both the Talmud and the Shulkhan Arukh (a sixteenth-century codification of Jewish law) were practiced by even "the most enlightened Jews of our time. The Talmud Jew is just as much the man of today as of yesterday."[50]

Although this translation of Rohling's work played a seminal role in the dissemination of the anti-Talmudic theme, the principal popularizer of the ritual murder theme in France was the "abbé" Henri Desportes, a seminarian from northern France who was a fanatical devotee of Drumont.[51] It is highly likely that Desportes was responsible for the 1888 French translation of a text by the Greek monk named Neophyte, who previously had been a rabbi. This text was titled *Le Sang chrétien dans les rites hébraïques de la synagogue moderne, révélations d'un néophyte, ex-rabbin, moine grec* (Christian blood in the Hebraic rites of the modern synagogue, revelations of a neophyte, ex-rabbi, Greek monk), and it had supposedly first appeared in Moldavian in 1803. In 1883, at the time of the furor over the Tiszaeszlár ritual murder trial in Hungary, it came out in an Italian translation to considerable fanfare in the French Catholic press.[52] The French translation was written under the pseudonym "JAB," and it bore a slightly modified title: *Le Sang chrétien dans les rites de la synagogue moderne* (Christian blood in the rites of the modern synagogue) (Paris: H. Gautier, 1888). It also included new material to make it relevant to a contemporary French audience. Although "JAB" has never been identified, similarities between this text and Desportes's subsequent work strongly suggest Desportes's authorship.[53]

In the introduction to *Le Sang chrétien*, JAB demonstrated the relevance of this text to the contemporary world, and he echoed the themes of *La France juive*. The Jews, he claimed, who had been condemned to wander the world because they bore the divine curse, today had become an "incontestable power" due to emancipation. Together with their Masonic allies, they ruled over "the Christian race." Throughout Europe they controlled the press and therefore public opinion. By means of their financial power, they had brought down the Union Générale, the Catholic banking house, in 1882,[54] and today they were threatening to ruin the Panama Canal Company as well. They had also begun to "penetrate all the administrations and governments of the world." Although there were only about seventy-five thousand Jews in France, JAB posited that nearly half of the eighty-six prefects were Jews. Above all, he reiterated Drumont's charge that Jews were responsible for the anticlerical laws: "It's the Jew [Alfred] Naquet who has overthrown the constitution of the family through the divorce law"; "It's the Jew Camille Sée who organized the lycées for young girls, where religion has been excluded from the classroom"; "It's the Jew [Ferdinand] Hérold, the prefect of the Seine, who has removed the crucifixes from Parisian schools."[55]

In order to carry out their anti-Catholic crusade, JAB insisted that Jews had been mandated by the Talmud to secure Christian blood. Since Jews today were no longer segregated from their Christian neighbors, it was imperative that Christians familiarize themselves with Jewish laws and rites so as "to defend ourselves against the outrages" of the Jews. In a long section titled "Historical Documents," JAB listed every ritual murder from 418 C.E. up to the present. These cases, he argued, proved beyond a doubt that "The Jews, even in our own day, make use of Christian blood in the fulfillment of their rites, in conformity with the prescriptions of their religion." It was time for "the people" to "break the chains and shake off the [Jewish] yoke, whose debris they'll jettison into the streams of blood."[56]

The books Desportes wrote under his own name further elaborated on these themes. Two of these works—Le Mystère du sang chez les Juifs de tous les temps (The Mystery of blood among the Jews of all time) (Paris: A. Savine, 1889) and Tué par les Juifs: Histoire d'un meurtre rituel (Killed by the Jews: History of a ritual murder) (Paris: A. Savine, 1890)—bore prefaces by Drumont, and Le Mystère du sang was dedicated to the antisemitic leader. In his preface, Drumont praised Desportes for having amassed "a considerable number of unimpeachable, undeniable facts" to prove the materiality of "this bloody sacrifice." Although witnesses to these events were no longer alive, Drumont maintained that the "facts" of these crimes were attested to by numerous historical artifacts: works of art, sculptures, stained glass windows, and especially trial testimonies. Most importantly, he proclaimed, Desportes's book proved once and for all that ritual murder was not a relic of the distant past; rather, these crimes were being committed in the heart of Christian Europe at this very moment.[57]

The text of Le Mystère du sang was, if anything, even more violent than Drumont's preface, a fact that ought to dispel any notion of the supposedly more moderate tone of Catholic texts. Here Desportes launched into a vicious attack on the Talmud, which he sharply distinguished from the Bible. The Bible, he claimed, was a work of perfection written by God. The Talmud, however, was a book of ignominy, which encouraged Jews to engage in vice, idolatry, and "abominations," including the sacrifice of their own children and the consumption of human blood. Above all, as Neophyte's book proved, the Talmud commanded Jews to hate Christians and to persecute them. That was why the Pharisees had killed Jesus, and that was also why Jews had ruthlessly massacred Christians throughout the Middle Ages.[58]

Most importantly, the Talmud commanded Jews to engage in ritual murder. According to Desportes, from the beginning of the Jewish dispersion up to the present, Jews had brutally assassinated Christian children to use their blood for Jewish rituals. These murders, he claimed, were not isolated acts; rather they were "national . . . crimes, observed and practiced by the entire Jewish people." Although Desportes conceded that there was nothing in the Talmud that explicitly commanded Jews to commit ritual murder, nevertheless he maintained that this silence was only because the rabbis had excised the relevant portions of the Talmud to hide the hideous truth. And although Desportes admitted that Jews in the West no longer widely practiced ritual assassination, he insisted that they now employed a new tactic to "poison" Christian souls: anticlerical legislation.[59]

The publication of Le Mystère du sang embroiled Desportes in a conflict with his superior in Rouen, Msgr. Léon-Benoît-Charles Thomas, who expelled the seminarian from the diocese for having written this tract. It also provoked an acrimonious polemic with Isidore Cahen, editor-in-chief of the Jewish weekly Archives israélites. And ultimately, it proved embarrassing to the Vatican, since the Pope had conferred a papal benediction on Desportes, who had sent the Vatican two copies of his book. Whether this benediction signaled that the "Pope greatly approves of his work on the horrible custom of the rabbinical Jews," as Desportes boasted to the press,[60] or whether it was merely a form letter, as Cardinal Mariano Rampolla, the papal secretary of state, explained to Cardinal Henry Edward Manning, the archbishop of Westminster, who had intervened with the Vatican at the behest of enraged Jewish leaders, is not clear.[61] What is clear, however, is that Desportes parlayed this papal benediction into a claim that he had the backing of the Vatican and that Cahen was sorely mistaken in claiming that Desportes spoke for no one but himself.[62]

This dispute paved the way for the next collaborative effort undertaken by Desportes and Drumont in 1890, a brochure charmingly titled Tué par les Juifs (Killed by the Jews). This work was addressed "To the Jew Isidore Cahen, Director of the Archives israélites," and in the preface Desportes refuted Cahen's charges regarding Le Mystère du sang. Here Desportes explained that he had not been disciplined by Msgr. Thomas because of this text or even because of his antisemitism. Rather, he insisted, Thomas had been eager to maintain good relations with the Jewish prefect of the Nord, Ernest Hendlé, because he was hoping to be named a cardinal and needed Hendlé's support. Furthermore, he claimed that Thomas was not opposed to antisemitism, as Cahen had suggested, and he cited the Pope's "laudatory benediction" as proof of Vatican support.[63]

In addition to refuting Cahen's claims, the other aim of *Tué par les Juifs* was to provide a contemporary example of ritual murder. Even before the book appeared in October 1890, Drumont and Desportes had begun to disseminate a new ritual murder accusation leveled by a Christian woman from Damascus named Jemilé Abd el Nour. In a letter written to Drumont in May 1890, Abd el Nour accused the Jewish community of Damascus of having ritually assassinated her son during Passover. According to her account, although eighteen doctors had performed an autopsy and knew the truth, the Ottoman authorities had hushed up the matter, since they feared an outbreak of interethnic disturbances. She therefore was appealing to Drumont as a man who was "unafraid to tell the truth."[64]

Whether Drumont and Desportes had concocted this affair from the start is not clear, but once this accusation had been leveled, they exploited it to the hilt. In May of 1890 the Paris police noted that the Ligue antisémitique de France (LAF),[65] led by Drumont, Guérin, and the Marquis de Morès, was posting placards throughout the city warning mothers with children under the age of seven to beware of ritual murder.[66] In addition, Drumont and Desportes persuaded the Catholic press in Paris and the provinces to reprint the mother's allegations as indisputable fact. Although Isidore Cahen again challenged these assertions, since there were neither witnesses nor any corroborating evidence, these provincial papers, especially in the staunchly Catholic region of the Nord, fiercely defended their stance.[67]

In the text of *Tué par les Juifs*, Desportes reaffirmed the veracity of Abd el Nour's charge, and he suggested that other ritual murders had occurred in recent years. These murders and their cover-up demonstrated that the character of the Jews had not changed one iota since the time of Christ. According to Desportes, "Since the great sacrifice of Calvary, the Jews . . . have never ceased shedding the blood of the disciples of Christ." There was only one solution to this horrific problem: Jews needed to be either expelled or reinterned in ghettos.[68]

Despite the efforts of Desportes and Drumont to ignite a conflagration over this incident, this story never grabbed the wider public's attention. By contrast, it received considerable attention in the Catholic press. Indeed, the coverage was so inflammatory that Rabbi Emile Cahen of Lille requested the Archbishop of Cambrai to intervene to pressure two Catholic papers in that city to tamp down their rhetoric, but apparently to no avail.[69] Nor did the Archbishop of Cambrai, nor any member of the French Church hierarchy for that matter, ever publicly denounce Desportes's inflammatory charges. The only prelate to do so was Cardinal Manning, a British citizen. In France, the ritual murder charge would not be publicly condemned by any high-ranking cleric until 1907.[70]

The works of Rohling, JAB, and Desportes provided a foundation for a series of violent Catholic works that appeared during the years prior to the eruption of the Dreyfus affair. These texts were filled with rants against the Talmud and accusations of ritual murder, and they all paid tribute to Drumont, despite the fact that the antisemitic leader was rapidly losing favor in the eyes of the Church hierarchy. According to one of these books, *Le Juif: Voilà l'ennemi! Appel aux Catholiques* (The Jew: Here's the Enemy! A Call to Catholics) (Paris: A. Savine, 1890), by a certain Dr. Martinez, Jews were "harmful beings by their very essence," whose character had been shaped by the Talmud. Their goal was to "crush the Goyim" and to set themselves up as the "supreme authority" over all other peoples of the world. Only one people was to be exempted from this fate: Christians, since they were slated for an even worse fate, extermination, either directly through ritual murder or indirectly through anticlerical legislation. To counter this threat, Martinez recommended reimplementing the entire gamut of medieval anti-Jewish restrictions, including bans on Jews holding public office and even stipulations that Jews be forced to wear distinctive garb. Since he recognized, however, that the state was unlikely to adopt this strategy, he urged Catholics to undertake a war of self-defense—a "holy war" or "war of extermination" as he called it. To be sure, he acknowledged that some "innocent" Jews might be swept away in this battle, but he deemed such causalities the "harsh necessity" of war.[71]

Father Isidore Bertrand, an archconservative from the Dauphiné in southeastern France, similarly railed against Jews for having imposed on Christians the "demoralizing divorce law" and the "Godless school" in a book titled *Un Monde fin de siècle* (An End of the Century World) (Paris: Bloud et Barral, 1891). Indeed, he claimed, the entire anticlerical program of the Third Republic had "issued forth from the Synagogue." How, he asked, had Jews achieved this immense power? Once again the answer was clear—the Talmud, which shared nothing in common with the Old Testament. Bertrand even declared that "[t]he God of the Talmud resembles not at all the one we worship." He further maintained that even the most assimilated Jews adhered to the "insanities of the Talmud." No matter how hard the Jew tried to free himself from the Talmud, "[h]e is riveted to his doctrines, like the ball is riveted to the foot of a galley slave." His ultimate goal was "the triumph of semitism" and "the reconstitution of Jewish power upon the ruins of Christianism." Due to their persecution, Catholics had become an oppressed population in their own country.[72]

Under these circumstances, Bertrand urged his coreligionists to fight tooth and nail against "these fin-de-siècle bandits." To be sure, as a priest, he still held out some hope for conversion. As he argued, "Only baptismal waters, received with faith, have the power to transfigure and replace in him the aspirations of the Christian for those of the semite." Nevertheless, although Bertrand's book was well over four hundred pages long, the theme of conversion scarcely figured at all. Rather, Bertrand fully endorsed Drumont's program. He seconded Drumont's appeal to boycott Jewish businesses, and he expressed no qualms about Drumont's appeals to confiscate Jewish assets, since these had been acquired through fraud and had been sanctioned by numerous medieval precedents. Although Bertrand paid lip service to the Vatican's policy of Ralliement and maintained that he did not oppose the republican form of government per se, nevertheless he insisted that as long as the Republic persisted in its anticlerical policies, Catholics were obligated to topple this satanic regime. They could begin by working through the ballot box, but if that strategy failed, Bertrand urged them to take up arms. As he declared, "For the freemason crossbred with the semite, fear of the cane marks the beginning of wisdom."[73]

Another venomous work that expressed these themes was Msgr. Léon Meurin's *La Franc-Maçonnerie: Synagogue de Satan* (Freemasonry: Synagogue of Satan) (Paris: V. Retaux et fils, 1893). Meurin, who was the Jesuit archbishop of Port Louis in Mauritius, compared the events of the nineteenth century to a tornado that had swept across his island. Although he focused less on the Talmud than on the Kabbalah, the Jewish mystical tradition, which he blamed for modern pantheism by which he meant atheism, he too claimed that Jews and Masons had banded together to wage "a bitter fight. . . . against Christ and his Church." Furthermore, he declared that the Jewish-Masonic alliance was the heir of every heresy that had ever bedeviled the Church. All of these groups were agents of Lucifer, the Antichrist, and they were motivated by "an indescribable rage against God and against all those who believe in God." Their goal was to "annihilate Christianism" in order to establish the reign of man over the reign of God.[74]

Meurin too evoked the specter of "the establishment of a universal judeo-masonic empire," bent on destroying the Vatican in order to erect a counter-Vatican headed by a "Jewish and satanic pontiff."[75] To achieve this goal, he echoed Desportes and Martinez in arguing that the enemies of the Church had two chief weapons at their disposal: ritual murder and anticlerical legislation. According to Meurin, Jews hated Christians to such an extent that they routinely resorted to ritual murder. As he recounted, every year during the Jewish festival of Purim, Jews killed a Christian child to commemorate the hanging of their archrival Haman in ancient Persia. They subsequently sprinkled this child's blood into the dough they used to bake *hamentaschen*, the triangular pastries made for the holiday, which they then distributed to Christians as gifts.[76]

But Jews had a second weapon in their arsenal as well: anticlerical legislation. The Jewish-Masonic clique in power, he declared, already had succeeded in subjugating Christians: they had imposed "atheistic education" on a Catholic nation; they had violated the sanctity of marriage through the introduction of "Jewish divorce"; and they had infringed on freedom of religion by imposing "revolting prohibitions" against public displays of Christianity, such as crucifixes and religious processions. They also had stolen Church property through discriminatory taxes, and they had systematically excluded Catholics from civil service posts. Ultimately, Meurin argued, this Jewish-Masonic cabal had radically inverted all moral values. For them, "God is Satan, Satan is God; Good is Bad, Bad is Good; Virtue is Vice, Vice is Virtue, etc. . . ."[77]

Finally, in the mid-1890s a wave of Catholic antisemitic works appeared that had originally been submitted for the 1895 essay contest sponsored by Drumont's paper, the *Libre Parole*, on the subject: "The practical means of arriving at the annihilation of Jewish power in France, with the Jewish danger considered from the point of view of race and not from the religious point of view." Priests penned a striking number of the submissions to the contest. For the sake of brevity only two of these will be discussed here: Father (Julien) Constant's *Les Juifs devant l'Eglise et l'Histoire* (The Jews Before the Church and History) (Paris: Gaume et Cie, 1896) and A. Puig's (abbé Baruteil-Puig's) *Solution de la question juive: La race de vipères et le rameau d'olivier* (Solution to the Jewish Question: The Race of Vipers and the Olive Branch) (Paris: Delhomme et Briguet, 1897).[78]

Constant's book bore no indication that it had been an entry in the *Libre Parole* contest, nor did it win a prize. It is nevertheless fairly certain that this text, which bore the imprimatur of the head of the Dominican order, was written for this end, since it relied entirely on Drumont's account of Jewish history and melded Drumont's antisemitism with the Church's theological stance on Jews and Judaism. Constant's chief argument focused on the need to revive medieval Christian anti-Jewish legislation. If such legislation were not resuscitated immediately, he warned, Christians risked being "devoured" by Jews. Following Drumont, Constant insisted that the "Jewish question" today had nothing to do with religion, since Judaism no longer constituted a religion. Once

Jews opted for the Talmud over the Gospels, they became a people, a nation, and as such they were unassimilable. Jews could never become French, not even through an act of naturalization. As Constant declared, addressing Jews directly: "Before and after [an act of naturalization], you're a Jew and you'll never be anything other than a Jew."[79]

Although Constant acknowledged that Jews had clung to their religion because of persecution, nevertheless he insisted that they had brought this persecution on themselves by following the immoral precepts of the Talmud. Constant repeated the charge that the Talmud encouraged Jews to cheat, lie to, and even kill Christians; therefore, criminality was rooted in their very nature. Indeed, he declared, the Talmud had been given to the Jews not by God or even Moses, but by the rabbis — the "ministers of the devil." The Talmud constituted an "outrage, blasphemy and destruction" against the Decalogue, which had now passed into Christian hands. "This cursed tradition" furthermore instructed Jews to hate Christians and the Christian state. In the eyes of Jews, "The Christian state is more abominable than any infidel state," and the Talmud expressly encouraged Jews to "rob and kill the Christian," especially through ritual murder. According to Constant, the fact that so many cases of ritual murder had been recorded throughout history constituted sufficient proof that this crime had repeatedly been committed. Although the Church had never shed a drop of Jewish blood, the Jews, Constant declared, "have shed streams of Christian blood, whenever and wherever they have been the masters," although precisely when these bloodlettings had occurred was never specified. Their secret aspiration was to destroy the Church and bring about "the ruin of the Christian."[80]

In their "war to the death" against the Church and the Christian state, the Jews were willing to use any and all means. Even converts could not be trusted, since the Talmud specifically commanded that Jews feign conversion in order to infiltrate Christian society and corrode it from within. Ultimately, Christians and Jews had nothing in common with one another; they were two entirely different species of being. As a result, Constant proclaimed, "The Jewish nationality is the enemy of the Christian nationality. The Jew, in refusing any fusion, any assimilation with the people among whom he is a guest, can only constitute for that people . . . an imminent peril." And, in an allusion to the recent conviction of Captain Alfred Dreyfus by a military court in January 1895, he added, "No feeling of patriotism attaches the Jew to the nation that has received him, treason is always lurking in his heart, and only awaits a petitioner."[81]

Again following Drumont, Constant maintained that Jews had already seized half of the nation's wealth, and he warned that if preventative measures were not implemented immediately, "thirty-six million French Christians" soon would be living in a "Jewish state." Were that to happen, their status would sink to the level of colonial subjects, "slaves and pariahs of the Jew, exploited by the Jew . . . skinned alive by the Jew." The Jews, he declared, should be expelled, or if that proved unworkable, more radical solutions, perhaps even a "revolution," might be warranted. Short of these remedies, however, Constant recommended reviving medieval anti-Jewish restrictions. He specifically urged the confiscation of the Jews' "oppressive fortunes" to curtail "the tyrannies of capitalism" that were crushing small-scale property owners; waging economic boycotts against Jewish enterprises; and reinstating ghettos, which he likened to internment camps where Jews would be placed under strict police surveillance and where relations between Jews and Christians would be strictly monitored. He expressed particular consternation about sexual relations between Jews and Christians, since he believed that Jewish women, and especially prostitutes, were seeking to destroy Christians through moral depravity. To radically reduce social contact, he recommended the reintroduction of the *rouelle*, or yellow badge.[82]

Finally, Constant demanded the revocation of Jewish emancipation. It was intolerable, he claimed, for Jews to hold civil and military service posts that placed them in positions of superiority vis-à-vis Christians. He also recommended that Jews be barred from a wide range of liberal professions, including law, medicine, and pharmacology. Most importantly, they should be denied the rights of citizenship "on Christian land." Constant conceded that some people might find these ideas intolerant, but he admitted that the Church was an "essentially intolerant" institution. In any case, since Jews had initiated a war against the Church, these measures were purely defensive.[83]

Although Constant's arguments were not original, his tone was more violent than previous works. To be sure, he did not speak of a war between semites and aryans, but his tract was peppered with racial language. Constant described Jews as a "contagion" and a "parasitical excrescence," and he frequently compared them to Judas. He also alluded to "the native perfidy of the race." Linking these racial traits to their socioeconomic character, he added, "Wealth is the defining characteristic of the Jew, just as the hump is the defining characteristic of the camel, just as *reptileness* is the defining characteristic of the serpent." He concluded by declaring, "The Jews of Drumont are the Jews of history."[84]

By far, the most violent of these texts was A. Puig's, *Solution de la question juive* (Solution to the Jewish Question), which won third place in the *Libre Parole* essay contest. In contrast to the other works discussed in this chapter, which were all written by right-wing Catholics, Puig, whose real name was abbé Pierre Baruteil, was a Christian Democrat, and as such, he supported democracy and opposed capitalism. Unlike the socialists, however, he identified capitalist exploitation only with Jews, and he believed that a more just social order would emerge from class conciliation based on Christian values of charity as opposed to class conflict. Indeed, Puig had attended the Christian Democratic Congress in Lyon in 1896, where Drumont was the featured speaker.[85] Hence, despite the sharp divide between conservative Catholics and Christian Democrats and Social Catholics on the "social question," their views on the "Jewish question" converged.

Although Puig was a priest who later taught theology at the Catholic Institute in Paris, he described Jews not as adherents of a religious denomination, but as members of a nation and even a race. He referred to Jews alternately as a "degenerate race," "vampires," "serpents," "race of vipers born of the Devil," and "vermin of humanity." Physically and morally they were degenerate beings. Physically, he claimed, they suffered from a host of disfiguring and debilitating diseases: scabies, ulcers, scrofula, dysentery, and anemia, and he echoed Drumont in asserting that they exuded "a stinking odor." Morally, he contended, their values were "incompatible with our principles of civilization"; they were the "irreconcilable enemy" of Catholics. Was any other "race," he asked, "more monstrous from the moral point of view?" Jews collectively shared a "horrible character . . . inclined to revolt . . . hard and bloodthirsty toward everything not Jewish."[86]

Where did this moral decrepitude come from? Once again, the answer was clear: the Talmud, or "the Jewish system" as Puig called it. Because of the Talmud, Jews had been raised to hate Christians and regard them as "offspring of cattle." As a result, they had never ceased waging a war of "extermination" against Christians, and Puig followed JAB in providing a long list of ritual murders from ancient times to the present. Like Martinez and Meurin, he too claimed that Jews possessed two principal weapons: ritual murder and anticlerical legislation. Regarding ritual murder, he declared, "They kill without compassion their own children, they eat, and what they're eating is human entrails; they drink, and it's the blood of human victims!" And he repeated Drumont's contention that "the existence of ancient Israel was nothing more than a perpetual battle between Molochism and Jehovism." These bloody practices, he maintained, had become especially pronounced after Jews rejected Jesus. From that time on "the spirit of superstition snuffed out the spirit of religion and the most hideous rites became the prerogative of the synagogue." Ultimately, Puig maintained, Talmudic Jews wreaked irreparable harm on the world; nothing can justify "the evils they inflict on us, the disasters they provoke."[87]

Yet Puig acknowledged that Jews today relied chiefly on their second weapon—anticlericalism. Since the Third Republic had come to power, Jews and their Masonic allies had conducted a crusade "against the beliefs and religion of the immense majority of Frenchmen." As a result, he reiterated the oft-repeated claim that thirty-six million French Catholics were living "in a Jewish country." Despite the republican motto of "liberty, equality, and fraternity," these ideals were a complete sham. The real aim of the Jews was to conquer not only France but the entire world. Their goal was to "exterminate the best" among the "goyim" and to subjugate all others to a life of slavery. If Christians ever acquired an inkling of the fate Jews had in store for them, they would rise up and exterminate them all.[88]

To salvage the last vestiges of Catholic religious liberties, Puig called on Catholics to wake up and organize a counterassault, and he laid out three strategies to combat the Jewish threat. First, he pointed to the strategy of assimilation, by which he meant conversion. In his view, however, conversion could never be effective, since as Drumont had declared, the Talmud "is imprinted on their brain by the law of heredity." Just as the Marranos of Spain and Portugal had falsely converted in the fifteenth and sixteenth centuries in order to infiltrate Christian society, so too converts today remained bound to their ancestral roots since "the race is everywhere the same."[89]

Puig's second possible solution to the Jewish problem was expulsion. Although he endorsed this option several times in his text, he retreated from it in his conclusion, perhaps due to pressure from his superiors. Indeed, in the book's conclusion he stated that were expulsion to be carried out, it would need to be executed in a "legal" fashion, with the approval of both houses of parliament as well as the head of state.

Finally, Puig turned to the third alternative: anti-Jewish legislation. This option, he concluded, was best suited to the current circumstances. Although these laws needed to be enforced in a "humane" fashion, they nevertheless had to be sufficiently severe to protect the Christian population. Puig therefore recommended reimplementing the bans on intermarriage between Christians and members of the "Jewish race," on Christians socializing with Jews, on Jews holding public office, and on Jews hiring Christian servants. He also recommended that Jews be required to wear distinctive clothing, including the *rouelle*, and he echoed Drumont's call to confiscate Jewish assets and property.[90]

For some Catholic commentators, Puig's book exceeded the bounds of acceptable Christian theology, but not because of its violent rhetoric. Rather, as abbé A. Boué commented in a collective review of the works submitted for the *Libre Parole* essay contest in the Jesuit periodical *Études*, what was objectionable about Puig's treatise was his treatment of the ancient Israelites of the

Old Testament. As Boué asked, "Must the hatred of Jewish domination make us extend our resentment all the way back to the time of father Abraham?"[91] According to Boué, Puig had apparently forgotten "that the Jewish people, in spite of its faults, was the chosen people of God." By contrast, however, Boué had no problem whatsoever with Puig's treatment of the Talmud. Indeed, he fully agreed that the Talmud constituted the constitution not only of medieval Jewry, but of modern Jewry as well. As Boué argued, one had to delineate clearly between "religious Judaism, which was the guardian of the early revelation of the ancestor of Christianism" and "modern 'juiverie,' born of the evil instinct of the race and encouraged by the Talmud, which is nothing but the opposite of the Bible."

Boué clearly agreed that the reintroduction of medieval anti-Jewish legislation — Puig's supposed "olive branch" — was indeed the best solution to the "Jewish problem." Still, Boué concluded that none of these works compared to the masterpieces of Drumont himself. As he proclaimed, Drumont was "a thinker at the same time as an artist." Moreover, Boué insisted that Drumont, in contrast to Puig, had never strayed from acceptable Christian theological views regarding the Jewish question, despite the fact that Puig's account of Old Testament Jews rested entirely on *La France juive.*

To conclude, this tremendous outburst of clerical antisemitism in the 1880s and 1890s was not merely a continuation of medieval Christian antisemitism. Rather, it needs to be seen as a central component of Catholic hostility to the Third Republic and especially to the radical secularization program. There already had been a ratcheting up of Catholic antisemitic rhetoric in the early 1880s when the anticlerical program was first implemented, but Drumont's arrival on the scene dramatically escalated this trend. Not only did Drumont's rants against the republican state help coalesce Catholic rage that previously had been inchoate, but also many Catholics envisioned Drumont as the leader of a political campaign to topple the secular state. Drumontian antisemitism focused not only on the "social question" — the degree to which the state ought to curb the excesses of laissez-faire capitalism to protect workers and small-scale property owners — but it also focused on the religious question — the extent to which the state and society ought to retain a Christian character. As Desportes explained, Jews today were no longer primarily interested in killing Christian bodies; rather, their goal was to kill Christian souls through anticlerical legislation. To be sure, the vast majority of anticlerical politicians in the Third Republic were not Jews.[92] Nevertheless, Jews were sufficiently well represented among anticlerical politicians and especially publicists for this claim to ring true for the majority of committed Catholics.

Hence, this Catholic antisemitic rhetoric, which repeatedly alluded to the need to fight a "war to the death" against the secularists, needs to be understood within the context of the late-nineteenth-century anticlerical battles or "culture wars," to use the term coined by Christopher Clark and Wolfram Kaiser.[93] But whereas these "culture wars" were of limited duration in Wilhelminian Germany, in France they dragged on for over two decades despite potentially moderating forces, such as the Ralliement or the growing rift between the Vatican and Drumont. Clearly these moderating forces had little effect on the lower clergy, whom Drumont repeatedly acknowledged as the main bastion of his movement,[94] but they apparently had little impact even on the bishops. Indeed, the majority of them agreed with the conservative archbishop of Aix, Msgr. François Xavier Gouthe-Soulard, who famously declared in 1893 that "we are not living in a republic, but in freemasonry."[95] According to Gouthe-Soulard, the Pope had distinguished between the *form* of the republic and its *content*: the laws, the institutions, and the personnel. Although Gouthe-Soulard conceded that Catholics were willing to accept the republican form of government, never, he insisted, would they accept this republic—the republic of the Masons and Jews. The institutions, laws, and personnel of this republic needed to be swept away in order to create a Catholic republic.[96] As a result of this attitude, even high-ranking clerics generally were pleased to see Drumont leading a campaign against the Jewish-Masonic state, despite their disapproval of his tactics and violent rhetoric.

Whereas in Germany the leadership of the Catholic Center Party eventually took a strong stance against antisemitism in the 1880s and 1890s, in France only a handful of Catholics, such as Anatole Leroy-Beaulieu, spoke out against it.[97] As we have seen with regard to Desportes, although he was disciplined by his superior, Msgr. Thomas, neither Thomas nor any other French bishop publicly denounced the seminarian's violent antisemitism, and no representative of the French Church hierarchy spoke out publicly against ritual murder until the early twentieth century.[98] This silence was partly because most members of the clergy continued to see Drumont as a spokesman for Catholic values, despite his racism and violent rhetoric. Furthermore, the majority of them agreed with Drumont's ultimate goal—the overthrow of the liberal republic. The fact that, of all the clerical publicists mentioned in this essay, only Desportes was sanctioned by his superior speaks volumes about the degree of tacit support Drumont's campaign had garnered in official Catholic circles. Moreover, this brand of violent and racial Catholic antisemitism was pervasive. It surfaced repeatedly in the Assumptionist newspaper *La Croix*, which dubbed itself "France's most anti-Jewish newspaper,"[99] and its sister publication, the illustrated weekly

Le Pèlerin (The Pilgrim). Through its numerous provincial editions, La Croix had reached over 200,000 readers by the early 1890s, even in remote rural areas, and Le Pèlerin, too, had a readership of 140,000.[100] But similar rhetoric pervaded nearly every organ of the Catholic press, including the newspapers L'Univers, La Vérité, and Le Monde, as well as prestigious revues such as Études. It also surfaced repeatedly in speeches at Catholic congresses,[101] as well as in the weekly diocesan bulletins, the Semaines religieuses.[102] Even the most violent of Catholic antisemitic charges—ritual murder accusations and anti-Talmudic diatribes—were common fare. Indeed, these charges were so widespread at the time of the Xanten blood libel trial in Germany in 1892 that the chief rabbi of France, Zadoc Kahn, felt compelled to refute them publicly, and his protest was published on the front page of the Libre Parole.[103]

Although some historians have attempted to map French antisemitism, arguing that it was stronger in some regions than in others,[104] the brand of militant Catholic antisemitism discussed here existed everywhere in France and, indeed, throughout Catholic Europe.[105] To be sure, it is likely that the vast majority of the French population, despite being nominally Catholic, did not adhere to these ideas; indeed, many of them had become alienated from the Church.[106] But that is precisely the point; it was in response to this growing alienation and indifference that committed Catholics felt the need to wage a crusade to recoup turf lost since the French Revolution, and especially since the late 1870s, when the republicans came to power and implemented their anticlerical program. From the vantage point of committed Catholics—clergy and laity alike—the war against the Jews, Freemasons, and Protestants, or "the Syndicate," as they were collectively dubbed during the Dreyfus affair, constituted the decisive battle against the rising tides of secularism, liberalism, and materialism, which had sharply reduced the role of religion in public life.

It is true that this Catholic antisemitism remained largely rhetorical, at least during the 1880s and early 1890s.[107] Nevertheless, this rhetoric ultimately inspired anti-Jewish action. In 1895 when several antisemitic deputies put forth a proposal in parliament to limit the role of Jews in civil and military service, citing the disproportionate number of Jews in the administration and claiming that Jews could never be French, Catholic publicists enthusiastically endorsed these measures.[108] Moreover, Catholic groups such as the abbé Theodore Garnier's nationalist league, the Union Nationale, created in 1892 to support the Ralliement and elect conservatives to office to repeal the anticlerical legislation and create a Christian republic, worked hand in hand with the LAF.[109] Finally, when anti-Jewish riots linked to the Dreyfus affair erupted throughout France in 1898, the police repeatedly singled out members of Catholic youth groups as

Ultimate Resource, in *Le Pèlerin*, no. 1180 (August 13, 1989): 16.

Courtesy of the Bibliothèque Nationale de France.

the principal instigators.[110] Although the Church hierarchy and even the Vatican acted behind the scenes to quell this anti-Jewish violence, largely because they feared an anti-Catholic backlash, most Catholic youths were unable to comprehend why such violence was unacceptable, since they had been shouting "Death to the Jews" for years without incurring the slightest reprimand. From their perspective, this physical violence was the logical culmination of this rhetoric.[111]

Finally, we need to move away from the oft-made distinction between religious antisemitism or anti-Judaism, as it is frequently called, and modern antisemitism, which generally is considered to be a secular movement.[112] Religious personnel, both clergy and laity, played a significant role in the dissemination of radical racial antisemitism throughout Europe, and indeed, I would suggest that these groups, at least in predominantly Catholic countries such as France or Austria-Hungary, were responsible for some of the most extreme brands of antisemitism, including the dissemination of violent apocalyptic conspiracy theories, such as the *Protocols of the Elders of Zion*. (The speech of Sir John Readclif, which was reprinted endlessly in the Catholic press in the 1890s, was an early prototype of the *Protocols*,[113] and the French version of the *Protocols*, published in 1920, was edited by a priest, Msgr. Ernest Jouin.[114]) These violent apocalyptic visions informed Austrian antisemitism at the time that Hitler was coming of age, and it is fairly certain that the "redemptive antisemitism" described by Saul Friedlander in his study of Nazi antisemitism stemmed largely from Catholic sources.[115] Simply because these sources arose from religious circles does not mean they were not modern; nor does it mean that they were not violent or racial. Indeed, to argue that the character of the Jews had been molded by the Talmud over the course of generations, whether or not they were observant, needs to be seen as a Catholic variant of racism. Precisely this form of racism became prevalent in France. Although this rhetoric subsided after 1905 with the separation of church and state, it nevertheless persisted in extreme right-wing circles well into the 1930s and 1940s. In his famous 1936 speech in which he denounced Léon Blum's appointment to the premiership, Xavier Vallat, a prominent right-wing deputy and member of both the nationalist league, the Croix de Feu, and the ultra right-wing Ligue Franc-Catholique, declared that Blum's "ascendance to power is incontestably a historic date. For the first time this old Gallo-Roman country will be governed by a Jew." Vallat then claimed that although he personally was not opposed to members of the "Jewish race" residing in France, he could not abide their being allowed to hold high public office, since "in order to govern this peasant nation that is France, it's preferable to have someone whose origins, no matter how modest, disappear into the bowels of our soil, rather than a subtle talmudist."[116] Moreover, in 1941, after Vallat had been appointed Vichy's first commissioner general for Jewish affairs, he reiterated the view that the character of "the Jew" had been formed by "the Law and the Talmud." These forces, he maintained, "have shaped him more powerfully than blood or climatic variation."[117] Hence, as historians Michael Marrus and Robert Paxton have commented, for those who formulated Jewish policy at Vichy "race and religion were inextricably intermingled."[118]

In sum, if we continue to ignore the role of religion in the rise of modern antisemitism, or to differentiate religious anti-Jewish hostility from economic and political antisemitism, we risk failing to understand the apocalyptic and exterminationist aspects of this hatred. The genocidal impetus arose not only from eugenics; rather, as the works discussed above suggest, Catholics, at least in this period, did not hesitate to use the language of "annihilation" and "extermination," language they justified by pointing to the threat Jews posed to Christendom. Moreover, although not rooted in science, this rhetoric was clearly racial, as illustrated by these incessant rants against the Talmud. We therefore need to focus on the interaction of this religiously informed antisemitism with the political and economic strands of the prejudice, since it was precisely this interaction that made antisemitism so virulent and embedded it within broader nationalist movements.

"L'OSSERVATORE CATTOLICO" AND DAVIDE ALBERTARIO CATHOLIC PUBLIC RELATIONS AND ANTISEMITIC PROPAGANDA IN MILAN

Blaming Jews for being stubborn unbelievers will not bring the masses into the movement.
— *Max Horkheimer and Theodor W. Adorno,*
   Dialectic of the Enlightenment

Horkheimer and Adorno added to their observation about the language of political antisemitism the remark that "religious hostility" has not yet been completely extinguished. "It had not been abolished, but was instead embedded in society as a 'cultural legacy.'" This dialectic of religious Jew hatred and secular antisemitism shaped not only the rhetoric of political antisemitism, but also paradoxically the very language of the Church in a time of social upheaval in the nineteenth century.

In the second volume of his overview of contemporary Jewish history published in 1910, the Jewish historian Martin Philippson focused on the origin and development of antisemitism in Europe. Philippson, an attentive observer, pointed out that in a speech from the early 1870s, Pope Pius IX had attacked Jewish journalists and suggested that Jews only "surrendered to the love of money." The papal charges, Philippson noted, anticipated the language of secular antisemitism far more than they drew on the repertoire of religious Jew hatred. For Philippson, "the signal" for the beginning of this new war against Jewry had been "given by the highest office of the Catholic Christianity, Pope Pius IX. This was the moment when modern antisemitism was born."[1]

In this context, Philippson emphasized in particular the importance of the Catholic ultramontane press in the new battle against Jewry. The mouthpiece of the Vatican, *La Civiltà Cattolica* (Catholic Civilization), played an influential role in the dissemination of the language of antisemitism.[2] In the intransigent Church circles close to the Holy See, antisemitism became a cultural code, in which the new language of antisemitism replaced the traditional themes of Christian hatred of Jews.[3]

In the following, I will examine this dialectic using the example of *L'Osservatore Cattolico* (Catholic Observer), a newspaper founded in 1864 in Milan and directed from 1869 to 1893 by Father Davide Albertario (1846–1902).[4] It was in Milan, then, that one of the most virulently antisemitic Catholic publications was produced under Albertario's editorship and where factions of the church came to view Jews, socialists, and liberals as enemies of Catholicism. Through a discussion of Albertario and the Catholic Church in Milan, this chapter will consider the promotion of antisemitism within the Milan church in particular and Italian Catholicism more generally; as this chapter shows, Albertario's activity in Milan attracted attention far beyond the Italian peninsula. At the center of this analysis I pose the question of whether conflicts broke out inside the Catholic Church over this issue, and if so, which specific positions in the debates were promoted by *L'Osservatore Cattolico*.[5]

After a brief overview of Italian historiography and the question of antisemitism, the first section will outline Church history in the context of the city of Milan, the founding of *L'Osservatore Cattolico*, and the biography of its chief editor, Davide Albertario. In the second section, I analyze important antisemitic articles from this publication, and the third part introduces this paper's campaign against ritual murders allegedly carried out by Jews. Through its anti-Jewish campaign, this Milan Catholic newspaper became widely known throughout Europe. The final section will analyze the reporting of this newspaper in the context of the dialectic of traditional religious hostility toward Jews and secular antisemitism.

Italy has been widely disregarded in historical research on European antisemitism,[6] and Italian historiography, in turn, has long ignored antisemitism. Again and again Italian historians have cited the eminent historian Arnaldo Momigliano, who asserted in 1933 that antisemitism did not exist in Italy.[7] His position gained broad acceptance in postwar Italian historiography, in part because Antonio Gramsci had referred to it in his prison notebooks.[8] Only in the mid-1970s did the Italian-American historian Andrew M. Canepa begin to draw attention to the long history of Jewish-Catholic conflict in Italy,[9] pointing in particular to the emergence of antisemitic voices in Italy during the liberal era.[10] Taking up these lines of interpretation, the Italian historian Mario Toscano has opened new directions for Italian historiography in a number of important articles regarding Jewish history and antisemitism in Italy.[11] Canepa also had emphasized the central role of the Catholic Church in the emergence of antisemitism in Italy.[12] As a result, the conflict between the Church and the new Italian national state received more attention in historiography on the emergence of antisemitism in Italy.[13] Recent debates are placing even greater emphasis on religious factors.[14] In my chapter, however, I would instead like to consider the secular origin of Catholic antisemitism through an examination of Albertario, *L'Osservatore Cattolico*, and the Catholic Church in Milan.

■ Milan came under Habsburg rule in the early eighteenth century, and after a brief interruption in the age of Napoleon, it again belonged to the Habsburgs. The Milanese tried, unsuccessfully, to break free in 1848.[15] Ten years later, in the Italian war of independence, Milan threw off Austrian dominance and was incorporated into the newly established Italian state.[16]

For the Catholic Church, these political changes raised fundamental challenges. The first stemmed from the profoundly liberal character of the new Italian national state, which aimed to separate church and state. Second, the foundation of the national state was directed against the secular rule of the Church within the Papal States. Already in 1864, in the aftermath of the first successes of the Piedmont-led path to national unification, Pope Pius IX, who had been considered sympathetic to liberal ideas before the revolution of 1848, had issued his encyclical "Quanta Cura." This pronouncement placed the papacy vigorously against all liberal tendencies of the time. After the conquest and integration of the Papal States into the Kingdom of Italy in 1870, the Pope, limited to the small and newly established state in the Vatican, adopted a profoundly conservative and antiliberal policy.[17] The Vatican became the stronghold of uncompromising and unyielding political opposition to the new nation-state of Italy.[18] Above all, Pius IX opposed any participation of Italian Catholics in political life,[19] and the Catholic media began an intensive war against Jewry.[20]

Sharp divisions existed among the Milanese Catholic clergy. Despite papal opposition, liberalism had deep roots in Milan even within the Catholic Church. Many priests had participated in the 1848 uprising against Habsburg rule and had taken active roles in the battles of the "Five Days" in March 1848. Within the Milanese clergy, the influence of the neo-Guelph idea, the prerevolutionary Catholic movement that was both liberal and anti-Habsburg, was also strong, and it remained so even after Italian unification. Broad sectors of the clergy therefore supported a more liberal Catholicism against the intransigent line taken by the Pope.[21] In particular, the theology of Antonio Rosmini-Serbati (1792–1855) enjoyed great popularity in Catholic circles in Milan. Rosmini-Serbati had endeavored to integrate the national demands of the age with Christian traditions, and for this the Vatican opposed him.[22] In 1859, following the end of Habsburg rule and the addition of Lombardy to the new Italian kingdom, the moderate liberal wing of the Milan clergy founded the *Società ecclesiastica* and, in the following year, the journal *Il Conciliatore:*

Foglio religioso (The Conciliator: A Religious Paper), which became the official voice of this newly established liberal clerical association.[23]

The opposition of more conservative factions of the clergy to Italian unification left liberals isolated. In May 1859 the Archbishop of Milan, Carlo Bartolomeo Romilli (1795–1859), had passed away. The new Piedmontese ruler rejected the Pope's conservative choice for Romilli's successor. As a result, Carlo Caccia Dominioni (1802–1866), an adherent of the Vatican's antiliberal position, carried on the office of the Milan archbishop on an interim basis. Caccia Dominioni refused to participate in the national Italian holiday in 1861 to celebrate Italian unification and prohibited the recital of a "Te Deum" in the Milan Cathedral. After this act of protest, he left town and continued to document the unmistakable position of the clergy against the new state.[24] In the civil society of Milan, however, the Catholic Church soon lost support, and the renewed ruling class of the town organized itself outside the realm of the church.[25] The Vatican's faction in particular experienced a clear and unmistakable decline within local civil society. While attending theatrical performances, for example, conservative clergy were often forced to leave the theaters, which was sometimes only possible under police protection.[26] The church as a whole lost influence on civil society, and consequently the influence of the clergy in Milan declined in the course of the nineteenth century.[27]

Yet the conservatives did not go away. Caccia Dominioni continued to work energetically against liberal institutions, shutting down the *Società ecclesiastica* and banning its publication of *Il Conciliatore*. In response, priests who promoted a reconciliation of Church and state founded a new publication, *Il Carroccio* (The Chariot), named after a symbol of the medieval North Italian City League. Caccia Dominioni, supported emphatically by Pope Pius IX, then retaliated and went on the offensive against the liberal clergy in Milan, encouraging the founding of a new publication to support this struggle. The publication *L'Osservatore Cattolico* (Catholic Observer) appeared in December 1864 and was led by Giuseppe Marinoni, a priest, and Felice Vittadini, a seminary docent. Soon another priest, Enrico Massara, joined the editorial staff of the paper. Above all, this paper was devoted to the local struggle against the liberal clergy, especially the adherents of the theology of Antonio Rosmini. At the same time, the paper combatted the political culture of liberal Italy as a whole.

The founding of the *Osservatore Cattolico*, then, can be understood as an expression of the conflict within the Catholic Church about the appropriate role of the Church in a changed world. The new Italian nation-state, insisted the *Osservatore Cattolico* again and again, undermined religious unity and devastated the social order. Liberalism and its contempt for the faith and for Christian morality had led to social breakdown and an increase in suicide, alcohol-ism, and crime.[28] Pius IX expressly supported this new paper and its positions, and the Pope even made his own contributions to the journal. The liberal state, for its part, turned to repression to counter the conservative clergy and their conservative paper. Many antiliberal priests were arrested. Caccia Dominioni himself was, for a short time, placed under house arrest.[29]

Caccia Dominioni died in 1866, and the following year the Archbishop of Milan, appointed by the Pope but rejected by the Italian state, also passed away. It appeared that the liberal camp had finally gained the upper hand within the Milan clergy, because Luigi Nazari di Calabiana (1806–1893), a priest believed to support reconciliation between state and Church, became the Archbishop of Milan. In 1848 the king of Piedmont had named Luigi Nazari di Calabiana a senator for life, and the year after his appointment as archbishop, King Vittorio Emanuele II decorated him with the order *Ordine Supremo della Santissima Annunziata*, the highest award of the Italian dynasty. The appointment of Calabiana sparked a conflict between the administration of the diocese and *L'Osservatore Cattolico*. This conflict intensified in 1869 when the extremely conservative Davide Albertario joined the editorial staff of *L'Osservatore Cattolico* and made the publication a militant conservative organ against the moderate clergy.[30]

Davide Albertario was born in 1846 in the Lombard province of Pavia into a peasant family.[31] He entered the bishop's college in his hometown and began studying to become a priest. He continued his studies in Milan, where he witnessed the repression of Caccia Dominioni and the intransigent clergy. After the completion of his theological studies at the papal Gregorian University in Rome, he was ordained a priest in Milan.[32] Immediately after attaining the priestly robes, Albertario felt called to become a journalist and joined the editorial staff of *L'Osservatore Cattolico*.[33]

There Albertario fulfilled his mission to defend the pope and to engage in a bitter struggle against liberalism and the Italian monarchy. This struggle sharpened with the military occupation of Rome by troops of the young Italian state on September 20, 1870, and the declaration by the pope that he was now a prisoner in the Vatican. In addition to these outside conflicts, the First Vatican Council and the declaration of papal infallibility gave rise to further divisions within the Catholic Church. While Davide Albertario and the *Osservatore Cattolico* represented the position of the papacy, the Archbishop of Milan was among those opposed to the Vatican Council.

The attacks by the *Osservatore Cattolico* on liberalism sharpened again in the middle of the 1870s. According to the *Osservatore Cattolico*, liberalism had enthroned immorality, and liberals had transformed contempt for morality into an instrument of their tyranny.[34] The paper argued that an anti-Catholic spirit had gained ground not only in Italy but also all over Europe.[35] In the following decades, Albertario continued to engage with the "social question" and was sentenced to three months in jail in 1898 for social agitation.

The mission of Davide Albertario was distinguished further by his animosity toward Jews. When King Vittorio Emanuele II died in January 1878, Albertario raised the conflicts within the Milan diocese to new heights of tension with a sarcastic tribute to the deceased Italian king that incensed not only the liberal political elites of the city, but also the moderates within the Milan clergy.[36] Some of those offended by the mock tribute organized a petition against the *Osservatore Cattolico,* and in response Archbishop Calabiana demanded that the newspaper be shut down. Davide Albertario then went to Rome to ask the pope for support, whereupon the archbishop was forced to rescind his order to close the *Osservatore Cattolico.* In February 1878, Pope Pius IX died, and Albertario feared that he would lose papal backing. A new conflict between the *Osservatore Cattolico* and *Lo Spettatore Cattolico* (The Catholic Spectator), a liberal Catholic publication founded in Milan in 1876, provided Archbishop Calabiana another opportunity, and in May 1878 he ordered Albertario's paper to cease publication. The new Pope Leo XIII, however, sought to mediate between the two camps and created a commission to investigate the conflict within the church in Milan. It was against this backdrop that Albertario began to introduce antisemitic elements into his agitation, despite the fact that Milan had a very small Jewish population.

The Jews of Milan had been expelled and readmitted several times throughout the Middle Ages. The community's position became more stable at the beginning of the eighteenth century.[37] The Jewish community of Milan remained small well into the mid-nineteenth century. In 1840 the community had only two hundred members; in 1861 Milan's three hundred Jews represented only 0.1 percent of the city's population.[38] According to the studies of Sara Sinigaglia, in the first half of the nineteenth century, 41 percent of the Milan Jews were shopkeepers, 20 percent were well-off persons, 6.5 percent worked as craftsmen, 5.2 percent were lawyers, 5.2 percent were merchants, 4.7 percent made a living as tailors, 3.2 percent were teachers or intellectuals, 2.7 percent were artists or actors, 1.6 percent of Milan's Jews labored as domestic servants, 1.3 percent were bankers, 1.3 percent were cooks, another ⅓ percent were engineers, 0.8 percent of the Jewish population of Milan served employees, and 0.8 percent of the city's Jews were doctors.[39] But Italian unification and the rapid growth of northern Italy's economy soon placed Milan at the core of the new state's industrial and commercial development. The Jewish population of Milan rose from around one thousand in 1881 to three thousand in 1900, so that the percentage of the total population increased from 0.3 percent to 0.6 percent.[40] This also caused a considerable increase in the role of the Jews within the local economy and in the Milan banking sector.[41]

Since there had been no Jewish community in Milan during the era when other Italian towns had established ghettos, Milan had no tradition of geographical separation. In the second half of the nineteenth century, around half of the Jewish population resided in the center of the town, along with the upper classes and the ancient families of Milan. Most of the remaining Jewish population lived in the middle-class quarters to the north and southwest of the Duomo, Milan's magnificent cathedral. Few Jews lived in the lower-class housing districts to the southeast of the Duomo.[42]

The constitution of the United Kingdom of Italy granted full emancipation to Jews, and Milan Jewry found broad acceptance within civil society and public culture. They were represented in the municipal council, and some wealthy Milan Jews had been decorated with medals and knighted by the Italian king.[43] This broad presence in urban life and the social advancement of the Milan Jews, however, did not give rise to antisemitic sentiments in middle-class circles or among the working classes. The predominantly liberal public sphere resisted anti-Jewish attitudes in any form. Even craftsmen and shopkeepers, who were among the social groups most attracted to antisemitism elsewhere in Europe (as in Vienna and Berlin, to give two examples), did not seem susceptible to antisemitic attitudes in Milan.[44] Antisemitism in Milan was instead closely related to the Catholic Church, and as the Church had placed itself politically and culturally in opposition to the new Italy, it had lost influence on public opinion in Milan and many other Italian cities.

In sharp contrast to other Italian regions and towns, in Milan much of the local clergy had supported liberalism and the movement for independence in 1848 and beyond, which put them in sharp opposition to official pontifical policy. Anti-Jewish attitudes, therefore, had not become apparent in the Milan Catholic church. This liberalism, however, elicited the strong opposition of the papacy and of the ultramontane wing of the Milan clergy. The original incubator of Catholic attacks on liberal political culture and on the Jews was, of course, the "infallible" Pope Pius IX and the Vatican. The ultramontane wing of the Milan church promoted this struggle, joining those Catholic parishes in Italy such as Mantua, which supported firmly the intransigent fight against the spirit of the age and against Jewish emancipation.[45] In Milan, one of the most rabid supporters of this position would be Father Davide Albertario.

■ Davide Albertario was motivated above all else by his unbridled hatred of liberalism, "the sin of the present era." He formulated this view forcefully in a speech in Bergamo in 1877. In order to battle this enemy energetically, Albertario asserted, "[W]e must hate it," but with a "rational hatred": "We must hate it with all the power of our spirit, always hate it, hate with the mind, with deeds, with words, hate it in such a way that this hatred becomes our nature . . . we must hate it so much that the hatred of liberalism is equal to our faith in and love of God."[46] For Albertario, hatred of liberalism came first, and this speech included only one antisemitic passage. Even thirty years later, in his memoirs of his prison time in 1898, Albertario abstained from antisemitic diatribes.[47] In a speech delivered to a gathering of the early Christian Democratic movement in Milan in February 1901, for example, he focused on Christian democracy and the social question. In this speech, socialism was the central enemy, and Albertario did not make any accusations against the Jews.[48]

In the last decades of the nineteenth century, however, Albertario's *L'Osservatore Cattolico* had become, alongside the Vatican's *Civiltà Cattolica* and *Il Cittadino di Mantova*, one of the most virulently antisemitic publications in liberal Italy.[49] What characterized the antisemitic rhetoric in this Milanese newspaper was that religious themes did not stand at the center. Certainly, Albertario at times fell back to religious motifs and some false Talmud exegesis, as in the "Letter to the Member of Parliament Toscanelli," published in the *Osservatore Cattolico* in 1891.[50] Still, the attacks of this Catholic journal were directed foremost against Jews as citizens and the roles they played in the changing world, including their alleged prominence in the economy, sciences, and journalism.[51] In October 1879, at the same moment when in Berlin the new themes in the language of antisemitism had provoked a public controversy, an article on liberal journalism and the Jews in *L'Osservatore Cattolico* lamented that the press in Vienna was in the hands of Jews and that the liberal newspapers of Italy also were gradually falling under Jewish control.[52] Catholics, it argued, needed to recognize the importance of having a specifically Catholic press.

The *Osservatore Cattolico* was in agreement with antisemites across Europe who were particularly incensed over the principle established at the 1878 Berlin Congress that the emancipation of the Jews was a requirement for international legal and diplomatic recognition of new European states. The specific issue concerned Romania. The *Osservatore Cattolico* published an excerpt from a memorandum by the Romanian Foreign Minister Vasile Boerescu, who stressed that Romania was the European country with the most Jews.[53] He warned, moreover, that should the demands of European diplomacy embodied in the Berlin Congress be fulfilled and Jews granted equality, Romania would fall into slavery.[54] The result would be an indescribable tragedy. The *Osservatore Cattolico* did not take this opportunity to remind Bismarck about his own demands in 1847 that Jews be excluded from society. The Jews, the paper argued, had the money, and money determined the outcomes of diplomacy.

In November 1885 Albertario published "The Jews in the World" in *Osservatore Cattolico*. In an ironic style, he employed vague references to race, noting that "this lovely race of individuals" had expanded to a global population of 6,377,602. Continuing in his ironic tone, he noted that "to all of our luck and to general happiness," 26,289 Jews lived in Italy. They are truly, he claimed, our masters, just as they have become the masters of Austria-Hungary, Germany, and France. Using another theme from the language of secular antisemitism, the *Osservatore* "revealed" that Jews dominated the lodges of the Freemasons. The Freemasons, he continued, had imported liberalism into Italy, which the Jews had used to dominate "parliament, journalism, and the family, yes, everything." However, with this, the spectrum of antisemitic themes was not yet complete, and so Albertario continued: "The Jew is lord of gold," and since gold rules the world, "the Jew is the universal ruler."[55] In a piece on the Jewish question in France, the *Osservatore Cattolico* again emphasized that liberalism had delivered the people into the hands of the greedy, usurious, and hypocritical Jews.[56]

In the 1890s the *Osservatore Cattolico* paid close attention to the Dreyfus affair. Just a few days after the indictment, the paper stressed that "Captain Dreyfus . . . is a JEW." The word "Jew" was highlighted and printed in uppercase letters. The middle of this sentence insisted that Dreyfus had "betrayed the army and his country" and, according this newspaper of Italian Catholics, "sold military secrets to the Germans and to Italy." In the next sentence, again drawing from the vocabulary of secular antisemitism, the article claimed that it was no surprise that Jews betrayed Christian nations — the Christian author of this article inserted the adjective "Christian" — since "they have no fatherland." A series of reports and articles about the Dreyfus affair followed this brief but revealing piece.[57]

As the year 1900 approached, Albertario and a younger generation of Catholic journalists began to accentuate more strongly social and political issues. Unsurprisingly, the *Osservatore Cattolico* closely followed the development of the Christian Social Party in Austria. The elections for the Vienna city council on April 5, 1895, resulted in a clear victory for the Christian Socials.[58] Immediately following the election, a brief article in the *Osservatore Cattolico* asserted that the capital of Vienna was falling into the hands of the Jews. This "fact," the paper declared, made the electoral victory of Vienna's antisemites — as the

Christian Socials were deemed by Catholic journalists in Milan—all the more astounding.[59]

Under the heading "Social Movement," the *Osservatore Cattolico* summarized its understanding of antisemitism by defining it as an integral part of broader social questions. Coming back again to the hatred of liberalism, the article asserted that "semitism"—meaning for the writer the supremacy of gold—was desired by liberalism. "The Jews possess," the article continued, "almost all of the big banks, and is taking possession of the mid-sized banks," and after all, "who owns the money, owns the press, and who owns the press, has the power."[60] The Milan Catholic newspaper proclaimed that the papacy repeatedly had saved Jews from persecution. Therefore, the paper insisted, the origin of antisemitism could not lie in religious conflict. Instead, the Jews had brought it on themselves. Antisemitism must, through the institution of laws, prevent the Jewish vampire from pressing down like a boulder on the stomach of the people. Only then, according to the *Osservatore Cattolico*, would the people be freed of this social plague.[61]

No matter was too small for *L'Osservatore Cattolico*. In 1901, for example, the engineer and vice mayor of Ferrara, Eugenio Righini, published an extensive work on "antisemitism and semitism" in Italian politics.[62] Although not free of ambivalent formulations—the author lamented the "Jewish influence" on the press, for example—Righini's book denounced antisemitism. Therefore Righini's publication received positive reviews in the Jewish press of Italy.[63] The *Osservatore Cattolico* praised the author for grappling with such an important topic, but it denounced Righini for doing so with insufficient understanding and one-sided observations.[64]

After the bloody suppression of the Milan food riots and demonstrations of May 1898,[65] the *Osservatore Cattolico* took an even clearer anticapitalist position, interpreting these disturbances and the ensuing crackdown through the prism of antisemitism. In 1901 an article appeared with the title "Jewish Capitalism." In this piece, the paper articulated again the nonreligious themes of Catholic antisemitism. Once more, the *Osservatore Cattolico* railed against the rise of the House of Rothschild, which ruled the capitals (and capital) of Europe. One had to be completely blind, the paper insisted, to overlook the enormous damage done to society by Jewish capital.[66] As we have seen, Davide Albertario sometimes downplayed antisemitism in his public speeches. But the paper he had helped to shape, the leading Catholic paper of Milan, showed no such restraint.

■ These hateful tirades and attacks on Jews were not the source of the *Osservatore Cattolico*'s great notoriety in Europe as a whole, particularly among European antisemites. The paper's intensive campaigns against alleged ritual murders committed by Jews in 1891 and 1892 dramatically raised the *Osservatore Cattolico*'s profile far beyond the borders of Italy.[67] By revitalizing these old legends, European antisemites tried to invent an antisemitic tradition and thereby legitimate their own hatred of Jews. At this particular moment, Albertario threw himself into this anti-Jewish campaign promoted by German and other European antisemites. Albertario and his journal's extreme antisemitic rhetoric did not succeed in winning over Milanese and Italian opinion, but rather pushed the *Osservatore Cattolico* further to the margins.

Albertario's anti-Jewish crusade, focused on ritual murder charges, has been intensively studied by Annalisa Di Fant,[68] an Italian historian who has published widely on antisemitism in the Italian Catholic press of the nineteenth century.[69] The following section draws on Di Fant's work. At the height of this campaign, as Di Fant has noted, the *Osservatore Cattolico* published antisemitic articles on an almost-daily basis.[70] As late as 1927, the *Jewish Lexicon*'s entry on "Blood Libel" noted that "the *Osservatore Catolico* [sic] in 1892, plagiarizing from other antisemitic pamphlets," published "a list of 154 allegedly attempted and accomplished 'Ritual Murders.'"[71]

It is revealing that Albertario did not begin writing on this theme in the *Osservatore Cattolico* in 1882, when the accusation in the Hungarian town of Tiszaeszlár unleashed a European-wide debate on the ritual murder legend.[72] The sensational lawsuit brought by the theologian August Rohling against the Austrian Rabbi Josef Samuel Bloch over Bloch's public attacks on the former's "scholarship" on ritual murder had a wide resonance in the European public sphere in this period. Yet the Rohling-Bloch battle also failed to inspire Albertario to write on this theme.[73] Albertario's attention was drawn to the question of the blood libel by a minor occurrence that took place in 1888. In Breslau, an aspiring rabbi was accused of taking blood from an eight-year-old Christian boy for ritual purposes,[74] an incident that did not follow the usual pattern of ritual murder charges insofar as the child was too old and not murdered.[75] It is not clear why this case aroused Albertario's interest. Perhaps his German correspondents had made Albertario aware of the case. A decade later, the extreme German antisemite Max Liebermann von Sonnenberg still remembered the Breslau incident.[76] It is also significant that Albertario's new antisemitic campaign began shortly after Leo XIII had appointed to the post of Vatican State Secretary Mariano Rampolla (1843–1913), the papal nuncio in Madrid who was well-known for his outspoken antisemitic views.[77] Rampolla strongly backed Albertario and his intransigent newspaper.

The next case that drew the attention of *L'Osservatore Cattolico* took place in 1890. On Easter Monday in Damascus, a young Christian boy—again, a boy and not an infant—went missing. The body was soon found in a well. It was reported that the blood had been drained from it, and the rumor of ritual murder spread.[78] The importance of this location was clear: a ritual murder accusation in 1840 in Damascus had revived European interest in this medieval legend.[79] The *Osservatore Cattolico* pursued rumors about the alleged Jewish blood rites in Damascus with great interest.[80] The Milan paper amalgamated themes from secular antisemitism with ritual murder. The paper portrayed Jews as cosmopolitan vampires who sucked the blood from society and its material goods.[81] Only a few days later, the Milan Catholic journal wrote that the entire Christian era was marked by this terrible stigma of Jewish ritual murders. The paper printed a long list of supposed ritual murders and blood libels from the fifth century to the present. This list, which was based on contemporary antisemitic literature and the *Civiltà Cattolica*, was the same list mentioned in the *Jewish Lexicon*.[82]

Albertario's intensive campaign against Jews became increasingly strident at the very moment when German antisemites took notice of the *Osservatore Cattolico* and considered using this paper for their own purposes. The context for German interest in this Italian-Catholic paper was the refutation of the blood libel written by a Protestant theologian at the University of Berlin, Hermann Leberecht Strack (1848–1922). Strack had debunked the ritual murder legend in response to the blood libel rumors that broke out on the Greek island of Corfu in 1891.[83] Strack had wanted to help cure the "terrible disease of superstitious belief" in the Jewish blood legend.[84] German antisemites commenced a sharp campaign against Strack in one of the most influential antisemitic German newspapers of that time, the *Staatsbürgerzeitung*.[85] They also gravitated toward *L'Osservatore Cattolico*, which itself had already reported in great detail about the eruption of the ritual murder accusations on Corfu.[86] German antisemites in turn offered the Milan paper reports on other supposed incidents of ritual murder. These appeared in *L'Osservatore Cattolico* under the heading "Letters from Berlin."[87] German antisemitic publications then cited the *Osservatore Cattolico*'s reports as evidence that ritual murder charges sported the seal of approval of an international Catholic paper.[88]

In March and April 1892 the *Osservatore Cattolico* published a series of eighteen stories on the certainty of the ritual character of Jewish murders. The paper cited an international array of antisemitic literature that ran from August

Rohling to Henri Roger Gougenot des Mousseaux, through the relevant articles of *Civiltà Cattolica*, and finally, to the writings of Edouard Drumont.[89] This campaign sparked a violent controversy in the Milan public sphere. The liberal newspaper of the city, *Corriere della Sera*, made serious allegations against *L'Osservatore Cattolico*'s campaign. In July, the Catholic newspaper challenged *Corriere della Sera* by offering a large reward should anyone prove false the charge that Jews committed ritual murders.[90] The German antisemitic *Staatsbürgerzeitung* reported on this challenge just a few days later.[91] Hermann Strack declared himself ready to deliver the necessary proof on the condition that an independent commission judge his manuscript. After the *Osservatore Cattolico* appointed August Rohling, who had become famous for his antisemitic writings on the alleged truth of the ritual murder accusations, Stack retracted his offer.[92] Instead, Strack published a new edition of his treatise on the superstitious belief in the blood libel in which he included a detailed chapter on the campaign by *L'Osservatore Cattolico*.[93] German informants also supplied the *Osservatore* with information about the ritual murder accusation that arose in the small village of Xanten in the Lower Rhineland in June 1891.[94] On August 6, just one day before violent physical assaults against Jews and their homes and stores broke out in Xanten, the *Osservatore* declared that the more Jews endeavored to insist falsely that they had never committed ritual murder, the more clearly evidence of such murders would reach the light of day.[95] The *Osservatore* published a series of short notices about Xanten in the first three weeks of September and returned to the issue with two extensive and detailed articles in the last week of the month.[96]

The theological journal of the Milan archbishopric, *La Scuola cattolica*, took on the subject and reported on the debate between Albertario and Strack.[97] In reply, in April 1893 the *Osservatore Cattolico* commented on the dispute the newspaper had with Hermann Strack and declared that its own opposition to the Jews had nothing in common with German antisemitism. The *Osservatore Cattolico* insisted that its own brand of antisemitism rejected any form of physical violence. The same article, distancing *Osservatore Cattolico*'s refined version of antisemitism from the barbaric German version, complained of the mafia-like character of the Jews and depicted them as a cancer infecting the body of society.[98]

The April 1893 article marked the sudden end of the vigorous campaign against alleged Jewish ritual murder championed by Albertario and the *Osservatore Cattolico*.[99] The paper's campaign against alleged Jewish ritual murder had lasted only two years. Albertario was forced to recognize that in liberal Milan he was unable to succeed with this harsh antisemitic rhetoric and with this revival of medieval legends. In fact, despite the persistent campaign and the constant stream of stories "documenting" alleged ritual murders, not a single case of blood libel accusations had occurred in Milan. Accusing the Jews on the basis of these medieval legends simply did not incite the people of Milan.

The Milan Catholic paper did continue to publish antisemitic articles; however, they were no longer focused on the blood libel accusation, and the campaign against Jews receded in favor of a new attention to social issues. In the meantime, the editorial committee of *Osservatore Cattolico* had experienced a fundamental generational change since the end of the 1880s.[100] The new generation of collaborators included lay Catholics. These lay journalists were equally convinced of the primacy of the papacy and fully committed to the pope's intransigent position. The politics of these new editors, however, had been shaped by the social engagement of Catholic associations. They also no longer questioned the existence of or directly opposed the Italian nation-state.[101] The most important figure in this younger generation of editors was the journalist and politician Filippo Meda (1869–1939), who assumed direction in 1893 after the end of the campaign of the blood libel accusation. Although Meda continued to declare unconditional submission to the Pope and his intransigent policy, his main concern was no longer the Church's battle against the national state. He focused instead on the Christianization of politics. The battle against the Jews was no longer at the center of his — or the *Osservatore Cattolico*'s–interest.

■ Under Meda's editorial control, antisemitic reports and editorials continued to be published in the *Osservatore Cattolico*. However, the editors tried to link them more closely to social issues and contemporary politics. The general antagonism between Church and state in liberal Italy clearly influenced the antisemitism emanating from elements within the Catholic Church in Milan. The Vatican itself played a decisive role in supporting *L'Osservatore Cattolico*. In Milan, however, the inner-Catholic conflict between liberal and intransigent members of the clergy exacerbated the situation, creating the journalistic space for the expression of Albertario's ferocious antisemitic rhetoric. When it became clear that ritual murder charges did not "bring the masses into the movement,"[102] a new generation of Catholic journalists associated with *L'Osservatore Cattolico* curtailed antisemitic agitation. With this turn away from strident antisemitic rhetoric came an increase in the circulation of the journal. In the years of Albertario the paper had a circulation of two thousand copies. By 1900, under the direction of Meda, the circulation had increased to eight thousand.

The dialectic of religious Jew hatred and secular antisemitism in the propaganda of the intransigent Milan Catholics reveals a break within the religious tradition itself. The allegations that had made their way from Damascus via Breslau to Xanten and were raised again and again in 1891 and 1892 in the *Osservatore Cattolico* did not correspond in any way to the traditional narrative of a ritual murder. Instead, the reports wove together fragments of this old tale to legitimate a new hatred against Jews.[103] After the campaign against ritual murder ended, the younger generation in the leadership of this intransigent Catholic newspaper of Milan returned to the language of secular antisemitism and used it as a weapon in the battle against liberalism, socialism, and capitalism. This antisemitic propaganda was not based on religious antagonism, but rather reflected conflicts within the Catholic Church itself. Factions within the Catholic Church responded with antisemitic agitation to the problems they had in defining their new role in a fundamentally changed world. For them, the Jews served as a cipher for social tensions, political uncertainty, alienation, and mental confusion in the emerging and bewildering industrial society.

PART 2

LOCAL VIOLENCE AND "ETHNIC" POLITICS

IULIA ONAC

THE BRUSTUROASA UPRISING IN ROMANIA

An episode that is sad to remember, the 1885 Brusturoasa Uprising needs to be added to the list of violent acts against Jews in Romania. In Brusturoasa, a small village in Moldavia, peasants turned on their Jewish neighbors. The local priest instigated the violence, and other elites in the village did nothing to stop it. The anger of the local peasantry, born of a deplorable economic situation, was quickly directed against Brusturoasa's Jews, whom the peasants blamed for their plight. The result of this violent episode was the expulsion of the entire Jewish population from the village of Brusturoasa.

Antisemitism as physical violence, whether collective or individual, has frequently manifested itself in modern Romania. Within Romania, synthetic works on Jewish history by Carol Iancu and Victor Neuman have examined aspects of this violence.[1] The history of antisemitism in Romania also has attracted the attention of scholars working outside the country, including Mariana Hausleitner, Dietmar Müller, Raphael Vago, and Beate Welter.[2] The pages of these works show plainly that in modern Romania, as in the rest of Europe, antisemitism had a violent component that revealed itself in unprecedented brutality and cruelty.

Until now, scholars have all but ignored the Brusturoasa Uprising. Yet what took place in Brusturoasa in 1885 anticipates much of what happened on a much larger scale in 1907, when one of the most bloody peasant uprisings in the history of modern Europe shook Romania.[3] In both cases the underlying cause was the poor condition of the peasants. But the uprisings also needed leaders (village priests, mayors, and teachers) to instigate the violence, as well as victims of the peasants' wrath (Jews). The important role played by emblematic figures of the Romanian village during this period emerges clearly from this analysis of Brusturoasa.

■ THE ROMANIAN CONTEXT

To understand and better integrate this episode into the history of antisemitism, it is necessary to discuss the close relationship between Romanian statehood, international human rights, and the severe social dislocation that accompanied the arrival of capitalist agriculture in rural eastern Europe. Modern Romania began to take shape between the onset of the Greek War of Independence in 1821 and the Revolutions of 1848. Both internal and external factors influenced this process. The union of Wallachia and Moldavia in 1859, combined with the support of the Great Powers, resulted in the creation of modern Romania. The era that followed, which lasted through the end of the First World War, overlapped with the modernization of the Romanian state, society, and economy. During this time, Romania developed rapidly. Industrialization took off, although it was still too undeveloped to provide opportunities for all those seeking work, which resulted in an excess of unskilled labor and kept wages at a low level. Significant migration nonetheless began to the capital of Bucharest, the Danube port cities of Galaţi, and the new center of the oil industry, Ploieşti. Beginning in 1869, railroads slowly spread across the country. In spite of this diversification, the Romanian economy and society remained closely linked to agriculture.[4]

These structural conditions in turn shaped daily relations among different ethnic and religious groups. In particular, they deeply affected the lives of Jews in the region. An active element in economic life, Jews contributed significantly to Romania's modernization as craftsmen, industrialists, merchants, bankers, and medical doctors. State building and economic transformation, in short, greatly influenced the place of Jews in the Romanian society.

Demographic changes also had an important impact. The number of Jews in Romania was small but significant. In 1861 Wallachia and Moldavia combined had 3,790,000 inhabitants. By 1899, when the last prewar census was taken, the population had reached 5,957,000 inhabitants, an increase of 57 percent.[5] The growth in the Jewish population during the same time was closer to 100 percent. According to statistics published in the *American Jewish Year Book*, some 269,015 Jews lived in Romania (4.5 percent of the total) around 1900.[6] Much of this population was concentrated in Moldavia, where Jews comprised about 10 percent of the province's total population. Many Romanian Jews came from the Russian Empire, drawn by agreements with Romanian noble landowners, who granted Jews economic privileges, provided land for synagogues and cemeteries, and allowed tax deductions for a certain number of years. In some cases, this resulted in settlements where the majority of the population was Jewish, a fact that often angered the surrounding Orthodox Christian population.

The Great Powers also helped to define the place of Jews in Romania. As a consequence of the 1878 Berlin Congress, Jews living in Romania, who until then could not become citizens because they were not Christians, could now enjoy civil rights based on the revised Article 7 of the Constitution. This article opened the door to Jews naturalizing and acquiring Romanian citizenship. The process itself, however, was cumbersome and flawed, and the Romanian Parliament was hostile to the integration of Jews. In fact, only eighty-five Jews became Romanian citizens between 1879 and 1900.[7] Romania's political and intellectual elite considered Jews to be foreigners without political rights. Nearly two hundred additional laws, decrees, and ministerial orders adopted between 1878 and 1914 aimed to exclude Jews from the main sectors of economic and professional life, including education, the military, and the professions.[8] The large number of Jewish merchants and craftsmen in the Romanian economy was largely because these were some of the few remaining areas in which Jews could secure a living.

In the nineteenth century, agriculture continued to form the basis of the Romanian economy. The vast majority of the population (about 85 percent) worked on the land. By the early 1900s Romania was the world's third largest exporter of corn, the fourth of wheat, and the fifth of other cereals. In 1912 food exports represented fully 75.7 percent of total exports and two-thirds the total national income.[9] Even so, the situation of the peasantry did not improve. While 4,171 large landowners owned 3,787,192 hectares of land, 1,010,302 peasants owned just 3,319,695 hectares.[10] In other words, the disproportion was huge: one million peasants combined owned less land than a few thousand wealthy landowners. Although attempts were made to facilitate the purchase of land by peasants, most continued to lease land from the big landowners or their intermediaries. These intermediaries were the leaseholders (arendași), who extended their administrative power over a large part of the land. Leaseholders paid a fixed amount of money to the landowners and in turn tried to cover their costs (and perhaps make a profit) by squeezing as much money as possible out of the peasantry. The Jewish presence as leaseholders was highly visible, especially in Moldavia, where 61 percent of arable land was managed by Jews. In 1904 the Fischer Brothers alone leased 138,424 hectares in Moldavia.[11]

The two questions—the peasant one and the Jewish one—thus became intertwined in Romania in the late nineteenth century. The two oppressed groups were so closely linked that it was impossible for one not to influence the other. The Romanian political classes not only failed to provide solutions to these problems but also, on the contrary, exacerbated social tensions between the two groups. These conflicts played themselves out on the state level and, as the case of Brusturoasa shows, in villages as well.

In addition to the structural problems just outlined, the uprising in Brusturoasa also had local causes. It began when the personal interests of a small number of individuals intersected with the anger and frustration of the peasantry. Brusturoasa was a small village in Bacău County in Moldavia. Around one hundred Orthodox Christian families lived there, in addition to thirty Jewish families.[12] In 1885 the village also had a handful of laborers from Austria-Hungary, who had been employed to mow hay in the region. The village had a new Orthodox church, built in 1871 on the foundations of the former wooden one. But it was also isolated: Brusturoasa lay deep in a valley on the eastern slopes of the Carpathians, more than eighty kilometers from the county seat and two hundred kilometers from Iași. The village had little arable land but several pastures and around forty small sawmills (some could be worked by only one man). Forestry thus was the main source of income for the residents of Brusturoasa. The arrival of the railroad to the nearby town of Târgu Ocna promised even more economic advantages for the peasant exploiters of the forest.

But the peasant workers soon had their dreams shattered when a Jew named David Grünberg became the new leaseholder in Brusturoasa. A native of Bacău County, Grünberg had lived in Brusturoasa for years and had established a paraffin factory and drilled for oil in the region. Yet, as the new leaseholder, he helped reignite an older dispute between the peasants and a local landowner that would then contribute to the start of the anti-Jewish revolt. Years before, the peasants had sued the landowner Ghica Comămășteanu to regain land that had been taken away from them forty years earlier. They already had spent between one thousand and fifteen hundred lei, but in 1885 the lawsuit had not yet been resolved. The village priest would use anger over the lawsuit's expenses and lack of resolution to urge the peasants to violence.[13] The priest Nicolae Teodoreanu, whose brother Mihalache Popovici was Brusturoasa's mayor, had leased a part of the forest and also controlled many of the sawmills that processed the wood. Teodoreanu's interest was directly affected by Grünberg, who now leased from Comămășteanu the forests on both the left and right sides of his property. In addition, the new leaseholder used mechanical saws to process the wood, which offered much greater efficiency. The priest's interests were seriously affected.

Father Teodoreanu quickly understood that the disaffected peasants could help him in his conflict with his rival. Determined to take advantage of this situation, he said to the peasants that "if they will provoke disturbances and if they will prevent in one way or another the normal path of things, then they could influence the court case because the landowner would give up the lawsuit and they would thereby gain huge, untouched forests."[14] In other words, Teodoreanu promised the peasants that agitation would lead the landowner Comămășteanu to concede the lawsuit and return their land. In this way, the entire episode started with intimidation and then with violent actions, not because of religious hatred, but because of a greedy priest's desire to protect his own economic interests.[15]

The spark came in early July 1885. The Christian residents of Brusturoasa, led by the mayor and the communal counselors, broke the windows of several Jewish-owned houses and even fired a gun at the leaseholder's home, hitting just above his bedroom.[16] Instead of taking action, the village authorities supported the vandals; they reported to the prefecture in Bacău only that for the past several days gangs of inhabitants had roamed through the village and committed criminal acts, but that the police, whom the crowd welcomed with stones, could not stop them. What is more, none of the criminals were identified. The prefect characterized the actions described in the report as "inadmissible in a rural commune."[17] As a consequence of the actions of the mayor and his counselors, the prefect dissolved the communal council of Brusturoasa. The dissolution took place, but it was just a palliative act and did not remedy the situation. The real instigator and author of the revolt was the priest Teodoreanu. At a market in Cășan, a settlement next to Brusturoasa, the priest had said the following to two witnesses, Ionica Popa and Toder Haluța: "You will see in two, three days what will happen in Brusturoasa when the Germans have finished mowing the hay."[18] The moment chosen—the end of the hay mowing—was convenient for the rioters, because it came after the expected departure of the workers who had come from Austria-Hungary and ensured that the Austro-Hungarian authorities would not become involved.

Further anti-Jewish violence began on August 15, on the feast of the Assumption of Mary. Several inhabitants of the village, including the now ex-mayor Mihalache Popovici, spent the entire day in N. Roșu's tavern drinking and cursing the Jews. As their minds became clouded by alcohol and filled with accusations against the Jews, they decided to take action. The violence started when they attacked the house of Ițic Leib, a wealthy Jew born in the commune. After futile attempts to enter his house using the front door and windows, the growing gang of rioters finally broke in the back door, forcing Leib, his wife, and four children to flee. The damage to his house totaled around four thousand lei.[19]

The scenario repeated itself on August 16, when the mass of rioters attacked another Jew, Moise Adelștein, who was living at the house of Spiridon Pădureanu, an Orthodox inhabitant of Brusturoasa. Pădureanu defended Adelștein against the enraged people, something that he had done in the past as well. As before, he stood in front of the villagers and asked them to leave Adelștein in peace and assured them that if this did not happen, he would physically defend him. Things took an unexpected turn when one of the rioters, Costache Sava, not taking the warning seriously, was wounded by a shot from Pădureanu's rifle (Sava would die from his wounds the next day). Frightened, the band of villagers started to run away, now being chased by Pădureanu and other inhabitants of the house. They managed to catch one of the agitators and handed him over to the commune's authorities, but he was released on the spot without any further action.

The aggressors included the former mayor, who feared that an investigation could show his role in what had happened. In response, he decided to repeat the events on a larger scale to disguise the truth. This caused the outbreak of full-scale violence on August 18 and 19, when people from surrounding villages joined the inhabitants of Brusturoasa in attacking the Jews. At their head, remarkably, was the priest Teodoreanu, disguised as a "Polish Jew" (the sources do not describe this costume, but presumably it was some kind of caricature of traditional Jewish dress).[20] As they moved through the village, the priest stopped in front of each home inhabited by Jews and told the rioters what they could loot from the houses. The aim was to regulate the robbery, the distribution of property, and the expulsion of Jews from the village.[21]

The evening of August 19 spelled the end of Jewish-Romanian cohabitation in the village of Brusturoasa. The rioters, having divided into gangs of twenty people, violently attacked the Jews' houses. Destroying and plundering Jewish property and beating and hitting women and children in their way, the aggressors gathered all of the victims in one place and with terror and violence forced them out of the village. Powerless and humiliated, 30 families—129 Jews[22]—were escorted by 200 people, who ensured that none of the Jews returned to the village.[23] The next morning, having been expelled from the village, exposed to the elements, and left in the middle of the road with only a few possessions they had saved from their homes, the Jews of Brusturoasa had to pay carters for their transportation costs to the nearest town, adding to their humiliation. As if this was not enough, a banner with the following inscription was placed at the edge of the village: "It is forbidden for any Jew to enter the village, or he will not escape in one piece."[24]

An eyewitness described the scene of suffering he found in Brusturoasa:

Monday Morning, August 20. You could see the mess with a broken heart. I am unable to describe the grief that dominated the women and children.

About one hundred and thirty souls were lying on the ground in the middle of the road and any Romanian passersby mocked them. At Asău, twenty minutes from there, I found out that the mayor of this commune had sent fifty policemen to harass [the Jews] and to force them to go to Comănești. So I decided to ride there, along with a friend, with the purpose of not letting any harm come to them if we could. I reached them, and I could not stop my tears and I was crying out loud, such a sad impression they produced on me, these maltreated people, lying in the middle of the road, among them around fifty small children, some of them just one year old, next to their mothers, crying because of the cold, while their mothers were crying from sadness. Not far from them, the tired men were sleeping lying on the ground because of their hardships. I was deeply moved inside my soul.[25]

The suffering and the humiliation of the Jews in Brusturoasa did not end there. From Moinești, the last place they stopped, they sent letters to the government and also to some newspapers:

Since the 15th of this month we are victims of the revolutionary movements in Brusturoasa, Bacău County. We are maltreated, plundered, taken by force from the commune by rioters, and hurled on the road with our children and the few possessions allowed by the rioters, who are more than three hundred. The administration, although it received complaints and reports about these robberies and brutal beatings, answers that it has no army and cannot do anything. Please Mr. Editor, please take up our defense by asking for an investigation of the facts and for the restoration of public order. The victims are over thirty families.[26]

At the same time some of the foreign workers, Austro-Hungarian citizens, who had been brought to the region to work in the forests, likewise addressed complaints to their legation in Bucharest, which in turn contacted the Romanian Ministry of Internal Affairs. Following these complaints, the government launched an investigation of the events at Brusturoasa.

The investigation was conducted by the director of the ministry of internal affairs, the Bacău County prefect, and a magistrate. They were instructed to head to Brusturoasa on short notice. Passing through Văsăiești and meeting with the victims of the Brusturoasa violence, the prefect was moved to tears by the pathetic state in which he found them. The investigators arrived in Brusturoasa on August 21 and were housed with Father Teodoreanu, who was suspected to be leader of the revolt.[27] The priest, summoning his courage and taking advantage of the situation, had a meeting with the prefect and the magistrate. Afterward he addressed the villagers and told them not to worry, because "no action will be taken, so follow your path and do not deviate from it."[28] The scope of the investigation was limited as much as possible. Simply put, the investigators did not ask hard questions and hoped to avoid creating a stir in the press. Instead, the investigators persuaded the leaseholder to make certain concessions to the inhabitants of the village. But just one witness was heard concerning the plundering and the excesses against Jews. The investigators did, however, permit Jews to return to the village.

■   EXPLANATIONS OF THE VIOLENCE

Against the wishes of the Romanian authorities, the revolt in Brusturoasa generated interest on a national scale. The Romanian Jewish press and newspapers in the capital of Bucharest commented on the episode. An illuminating analysis of Brusturoasa came in an article from the newspaper *Lupta* (The Struggle), a liberal opposition paper edited in Bucharest by Gheorghe Panu.[29] The article's anonymous author, who hesitated to call the events an "uprising," instead stressed the social origins of the violence. In particular, the article identified the initial cause of the violence as the installation of mechanical saws by the leaseholder David Grünberg. This had led to several important consequences. When he had installed the new saws, Grünberg "took the old ones from the hands of the peasants" and invited them to work as his employees.[30] The obvious repercussion of this measure was that a sizeable part of the local peasantry, about one hundred men, remained without jobs. They refused to give up what they saw as their freedom of work; indeed, they considered themselves the owners of the forests (as they had claimed in their ongoing lawsuit against the owner of the Comămășteanu estate). As a consequence, the leaseholder was forced to bring in foreign workers, Hungarians from Transylvania, to work with the mechanical saws. The article in *Lupta* also pointed to the locals' anger that since the Adjud-Târgu Ocna railroad had opened, trade in timber had grown significantly and Grünberg was making the best of it.[31]

Seen in this light, economic tensions formed the background to the Brusturoasa uprising. But so too did antisemitism, which had deep roots among the Romanian peasantry. Many peasants had direct contact with Jewish leaseholders. Landlords preferred Jewish leaseholders because of their "diligence" and "seriousness." Yet the figures show that the number of Jewish leaseholders was not so high.[32] They were more common in Moldavia than Wallachia, but overall most leaseholders were Orthodox Romanians, and they also included some Greeks and other nationalities. According to statistics from 1907, the total number of leaseholders was 3,332, of whom 2,417 were Orthodox Romanians,

472 Romanian Jews, and 443 foreigners. The number of leaseholders who had over 4,000 hectares was 132, of whom 77 were Orthodox, 28 Jews, and 27 foreigners. Of the total leased land of 2,334,145 hectares, Jews administered 18.87 percent, Orthodox Romanians 63.34 percent, and foreigners 17.97 percent. It is clear that Jews were far from constituting the majority of leaseholders, no matter what the antisemitic press claimed and many people believed. Yet there were some large Jewish leaseholds: not without reason, the Fischer Brothers' vast leasehold was called "Fischerland."

Antisemites and their sympathizers nonetheless popularized the discourse of Jewish leaseholders as "a plague that spread on the ancestral land."[33] Antisemites recognized that the leaseholder was one of the best figures with which to channel the peasants' anger at the status quo. The Jews' opponents successfully exploited the position that the leaseholders held as intermediaries between Romanian peasants and the Romanian landowners. In this way, Romanian peasants, who had no direct contact with the landowners who oppressed them, instead focused their discontent on the Jewish leaseholders. Jews, in short, were made into scapegoats.

Unsurprisingly, in the wake of the violence in Brusturoasa some contemporary newspapers also justified the rioters' actions by presenting the local Jewish leaseholder as "inhuman."[34] This image had little to do with reality. The leaseholder, David Grünberg, had been active in the village for decades. He had built the first paraffin factory in Brusturoasa in 1867, and later he started drilling oil wells using efficient drilling machines, which allowed a systematic exploitation of the resource.[35] In recognition of these contributions and the many jobs he had brought to the village, Grünberg received from the mayor of Brusturoasa and the subprefecture of Tazlău de Sus a certificate to be used for "his necessities" (that is, for his protection) for the entire period of the revolt. This leaseholder, as well as his son, who was described in the antisemitic press as a great exploiter of the peasants, thus were not only spared the fury of the masses, but also were offered protection for their safety.[36] But if the village elites were not opposed to Grünberg, they did oppose his mechanical saws. In spurring the peasants to violence, the village leaders hoped to create anarchy to stop the work of the saws.[37] The commission sent to investigate the events of August 16 to 20 treated this central fact superficially.

From the beginning, village leaders in Brusturoasa used the peasant masses as an instrument to solve their personal problems. The priest, the mayor, and the teacher did not try to calm tensions, but in fact were initiators of the revolt. The role of the village leaders in the August 1885 events in Brusturoasa is typical for modern Romania. Numerous documents show that these characters of the Romanian village were often the most reliable supporters of antisemitic movements. For example, priests played a prominent role at the Antisemitic Congress in Bucharest in 1886, as well as in the Universal Antisemitic Alliance (*Alliance Anti-semitique Universelle*), an organization founded in 1895. Other leagues and organizations, more or less antisemitic, could also count on priests' support whenever they launched antisemitic initiatives. In 1913, for example, the influential League for the Cultural Unity of All Romanians (*Liga pentru Unitatea Culturală a tuturor Românilor*) issued an appeal to village priests and teachers, calling on these two groups to defend the country by collecting signatures in support of the Jews' expulsion from Romania.[38]

In Brusturoasa, village elites were at the center of the violence from the beginning to its end. The influence of the priest in the Brusturoasa uprising was decisive. Father Teodoreanu was the main instigator of the uprising and used his position to canalize the discontent of the peasants against Jews. It is no coincidence that the Romanian Orthodox Church itself never took an official stance on the treatment of Jews, or at least it never made public its views in newspapers during this era.[39] The mayor, another authority in the village, responded to news about the violence by not taking any action against the agitators; indeed, he later worked to conceal events he had been part of by encouraging further plunder and violence. Finally, the authorities responsible for public order also did nothing to quell the violence in Brusturoasa. The deputy commander of the garrison was seen on August 18 roaming through the village and urging people to take part in the revolt.[40] Instead of stopping the rumors and the agitation, individuals with authority and power in the village only made the violence worse.

Under such conditions, who might have defended the Jews? The investigators sent by the minister of internal affairs? It has been mentioned above that the investigators limited themselves to securing some concessions for the local peasants in return for allowing the Jews to come back to the village. But they did this without hearing testimony from the actual victims. Could the landowner Ghica Comămăşteanu have stood up for the Jews of Brusturoasa? He neither intervened on the behalf of the Jews nor showed up there in the first place.

The Brusturoasa uprising instead followed a general pattern of agitation against Jews characteristic of late nineteenth-century Romania. Such events often began with a meeting at which a small number of Orthodox Christian men aired their grievances against Jews. Then followed public agitation, in which crowds gathered and headed toward Jewish-owned buildings. The crowds directed their anger at individual Jews in the streets or toward Jewish shops and houses. Another feature of these events was that many of them took place under the indifferent eyes of the police or other authorities, who intervened too late or not at all. In 1897, for example, after debates in Parliament about whether Jews should serve in the Romanian army, gangs of students vandalized the Jewish quarter of Bucharest under the "benevolent gaze of the police." Only after many synagogues, shops, and houses had been damaged did the police intervene.[41]

■   THE VICTIMS

The situation of the Brusturoasa Jews was most unfavorable. Beaten, dispossessed of their belongings, thrown out of the village by force, and left in the middle of the road with their wives and children, they appealed to the ministry of internal affairs, hoping for some restitution. The contents of their petitions show their difficult situation in Brusturoasa and also bring to light their relationship with the Romanian authorities and the peasants of the village. The petitions stress that the Jews' relationship with their fellow Orthodox villagers was a normal one, similar to two neighbors who know each other well. We should not assume that the Orthodox Romanian population had a long-cultivated or inborn hatred against Jews or that the village Jews viewed the Romanians with antagonism. Their daily relationships were mostly unremarkable, even if from time to time disturbances did occur against Jews in Romania. But these incidents were often organized by village leaders, who pushed the population to undertake violent acts such as the uprising of Brusturoasa. The petitions written by Brusturoasa's Jews provide evidence of these relationships. One reads as follows:

> Like others who were born in this village and others who have lived here for 30 to 40 years, we had no reason until today to complain against our Christian cohabitants, with whom we lived and still live in the most intimate relations of friendship. We do not file this complaint against them at this time; but on the contrary, we have a cherished belief that here in this game there is the antagonistic hand and agitation of a certain individual, who tries to make a profit and help his own affairs from the revolt, for which he stirred against us the ones who would not even think to do us any harm, and what is more he committed excesses like the actual ones against our persons and property.[42]

One contemporary observer went so far as to claim that "[i]n the case of Brusturoasa uprising, the persecution [of Jews] was superficial, the Romanian people had no part in it, but only the authorities."[43] In addition to the petition, the good relationship between the Orthodox villagers and the Jews is shown in the testimonies given by Jewish residents such as Moise Grünberg, Moșe Tenen-țof, Moise Adelștein, Iancu Buium, and Samule Veissman (whom Spiridon Pă-dureanu had protected). They recalled the good relations they had with local Orthodox and the help they had received from neighbors in those critical days of August 16 to 20. Another Brusturoasa Jew, Moses Gaster, wrote about the good relations he had with the Romanians: "This [violence] turns upside down my entire popular psychology, as never a Jew complained or could complain against the Romanian people, who are gentle and innocent by nature. I am sure that not one Jew could be found in the Romanian country who would not protest against the slandering assertions of certain journalists, who say that the Jews complain against the Romanian people. I underline these words!"[44] Brusturoasa's Jews obviously had good reasons not to complain about their Christian neighbors in petitions to the government. But one could also point to the fact that the majority of Jews in Brusturoasa were reasonably well-to-do, established for a long time, or born in Brusturoasa, where they had numerous relatives and ran a range of businesses. As such, Jews did not represent a finan-cial burden on the village. Nor were they easily marked as "outsiders."

The expulsion, plunder, and mistreatment of the Jewish community were not the only consequences of the uprising in Brusturoasa. The episode had sig-nificant long-term consequences for some individuals, including Moses Gaster, Elias Schwarzfeld, Isac Auerbach, and Marcu Brociner, all of whom were ordered to leave Romania within twenty-four hours in accordance with Article I of the 1881 law on foreigners.[45] Although the law had originally targeted Rus-sian nihilists who found shelter in Romania after the attack on Tsar Alexan-der II, increasingly it was used against foreign Jews resident in Romania. Be-tween 1880 and 1894, 163 of the 859 individuals expelled from Romania were Jews (19 percent of the total); between 1894 and 1904, 1,177 of 6,529 expellees were Jews (18 percent).

The case of Moses Gaster is instructive. Gaster (1856–1939) was born in Bucharest to a Dutch Jewish family that had come to Romania. At nineteen, having attended both the prestigious Gheorghe Lazăr School and the Matei Basarab School in Bucharest, he continued his studies at the Saint Sava Na-tional College, also in Bucharest. He then attended the Jewish Seminary in Breslau, where his teachers included the celebrated Jewish historian Heinrich Graetz. Returning to Romania, he taught at the University of Bucharest and published widely on Romanian literature and folklore. In 1885 he published the article "The Revolt in Brusturoasa," in which he denounced the incitement of the peasants to antisemitic action and the diversionary actions of the government, with their aim of covering up the local violence. At the insistence of Dimitrie Sturdza, Romanian minister of religion and education, Gaster was then expelled along with other Jewish leaders.[46] Gaster first went to Paris and then to London, where he became a highly respected rabbi in the London Sephardic community.

Another prominent Jewish leader affected by the Brusturoasa uprising was Elias Schwarzfeld. Schwarzfeld (or Schwartzfeld, 1855–1915) had been born in Moldova, in the Russian Empire, but soon moved to Romania. His work focused on the Romanian Jewish community. He also was known as a political activist. Concerned about his coreligionists, Schwarzfeld could not stay neutral in the summer of 1885. His article, "The Truth about the Brusturoasa Revolt," created a great stir in the Romanian press, just as Gaster's article had done. The two articles, far from being polemical, attempted to describe in an objective way what had happened in Brusturoasa. As such, they represent two of the most credible sources about the uprising. Like Gaster, Schwarzfeld was expelled from the country following his journalistic intervention. The expulsion of these two men and of many other Jewish intellectuals was made without any explanation. For example, in the October 19, 1885, edition of *Universul*, one of the most successful of Bucharest's daily newspapers, a short notice appeared about the expulsions, but it did not explain why they had taken place. The government was silent on this matter: "They happen just as you have seen. The reasons are secret and cannot be communicated to the mob."[47]

These two articles about the Brusturoasa uprising were only part of the story. True, they did make things uncomfortable for the political classes, but other factors also help explain the expulsions of Gaster, Schwarzfeld, and other Jewish leaders. As unofficial representatives of the Jewish minority, Gaster and Schwarzfeld had many contacts with influential Europeans whom they had asked to help the Jews in Romania. That Romanian Jews had earlier sent a delegation to Lord Salisbury in London and that Armand Levy had come to Bucharest as an emissary of France's Alliance Israelite to open a branch of the organization there had angered officials in the Romanian government, as well as members of parliament, who feared that Jews would "defame" Romania in the eyes of the West. Schwartzfeld correctly assessed the situation: "The law on foreigners, in accord with Article 7 of the Constitution, has made the Jew a thing, a bundle, that one throws away and rejects anywhere one wants, a man without hearth or home, a *Vogelfrei*."[48]

CONCLUSION

The tragic end of the Jewish community in Brusturoasa caused more than 30 families—or about 129 persons—to be expelled. The revolt itself was not so much against the Jews in general but against those who threatened the personal interests of the village's leaders, with the heart of the conflict being the question of the forests. The people from the village would not have started a revolt against their neighbors without instigation "from above." That the population was so easily stirred, however, spoke to the endurance of older, anti-Jewish stereotypes. As the historian Andrei Oişteanu has shown, negative images of Jews—seen as both physically (beards and sidelocks) and morally (dishonest business practices) distinct from Christians—were widespread in Romania.[49] But the particular situation of the peasants in villages such as Brusturoasa also played a role. The peasants were angry at the landowner, who had "taken" their land forty years earlier, and at the leaseholder, with his new mechanical saws. One could say that the "peasant question" in this case was analogous to the labor question in western Europe. The relations between the employed peasants and the landowners and leaseholders were as grave as those between industrial workers and employers in large European urban centers. But because the peasants had no direct contact with the landowner or the leaseholder, they vented their fury and dissatisfaction against the Jews in the village. The result in Brusturoasa was chilling. In Schwarzfeld's words, it was "until now, unparalleled, for the peasant inhabitants to rise against the Jews and expel them from the village."[50]

The other important aspect of the case is the role of Romanian elites, both in the village and in the cities. It is striking that in Romania, where the political class and the intellectuals overlapped, both groups often were the most ardent supporters of antisemitism. This phenomenon was not limited to the prewar period.[51] Why this lasting anger among the elites against the Jews? In part it was because Jews were a convenient scapegoat and an unprotected minority in Romania. Under Ottoman rule, economically and politically influential Greeks had been the most resented minority. Following independence, Jews served this role, in part because they were seen as "foreign" and in part because of their economic function within Romanian society. The Great Powers did little to help. By making Romanian independence contingent on Romania introducing changes to its constitution regarding Jews' citizenship, the 1878 Congress of Berlin angered many Orthodox Romanian politicians and intellectuals, who were sensitive to every perceived slight to Romanian sovereignty.

But the fact that a younger generation of intellectuals, many of them educated in major European capitals such as Berlin, Vienna, and Paris, was also receptive to antisemitic ideas, suggests that antisemitism among the elites would not go away. In Romania, as in much of Europe, antisemitism went hand in hand with nationalism. Increasingly, many Romanian elites came to the position that Jews had no place in Romania; they were seen as a threat to the very existence of the young Romanian state. To be a good Romanian patriot, it followed, meant to be antisemitic. Certainly this was the lesson of the tragic events in the village of Brusturoasa.

MICHAL FRANKL

FROM BOYCOTT TO RIOT
THE MORAVIAN ANTI-JEWISH
VIOLENCE OF 1899 AND ITS
BACKGROUND

Starting in mid-October 1899, the Bohemian Lands[1] ex-
perienced one of the most extensive and violent popular protests in its history.
Triggered by conflict between Czech and German nationalists, Czech politicians
and activists sought to mobilize the masses to express their outrage against
the repeal of language ordinances designed to place Czech on a more equal
footing with German in the state administration. However, in most cases, the
nationalist demonstrations and protest marches quickly turned into aggressive
anti-Jewish riots. Across the Bohemian Lands, drunken rioters shouted anti-
Jewish slogans, smashed windows, pillaged, and looted; extortion and arson
were widespread.

Recent historiography has provided fresh insights into and new interpretations of anti-Jewish violence in modern Europe. Historians of antisemitism
generally agree that violent anti-Jewish crowds should not be understood as
"primitive" mobs guided solely by traditional prejudice or lust for plunder and
enrichment. Violence against Jews needs to be analyzed in terms of its causes,
symbolism, and structure. "Revisionist" historiography on antisemitism also
has challenged simplified interpretations explaining the violence (especially in
Russia) by the (in)action of the state.[2] The most comprehensive interpretative
template, the concept of "exclusionary violence," was empirically based on the
analysis of anti-Jewish violence in modern Germany and methodologically inspired by scholarly approaches to racial violence in the United States and elsewhere. In contrast to the "emancipatory" riots of a minority against the state or
an oppressive majority, the "exclusionary" riot is defined as a case of violence
directed against a minority based on prejudice or driven by antisemitic propaganda. "Exclusionary" pogroms are preceded by a perceived shift in power in

The author expresses his gratitude to Michael L. Miller and Daniel Unowsky for their
thoughtful comments on drafts of this chapter. Parts of the text were created within the
Czech Science Foundation–sponsored project "State Building without Antisemitism? Antisemitism in the Czech Lands and Slovakia, 1917–1923," No. P410/11/2146.

favor of the minority and a cooling of social relations between the in-group and the out-group. Such violence is meant to reassert, through a symbolic and violent performance, the outsider status of the minority. "Exclusionary" riots are characterized by an asymmetry of power between the majority and the excluded minority and most often by a low level of organization.[3]

While building on the existing research and drawing on the concept of "exclusionary" violence, this chapter seeks to extend it in two ways. First, the setting of the violence in an ethnically mixed territory and against the background of an intensifying (and increasingly aggressive) nationality conflict between Czechs and Germans in the Bohemian Lands provides a specific context for this case of "exclusionary" violence. Moreover, the chapter draws our attention to the importance of the local, in this case Moravian, context and offers an opportunity for an in-depth look at the interplay between the local or regional and the national aspects of the riots and the propaganda that preceded them.

In this way, this chapter also aims to challenge the usual interpretations of the 1899 riots (and by extension late nineteenth-century Czech antisemitism). It is striking how close the positions in recent scholarly works are to the views put forward by contemporary Czech nationalists in 1899.[4] Czech commentators generally saw the violence as part of a legitimate national protest against the oppressive Habsburg state and against German dominance. Czech antisemitism and anti-Jewish violence were described as a by-product of the ever more radicalized conflict between Czech and German nationalists and as a reaction to the alleged German political and cultural loyalty of Bohemian and Moravian Jews. For a long time, this subordination of the history of Czech antisemitism to the nationality conflict prevented critical research into its causes and forms. Even though the Bohemian Lands have been analyzed by many historians of modern nationalism as a kind of laboratory of nationality conflict, antisemitism has figured in this research only as a marginal subject. Therefore, this chapter aims to challenge the prevailing view of Czech antisemitism as secondary to the rise of the nationality conflict and to the anti-German passions and policies of Czech politicians and activists. Instead, it aims to provide a more balanced analysis of the dynamic interaction of modern nationalism and antisemitism.

The chapter seeks to decode and understand the Moravian anti-Jewish violence of 1899 not only against the broader pattern of the rise of modern political antisemitism, but also with a view to specific aspects of the relationship between Jews and Christians in Moravia. Even though serious demonstrations and incidents occurred in a number of Bohemian communities, including Prague, the epicenter was Moravia, where the most violent and widely discussed incidents took place. Therefore, the riots were generally referred to as "Moravian."

Moreover, the most excessive attacks on Jews took place in a relatively small region of Haná (or Hanna in German) in central Moravia, to the east of Olomouc/Olmütz. In order to understand the character of the riots, it becomes necessary to look into the features that marked the cohabitation of Jews and Christians in smaller Moravian towns and the strategies that local Czech nationalists and antisemites chose in their attempts to demarcate the national territory and apply ethnic standards in the local economy. Significantly, in 1899, many Moravian Jews still lived in separate Jewish administrative units, the so-called "political Jewish communities," and many of them still played a traditional role in the economy. The chapter therefore starts with a short account of the larger riots, continues by looking at how the politics of nationality conflict contributed to the escalation of antisemitic violence, and finally places the riots into the context of local politics and nationalist campaigns.

■   PROTEST INTO VIOLENCE

While the cohabitation of Jews and Christians in Moravia was never without tension and occasional violence, the extent and the dramatic character of the 1899 riots were extraordinary and without parallel in the nineteenth century. The anti-Jewish riots of the revolutionary year 1848–1849, conflicts surrounding the participation of Jews in citizens' guards (for instance, in Prostějov/Prossnitz), and tensions around Jewish emancipation were much more limited and can be described as isolated rituals of exclusion.[5] Even the more extensive wave of attacks in several Moravian towns in May 1850, directed against Jewish emancipation and related to the attempts to amalgamate separate Jewish townships with "Christian" towns, were much less violent than the 1899 riots.[6] The 1866 Bohemian rural riots mostly avoided Moravia.[7] The wave of anti-Jewish violence of 1881 to 1882, inspired by the growth of political antisemitism in other countries or regions, including the Russian pogroms and the subsequent Hungarian riots, was characterized by isolated, small incidents, such as window smashing. In 1887 anti-Jewish riots broke out in Kojetín following an accusation of ritual murder.[8] However, it was only the 1897 disorders (which were regionally more concentrated in Bohemia) and the 1899 "Moravian" riots that took place at one time over a wide territory and with an unprecedented mobilizing effect on the Czech public.

Drawing on reports published in Czech language newspapers, historians Helena Krejčová and Alena Míšková have listed 265 demonstrations and violent incidents that occurred in 177 communities and described 160 (or two-thirds) of them as purely anti-Jewish.[9] This statistical overview must be considered incomplete since the press did not record many minor incidents in smaller villages, which can be partially documented based on archival sources.

The October 1899 incidents in the Moravian towns of Holešov/Holleschau, Vsetín/Wsetin, and Přerov/Prerau,[10] all three located close to each other and southeast of the city of Olomouc, witnessed the most serious and controversial riots and deserve a detailed description. In Přerov, the wave of violence began in the aftermath of a large "private," closed-door meeting called by a local nationalist association to which, however, nonmembers and people from outside the town had been admitted. Later, a crowd of demonstrators numbering approximately three thousand moved through the town and sang national songs. When the crowd refused to disperse, military forces stationed in the town were quickly called in and took action, wounding several people. The violent rioters still refused to disperse, resisted the soldiers, and pelted them with stones and firecrackers. Later, several groups of rioters smashed windows in most of the Jewish houses in the town.[11] Many disturbances in the Bohemian Lands followed a similar pattern.

In Vsetín, events on the evening of October 24, 1899, likewise started with a Czech nationalist gathering. Organized by the Czech association *Snaha* (Endeavor) and the Czech representative in the Moravian Diet, Karel Bubela, the gathering quickly turned into an anti-Jewish riot. According to a report by an official from Vsetín, a crowd of some five hundred people gathered in an attempt to storm and demolish the synagogue. Rocks flew into the windows of the neoclassical "Israelite Temple" built only two years before.[12] The gendarmes pushed back the mob, which consisted of people of different genders and ages. The crowd then divided into smaller groups and smashed most of the windows in the shops, houses, and flats used by Jews. The rioters also broke into several Jewish shops to loot goods and money. The crowd regrouped in front of Josef Glesinger's (kosher) restaurant, where they smashed the windows. After several hours, the rowdies broke into the yard of the adjoining distillery. The gendarmerie was insufficient to stop the crowd. Many rioters, under the influence of alcohol, became aggressive and began to stone the gendarmes. The outnumbered gendarmes eventually resorted to the use of firearms: two rioters fell, a third looter succumbed to his wounds on the way to the doctor, two others were seriously wounded, and another twelve people received minor injuries. As was often the case with riots in the late Habsburg Monarchy, the tiny local police force was utterly incapable of restoring order, and the violence was suppressed only following the arrival of the army.[13]

The riots in Holešov were the most violent of the 1899 anti-Jewish attacks in

Moravia—and the ones about which the accounts of witnesses, officials, jour-nalists, and politicians diverge the most. The lack of reliable reports on the events in Holešov probably has to do with the fact that the district captain be-haved in a rather passive way and did not witness at least some of the riots; the testimony of Jewish police officers was also considered unreliable after a brawl with a member of the local elites. Therefore, the reports by Czech and Jewish witnesses correspond with each other in time and place, but they vary sharply in the description of causes and of the course of events.

On Saturday afternoon, October 21, groups started to gather in Holešov and sing Czech nationalist songs: "Hej Slované" (Hey Slavs) and "Kde domov můj?" (Where is my home?). A little later two people, a father and son, were imprisoned for offensive behavior in the Jewish town (the separate "political community"). The leadership of the Jewish community perceived the increas-ingly volatile situation and feared anti-Jewish violence. Therefore, the mayor of the Jewish town decided to reinforce the Jewish police with a group of strong young men. Around midnight, the well-known local Czech publisher Lambert Klabusay accompanied one of his employees who lived in the Jewish town on his way home from a pub. Allegedly, Klabusay wanted to make sure that his colleague got home safely. This claim is impossible to verify. Because Klabusay's drunk coworker was singing loudly, the police of the Jewish town, along with its mayor, Salomon Zwillinger, confronted them. Klabusay was well known for his antisemitism, for selling antisemitic booklets, and for distributing anti-semitic leaflets. Most likely, the Jewish policemen believed that Klabusay and his accomplice were about to provoke a pogrom.

It is not clear from the available testimonies what exactly happened at this fateful moment. While the Czech side claimed that the Jewish police beat Kla-busay and his friend without any explanation or questions, a Jewish citizen stated that Zwillinger first called on Klabusay to behave calmly. Whatever hap-pened, the event illustrated the great tension and the effects of the antisemitic propaganda in the town. The bloodied publisher was taken to a doctor, where several light wounds were treated; he was said to be injured so badly that he could not return to work for three weeks. Zwillinger and his friends later were sentenced to short prison terms for this attack. As a prominent journalist and publisher, Klabusay belonged to the local elite, and the news of his mistreat-ment sparked a great deal of anger among the local population. An attack by a Jewish group on a Christian also might have been seen as a sign of Jews de-parting from their traditional roles, threatening a shift in power relations to the disadvantage of Christians. The next morning, Klabusay's bloodied shirt and tie were exhibited in a hotel on the main square, which belonged to the town mayor, František Pokorný. The items attracted huge crowds, and leaflets circulated announcing an anti-Jewish riot at eight o'clock in the evening. Klabusay's employees allegedly talked to the crowd and spread antisemitic accusations. On Sunday afternoon, large numbers of inhabitants gathered in groups in the Jewish town as well as on the main ("Christian") town square, and the atmosphere became explosive.

The violence started with an attack on the taproom of Abraham Grätzer on the main square, in sight of Klabusay's bloody clothing. Again, accounts of the event differ dramatically depending on who is doing the telling. In the Czech narrative, the riots were triggered by an event common in small towns like Holešov: an inebriated person was thrown out of Abraham Grätzer's taproom. When the tavern keeper demanded compensation for a glass door broken as the drunkard was driven out, a large crowd gathered and smashed all the windows. However, Grätzer himself offered a different account of events. He described a fight between two of his (drunk) guests, which ended by one throwing the other out of the pub; the town police then imprisoned the drunkard. At this moment, Grätzer noticed a large crowd in front of Pokorný's hotel looking at Klabusay's clothes, decided to close his pub, and with some difficulty drove out all of the guests just as people started to gather. Grätzer then witnessed a group of 150 students leaving Pokorný's house and gathering in front of his pub. The young men shouted anti-Jewish slogans, tried to break into Grätzer's house, and threatened his family. Grätzer escaped through the back and called for help from the rather passive district captain; in the meantime, his son returned home and managed to push the most violent intruders out. Afterward, the students started to throw stones at the house while two city policemen calmly looked on.[14]

Subsequently, the crowd moved to the Jewish town, and a large-scale attack on Jewish pubs, shops, and houses followed. The district captain attributed the outbreak to a small group of radicals and rowdies; alcohol consumed partly in Jewish taverns also played a major role. One of the rioters even died as a consequence of heavy drinking a few days later. The five gendarmes dispatched to put down the violence fired into the crowd killing two people (who were probably bystanders) on the spot. A third died later of gunshot wounds. As a consequence, the crowd became even more violent, destroying and pillaging Jewish property, and it returned to the main square to set Grätzer's house on fire. Interestingly, according to Grätzer's testimony, the pub itself survived whereas his flat and a "laboratory" were destroyed. The frightened gendarmes retreated to their barracks. Law and order was restored only with the arrival of the army.

The gendarmes later were accused of shooting innocent bystanders and of unprofessional behavior in that they cut off the escape route of the crowd away from the Jewish town and therefore prevented the rioters from leaving. Some questions were never fully answered, including, most importantly, just who, apart from the gendarmes, shot into the crowd with ammunition that was not standard issue for the gendarmerie.[15] (A Jewish policeman named Bernhard Ehrlich was investigated for allegedly firing into the crowd from his house and injuring a Christian woman.)[16]

Two days later, during the funeral of the victims, some three thousand people gathered. As a nineteen-year-old shoemaker rushed to the funeral and tried to break a military cordon, he was wounded by a soldier wielding a bayonet and later died. This incident led to a new round of violence against the army, gendarmerie, and local Jews. The riots had a profound effect on relations between Jews and Christians in the town. Hundreds of Holešov Jews, reportedly fearing further violence, at least temporarily fled the town.[17]

Examples of less-serious cases of violence can complete the picture of the 1899 Moravian riots. In the days following the Vsetín riot and only a few kilometers away, a group of military reservists (on their way from a regular military inspection in Vsetín), entered the pub of Moritz Morvai in the small village of Hovězí. They verbally intimidated the Jewish innkeeper and his family, threatening them and singing popular anti-Jewish songs. After being forced to vacate the pub by a local gendarme, the drunkards smashed Morvai's windows.[18] In the village of Dřevohostice, not far from Přerov, unknown attackers repeatedly threw rocks at the windows of Edmund and Ferdinand Fried.[19]

■   NATIONALITY CONFLICT AND ANTISEMITISM

Of all contemporary interpreters and commentators of the Moravian riots, Jan Žáček, a Czech nationalist representative to the Reichsrat, the Vienna parliament, and the leader of the Moravian Old Czech Party, provided the most consistent and elaborate account. Žáček represented some of the towns in which the riots took place (among them Přerov) and travelled to the locations of the riots to collect firsthand accounts from Czech nationalist elites as he was preparing his address. In a long, eloquent, and passionate speech to the Reichsrat, he challenged government accounts as well as reports in the Austro-German press and described the riots as largely nonviolent demonstrations triggered by the unjust repeal of the language ordinances. Having blamed government behavior for sparking the demonstrations, he expanded this interpretation to the escalation of violence itself: it was the gendarmerie or army that, by its lack of professionalism and unwarranted harshness, had provoked the worst violence and destruction of Jewish property. For instance, in stark contradiction to the official reports, he claimed that no serious damage was done in Holešov prior to the fatal shooting into the crowd. It was only the two unnecessary salvos that sparked the destruction and created the state of lawlessness. (Some contemporary propagandists developed this argument further and claimed that the government intentionally provoked the violence in order to justify a harsh clampdown on Czechs.)

Nothing disturbed Žáček more than reports — paradoxically put forward by both liberals and antisemites — that depicted the riots as a consequence of antisemitic sentiments and propaganda among the Czech (Moravian) people. For instance, the Viennese liberal *Neue Freie Presse*, the most influential Austrian newspaper of the time, highlighted Moravian antisemitism in its editorials and called for more empathy for the real victims: the plundered, robbed Jews.[20] Žáček repeatedly and emphatically rejected the accusation that antisemitism could have been the root cause of the unrest. The protests had been no "ordinary *Judenhetze*," he wanted to believe (as far as we know, Žáček did not support political antisemitism). Interestingly, at one point the Viennese Christian Social antisemite Hermann Bielohlawek interrupted Žáček: "Don't be afraid, Herr Doctor! You don't have to be frightened [to talk about antisemitism], nothing will happen to you!"[21] In his speech, Ernst Schneider, a Viennese Christian Social known for his rabid antisemitism and his attempts to "investigate" various accusations of ritual murder, many of them in the Bohemian Lands, offered an antisemitic interpretation of the events and hailed the anti-Jewish views of the Moravians. Schneider's speech was quickly translated into Czech and published as a booklet by two different groups of Czech antisemites.[22] The debate in the Vienna parliament thus highlighted the tension between the two most common explanations of the violence: the nationality conflict between Czechs and Germans (Žáček) and antisemitism (Bielohlawek, Schneider). Any attempt to analyze the riots therefore must examine the interplay between the two phenomena.

There can be no doubt that many of the 1899 riots started as nationalist protest demonstrations only to quickly degrade into anti-Jewish violence and looting. However, in Czech historiography (often following Žáček's narrative), the national conflict has consistently been given more weight as an explanation of the violent action than Czech antisemitism. Similar views have been expressed in recent works, most notably in Zdeněk Fišer's book on the Holešov pogroms.[23] However, while the nationality conflict was an important factor, by itself it is not sufficient to explain the anti-Jewish turn of the violence.

Moreover, the 1899 riots were similar to the previous major wave of Czech anti-Jewish violence: the riots of December 1897. In both cases, the immediate cause of the demonstrations and riots was related to the culmination of the long-standing conflict between Czech and German nationalists in the Bohemian Lands and in Cisleithania regarding the use of language in the state administration. At the heart of the controversy stood the language ordinances issued in 1897 in exchange for Czech political support by the government of Kazimierz Badeni. According to these guidelines, most state officials in Bohemia and Moravia would be required to conduct business in (and therefore have knowledge of) both Czech and German. Following months of aggressive political propaganda and demonstrations by German nationalists, Badeni resigned in November 1897. In March 1898 the government of Franz Thun, in an attempt to find middle ground, issued a milder version of the ordinances. The immediate trigger of the Moravian riots of autumn 1899 was Thun's resignation and the repeal of his language accords by the new government of Manfred von Clary-Aldringen. Both the 1897 resignation of Badeni and the 1899 repeal of the language ordinances were followed by anti-German and increasingly anti-Jewish riots. Whereas in 1897 the epicenter of the protests was Prague, two years later the most violent clashes occurred in small Moravian towns.

The nationalist gatherings and demonstrations, which in most cases started the chain of events, were mainly intended as a protest against the government or the Habsburg state that—from the Czech nationalist perspective—had denied the Czech nation its legitimate rights. Antigovernmental slogans were voiced and leaflets and posters distributed. For instance, a popular leaflet imitating a funeral notice stated "Spravedlnost † v Rakousku odvoláním jazykových nařízení" ("Justice † [has passed away] in Austria with the revocation of the language ordinances").[24] Therefore, the immediate cause for the start of the 1899 riots has to be located outside the standard arsenal of antisemitic images and propaganda. The trigger was the repeal of the language ordinances, which Czech politicians wanted to denounce in a demonstrative way. The events were organized by Czech nationalist elites, often under the auspices or active participation of mayors and other local dignitaries. In the village of Rouchovany, for instance, the mayor participated in the demonstration and demanded the release of arrested rioters. In Holešov, the mayor allowed Klabusay's items to be displayed in his hotel, and the whole municipal council took part in the demonstrative funeral of the victims of the previous round of the riots. In Vsetín, the local Czech nationalist association Snaha and its leader Karel Kubela organized and supported the original demonstration, only to find themselves unable to control the crowd and stop the anti-Jewish violence that quickly erupted. The high spirits at the marches and gatherings were often fueled by singing Czech nationalist songs, such as "Hej Slované" and "Kde domov můj?"

The tempo of the transformation of a nationalist protest into a clear-cut anti-Jewish pogrom was remarkable and not lost on contemporaries. In fact, few institutions that symbolized the German presence, such as German clubs and associations, theaters, businesses, or schools with German language of instruction, were physically targeted in Moravia. Even though attacks on Jews had previously accompanied anti-German protests and demonstrations, the intensity of the 1899 attacks on synagogues, Jewish shops, taverns, and homes came as a profound shock. This fact not only testifies to the intensity of anti-semitic propaganda at the time, but also to its mobilizing effects on wide circles of the population. Therefore, the way antisemitism merged into the discourse and practice of the nationality conflict requires more attention. To explain this phenomenon, however, it is necessary to look beyond the usual narrative that would treat the—real or imagined—German cultural and political loyalties of Bohemian and Moravian Jews as the cause of anti-Jewish words and acts.

Many scholars of modern antisemitism have argued for an intrinsic connection between nationalism and antisemitism in the Bohemian Lands and differentiated between the German (or German-Austrian) "racial" and Czech "national," "economic," or "religious" anti-Semitism.[25] Czech antisemites of the 1880s and most of the 1890s, however, were rarely motivated by the nationality conflict and, in contrast to liberal nationalists, prioritized social and economic issues and various ethnonational concepts ahead of the conflict with the Germans. For them, the internal enemy—the Jew—and not the external enemy—the German—was viewed as the cause of all of society's ills. In the context of efforts by many European antisemites to create an international antisemitic movement, the supporters of antisemitism in the Bohemian Lands claimed that fighting the Germans was a counterproductive effort, which only played into the hands of the Jews. For instance, this idea was visualized by a caricature published in one of the Moravian antisemitic newspapers of the time, the *Brněnský Drak* (The Brno Dragon), which showed a Czech and a German fighting over a cow while a Jew can be seen milking (and hence profiting from) it.[26]

The rise of Czech antisemitism in the 1890s was related to internal cleavages in Czech society. Antisemitism became one of the central forces on the ideological spectrum in Czech politics in the late 1890s following the introduction of the limited general franchise and in reaction to the first electoral inroads by the Czech branch of Austrian social democracy. During the Reichsrat elections of February and March 1897, Czech nationalist and "clerical" political parties increasingly adopted antisemitism. They depicted social democracy as a tool in the hands of the worldwide Jewish conspiracy. Following the elections, more antisemitic political parties came to play a role in Czech politics (the State

Rights Party, the National Social Party), and activists founded *Národní obrana* (National Defense), an organization modeled on national defense leagues and committed to promoting economic boycotts of Jews as well as Germans. Antisemitism increasingly functioned as a cultural code or common denominator for the broad camp of antiliberal and antisocialist nationalist groups and political parties.[27]

The alignment between the two causes—nationalism and antisemitism—followed not only from the Badeni crisis and the radicalization of the nationality conflict. This shift also reflected the new position of antisemitism as a result of the corrosion of the old national-liberal political parties and the rise of socialist groups. Antisemitism was now coded as a Czech nationalist program, in opposition to the international and allegedly antinational social democracy. Meanwhile, the dreams of creating an international antisemitic movement in Central Europe had faded away, and antisemitic groups in different countries stood increasingly in conflict. A clear illustration of this fact was the change of heart of Karl Lueger's Christian Socials in Vienna, who used to be more open to cooperation with Czech antisemitic groups and wished to attract Czech lower middle-class voters in Vienna. In November 1897, however, the Christian Socials contributed to the fall of the government of Kazimierz Badeni and thus alienated most Czech antisemites.

The newfound compatibility between the practice of the nationality conflict and antisemitism gave the 1897 and 1899 riots increased power. Moreover, the 1897 and 1899 riots became a template for future protests such as the anti-German and anti-Jewish demonstrations and looting in Prague in December 1918 and November 1920, which followed the same rituals of mass violence.[28] The close integration of both ideological elements during the 1899 riots can be illustrated with a number of examples. In Velká Bíteš, a small town in Moravia close to Brno/Brünn, some fifty to sixty young men (who are described in the gendarmerie report as members of the Czech nationalist gymnastics organization Sokol) organized a march through the town on November 29, when they shouted both anti-Jewish and antigovernmental slogans ("hanba židům a hanba vládě" / "shame on Jews and shame on the government").[29]

The nationalist departure provided a degree of legitimization that antisemitic ideology or isolated antisemitic incidents never could achieve. The anti-Jewish violence became so strong not despite the initial causes, but because of the approval provided by Czech political leadership, emanating from the Czech national case against the Germans. The power of this mobilization could have been measured in the size of the crowds that in some places included half of the population (even if part of the rioters certainly came from the surrounding countryside). The three thousand people participating in the funeral of the Holešov victims, for example, constituted about two-thirds of all non-Jewish inhabitants of the town. In his report, the district captain of Přerov described the demonstration in his town as simply "colossal."[30]

In many respects, the 1899 Moravian riots fit the definition of "exclusionary" violence. However, from the subjective point of view of the rioting Czechs, the riots were part of the struggle for equal rights in German-dominated Cisleithania and for the emancipation (or *obrození*, "rebirth" in Czech) of the Czech nation. Indeed, most cases of anti-Jewish violence in the age of emancipation included an element of a protest against the state or the government (which allegedly protected Jews).[31] However, the declared "emancipatory" character of the struggle for national rights also included legitimization from above by a national elite. It was this justification that gave the 1899 Moravian variant of the "exclusionary" riot increased strength and violence.

■   THE HILSNER AFFAIR

If something was conspicuously missing in Žáček's Reichsrat speech, it was the Hilsner affair, an accusation of Jewish ritual murder that caused a great deal of public excitement. In the autumn of 1899, Žáček's antisemitic colleagues frequently referred to the Hilsner affair in speeches on the floor of the Reichsrat.[32] It was no surprise to the members of parliament when Ernst Schneider developed his Reichsrat speech into a lengthy diatribe based on this accusation of ritual murder.

The trial of Leopold Hilsner for the alleged ritual murder of a Christian girl in Polná (a small Bohemian town close to Moravia) took place just weeks before the outbreak of violence in Moravia. The Hilsner affair divided the politically active Czech public into two camps, and it is believed to be the only case—out of the many similar accusations in Cisleithania—in which the Jewish defendant was found guilty. The case started with a brutal and most likely sexually motivated murder of a Christian girl, Anežka Hrůzová, in a nearby forest around Easter 1899. Immediately after the discovery of her mutilated body, local inhabitants started to speculate about the "Jewish" character of the crime and eventually pointed—without any evidence—to a young Jewish vagrant named Leopold Hilsner. Hilsner was detained and eventually sentenced to death. The evidence against him was based mostly on local citizens suddenly "remembering" to have seen the missing pieces of evidence. The outcome of the trial would not have been possible without the rise of Czech political antisemitism in the preceding years and months. In the antisemitic propaganda, which grew stronger after the 1897 Reichsrat elections, the accusation of ritual murder was used as a metaphor for the alleged world Jewish conspiracy against the Czech nation and the world of nations more generally.[33] The images of Hilsner draining the Christian girl of blood and of social democrats undermining the integrity of the nation complemented each other. Hilsner lost his appeal in 1900, and his sentence was commuted to life by the emperor. Eventually, he spent almost twenty years in jail for a crime he did not commit.[34]

The affair and the trial proved to be a powerful catalyst for Czech antisemitism. The stream of popular pamphlets, songs, and similar accusations testifies to the immense attraction of the "sensational" murder and of the blood libel accusation. Moreover, the language and symbolism of the ritual murder, with its emotional power and references to traditional anti-Jewish imagery, made the more abstract antisemitic program comprehensible to those classes that were traditionally less mobilized by political issues. The trial was closely watched by the media,[35] and the courtroom filled with journalists and politicians. As the 1899 riots unfolded, Thomas G. Masaryk publicly discussed Hilsner's case, criticizing the biased investigation and calling for a revision of the trial.[36]

Therefore, it is no exaggeration to say that the sentiments created by this ritual murder accusation and by the trial in September 1899 seriously contributed to the anti-Jewish atmosphere during the October demonstrations. Not surprisingly, references to Hilsner and the trial were omnipresent during the riots. In Holešov, for instance, local authorities investigated several cases of schoolchildren harassing their Jewish schoolmates. A Christian student was documented to have taunted his Jewish classmate: "Hilsner is your uncle!"[37] The bloody shirt and tie of Klabusay, the antisemitic owner of the local printing shop, was exhibited next to a large figure made of papier-mâché and described by an inscription "Hilsner bez provazu" ("Hilsner without a rope"), referring to the popular images of a hanging figure of Leopold Hilsner.[38] In Třebíč/Trebitsch, the false "news" that Hilsner's mother now resided in town (having been forced out of Polná) had a powerful effect on the Czech public. During the riots, in the south Moravian town of Göding/Hodonín, a rumor that Karel Baxa was about to visit was sufficient to set local authorities, the local army unit, and the police on alert.[39] Baxa was a lawyer and a radical Czech politician and nationalist. During the Hilsner trial, he had served as a private attorney to the mother of the murdered girl and systematically manipulated the court to spread antisemitism.

Yet, to explain the power of the 1899 riots, we need to look at another significant element. The success of the accusation would not have been conceivable had antisemitism not become part of the identity of the local Czech community in Polná, which stood together to describe the crime as a Jewish one and fabricated much of the evidence against Hilsner. However, the formation of a local anti-Jewish identity and the integration of antisemitism into local politics was characteristic of many Moravian towns over the course of the preceding two decades.

■ ANTISEMITIC TOPOGRAPHY

The intensity of the Moravian anti-Jewish riots also needs to be viewed against the already established pattern of antisemitism in political and national conflicts in many towns in Moravia. Beginning in the 1880s, several Moravian towns became the settings for intense conflicts between Czech and German nationalists as the Czech national party strove to wrest communal power from German-speaking liberals who had been, up to that point, privileged by their economic, social, and political advantages. Certainly, there were parallels in many other cities and towns in east central Europe in this period; however, Moravia was in some respects unique. First, unlike Bohemia, it was a more mixed region. Here, Czech and German speakers were less separated geographically than elsewhere in the Bohemian lands. According to the 1900 census, 1,727,270 Moravians (71.4 percent) declared Czech as their "language of daily use" and 675,492 German (27.9 percent); 44,255 (1.8 percent) of Moravians identified themselves as Jewish by religion.[40]

Moravia had been home to significant Jewish communities and famous yeshivas since the Middle Ages. In the fifteenth century, Moravian Jews had been expelled from royal towns; subsequently, many strong and vibrant communities were created in smaller towns such as Holešov, Boskovice/Boskowitz, Třebíč, and Mikulov/Nikolsburg. Many Jews from these communities migrated into new economic and industrial centers such as Vienna or Brno and Moravská Ostrava/Mährisch Ostrau in Moravia in the second half of the nineteenth century. Still, the older communities kept much of their integrity. Many also functioned as "political," self-administrative units with independent municipal councils, mayors, police, schools, and municipal elections. Thus in many smaller towns in Moravia, two "political" communities existed next to each other: a larger "Christian" and a smaller "Jewish" administration. Starting in the 1860s, these autonomous Jewish communities became pawns in the political game of Austrian-German liberals, who profited from the existence of these culturally pro-German and predominantly liberal townships and used them to bolster their position during the elections in the urban curia.[41]

The separate Jewish settlement areas, or "ghettos," were relatively new. They were only firmly established in the 1720s as a consequence of the state policy of separation that required Jews in many towns to move to designated areas away from churches and Christian processions. However, in the second half of the nineteenth century, the lines of division began to blur as some Jews migrated to the "Christian" parts of the town; Jewish businessmen who played important roles in local economies moved to town centers, opened shops, and acquired houses. They often faced distrust and protests by Christian inhabitants. The former ghettos became populated by impoverished classes of both confessions. Jewish "political" communities, however, managed to keep their Jewish identity and to support separate "Jewish" schools and other institutions.

According to the census of 1890 and an 1898 survey, 27 Jewish "political" communities still existed in Moravia, housing more than 16,000 inhabitants. However, Jews made up only 55 percent of the population in these communities, and 70 percent of the inhabitants declared German as their language of daily use. Of the almost 118,000 inhabitants of the parallel "Christian" towns, almost 6,000 (or 5 percent) declared themselves Jewish by religion and 24 percent claimed German as their language of daily use.[42] Apart from long-standing animosity and the rise of Moravian antisemitism, the wish of the Jewish communities to preserve their German cultural identity figured prominently among the reasons for the persistence of this administrative anomaly. The preference for German as the language of education, administration, and business was not, however, an expression of a German nationalist orientation among the Jews of Moravia, but rather a sign of their continued adherence to the tradition of the German-Jewish *Haskalah* (Jewish Enlightenment) and to the form of German liberalism that was associated with emancipation of Jews. Most of the Jewish "political" communities survived until the end of the First World War, and this anachronism was not abolished until the formation of the new Czechoslovak state, which had no interest in preserving the largely culturally German parts of towns as separate communities.[43]

The German character of the Jewish towns, but even more that of the Jews living in the "Christian" communities, was considered an offence by Czech nationalists who strived to create linguistically and nationally homogeneous communities. Even Žáček (in the speech described above) interpreted the anti-Jewish sentiments and actions of Czechs as deriving solely from Jewish support of German dominance in a number of Moravian towns: "No, gentlemen, nowhere do Jews walk hand in hand with Czechs, everywhere they stand as political antagonists of the Bohemian [that is, Czech] people." Only when Jews, who as a community had previously voted for German-oriented political parties instead of abstaining or yielding to Czech pressure, shifted their support would the strength of "Germandom fall in these towns."[44]

It was no coincidence that most of the intensive confrontations during the riots of 1899 occurred in the places of traditional Jewish settlement (although not all had "political" Jewish communities) and not in the new Moravian centers that attracted Jewish immigration, such as the industrial cities of Moravská Ostrava/Mährisch Ostrau and Brno/Brünn. Not unlike Polná, Holešov and similar places had experienced little industrial and commercial development. They retained instead a more traditional small-town social structure. These small-town Christian and Jewish communities were in decline compared to the new industrial and commercial centers. Most Jews in these communities performed traditional economic functions as traders, shop owners, innkeepers, factory owners, or peddlers.

The Moravian antisemitic campaigns made use of the weaknesses of the curial electoral system, which weighted the votes of different groups of eligible voters based on their economic, social, and educational standing. Thus, voters in communal elections usually were divided into three groups, each paying one-third of the communal taxes. The first curia was the domain of a few members of the local economic elite, the second comprised local businessmen, smaller entrepreneurs, and members of the *Bildungsbürgertum* such as teachers and priests. All other eligible voters constituted the third and largest curia. Usually in the disputed towns, with the third curia firmly in their hands and the first one out of reach, Czech nationalists would concentrate on "conquering" the second curia.

Harassment of Jewish voters, who—because of their strong position in business and industry—were influential in the second curia, was therefore not only an expression of antisemitism, but also an effective electoral strategy. The economic boycott of an ethnic group developed into a useful tool in electoral campaigns and contributed much to the integration of antisemitism into local politics in Cisleithania. It can be argued that the first inroads political antisemitism made in Cisleithania were on the communal level, as antisemitic groups fought against liberal dominance. Only later, around 1897, did antisemitism gain an important function in Cisleithanianation-wide politics.

A model anti-Jewish boycott by Moravian Czech nationalists took place in the town of Prostějov/Prossnitz. In this town, actions by the Czech national movement beginning in the early 1880s finally succeeded in ushering in Czech dominance of the town hall by 1892–1893. As a rule, anti-Jewish agitation intensified before local or parliamentary elections and included calls for boycotts propagated through the *Hlasy z Hané* newspaper[45] as well as public meetings during which speakers urged farmers from the countryside not to purchase goods from the alleged enemies of the Czech nation. The propagandists made full use of the *svůj k svému* slogan (roughly: "each to his own"), which became the symbol of exclusive economic nationalism and of campaigns against Jews and Germans in the economy. The drive against Jewish businesspeople reached its climax between 1890, when the Czech party lost the election to the Moravian diet in Prostějov, and 1892, when the same party finally took over the communal administration. The Prostějov model was replicated over the following years in several Moravian towns (for instance, in Kyjov/Gaya, Litovel/ Littau, and Vyškov/Wischau), and anti-Jewish boycott campaigns were firmly established as a legitimate tool in the Czech nationalists' fight for communal power.[46] Nowhere in the Bohemian Lands did the anti-Jewish economic boycotts become as intensive and forceful as in these small Moravian towns.

How, then, were nationalists able to mark certain shops or pubs as antinational and enemy businesses? A general, impersonal, anti-Jewish propaganda apparently was not sufficient because—the animosity to Jews notwithstanding—locals were used to conducting business with Jews and thereby accepted their role in the local economy. The nationalists needed to locate Jews and other enemies on the national map of the community, to label individual shops and businesses as hostile, and to enforce national discipline in economic behavior. According to law, calls for boycotts of certain groups of individuals based on their ethnicity were illegal; however, in practice this ban was bypassed in several ways. One was to mark "friendly" businesses as Czech and Christian: the National Party in Prostějov invited Czech shopkeepers from other places to open "Christian" stores in the town and then supported them. The association of "Christian" shopkeepers in Prostějov, however, was involved in boycott propaganda in the countryside. Czech nationalists published lists and address books of Czech and Christian businesses and warned readers of the nationalist press against frequenting stores run by "enemies" of the Czech nation. Nationalists also took advantage of the fact that voter lists and ballot choices were not secret: by publicizing lists of citizens who voted against the Czech party, the nationalist propagandists achieved the same result.[47]

The effect of the antisemitic boycott campaigns extended beyond the communities where Czech nationalists fought against the German administration (Holešov, among other places affected by the 1899 riots, had a Czech communal administration) and can be seen as part of the broader phenomenon of the rise of antiliberal and antisemitic politics. For instance, a faction of the Young Czech party in Kolín in Bohemia used antisemitism as a vehicle to fight the Czech liberal (Old Czech) community leadership from 1892 to 1893. Their antisemitic propaganda eventually culminated in an accusation of ritual murder and grew into extensive anti-Jewish riots suppressed by the army.[48] At roughly the same time, in the south Moravian region of Znojmo, the antisemitic Christian Social movement fought against the dominance of the well-entrenched German liberals, who were becoming increasingly nationalist. Local Christian Social organizations, under the direct influence and support of Karl Lueger's Viennese party, still united German- and Czech-speaking politicians and voters.[49] At this time, both Czech and German-Austrian antisemites hoped to create a large movement spanning linguistic and national boundaries.

Antisemites blamed Jews for inflaming the nationality conflicts in order to profit at the expense of both Czechs and Germans. One of the areas of cooperation between Czech and Austrian (especially Viennese) antisemites was the propagation of the accusations of ritual murder; the Viennese Christian Social antisemitic "expert" Ernst Schneider was busy traveling around Bohemia and Moravia and documenting alleged Jewish ritual murders. In the same period (in 1893), Holešov experienced its own small blood libel when two Christian women, in two separate cases, accused local businessman David Tandler of an attempt to drain them of blood.[50]

The growth of antisemitism can be followed in a number of Moravian Czech-language newspapers. In the late 1880s and 1890s, many regional papers added antisemitism and boycott calls to their political campaigns. Two completely antisemitic Czech journals were published in Moravia at the time: *Brněnský drak* (Brno Dragon) in Brno and *Žihadlo* (Sting) in Kroměříž. *Žihadlo* was widely disseminated in the region where the 1899 riots were centered, including the nearby town of Holešov. Not only did the paper publish vicious anti-Jewish articles and describe Jews as promoters of the nationality conflict and enemies of both Czechs and Germans, it also actively attempted to organize Czech economic life in the region and to boycott Jews. In 1893 the paper's editor, Hugo Dvořák, acted as one of the main speakers at the founding meeting of a new "joint-stock Christian store" (*akciový křesťanský obchod*) in Kroměříž, which aimed to replace Jewish textile retailers.[51]

In 1894 Kroměříž was also the setting of the Moravian-wide meeting of the small traders' association (*živnostenský sjezd*) where at least some speakers openly expressed their antisemitism. Colleagues and antisemitic politicians from outside the area were invited, including Ernst Schneider. His presence, however, gave rise to dissent among the organizers, including Karel Adámek, a well-known Young Czech politician who stood close to antisemitism. Adámek turned against Schneider and apparently helped to prevent him from addressing the meeting. (Schneider's antisemitism was not the problem: Adámek and others resented Schneider's lack of command of Czech.) The traders' association in Kroměříž had honored the Viennese antisemite as a guest at a separate meeting, however.[52] More generally, Moravia, and especially its southern part where most of the more violent incidents took place in 1899, might have been influenced by the rise of Viennese antisemitism because of geographic proximity and migration. One can only speculate whether the antisemitic publisher Klabusay was inspired by his apprentice years in the Habsburg capital.[53]

The conflicts and riots of 1899 cannot be understood without taking into account the antisemitic campaigns of the preceding years and the specific antisemitic groups in the affected towns. In Holešov, for instance, the Jewish police who attacked Klabusay were certainly aware that he was known to publish and distribute antisemitic booklets (including an abridged version of August Rohling's infamous *Talmudjude*).[54] Moreover, Klabusay was one of the early promoters of the creation of the local small traders' organization and published its newspaper. Antisemitism seems to have been an undisputed and self-evident weapon in the ideological arsenal of the movement that aimed to force their Jewish competition out.

Echoes of the boycott movement were recorded during the 1899 riots. For instance, in Litovel/Littau, one of the towns in which the Czech national movement fought against the German town hall, the violence coincided with a campaign for municipal elections, bringing about an explosive atmosphere.[55] In Prostějov, leaflets with "*svůj k svému*" were distributed during the 1899 crisis.[56] Just after the riots, the mayor of Holešov, together with almost forty mayors or councilors from surrounding communities, issued a proclamation to the inhabitants of the Holešov district. While they opposed the anti-Jewish violence and described it as counterproductive (having only brought harm to Christians, including some deaths), they called for an economic boycott of Jews and for following the "*svůj k svému*" slogan.[57] Hence violence and the boycott were seen as sharing the same objectives; the latter was considered to be more effective. The proclaimed boycott therefore was a functional continuation of the anti-Jewish violence.

The boycotts of the 1880s and 1890s were instrumental in forging a pogrom atmosphere in two interconnected ways. First, a fundamental aspect of the antisemitic movement was to clearly define the group that was supposed to be boycotted. By mapping ethnicity and national allegiance onto the space of a town, Czech nationalists succeeded widely in defining the out-group and making it highly visible and concrete. The focus of the rioters on Jewish businesses of all kinds, much more than other symbols of Jewish presence such as synagogues, has to be attributed not only to the Jewish role in local economies, but mainly to the boycott campaigns. Historian Hannah Ahlheim, who examined the German boycott movement in the 1920s and 1930s, came to a similar conclusion and stressed the significance of the local as well as the fact that the boycotts helped to create a symbolic mental and antisemitic topography of the towns and villages: "the 'greedy Jew' was given a name, a face, and an address by the calls to boycott specific local stores."[58] In addition, the boycotts helped Moravian Czechs to internalize antisemitic ideology and, perhaps more importantly, to adopt day-to-day exclusionary patterns of behavior. While not all (and perhaps not even most) Czechs followed the nationalist logic in their economic (and other) choices, some did change their daily behavior to conform with nationalist and increasingly antisemitic prescriptions. The rioters of 1899 surely knew the ethnoreligious geography of their towns well and did not need much guidance about which places to target with their anger and stones.

The long-term impact of the antisemitic propaganda in Holešov and vicinity further illustrates the success of the late nineteenth-century nationalist and antisemitic campaigns. A few weeks after the end of the First World War and the establishment of the independent Czechoslovak Republic, anti-Jewish violence again came to Holešov. What is often inaccurately called the "last pogrom" in the Bohemian Lands was part of a wave of anti-Jewish riots, looting, and the forced sale of shops that followed the demise of the Habsburg Monarchy. However, the Holešov riot was the most lethal and extensive example of the Bohemian and Moravian anti-Jewish violence of 1918–1919. On the night of December 3, 1918, a group of soldiers stationed in Holešov, joined by several hundred locals, staged an extremely violent pogrom that left two Jews dead and dozens of shops and pubs looted and destroyed. The rioters cut off the telephone connection to the city and detained local gendarmes. Order was only restored the next morning.[59]

While many rioters were later punished, the exact reasons for the attacks were never clarified. The driving force had been an undisciplined army unit that came from the outside; however, many local inhabitants joined readily, and some clearly tried to settle accounts for the death or punishment of the 1899 rioters. One of the Jewish victims of the 1918 violence was Hugo Grätzer, son of the owner of the tavern demolished in 1899 and one of those who attacked Klabusay (who, on the other hand, was elected into the temporary National Council that took over administration in the town in 1918). Other participants sought revenge for the imprisonment of a group of Holešov youngsters accused of treason and allegedly denounced by local Jews during World War I.[60]

The 1918 riot differed in key respects from the events of 1899. It was more violent. Large numbers of armed soldiers took part and made ready use of their weapons. It took place amid extreme shortages of food, coal, and clothes, as well as among accusations of usury and speculation. In 1918 Czech national goals had largely been accomplished, but it was alleged Jewish behavior during the war and supposed Jewish disloyalty that were now under public scrutiny. However, the strength of the pogrom also indicates a continuity of antisemitic ideas between 1890s and the interwar Czechoslovak Republic. For at least some groups in Holešov, antisemitism had become an integral part of local identity.

Holešov soon would become one of the early centers of Czech fascism, which emerged at the end of 1922. The Holešov-based journal *Hanácká republika* (Haná Republic, later *Národní republika*, National Republic) published by Robert Mach spread nationalist, fascist, and antisemitic ideology in the region. The paper's articles and editorials described Jews as a force Germanizing the Moravian region of Slovač.[61] The movement also was a way to maintain local identity against the new and distant center of government and party politics in Prague. This regional form of fascism later continued in the organization Národopisná Morava (Ethnographic Moravia), which willingly cooperated in the antisemitic campaign in the Nazi-occupied "Protectorate of Bohemia and Moravia."[62]

As a Czech journalist toured Holešov in January 2012, he found the memory of the Holešov pogroms well and alive. Today, many inhabitants of the town seem genuinely interested in Jewish culture and history. Still, some of the people he interviewed expressed traditional antisemitic views and cited alleged Jewish Germanization of the town and economic exploitation as justification for the previous incidents of violence and for their own anti-Jewish attitudes.[63]

"AN ANTISEMITIC AFTERTASTE"
ANTI-JEWISH VIOLENCE
IN HABSBURG CROATIA

In the Habsburg Crownlands of Croatia and Slavonia, anti-Hungarian political protests broke out in the summer of 1883 and expanded into a full-blown social uprising of Croatian peasants. During the protests, anti-Jewish rumors circulated widely. Posters called for the Jews' expulsion. Jewish houses were attacked and their stores plundered. Jews reacted with fear and uncertainty. In March 1903 political protests aimed once again at Hungarian hegemony commenced in Zagreb and then spread throughout the region. The demonstrators demanded a reordering of Hungarian-Croatian financial arrangements. Soon after the first demonstrations, peasants and military forces clashed. Protesters attacked people seen as representing Hungarian domination and also confronted Jews. In many communities, Jews were threatened; and in some areas, as in 1883, Jewish homes and businesses were plundered and damaged. Another wave of violence accompanied the end of World War I and the establishment of the new Kingdom of the Serbs, Croats, and Slovenes. Social crisis and political instability led to destruction and looting in many parts of Croatia-Slavonia. Once more, violence took on an antisemitic character. Crowds plundered Jewish property, set Jewish homes on fire, and attacked synagogues.

On the basis of this brief sketch, it would be easy to assume, as many outside observers did at the time, that antisemitism in Croatia-Slavonia was incessant and inescapable, a "structural" condition that unfailingly showed itself during moments of crisis. One also could claim, as many Croatian leaders did then, that these antisemitic demonstrations were rare exceptions to a long history of good relations between Jews and Christians in the Crownlands. By focusing on the violent events of 1883 and 1903, this chapter looks much more closely at antisemitic violence in Croatia-Slavonia during the Dual Monarchy. I argue here that the anti-Jewish attacks in Croatia and Slavonia arose as a "by-product" of politically charged social and economic tensions. In contrast to other parts of the monarchy, such as Hungary, Galicia, or in the Slovak areas, anti-Jewish violence in Croatia-Slavonia was not initiated and directed solely against the Jews. There were always other causes and reasons for the politically and socially motivated violence; however, it is noteworthy that this violence always unfolded with an antisemitic "aftertaste." Why this was, how antisemitism manifested itself, and how contemporaries made sense of this "aftertaste" will be presented in this chapter.

Antisemitism is marginal in much Croatian historiography. Of course, some works on the Jewish history of this region refer to antisemitic incidents; however, for the most part, this scholarship tends to relativize these events.[1] Only two articles have appeared that deal explicitly with antisemitic violence in the Crownlands of Croatia and Slavonia.[2] In her 1957–1958 article, historian Miroslava Despot followed the course of the 1883 violence.[3] The Croatian historian Ljiljana Dobrovšak likewise focused on the violent anti-Jewish attacks of 1903 in an article published in 2005.[4] The two articles have much in common. Both engage systematically with the forms and locations of anti-Jewish violence. Yet both historians relativize the events and fail to consider them in connection with wider patterns of antisemitism.

As noted above, the occasions and causes of the outbreaks were not, in general, motivated primarily by anti-Jewish hatred. Still, the fact that this violence always developed antisemitic characteristics cannot be dismissed as merely contingent or unintentional. In the following, I want to demonstrate the potency of the antisemitic symbols and rhetoric that had developed and disseminated in "calmer" times and could, during moments of crisis, agitate crowds and be employed by political actors. The "sideshow" of anti-Jewish violence was intentional, because Jews became symbols and substitutes for the original targets of the violence. After briefly describing the position of Jews within Croatia-Slavonia, I will analyze the anti-Jewish riots of 1883 and 1903 in local terms, but always keeping in mind the wider transnational influences that informed them.

■ JEWS IN CROATIA-SLAVONIA

Over the course of the nineteenth century, Croatia and Slavonia—like other regions of the Habsburg monarchy—experienced many crises. These two crownlands, to which the Kingdom of Dalmatia was linked by history if not by administration, were controlled by Austria or Hungary for centuries.[5] During the 1848–1849 revolutions, the Croatian leadership hoped above all to be freed of the Hungarian yoke and to wrest greater autonomy for the Croatian lands from the Habsburgs. This was one of the central reasons why the Croatian Ban Josip Jelačić helped the Habsburgs to defeat the Hungarian revolution. In this revolutionary and politically unstable time, Croatia and Slavonia, like

Hungary, experienced anti-Jewish agitation, including calls for the expulsion of Jews from many towns, looting of Jewish stores, and a generally anti-Jewish atmosphere. The liberal-leaning Jelačić prevented serious attacks on Jews and expulsions from taking place.[6]

The political result of the revolutionary years was the so-called neoabsolutist regime in the Habsburg Monarchy. With the 1867 *Ausgleich* (Agreement) between Austria and Hungary, Croatia and Slavonia were assigned to the Hungarian half of the now constitutional Dual Monarchy of Austria-Hungary. In the following year, however, Croatians succeeded in securing the so-called little *Ausgleich* with Hungary, which guaranteed a measure of autonomy for Croatia and Slavonia in matters of inner administration, justice, religion, and education. Despite this treaty, which recognized the Croatian nation as a political entity and the Croatian language as the sole language of the bureaucracy, leading Hungarian political circles pursued a targeted "Magyarization" policy.[7] This policy was a clear violation of the Ausgleich and was designed to weaken further Croatian demands for autonomy in financial or economic matters. Magyarization, in short, ensured that Croatian-Hungarian relations remained strained until the collapse of Austria-Hungary in 1918. These tense relations erupted in 1883 and again in 1903.

This era nonetheless created new opportunities for Jews in Croatia-Slavonia. For a long time, Jews had occupied an uncertain position in society: their legal status was not clearly defined, and they were not equal citizens. Some individual Jews had managed to achieve a measure of economic and social success.[8] The 1868 agreement had left the question of Jewish emancipation to the Croatian authorities. Conflicts over the Ausgleich, as well as the dissolution and the obstruction of the work of the Croatian diet by the pro-Hungarian Ban Levin Rauch, hindered the completion of this work. In 1873 the Croatian diet granted Jews legal equality with Christians.[9]

As a result of emancipation, Jewish immigration to Croatia-Slavonia rose dramatically. In the 1860s several thousand Jews lived in these crownlands. By 1880 this figure had risen to 13,488 and by 1900 to around 20,000. Even with this growth, Jews remained a small minority, representing no more than 0.8 percent of the total population at the turn of the century. Most immigrants came from Hungary (76 percent of the total) and others from Austria (7 percent), Bosnia (6 percent), and Serbia (5 percent). For the most part they settled in urban areas.[10] From emancipation until the dissolution of the monarchy, Jews took part in all categories of social life in Croatia-Slavonia. Jews were members of city councils, representatives to the regional parliament, presidents of the chamber of commerce, chief state prosecutors, judges, and so on. In 1912 Croatia appointed its first Jewish chief justice of the province's supreme court.[11] Jews also made major contributions to the expansion of the Croatian economy.[12]

Croatian Jews were not only active in the political and economic realms, but also founded and supported numerous cultural associations. They created a network of charitable organizations in which Jewish women were particularly active.[13] At a time when 70 percent of Christian Croatians were illiterate, the portion of Croatian Jews unable to read and write was about 25 percent.[14] In 1910 the Jews of the town of Varaždin had the highest literacy rate (90.3 percent) of any Jewish community in the entire monarchy. The Jews of Osijeker ranked fourth (87.7 percent), behind the Hungarian communities of Pécs and Székesfehérvár and ahead of Budapest.[15] As a result, Jews were more highly educated than the Croatian and Serbian populations of Croatia-Slavonia, which opened up possibilities for Jews to succeed in the economy and the professions. Jews in this region enjoyed a relatively high social standing, and poverty was a rare occurrence among them.

Croatian Jews spoke a number of languages. On the 1900 census, some 42 percent listed German as their "mother tongue," 21 percent marked Hungarian, and 35 percent Croatian. Ten years later, 46 percent of Jews declared Croatian their mother tongue, and the percentage claiming Hungarian rose slightly to 22 percent. The steady number of Hungarian speakers reflected continued Jewish immigration from Hungary into Croatia as well as the ongoing Magyarization policies, which promoted the spread of the Hungarian language and privileged Hungarian speakers. But the decline in the number of Jews claiming to speak German as their "mother tongue" and the increase in those declaring themselves Croatian speakers also pointed to the growing acculturation of Jews within Croatian society.

For some Croatian leaders, Jews would always be outsiders. Under the influence of wider European antisemitic movements, in the 1880s some opposition politicians and activists began to employ anti-Jewish allegations and stereotypes in partisan struggles for power.[16] In the years that followed, the party press formulated and constantly propagated the image of "the Jew" as an exploiter, forever at odds with the Croatian nation and its culture. Until the dissolution of the Habsburg Monarchy in 1918, Jews were depicted as Germans or Hungarians who therefore represented "foreign" interests in Croatia and Slavonia.

■   1883

At the beginning of August 1883, violent demonstrations broke out first in the Croatian capital of Zagreb (as would also be the case in 1903) and eventually spread to much of Croatia-Slavonia. Attacks against Jews and their property took place in cities and in the countryside. An imprudent action by the Hungarian Finance Director Antal David provided the immediate cause for the 1883 rioting. In the summer of 1883, David replaced the coat of arms with a Croatian inscription on the facade of the finance building in Zagreb with one bearing both Croatian and Hungarian inscriptions. The opposition press vehemently denounced this act, which violated the Croatian-Hungarian Ausgleich.[17] At the same time, the opposition took advantage of the incident to mobilize the population against Hungarian hegemony.

In later years, these protests often would be interpreted as a kind of national uprising and national resistance against Hungary, because the spark that had ignited the events was a clear expression of the policy of Magyarization. In fact, the peasant population was much more concerned about the oppressive burden of taxation and the effects of a long-term agrarian crisis.[18] Whether or not the coat of arms had a Croatian or Hungarian inscription must have been of little concern to the largely illiterate peasantry.[19] Still, the uprising in Croatia caused a great deal of nervousness in Budapest and Vienna.[20] Intensive political maneuvering in Vienna led finally to the appointment of the Hungarian Count Károly (Dragutin) Khuen-Héderváry as Croatian ban in December 1883 and with him came the institution of a rigid political system.

Of great interest in this context is the question of why the violent upheaval of the peasants also took on an antisemitic character. Why did rioters attack Jews and Jewish homes and businesses in Zagreb and in the countryside? And how did the Croatian political parties react to the antisemitic riots?

The installation of the Hungarian-Croatian coat of arms was rejected across party lines. At the same time, nearly all of the political parties welcomed the protests and celebrated the mobilization of the population as a political demonstration against this violation of the Hungarian-Croatian Ausgleich and against Hungarian paternalism. The coat of arms was put up on the night of August 6–7. Several windows of the finance building were broken on the eighth, and demonstrations commenced on the eleventh. On August 15, the Catholic feast day celebrating the Assumption of Mary, clashes between demonstrators and the police resulted in one death.[21] Demonstrations took place in several other Croatian towns between the middle and end of August.[22] By the end of the month, violence had spread into the countryside.

In an article entitled "Unrest in Zagorje," *Pozor* (Attention), the organ of the Independent National Party and the most important Croatian daily newspaper, initially expressed shock and surprise at the violence in Zagorje, the rural region around Zagreb where the peasant unrest first broke out.[23] The Independent National Party represented the interests of the upper-middle classes and the Catholic hierarchy and was the most significant opposition party. From the early 1880s, the Independent National Party and its paper had been increasingly interested in the rise of political antisemitism across Europe. The party claimed to defend the rights of Christians and the Church against the Jews; the paper portrayed Jews as profiteers of liberalism and representatives of Hungarian interests. In 1883, then, it was not surprising that the paper began to express great sympathy for the condition of the peasantry. The ruling elites, it wrote, take the fruits of their fields and burden them with taxation, "And the Jew takes what the rulers leave behind." Peasants would gladly borrow on credit at reasonable interest rates, it continued, but such credit was nowhere to be found. Here, Jews would jump in and pretend not to demand any interest. However, after the harvest, they forced peasants to give up their wheat and wine at shamelessly low prices. *Pozor* then asked rhetorically whether incidents like those that took place in Zaborje should come as a surprise to anyone. Despite this seeming explanation of anti-Jewish violence, the article ended with a call to the "patriots of Zagorje" to restore calm as soon as possible.[24] The article did not directly address the rioting against Jews and also left aside the issue of the coat of arms. Instead, the author focused on the precarious position of the peasantry, blaming the Jews along with heavy taxation for the terrible social situation in the countryside.

The same issue of *Pozor* discussed an article published in the Hungarian newspaper *Nemzet* (Nation) and a brief report from the *Pester Lloyd* concerning the antisemitic outbreaks in Hungary. *Pozor* reported in far greater detail on violence against the Jews in Hungary than those in Croatia. This contrast reflected the paper's editorial position. During the riots in Croatia, the paper repeatedly called for calm and made little reference to specifically anti-Jewish attacks. *Pozor*, however, did report at length on the anti-Jewish incidents in Hungary.[25] The editors of *Pozor* clearly opposed antisemitic violence and preferred not to draw attention to evidence of Croatian antisemitism, even as they and the political opposition more broadly used the violence in Hungary to discredit Hungarian claims to cultural superiority and political supremacy. From the start, then, the Croatian opposition officially denounced violence against Jews, even as it drew attention away from antisemitic rhetoric and demonstrations at home.

With the spread of the unrest in Zagorje, a correspondent for *Pozor* reported that among the Croatian people voices could be heard calling, "Down with the Jews, leaders, and Hungarians!" According to the author, this call reflected beliefs deeply rooted in the collective consciousness of the people.[26] The editors noted, however, that nothing terrible would happen once the true cause of the unrest had been addressed, namely, the awful material conditions of the population.[27] For now, the paper called on its readers to restore order and calm.

In the weeks that followed, *Pozor* dealt with the political question of the removal of the coat of arms almost daily but published relatively little about the rioting in general or the attacks on Jews in particular. Thus it contained few reports of anti-Jewish attacks such as those that took place in the villages of Ivanec and Bednja, both to the north of Zagreb, where Jewish businesses were sacked in early September.[28] On September 3, a military unit stationed in the town of Sambor reported to the commander in Zagreb that the night before, some forty people had gathered and smashed the windows in the home of Josef Brückner, a Jewish resident. According to the military's report, the crowd attacked Brückner's home because Brückner had called in six Hussars as guards to protect him from rumored violence.[29] A few days later, *Pozor* published an article entitled "Alleged Riots against Jews."[30] The *Pozor* correspondent wrote contemptuously about Brückner, deeming him a "usurer" and "profiteer." The paper confirmed that the windows of his house had been broken; however, *Pozor* defined this as an "alleged" anti-Jewish incident. With this article, the paper confirmed once again its intention to minimize or even cast doubt on anti-Jewish attacks.

A similar pattern held when a crowd of around fifty protesters gathered in the center of Zagreb at the beginning of September. Suddenly, the rumor arose that the Jew Eduard M. Sachs had cast aspersions on Croatia. Inflamed by the rumor, the crowd broke the windows of the Prister, Baumgärtner, and Wasserthal homes, as well as those of the café owned by Heimbach.[31] *Pozor* regretted these events but blamed them on "foreign agitators."[32] The same edition also published a clarification from Eduard Sachs, who decidedly rejected the charges against him and warned that Croatia should not mimic the anti-Jewish atmosphere that then prevailed in Hungary.[33] The next day, *Pozor* explained to its readers "how antisemitism was imported." This article claimed that a bureaucrat in the Finance Direction by the name of Vučetić had incited the crowd in Zagreb against the Israelites. A second "inciter," according to the report, was the unemployed vagabond Benjamin Janežić. "Both of these little birds," reported *Pozor*, were being held by the authorities for questioning.[34]

With this article, which included no additional information about the persons involved or the motivations for their actions, *Pozor* again minimized the violent attacks against Jews and their property. The paper did not announce any other antisemitic incidents. It only reported on the trials of those involved in the attacks on Jewish homes. The paper quoted the defense attorney for the accused, Marijan Derenčin, who remarked that the riots were not antisemitic but political in nature, because the people were "upset and bitter."[35] The trials nonetheless ended with many convictions and prison sentences.[36]

Pozor had made great efforts to conceal or downplay antisemitic assaults in Croatia. When it was no longer possible to ignore the attacks in Zagreb, since the entire city already had heard about them, the paper expressed regret over the rioting. This limited coverage had several causes. First, the leading opposition party could not embrace the violence, since violence would have been seen as evidence of backwardness and would have undermined their struggle against Hungary. As part of this strategy, they wanted to situate anti-Jewish attacks exclusively in Hungary in order to challenge the Hungarian claims to modernity and liberalism. Antisemitic violence would put the Croats on an equal footing with the Hungarians. Only in this context can we understand the hesitant reporting on the antisemitic violence. Ivan Peršić, a contemporary journalist, confirmed this point: "The Croatian opposition did not at all like the fact that the riots took on an antisemitic character. 'Pozor' appealed to the community not to act incorrectly and to protect its good reputation so that the outside world would not view us as barbarians. Under no conditions can the Croatians allow the unrest to fall to the level of Vienna or Budapest, where the population steals and plunders."[37] Despite such concerns, *Pozor* clearly maintained an anti-Jewish perspective. This important newspaper never conclusively condemned the physical attacks on Jews or the anti-Jewish slogans heard in many locations. Anti-Jewish violence was denounced only because it undermined the political goals of the opposition and damaged the reputation of Croatia. The paper never condemned the attacks as assaults on equal citizens who were entitled to protection.

After the initial unrest and the subsequent resignation of Ban Ladislav Pejačević at the end of August, Vienna and Budapest agreed to appoint General Hermann Ramberg as the royal commissioner in Croatia, whose task it would be to restore law and order with the assistance of the military.[38] Only one undated report from Ramberg to Minister President Tisza still exists in the Croatian archives. In this document, presumably penned in the middle of September, Ramberg stated that "robbery and plundering of the Jews is increasing."[39] Other evidence confirms his view of developments. In Kraljevčani, a village southeast of Zagreb in the former Military Border (the region bordering the Ottoman Empire, long administered directly from Vienna and abolished only in 1881), crowds plundered the store of a Jewish trader and innkeeper, who had to promise that he would convert to Orthodox Christianity.[40] Clearly, some among the Serbian Orthodox population were participating in the demonstrations and the attacks on Jews. At the end of August, Jews in Nova Gradiška were threatened.[41] Anti-Jewish incidents also were reported to have taken place in Varaždin during the first days of September, and "antisemitic agitation" also took place in Jasenovac.[42] On the evening of September 8, journeymen smeared the slogan "Jewish pig get out" on Jewish homes in Novska.[43] Anti-Jewish violence, in short, broke out across wide swathes of Croatia-Slavonia.

The example of Bednja, a small town in northwestern Croatia, can help us understand this violence and how the authorities responded to it. Bednja had just over 1,500 inhabitants, nearly all of them Croatian-speaking Roman Catholics. A small number of Jews also lived in town, but they made up only a fraction of the population. This was the case in much of rural Croatia; in the county in which Bednja was located, 1,585 Jews lived among more than a quarter million Roman Catholics. As merchants and tavern keepers, however, Jews were highly visible. Locals had a clear sense of where Jews lived and worked. In Bednja in 1883, for example, peasants plundered and destroyed the businesses of David Fritz und Ignatz Hafner.[44] They also attacked Jewish residences and looted taverns. In the evening, an infantry company arrived in the town and energetically confronted the rioting peasants, shooting four of them.[45] According to a later report to the Hungarian government by Ostrožinski Ognjeslav Utješenović, the prefect of Varaždin County, earlier attacks against Jews and their property had occurred in the villages around Bednja. But Utješenović insisted that the Jews themselves had provided the reason for the destruction of their material possessions, because they engage in "excessive usury."[46] The prefect relayed other charges that the peasants had made against the Jews. Jews had attacked a peasant woman; another had cursed God, Jesus, and the Virgin Mary; the Jew David Fritz, who together with his family had received the protection of the village priest during the riots, reportedly had railed against the pastor because allegedly he would not give the Jews anything to eat.[47]

Available sources do not permit us to verify or disprove the veracity of such accusations. It can be safely assumed that tensions had long existed between Jews and Christians and that the small towns and villages discussed here were no exception. Despite this, the prefect's report must be read with caution. He was describing what he believed to be "popular opinion." Because he had to be careful with any criticism of Hungarian policies, he tended to blame the peasants instead of the problematic economic and financial policies of the government. Other evidence suggests that relations between Jews and Christians in Bednja cannot be described as wholly antagonistic. According to the journalist Rudolf Horvat, the peasants volunteered to help the Jews rebuild their houses and did not accept payment for this assistance.[48]

Another report from Prefect Utješenović repeated the assurance that the violence was not directed against the government or the political administration. The causes of the disaffection of the population, he claimed, stemmed from the collection of taxes, the "exaggerated usury of the Israelites," and the bureaucrats.[49] Certainly, the fact that some Jews offered credit to peasants contributed to the accusations made against them. Roman Catholics and Orthodox Christians also loaned money, but these creditors did not become objects of popular fury. Jews were easy targets. The peasants knew them, and Jews often belonged to the more prosperous elements in the Croatian countryside.

The most common form of attack against Jews was the smashing of windows on Jewish houses and businesses. The attacks by a group of rock-throwing youths in Zagreb have already been noted above.[50] Similar incidents took place in September in the Slavonian village of Podvinj and in Velika Gorica, a town near Zagreb.[51] The mayor of Velika Gorica demanded that the government immediately send soldiers.[52] The mayor of Koprivnica, a town in northern Croatia, likewise demanded military assistance. He and another city official wrote that the town was beset by a "general fear" and that the Jews were especially frightened.[53] To bolster his request for troops, the mayor included five notices with his plea to the government.[54] These notices were handwritten, illustrated on small sheets of paper, and amateurish. One had a black frame, like an obituary, and included a skull, a gallows, and a stylized map, on which "the Jewish land of Palestine" was written. The text on the notice read: "You accursed Jews, leave our land, we do not want to live with pigs. You multiply like rats." A second notice also sported a skull and carried the inscription "Jews need our blood, this is why they slaughtered the poor Christian Eszter in Hungary. Death and expulsion to all of the accursed Jews!" The third flyer insisted that "Jews have to be expelled, otherwise within a few years no one will be able to survive, because these accursed Jews dominate everything through their fraud; therefore, they should not be coddled so strike at them!" This flyer was signed "Istóczy," in a clear reference to the well-known Hungarian antisemitic politician. A fourth flyer titled "Announcement" charged that "In Jewish law it states: You need Christian blood and cannot live without it. So, BELOVED Christian, why should we sacrifice our Christian people to the accursed Jews? We do not need to do this. Out with the Jews. Long live our Istóczy!!!" The last of the flyers was written in pencil and began with a well-known but altered Croatian motto:[55] "Slap a rope around all of the Jews in the city. Only with united Croatian blood can we awaken our city against this Hungarian crap."[56]

While the language and images of the flyers clearly hinted at the limited abilities of their creators, the content of the notices only repeated widely disseminated antisemitic charges. That Christians were the victims of Jews fit neatly into a much older Roman Catholic tradition of anti-Judaism, one that had deep roots in Catholic Croatia. Other elements—calls for the expulsion of Jews and the affirmation of the ritual murder lie—suggested affinities with other antisemitic movements across the region. So too did the depictions of Jews as pigs, rats, and swindlers. It is not surprising that the mayor of Koprivnica wrote that the Jews of his town were unsettled by these flyers.

Anti-Jewish flyers like these appeared in many places in Croatia. At the end of September 1883, news reached the government that in the Slavonian village of Trnjani notices were found calling for a rebellion against the Jews.[57] The district chairman of Garčin clarified the situation a few days later: no such notices had been found in the area, and he asserted that the notice that had been found most likely was related to a personal feud.[58]

The appearance of these flyers underscored once again that the charges against Jews widely disseminated and believed in Hungary in the early 1880s in the context of the Tiszaeszlár ritual murder case were also well known and well received in Croatia-Slavonia. This transfer of antisemitic "knowledge" likely resulted from efforts by individuals who either were truly convinced of the vileness of Jews or viewed them as stand-ins for and symbols of a political and social order they resented. Moreover, these flyers revealed the intellectual wellspring from which the antisemitic attitudes so widely held at this time in Croatia and Slavonia arose: namely, supposedly Christian sentiments and social anxieties. In addition, Jews were described as "Hungarian crap," which illustrated the contradictory association of Hungary as both the source of antisemitism and at the same time the focus of Jews' loyalties.

Multiple copies of a placard that emerged in September 1882 in the east Slavonian town of Ilok clearly illustrate the powerful transnational influence of antisemitic accusations. This poster focused on the alleged ritual murder of Eszter Solymosi. In contrast to the handwritten flyers from the Koprivnica region described above, this one appeared to have been produced by a professional printer. Titled "The Blood Victim," it was printed in German, Hungarian, Czech, and Serbian. The high quality of the printing and the Serbian-Cyrillic lettering (as opposed to the Croatian-Latin script) make it probable that this poster did not originate in Croatia. It likely came from Hungary. The High Sheriff Julije Bubanović, in whose county the posters appeared, expressed his doubts to the government that the offending material came from Croatia. He also asserted that antisemitic agitation came to Croatia "from outside." He assured his superiors that there was no fear of antisemitic rioting in his county and that if any incidents did take place they would be "stifled as soon as they begin."[59] As we have seen, the authorities could not always control what happened on the ground.

The popularity of the German-language, Budapest-based, antisemitic publication *Rebach* (Profit), which attracted the attention of the Croatian authorities, also underscores the transnational dissemination and reception of antisemitic ideas.[60] In the middle of January 1883, Bubanović reported to the regional government in Zagreb on the spread of this publication, which had many subscribers and "indirectly inflamed antisemitism."[61] In the beginning of February, he sent three confiscated editions of *Rebach* to the government to provide his superiors with a sense of the threat to public order inherent in this publication.[62] In July the authorities in Nova Gradiška insisted that the government ban this publication, since more and more people were reading it and copies were available in stores and taverns. A priest from a nearby village assisted in the distribution of this antisemitic paper. The Jews of Nova Gradiška were greatly disturbed by this and began to avoid public events and some taverns.[63] In early September, at the time of the first attacks on Jews, *Rebach* was reported to have been sent free of charge to the inns of the Slavonian town of Okučani; however, these establishments did not want to accept delivery of these antisemitic papers.[64]

By 1883 anti-Jewish articles in the press, antisemitic flyers, and of course, violence against Jews and their property demonstrated that antisemitic ideas and demands were widespread in Croatia-Slavonia. Despite this reality, daily newspapers and other publications made conscious efforts to minimize their coverage of antisemitic incidents. The Croatian press rarely mentioned outbreaks of violence against Jews.[65] *Sriemski Hrvat* (Sriemer Croat), a daily paper close to Catholic circles, justified attacks against Jews by noting that Jews were generally viewed as Magyars.[66] "Jews in Croatia do not learn the national language; they consider themselves cosmopolitans, meaning people who do not see the land in which they live as their homeland. Neither the enlightened strata of the population nor the peasants sympathize with them." Furthermore, according to this paper, the "phenomenon" of attacks against Jews would soon pass and was wholly unlike the systematic attacks in Hungary. There Jews were killed and their homes plundered, "whereas in Croatia, at most windows were smashed or they [the Jews] had to pledge that they were good Croats."[67] The entire editorial slant of this paper justified or downplayed the anti-Jewish attacks. This important Catholic paper ignored the fact that the breaking of windows was accompanied by fear, threats, and the destruction of property.

In a similar spirit, *Sloboda* (Freedom), the press organ of the second opposition party, the Party of Rights, sought to portray barbaric acts of violence against Jews as exclusively the work of Hungarians. In the middle of September, this paper published an article about the anti-Jewish attacks in Zagreb. In this piece, the author expressed indignation that the deed was said to have an anti-semitic character. A few broken windows could not be called vandalism, the author insisted. "In any case, this act was only a necessary result of the brazen and condemnatory provocation from the Jewish side."[68] *Sloboda* declared that Jews could not be believed when they claimed to be good Croatians. "We know that, in the same way, Jews claim to be good Hungarians, good Germans, and so on, they are in fact nothing but excellent Jews; [. . .] Jews in Zagreb, with few ex-ceptions, constitute the strongest contingent of Germans in public and private life!"[69] In this way, *Sloboda* relativized the antisemitic attacks. Antisemitism as such, according to *Sloboda*, existed only in Hungary. The Jews attacked in Cro-atia were not, by this logic, victims of antisemitism. They had only themselves to blame, because they behaved un-Croatian and, therefore, had provoked the violent reaction of the people. Here the lines of argumentation put forth by the Party of Rights and by the Independent National Party converged. These politi-cal rivals both blamed "real" and "genuine" antisemitism on the Hungarians and insisted that the homemade Jew hatred in Croatia was the logical result of the Jews' own misbehavior and misconduct.

The divide between foreign antisemitism and native Jew hatred was typical for the Croatian political landscape at the beginning of the 1880s. The equa-tion of the new antisemitic movement with Hungarians (and to a lesser extent, Germans) served to undermine Hungarian claims to superiority and leadership over other peoples, such as the Croatians. In this context, it is not surprising that the Croatian press relativized antisemitic incidents and accused local Jews of being overly sensitive to every perceived slight. The opposition press repeat-edly denied that widespread anti-Jewish enmity existed in Croatia-Slavonia.

The liberal, progovernment press was just as restrained in its coverage of the unrest as the opposition. For example, in early September, *Narodne Novine* (National News), the official newspaper of the government, reported the attack on the trader Bachrach in Velika Gorica. It was known that the crowd had at-tacked Jews and also that the town's mayor had sent a message confirming this fact to Zagreb and calling for a regiment of the army. Yet the paper noted only that the participants broke windows, did not mention that Bachrach was Jew-ish, and insisted that one should not assume that the incident possessed in any way an "antisemitic nature."[70] The implicit message was that antisemitism had no basis in Croatia.

The liberal press also relativized the violence. It argued that violent anti-Hungarian demonstrations, the deployment of the army, the unfilled seat of the ban, and the suspended Diet had violated the constitution and justified protest against Hungarian hegemony. The government and opposition press was unified on this point. The difference was that the editors of *Narodne Novine* most certainly expressed sympathy for the situation of the Jews and, in the spirit of liberalism, defended the values of equality and humanity. *Narodne Novine* expressed this sympathy in a second article in the same edition, in which it reported on Jewish refugees from Hungary. The article ended with the assertion: "Thank God that our Croatian intelligentsia, which does not get involved with antisemitic agitation, is more progressive that some others. Croatian Jews should keep this in mind and not distance themselves from the Croatian nation."[71] Even as it represented liberal thought, the government press still felt obliged to issue a warning to Croatian Jews. In a time of national and social tension, the paper put Jews on notice to avoid "provocative" behavior and to show solidarity with the Croatians. With this article, the editors of the paper echoed a wider prejudice that Jews themselves were not Croatians.

Vienna's *Neue Freie Presse* (*NFP*) and the German-Jewish *Allgemeine Zeitung des Judentums* commented on the tendency of the Croatian press to refrain from reporting on antisemitic events at home. In the beginning of September, the *NFP* announced that *Pozor* had called on the population to exercise caution and had warned against antisemitic rabble-rousing.[72] In its evening edition on September 11, 1883, the *NFP* reported that the movement in Croatia had acquired an "antisemitic aftertaste." The paper mentioned a few localities in which violence against Jews had taken place.[73] In comparison to its coverage of anti-Jewish incidents in Hungary, however, the *NFP*'s reports about events in Croatia were limited. The reason for this was likely the fact that the *Neue Freie Presse* regularly commented favorably on the Croatian movement as a means of indirectly criticizing Hungarian policies. In mid-September, the *Allgemeine Zeitung des Judentums* also reported on the "antisemitic rabble-rousing" in Croatia[74] and emphasized that "the journals there warn of the shameful activities of the antisemites."[75]

Who had incited and called on the peasantry to attack Jewish property was never made clear. The authorities and the press repeatedly insisted that the antisemites came from Hungary and that the anti-Jewish agitation in Croatia was fueled "from outside." Hungarian media, however, at times declared Croats responsible for the unrest and riots.[76] The national-minded, intellectual strata of society looked for culprits outside of their own national camps. Certainly, one must assume that the antisemitic attacks in Hungary had an effect on the Croatian population and that there were individuals who brought news about ritual murder charges—like the Tiszaeszlár case—to Croatia and fed the largely illiterate peasant population with anti-Jewish propaganda.

The originators of the anti-Jewish notices were interested in both mobilizing the population and frightening the Jews. In contrast to the majority of the Croatian population, Jews could read and understand the flyers. That Jews hid themselves, asked for help, or stopped frequenting certain pubs "proved" to those who supported the antisemitic movement that their agitation had hit their target. The political parties and their newspaper outlets mixed together social and political protests with Jew hatred. In this way, even if no party newspaper specifically and directly called for antisemitic violence, they did create the connection between social grievances and Jewish culpability. Specific economic and social demands became identified with the importance and condition of the Jews in Croatia and Slavonia. Jewish responsibility and guilt for problems was considered self-evident and was not questioned. It was indicative of the mood in the 1880s that not one Croatian party newspaper explicitly defended the Jews.

■   1903
Twenty years later, similar protests swept across Croatia and Slavonia. In the beginning of the year, Austria and Hungary renewed the financial Ausgleich. During the negotiations, Croatians had hoped to change their own disadvantageous financial arrangements with Hungary.[77] When it became clear at the end of February 1903 that nothing would change, part of the Croatian opposition called for political protests. Demonstrations erupted in Zagreb in March, spread over much of the province in subsequent months, and reignited in 1904. The demonstrators demanded the financial independence of Croatia, opposed Hungarian domination, denounced the repressive policies of Ban Kheun-Héderváry, and rejected what many viewed as the systematic violation of the 1868 Croatian-Hungarian agreement.[78]

The political manifestations soon took on a violent character. In many locations, rioters attacked Jews and their property. At the end of April, a report was sent to the provincial government from the town of Bjelovar, to the east of Zagreb. According to the report, the pharmacist Eduard Suhomel had attempted to stir up the population against the Jews. He accused Kheun-Héderváry of having supported the Jews and of having harmed Croatia. Suhomel was arrested, and no violent outbreaks took place in Bjelovar.[79] From Varaždin, the local prosecutor's office reported to the state prosecutor in Zagreb that agitators had called for attacks on the district chairman and the "Jew Moses." The army was deployed, and several people were wounded. The prosecutor also reported that threats against the Jews had not abated.[80] In mid-May the prefect of Bjelovar-Križ district wrote to the provincial government that anti-Jewish rumors were spreading about upcoming anti-Jewish attacks. He assured the government, however, that he would prevent violence from breaking out.[81] In Sisak, a town southeast of Zagreb, the authorities failed to maintain calm. There, on the night of November 9–10 1903, more than one hundred people rioted. The former section chief for the Ministry of Religion and Education, Iso (Isidor) Kršnjavi, wrote in his memoirs that the Sisak demonstrations had "an antisemitic aftertaste."[82] According to a report from the state prosecutor from July 1903, the demonstrators had attacked the local train station and broken the windows of homes inhabited by bureaucrats and Jews. Janko Dujak, a book printer, was among the "intellectual instigators" of the unrest. He was arrested after suspicious flyers were discovered in his residence. Soon, however, he was released.[83] A German-language newspaper close to governing circles, *Die Drau* (Drava River), noted in two short news reports on the "antisemitic excesses" that the incriminating flyers were "antisemitic leaflets."[84] The report of the state prosecutor did not mention antisemitic leaflets and instead referred to materials that "doubtless" would further inflame already "feverish tempers." It is, therefore, highly probable that antisemitic writings were coursing through the area, as Dujak cultivated close ties with the antisemites around Grga Tuškan, a well-known and self-defined antisemitic agitator and politician from Sisak.[85]

In many locations throughout the province, peasants attacked symbols of Hungarian hegemony—such as train stations and the homes of government officials—which they linked to their poor economic conditions. Peasants also attacked Jews and their property. Businesses were plundered, windows smashed, and homes defaced with graffiti or feces.[86] In the town of Ludbreg, for example, rioters targeted both Christian and Jewish merchants and grocers, although Jews suffered greater damages.[87] The insurgents insulted and humiliated the rabbi of the Ludbreg Jewish community, Leopold Deutsch, by forcing him to walk through a pig field.[88]

Peasants also aimed their anger at targets such as train stations, inns, grocery stores, houses of government officials, and those supporting the National Party. In other words, not all of the violence was directed at Jewish-owned property; however, Jews made up a large number of those who worked on the railroad, in taverns, and in grocery stores. Many Jews supported the National Party. In the eyes of the demonstrators, then, Jews were natural targets.

In 1961 the Croatian historian Vaso Bogdanov wrote that the riots of the years 1903 and 1904 were expressions of "class warfare." The anti-Jewish attacks, he claimed, had nothing to do with antisemitism. Jews were assaulted not as Jews per se, but as capitalists.[89] In 2005 Croatian historian Ljiljana Dobrovšak concluded that the national movement was directed above all against Khuen-Héderváry, against the Hungarians, and against the grim economic conditions and that it "had no antisemitic character."[90] It can be demonstrated that neither the Croatian parties nor individual political activists called for attacks on Jews in 1903. Also, almost all of the press organs distanced themselves from the attacks. This allows for the conclusion that this kind of violence was not advocated by the national movement. However, the assaults on Jews and their property that took place all over the province must be understood as antisemitic.

Beginning most intensively in the mid-1890s, the Croatian political opposition and its press outlets created and disseminated throughout Croatia the image of the rich, exploitative Jew.[91] The most widely held stereotype of Jews presented them as the henchmen of the Germans and Hungarians, who enriched themselves at the expense of the Croatian people and sabotaged the Croats' national and political hopes. In this same period, Croatian Catholic journalists and clergy, inspired by the 1891 papal encyclical *Rerum Novarum* and Vienna's Christian Social Party and the Catholic People's Party in Hungary, attacked Jews as the propagators of liberalism. Zagreb's *Katolički List* published article and after article denouncing Jews for the death of Jesus and the more modern crimes of usury and the domination of big business. The paper warned against the power of the Jewish press and international Jewish organizations. The Catholic press depicted Jews as allies of the Hungarians and as threats to the Croatian nation.[92] It is, therefore, no surprise that the wide masses of the population, when facing an exceptional or crisis situation, took the opportunity to express their displeasure and anger and to go after those who for years had been depicted as responsible for their economic and political problems. The decade of anti-Jewish rhetoric fell on fertile ground, even if in the moment of crisis itself the opposition was cautious with its antisemitic expressions. By 1903 most of the population was already politically mobilized, so it was no longer necessary to employ antisemitic propaganda in order to encourage the masses to engage in anti-Jewish actions.

All of the opposition parties welcomed the protests of 1903. The opposition parties' papers rarely mentioned the associated violence and almost completely ignored attacks directed specifically at Jews. The Croatian party press had behaved in similar ways in 1883; however, they had reported on many cases of anti-Jewish assaults in that earlier wave of violence. In 1883, in the wake of the Tiszaeszlár affair, a widespread anti-Jewish atmosphere existed in Croatia. In 1903, in a very different context, the European press expressed outrage over the

Kishinev pogrom, as did the media in Croatia. This certainly contributed to the fact that reports of anti-Jewish violence in Croatia were greatly minimized. The notion that anti-Jewish violence could once again discredit the political demonstrations otherwise viewed by the opposition as legitimate was also present. The Croatian opposition had great expectations of the protests and demonstrations. The opposition hoped that the uprising would lead broader sectors of the population, above all the workers, to finally cast off Hungarian domination and help lead Croatia-Slavonia to greater autonomy. That the protests brought with them ever more frequent attacks on and threats to Jews was a result of the intensely antisemitic rhetoric of the opposition parties. As in 1883, pressures that had built up during "calmer" periods had exploded at a moment of intense political agitation and economic crisis.

■ CONCLUSION

The collapse of the Habsburg Monarchy brought to an end the old political order in Croatia in which the government had stood decisively against anti-Jewish violence. At the end of 1918 and the beginning of 1919, north Croatia experienced a "wave of antisemitic violence": intensely violent attacks, destruction, and looting.[93] Deserters and local peasants attacked Jews, charging them with responsibility for the war and the catastrophic postwar situation. The claim that Jews had profited from the war made the rounds. Strikingly, it now appeared that the new government approved of the plundering and destruction of Jewish property. The National Council, the provincial government, declared on November 3, 1918, that the Jews had increased their wealth significantly during the war.[94] Just two days before, the chair of the National Council had announced that the riots in northern Croatia were not antisemitic in character. The National Council declared that if antisemitic ideas did play a role in the violence, it would be only in limited instances and would be vigorously denounced.[95] This halfhearted announcement was obsolete two days later, when the same council justified the attacks on Jews with the claims of supposed Jewish war profiteering. The local National Council in Vrbanje, a small town in eastern Slavonia, announced at the beginning of December that Jews and the rich—unlike the peasants—had been spared all of the negative consequences of the war. A peasant could not understand why Jews and the rich still could decide for themselves how much tax they wanted to pay.[96] High officials publically charged Jews with contributing far too little to the newly levied "national tax."[97] With such statements, the authorities came close to conscious antisemitic resentment, in that they portrayed Jews as war profiteers and exploiters. In this way, they legitimated violent attacks on Jews and their property.

This form of violence occurred in so many locations in December 1918 that the Croatian Zionist publication *Židov* (The Jew) employed the word "pogrom" for the first time when referring to incidents taking place on Croatian-Slavonian territory.[98] The wave of violence continued systematically into the beginning of 1919. In Nova Gradiška, many Jewish homes were set on fire, and synagogues were plundered and so badly damaged that they had to be torn down.[99] People from the upper strata of society joined peasants in the plundering and even bought looted goods from them.[100]

Many Jewish families felt compelled to leave their hometowns and villages and flee to Zagreb. Some had been robbed of their livelihoods; others simply feared for their lives. However, Zagreb was not spared anti-Jewish measures. At the request of the Social Democratic Party, raids were conducted in stores to find hidden foodstuffs. It was more than a mere coincidence that most of the 120 stores searched belonged to Jews.[101] Even if Jewish stores were not the only ones affected by the attacks, the research undertaken by the historian Ivo Banac has made it clear that Jews and their property were the main targets of the rioters.[102] *Židov* rejected the assertion that anti-Jewish rioting was nothing more than a popular reaction in the face of famine: "This is not about a holy exasperation, or about revenge, or about a hungry people. The press, intellectuals, and officials have incited the population against the Jews for years and months and above all in the last few weeks. They provided the weapons and the schnapps. The pogrom began."[103] And again it was the anti-Jewish thought pattern, fomented for years, that came to the fore in a political and economic crisis.

The anti-Jewish violence in Croatia-Slavonia followed a pattern that historians and sociologists have recently termed "exclusionary violence." In the context of social unrest, the cultural construct of a Jewish threat was reactivated. The majority sought to "punish" the minority and justified its own actions as self-defense. The threats and application of violence were intended to unsettle the minority population and to worsen its social position.[104] In 1883 and again in 1903, the Croatian Jews were "punished" for their assumed cooperation with the Hungarians, for their alleged lack of loyalty to the Croatian nation, and for the supposed economic exploitation of the Croats. This message, propagated by the Croatian nationalist opposition for years, helped to shape acts of violence in crisis situations. Although the anti-Jewish incidents of 1903 did not have the intensity of those that occurred in 1883, these later attacks should not be minimized. Jews were not the accidental victims of this violence. By the 1890s, the opposition parties had made it clear that their struggle against liberalism, secularization, and modernization targeted everything and everyone they opposed. The political antisemitism of the opposition developed in the context of this struggle against the existing political and economic order. Croatian admiration for Karl Lueger and his Christian Social movement in Austria facilitated the legitimation of the employment of antisemitism in political battles against the status quo.

In the eyes of the Croatian opposition, Jews were to blame for all social and political problems. The Jews were depicted as active supporters of Hungarian rule. They were labeled as Magyars or Germans and therefore were responsible for Croatian problems. The image of the Jew as the symbol for all of Croatia's problems and difficulties had been promoted for decades and was transformed into concrete anti-Jewish action in times of crisis. Broad sectors of the political spectrum and of society as a whole had been sensitized to anti-Jewish hatred through political antisemitism and antisemitic rhetoric.

Antisemitism and the willingness to participate in anti-Jewish violence were based on the recognition and application of potent transnational anti-Jewish "knowledge" and anti-Jewish rhetoric. The anti-Jewish violence that took place in Croatia and Slavonia in the late nineteenth and early twentieth centuries showed the power of transnational antisemitic resentments and ideas. The Croatian press, individual actors, leaflets, and rumors broadcast this knowledge far and wide. Widely held stereotypes, spruced up with new political and social grievances—such as those that plagued many parts of the late Habsburg Monarchy–received a welcome reception in Croatia and Slavonia and took on concrete form in the violent waves of anti-Jewish riots that outlasted the fall of the Habsburg Monarchy itself.

PART 3

THE CIRCLE WIDENS

SAM JOHNSON

"TROUBLE IS YET COMING!"
THE BRITISH BROTHERS LEAGUE, IMMIGRATION, AND ANTI-JEWISH SENTIMENT IN LONDON'S EAST END, 1901–1903

In Great Britain, the period from the late nineteenth to the early twentieth century was suffused with an array of national, racial, social, and economic anxieties. Britishers, long exalted to "rule the waves," were no longer stridently confident about their position on the world stage, with the Empire seemingly under threat from an assortment of enemies, both real and imagined. Many became apparent, or were accentuated, as a result of recurrent military conflicts in South Africa, especially the Second Boer War of 1898–1902. Politicians of every hue expressed alarm about "national efficiency," as failings on the battlefield were linked inextricably to problems at home, ranging from urban overcrowding to the unhealthy condition of the working classes.[1] Naturally, efficiency questions also reached into the economic sphere, impelled, on the one hand, by that irritating upstart and relative newcomer, the United States of America, and on the other, by the impressive industrial challenge of Imperial Germany. One correspondent, writing to the right-wing, populist newspaper the *Daily Mail*, revealed that their first remark on entering any shop was "Show me no German goods!"[2]

It was in this nationally fraught and troubling context that British political and public opinion once again turned its attention to an internal concern, namely, the "destitute" or "pauper alien." From the late 1880s onward, both houses of parliament habitually considered whether it was necessary to implement restrictive legislation against a relentless flood of penniless immigrants, who apparently came to Britain to deny the native Anglo-Saxon work, dwelling, and food.[3] In the 1890s, in particular, the matter acquired increasing significance, with parliamentary debates and proposals for legislation occurring almost every year.[4] Similar anxieties were expressed at the other end of the social and political scale, when in 1895 the annual conference of the Trades' Union Congress passed a resolution that urged the implementation of restrictive legislation.[5] All this was to culminate in 1902 with the convening of the Royal Commission for Alien Immigration, the lengthy deliberations of which eventually resulted in the passing of the 1905 Aliens Act. This was Britain's first piece of immigrant legislation and, although it was not as restrictive as many had hoped, it aimed to exclude specific immigrant categories, especially those who arrived with barely any visible means of support.[6] At the time, it was claimed that Jews were not the Act's primary concern, but even a cursory glance at the political and popular discussion that underscored its passage illustrates that the reality was quite different.

Jews were unquestionably the primary focus of anti-alien anxiety, since this group and no other formed the principal source of immigration to the United Kingdom from the 1880s onward. Although there are no wholly reliable statistics, historians estimate that between 120,000 to 150,000 Jews arrived in the United Kingdom between 1880 and 1914, from Romania, Austria-Hungary, and the Russian empire. This demographic shift effectively doubled in size Britain's Jewish community, though at no point did it amount to more than 1 percent of the entire U.K. population.[7] In earlier decades, it was the Irish immigrant who bore the brunt of British domestic frustrations and fears, but by the late 1890s, despite regular protestations to the contrary, the term "destitute alien" unquestionably was synonymous with the immigrant Jew.[8] Moreover, when considering matters related to national (in)efficiency, it was the Jewish immigrant who undoubtedly represented one of the greatest "national dangers" of all.[9] By the early twentieth century, these concerns intensified, inextricably fusing a host of negative associations to the "alien Jew." In early 1901, for example, one newspaper from London's East End reported on its district's "foreign undesirables" and how, in turn, their presence was sowing the seeds of the antisemitic "disease" (though it claimed the British ramifications were not comparable with the "'Judenhetze' of the continent").[10] In this way, the immigrant Jew was to be doubly blamed: first, for intensifying the social and economic problems of the East End (with nationwide ramifications), and second, for encouraging the rise of an ideology whose reputation was sufficiently disreputable to condemn as continental.[11]

Within a few months of this gloomy diagnosis, anti-immigrant sentiment took a new turn in Britain, with the creation of a single-issue, mass political organization, the British Brothers League (BBL). Formed in the East End of London, where, not by happenstance, Britain's largest proportion of East European Jewish immigrants resided (60 to 70 per cent of the total settled there), it was driven by a vehement desire to exclude wholesale a further influx of "destitute aliens" from ever attempting to reach British shores.[12] Its outlook and agenda, informed by racial antisemitism, facilitated the dissemination of that continental "disease" so feared by the East End press. Although described as "protofascist" by one observer, the British Brothers League has merited little historiographical investigation.[13] In part this is a consequence of the supposed paucity of sources, since there is no surviving archival material belonging to the League itself. Likewise, its fleeting existence and notoriety (it apparently existed until 1923, but largely vanished from the public scene sometime in 1903), lack of durable influence, and failure to recruit any "brothers" beyond London, has rendered it of minor significance in the history of both British politics and anti-semitism.[14]

Surely, however, the League deserves reexamination, not least as there is plenty of documentary evidence that gives insight into its activities, membership, reach, and impact. In this regard, newspapers, especially the East London press, are hugely informative and useful, and not merely because they fill the many lacunae in our knowledge of the League. After all, in and of itself, the newspaper is vital to understanding the function and dissemination of popular, cultural, and political forms of antisemitism in the modern era. This chapter uses four East London newspapers: the *East End Observer*, the *East End Advertiser*, the *Eastern Argus and Hackney Times*, and the *East End News and London Shipping Chronicle*. All were politically independent, their coverage was geared largely to local issues, and East European immigration dominated their editorials and correspondence columns for many years. There are no extant circulation statistics, but they collectively served around one million East Enders.[15] The *Eastern Argus* was the only tabloid, its content and writing style less sophisticated than its contemporaries, though all were cheap and thus accessible to a broad social constituency.

The League was cognizant of the significance of the local press, and although it used other forms of propaganda, it was often via the newspaper, especially the weekly *East London Observer*, that it sought to promote itself. In this aspect, the League's leaders understood modern methods of persuasion and attempted to utilize them to the full. This extended to lively parades through the East End and a mass meeting in 1902, which were all accompanied by banners, patriotic songs, and more than a hint of violent confrontation. To what extent, though, was the BBL successful in recruiting local people to its cause? Were East Enders caught up in its campaign, and if so, who was attracted to it and why? Did it achieve any of its aims? What impact did it have in the East End of London, where, as one brother threatened in 1902, "Trouble is yet coming!"[16] How did Jews, in particular, respond to the creation and development of the League?

The historians who wrote the first important studies of the path to the 1905 Aliens Act argued that anti-Jewish sentiment in Britain before the First World War was essentially benign and unthreatening.[17] To paraphrase Anthony Julius, they deemed it of a type that merely wounded Jewish sensibilities, rather than one that promised to break Jewish bones.[18] In light of this interpretation, these historians argued it was xenophobia that motivated the clamor for anti-immigrant legislation in Britain at the turn of the twentieth century. Racial antisemitism, they argued, was an inconsequential phenomenon, the preserve of one or two fanatics.[19] The corollary to this, inevitably, was the reassuring notion that antisemitism of all kinds was an entirely continental phenomenon and had no significant place in British life. However, as this chapter demonstrates, at the turn of the twentieth century antisemitism maintained a real and tangible presence in London's East End, and its salient characteristics bore more than a passing resemblance to continental manifestations of anti-Jewish hatred. In other words, it ran way beyond the bounds of derisory humor, and the breaking of bones was not a wholly unimaginable possibility.

■ The East End of London, which in 1900 encompassed the metropolitan boroughs of Stepney, Bethnal Green, Shoreditch, Hackney, and Poplar, has a long history as a center of refuge and immigration, from French Protestant Huguenots in the seventeenth century, to Irish economic migrants in the eighteenth and nineteenth centuries, as well as Bangladeshis in the twentieth.[20] In the late nineteenth century, however, it was East European Jews who made up the largest immigrant group, although there were also large Italian and German communities. Seldom were these latter two groups the focus of hostility in the period under investigation. But for East London's Jewish residents, prejudice and intolerance were commonplace. Their social position and economic activities were under constant scrutiny, at the national and local levels. For example, a letter from "East Ender" to the *East End Observer*, published in January 1901, revealed the strength of anti-Jewish feeling in London, decreeing that "the chosen people are a menace to the people of England today, not to speak of other parts of the globe." Amongst a range of disagreeable characteristics and associations were "sweating dens, illicit spirit distilleries, and seething masses of blood-sucking landlords, besides gambling houses, under the guise of restaurants, and the money-grabbing propensities of those Shylocks."[21]

In many ways, the rhythms of anti-immigrant animosity ran hand in hand with the array of social problems to which the East End also was host. Overwhelmingly working class, the area soaked up local male labor in various industries, including sugar refineries, breweries, shipbuilding, and railways. In the upper reaches of the East End, the marshaling yards of Bishopsgate and Spitalfields stations, on the North London Railway, readied the transportation of the goods, luxury and commonplace, that arrived in East London via the

River Thames from all parts of the empire and every corner of the world. The vast docklands of the river provided the primary occupational opportunities for most men in the East End, largely as laborers who hauled cargo off the ships. The majority was employed on a casual, often hourly basis, and by the end of the nineteenth century, there was intense competition for just an hour or two's work per day.[22] Poorly paid and sometimes not paid at all, many thousands were condemned to live in overcrowded, unsanitary slum tenements, with crushing poverty the average lot. This was brought home visually via the so-called "poverty maps," produced in conjunction with Charles Booth's extensive social inquiry, *The Life and Labour of the People in London*.[23] The poorest dwellings and their inhabitants were identified as "vicious and semi-criminal."[24] Without doubt, violence of all kinds was interwoven into the everyday experience. In short, the East End was a dangerous, filthy, and desperate place. In many aspects, this was as much the case for Jews as for their Christian neighbors.

Although the material condition of immigrant Jews usually was indistinguishable from that of their neighbors, separateness was discernible in other aspects. The vast majority was Yiddish speaking and religiously orthodox, their patterns of day-to-day existence contained by Judaism's strictures. Jewish shops bore Yiddish signs, sold kosher comestibles, and opened on Sundays, a source of contention among many nominally Christian East Enders. For Jews, thirty to forty synagogues in the area serviced their religious needs, with a range of educational and philanthropic institutions playing key communal roles. In general, like their neighbors, East End Jews lived cheek by jowl, and large families slept, ate, and usually worked in the same one-room dwelling. As can be seen in the accompanying map, the Jewish presence could be traced along two key East End arteries: Whitechapel Road, Commercial Street, and their tributaries. It is little wonder that some observers, both Jewish and non-Jewish, described this part of London as a "ghetto," a hyperbolic, unhelpful term, as its existence was largely illusory.[25] To be sure, there was a Jewish concentration in some East End streets, especially in Whitechapel, but Jews also lived alongside Christians, their worlds not entirely isolated.

Occupationally, many Jews worked in small manufacturing trades, such as tailoring and shoe making, though some were shopkeepers and secondhand clothes dealers. Fewer were employed in the docks, and thus Jews rarely competed directly with their Christian neighbors for employment opportunities.[26] This did not, however, chime with contemporary perceptions. Many charges laid at Jewish immigrants claimed they deliberately undersold and priced non-Jews out of the marketplace and also were willing to accept low wages. Clearly, little could be deemed original in the anti-immigrant hostility of early

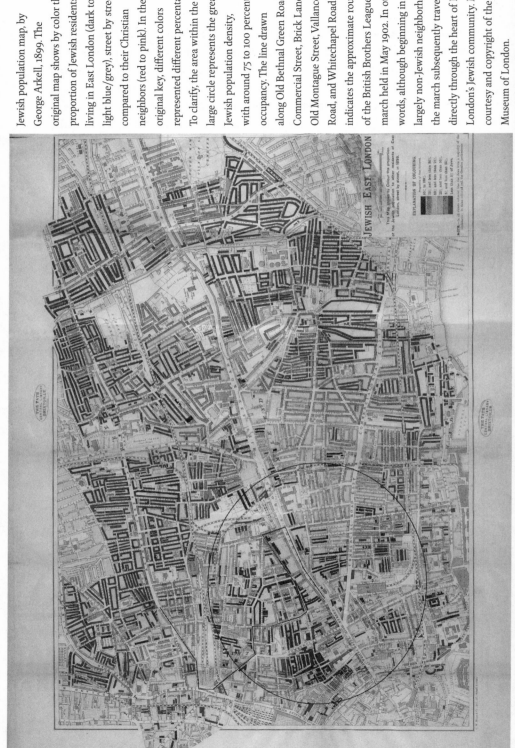

Jewish population map, by George Arkell, 1899. The original map shows by color the proportion of Jewish residents living in East London (dark to light blue/grey), street by street, compared to their Christian neighbors (red to pink). In the original key, different colors represented different percentages. To clarify, the area within the large circle represents the greatest Jewish population density, with around 75 to 100 percent occupancy. The line drawn along Old Bethnal Green Road, Commercial Street, Brick Lane, Old Montague Street, Vallance Road, and Whitechapel Road indicates the approximate route of the British Brothers League march held in May 1902. In other words, although beginning in a largely non-Jewish neighborhood, the march subsequently traversed directly through the heart of East London's Jewish community. Map courtesy and copyright of the Museum of London.

JEWISH EAST LONDON

This Map appears to Colour the proportion
of the Jewish population to other residents of East
London, street by street, in 1899.

EXPLANATION OF COLOURING:

95 to 100
75 and less than 95
50 and less than 75
25 and less than 50
5 and less than 25
Less than 5% of Jews.

NOTE. No full street in those coloured and has therein predominating twentieth-century East London. This theme, however, ran in tandem with increasing politicization, especially unionization, which alarmed the British establishment at recurrent intervals. The dock strike of 1889, for example, set the tone for generations of East End workers, who battled for basic living standards and employment rights.[27]

This, then, was the context in which the British Brothers League was founded in May 1901 by one William Stanley Shaw, a clerk in the City of London.[28] Given the wider concerns about British pride and self-worth, perhaps the League's appearance was an inevitable, if somewhat defensive, response. But in the East End, the agenda undoubtedly was informed by keenly felt local concerns, namely, the supposed Jewish threat to the ordinary working man. Indeed, though the organization's name betrayed little of its actual political intent, it was without question exclusively concerned with immigration. This was evident in the BBL's earliest propaganda, a poster pasted around the East End in the month of its founding:

> Thousands of paupers have for some time past been steadily pouring into London (settling chiefly in the east), driving English people out of their native parishes, and literally taking the bread out of English mouths. [...] How much more must a small country like England stand in need of similar restriction [as the United States]? The influx of foreign paupers (the sweepings of the continent of Europe) into London has given the landlords of the poorer quarters an opportunity of sweating their tenants and of exacting blood-money from them, in the form of exorbitant rents, an opportunity of which they have taken advantage to the full. The East End of London is rapidly becoming the dust-bin of Europe, into which all sorts of human refuse is shot. This is not a question of politics, still less of religion. It is of no consequence whether a foreign pauper believes in the Bible, the Talmud or the Koran.

Care was to taken to avoid direct reference to Jewish immigrants; but notwithstanding the denial in the final sentence, the references to "sweating," "blood-money," and "exorbitant," each an allusion to imagined Jewish business practices, undoubtedly indicated that Jews were the primary concern. This was certainly how one correspondent, "A British Working Man," interpreted this call to arms. In his letter to the *East End Observer*, he expressed the hope that the League would assist in preventing a "further influx of the Hebrew."[29]

From the outset there was no ambiguity about the League's agenda, or its methods, which were set to appeal to a largely emotional, rather than rational, response to Jewish immigration. This approach was amply underscored at the League's inaugural public meeting, held in the Stepney Meeting House (within a nonconformist church) on May 9, 1901. Variously billed as "stormy" and "lively" by the local press, the meeting brought together several interested parties.[30] The local political elite dominated the proceedings, and the meeting was chaired by the conservative MP for Mile End, Spencer Charrington. Almost every East End member of parliament was in attendance, with the significant exception of Jewish MP Stuart Samuel, who represented Whitechapel. In addition, several hundred (there are no precise figures in any report) working-class East Enders were present, including at least one trade union representative.

The most outspoken MP at the meeting was Major William Evans-Gordon (Stepney), who also personally defrayed the meeting's expenses. A renowned restrictionist, who later became a member of the Royal Commission on Alien Immigration, his speech claimed that anti-immigrant sentiment in the East End was not actuated by antisemitism.[31] It was evident, however, that many members of the audience saw the matter quite differently. Evans-Gordon was interrupted constantly, and at one point, "a working man [. . .] rushed up to the platform, and accused the speaker of having got into parliament by the help of the Jewish vote." A "great disturbance" followed, apparently caused by a "large body of socialists."[32] Isaac Solomons, secretary of the National Boot and Shoe Workers' Trade Union, proposed from the platform that "nothing short of the complete organization of the people themselves of their industry, and the public ownership by the nation of the means of life would solve the question at issue."[33] The obviously Jewish Solomons was heckled with shouts of "No more Jews!," "Sweater!" and "Go home!" His comrades responded by singing the "Marseillaise," which in turn prompted minor violence ("a sort of free fight") and the ejection of "some of the disturbing element."[34] Another audience interjection followed: "Suddenly, a working man rushed up to the platform and invited the meeting to vote on the question whether 'no more Jews should be brought into this country.' Hands went up wholesale; 'now against,' said the man, and one hand alone was held up. 'There you, you Jew, get down!' 'And this is the British Brotherhood,' said Mr. Solomons, who concluded amid groans and hisses."[35]

This, then, was the atmosphere in which the League débuted on the British political stage. While its leaders and those who stood on its platform, such as Evans-Gordon, claimed that the organization was not motivated by antisemitism, it was evident that its working-class supporters (its principal constituency) imagined things in those very terms. To be sure, the atmosphere of the meeting was, in many ways, entirely in keeping with the radical outlook of the East End and especially with the inherently controversial nature of the alien question.[36]

But the real truth as to why the League was created was plain enough. Immigration was a Jewish question in the United Kingdom, and the BBL represented a route to its solution, especially for the working classes of the East End. Subsequently, this was confirmed in a letter from a "British Brother" present at the Stepney meeting, which, in reflecting on the influx of "a dirty, money-grubbing population," threatened that unless the government intervened, "the time will come when there will be a flame kindled before which the antisemitism of the continent will pale."[37]

The League continued its agitation in much the same vein for the next twelve months, its noisy presence in East London undoubtedly serving to inspire ill feeling between Jews and their neighbors. Local newspaper editorials were supportive of the League's restrictive agenda, which no doubt encouraged a feeling of legitimacy among William Shaw and his associates. At the same time, it was held it up to considerable scrutiny. The League's name, for example, was a cause for regret, as it smacked "of a cheap appeal to insular prejudice and opinion."[38] Of more concern, though, was the absence of an executive committee, the question of whether the League was associated with an existing political party, and confusion with regard to its finances. In other words, where did it fit with the wider scheme of things and could it be deemed a serious organization? The presence of various parliamentarians at its inaugural meeting meant, temporarily at least, that it could not be instantly dismissed. Nevertheless, the answers that initially followed these questions were not particularly convincing. In matters of finance, for example, the League acknowledged only the personal assistance from Evans-Gordon and A. T. Williams, a member of the London County Council (LCC). In political matters, a letter from William Shaw refuted any suggestion that the League was an "appendage of the Conservative party." But little else was forthcoming.[39]

In early June 1901, the League published a manifesto, which dealt directly with issues about its structure. Addressed to the "working men of East London," with no reference to any parliamentary patronage, it was shot through with the same emotive phraseology and tone that was featured in its first poster and dominated the proceedings at Stepney. Urging an act of parliament, its exclusive concern was the "destitute" immigrant:

> Thousands of foreign paupers, unclean in their habits and possessing no code of morals—no sense of honour or decency—have for some time past been steadily pouring into London (settling chiefly in the East), driving English people out of their native parishes, and literally taking the bread out of English mouths. [. . .]

In order to force on legislation it is necessary to combine and to organise. A horde of men without a definite purpose and without organisation, are as helpless as babes; but a body of united and organised, resolute and determined Britishers, is apt to make itself a factor of considerable influence — and influence too strong to be ignored.

The organisation of the British Brothers League (open to all natural-born Englishmen, Irishmen, Scotsmen, or Welshmen) has been altered [it is not clear what from] as follows:

One hundred men will form a section.

Ten sections will form a ward.

A ward will thus constitute a thousand men.

The sections will be lettered A, B, C, D and so on. Wards will be numbered: First, Second, Third and so on.

Each section will elect a delegate to represent it on the Executive Committee [. . .]

The Executive Committee shall decide upon the general policy of the League. [. . .]

In order as far as possible to make the movement self-supporting a nominal entrance fee of sixpence is payable at the option of each member joining the League. No member need pay this unless he likes. Non-payment will not affect membership.[40]

Again, the notion that this agenda was about any immigrant other than the Jew can be dismissed outright. At stake was not merely the threat posed *per se* by immigration to "natural-born Englishmen Irishmen, Scotsmen [and] Welshmen," but the very character of the "foreign pauper" stood against all that was "British." And here, without question, "foreign pauper" was a metonymy for immigrant Jew. Both the East End working and political classes would have immediately understood the resonance of the phrase, whether they approved of it or not.

This short, uncomplicated manifesto, which described the League's vaguely militaristic configuration (at odds with any other British political party or grouping in this era), was directed toward the East End working man (there was no mention of women). Whilst Shaw acknowledged the support of MPs in newspaper correspondence, especially Evans-Gordon, working-class recruitment was an urgent matter, hence the fact that membership fees operated on a voluntary basis. The *East London Advertiser* predicted that this lax arrangement would ensure that the League was "foredoomed to failure."[41] But sixpence, although described as nominal, would have been a reasonable outlay for some working men, especially dock laborers with only intermittent employment. In this regard, the intention to recruit from the working classes is all the more significant when it is recalled that, before 1918, the franchise was available to less than 60 percent of all men (and of course, no women) in the United Kingdom. Many, if not most, of those who joined the BBL's ranks did not have the vote, including those who made up the executive committee, which was announced three weeks after the manifesto's appearance. All were working men, all lived in Stepney.[42]

The flurry of attention afforded the creation of the British Brothers League served, at least in the East End, to heighten press and public interest in the alien question. A series of articles commissioned by the *East End News and London Shipping Chronicle* was headlined with two striking phrases: "crucifying East London" and "a growing danger to London and the nation." The influx of aliens was so severe, so threatening, that it was described as a "plague" that was "killing London."[43] As usual, the unnamed correspondent claimed that in referring to "alien," he meant all immigrants, whether Jewish, Italian, French, Polish, or German. Yet the third article was exclusively about Jews, while the second related a conversation with a man named Mr. Benjamin, "a ragged patriarch with a long beard," with much emphasis placed on his "foreign" accent.[44] His surname, demeanor, and manner of speech (stereotyped Yiddish) indicated that he was neither French nor Polish nor Italian.[45]

The flurry of enthusiasm following the League's founding led to the creation of individual branches. The first were formed in October 1901 in Bromley and Bow, and Poplar.[46] In the following month, November 1901, it was Hackney and Bethnal Green's turn, with branches subsequently convened in Shoreditch, Stepney, St. George's-in-the-East, Limehouse, and Haggerston.[47] Some of these branches had their own individual badges and banners, guildlike trappings that served to underline the League's fraternal dimensions.[48] Unfortunately, none of these objects have survived, so one can only hypothesize about the imagery employed (perhaps, for instance, the Union flag played a central role). With the prominent exception of Whitechapel, where the largest proportion of the capital's Jews resided, the League could claim representation throughout the East End. Of course, this also indicated that the British Brothers League was utterly unsuccessful in recruiting beyond London, which effectively nullified its extravagant title.[49] By September 1902, membership was said to stand at 45,000, but undoubtedly this was an extravagant estimate, since reports about individual branches indicate that the number attending weekly meetings was usually less than a hundred.[50] Special events and meetings did, of course, draw larger numbers, but it rarely amounted to thousands. Nevertheless, the League could point to some measure of success, especially in the activities of the Hackney and Bethnal Green branches.

Both Hackney and Bethnal Green held weekly meetings in local public houses, the Baker's Arms and the Volunteer, which again underlined the largely working-class orientation of the League.[51] Hackney's meetings, in particular, were never staid events. In December 1901, a concert accompanied the proceedings, which became a regular feature.[52] A meeting in May 1902, with a "crowded attendance of both sexes" (one of the few mentions of female involvement), underlined the usefulness of musical accompaniment in generating a sense of belonging for League members. Popular songs were sung, giving proceedings more than a whiff of the music hall. The *Eastern Argus and Hackney Times* reported that "Mr. Jack Elliot created roars of laughter by his renderings of 'How can they tell I'm Irish?' and 'They fancy I'm a coon from Carolina.'"[53]

In February 1902 a further instillation of brotherly feeling was attempted with a "grand parade and marchout, headed by an efficient brass band and their banner, which caused quite a stir."[54] A few months later, the additional purpose of such a show of strength, with its accompanying militaristic echoes and masculine bonding, was highlighted by

> A parade and demonstration [which] traversed Old Bethnal Green Road, Commercial Street, Brick Lane, Old Montague Street, Vallance Road and Whitechapel Road. Their [members of the Hackney Branch] progress was witnessed by thousands of aliens, who offered some slight opposition in Brick Lane, but a strong posse of police kept order. In Old Montague Street the British Brothers, waving large banners and accompanied by a band, which played patriotic airs, such as "Britons never shall be slaves" [that is, "Rule Britannia"], gave vent to their feelings by shouting "Go back to Jerusalem." The British Brothers League intend holding a further procession through the Jewish quarters.[55]

The jeering cry of "go back to Jerusalem," as opposed to, say, Odessa, Kiev, or Lemberg, again underlined that immigrants were targeted because of their Jewishness, not their foreignness.

As shown on the map of Jewish London, which traces the route of this march, many of these streets contained the densest population of Jews in the East End (and for that matter, the whole of London). A deliberate choice was made here, to stomp noisily in front of Jewish residences, Jewish shops, and Jewish places of worship. Without question, it was a form of unsophisticated incitement (hence the police presence) and a macho procession, which presaged the nasty demonstrations attempted by Oswald Mosley's Blackshirts in the 1930s. The British Union of Fascists was resolutely challenged by the Jewish East End, most notably during the 1936 Battle of Cable Street, but in 1902 the Jewish opposition community was "slight."[56] This apparent Jewish impassiveness, however, may have been compounded by the fact that this demonstration took place on a Saturday afternoon. Nevertheless, it surely prompted ill feeling among the Jewish residents of Stepney and Whitechapel, and as will be discussed below, not all Jews were submissive in the face of BBL provocation. In January 1902 the League held its most successful public meeting, an occasion that represented the pinnacle of its activities in the East End. It convened in the Queen's Hall of the People's Palace, Mile End Road. Opened in 1887 by Queen Victoria, the People's Palace was an educational and recreational complex for East End working men and, after the First World War, women. An institution of many decades duration, it laid the foundations for the present Queen Mary College (part of the University of London); it housed a library, a technical school, swimming baths, and lecture rooms and offered evening classes. The Queen's Hall, with a capacity of three to four thousand was one of the largest East End spaces for political and other meetings.[57] In a sense, to claim such a venue was indicative of the local legitimacy the League commanded at this particular moment.

This was also the first (and last) BBL meeting to be advertised in the local press.[58] According to the *East End News and London Shipping Chronicle*, the Queen's Hall was "crowded to excess," while the *East London Observer* believed attendance to be around four thousand, the majority of whom were "Englishmen," though occasionally one could see the "squat features of the Russian exile."[59] Such were the numbers that around 260 stewards, "big, brawny stalwarts [and] dock labourers," were drafted to avoid the kind of disturbances that had featured in the 1901 Stepney meeting.[60] Indeed, two weeks earlier, an *ELO* editorial expressed the hope that there would be no trouble: "With the object of the promoters there will be much sympathy, though it is doubtful if the anti-alien party is adopting the best methods. There is an evil, but neither of the character nor of the proportions which have been represented. In fact, the demon of exaggeration is the real evil, for when the case breaks down reaction will set in, and the last state of East London may be worse than the first."[61] As it turned out, this concern was misplaced on the day of the meeting, for the burly stewards were primed to suppress any disturbance or dissent. And when, as in Stepney, "an angry alien arose from his seat to protest, he forthwith received the attention of the stewards and was unceremoniously bundled outside in the cold, biting atmosphere."[62] In contrast, the "demon of exaggeration" was afforded various degrees of encouragement by the meeting.

Besides the swift silencing of opponents, the League imprinted its image at the Queen's Hall in other ways. Once full, various League "battalions"— from Stepney, Hackney, Shoreditch, and Bethnal Green—entered the hall with great ceremony. "Carrying banners and singing national songs to the accompaniment of drums and divers kinds of musical instruments," such was the excited response to this commanding entrance; the "audience rose almost to excess as [the hall's] powerful organ pealed along to the strains of 'Soldiers of the Queen,' 'God bless the Prince of Wales,' 'There's no place like home'" and 'Rule Britannia.' The scene thus was set for a similarly enthusiastic welcome for the chairman, Major Evans-Gordon, "who was received with loud and prolonged cheers."[63] The fundamentals of the modern political rally were in abundant evidence.

This gathering, populated by several members of parliament, local East End and LCC councilors, was supported by correspondence from several members of the clergy, schoolteachers, and even the popular novelist Marie Corelli. It was the first (and last) meeting to draw attention to the League outside local boundaries. Three national newspapers, the *Daily Mail*, the *Daily Chronicle*, and most significantly, the *Times*, each published brief reports.[64] The *Daily Mail* emphasized Corelli's proposal that "committees of the British Brothers League should be formed in the large provincial towns." Given this and the ecstatic reception in the Queen's Hall, where every speaker was cheered and applauded, the BBL's leadership must have confidently expected that their influence would soon extend to other British cities. But this was not to be.

The January 1902 meeting also elicited the attention of the Jewish press. It had intermittently monitored the activities of the League since its creation in May 1901 and, naturally, was singularly unimpressed. The United Kingdom's leading national Jewish newspaper, the *Jewish Chronicle*, was terse in its response. It suggested that there was "very little British and nothing brotherly" about the League and was especially puzzled by the involvement of East London MPs, whose political success or failure, it reminded them, partially relied on the Jewish vote.[65] Its more popularly oriented counterpart, the *Jewish World* (also a national newspaper and often more confrontational than its establishment contemporary) could barely conceal its disdain: "The latest organisation for the purpose of resisting alien immigration has certainly some novel characteristics. It bears the grandiose title of 'British Brothers League.' The figure ten forms a rather conspicuous feature in the association. Every group of ten elects a leader, and every ten leaders elect another chief and so on. These lordlings will bear military designations, and there will probably be a martial spirit pervading the host. When their effective operation will begin we know not."[66]

For the most part, however, until the January 1902 meeting, the League merited little comment, even in the Jewish press. But given the numbers in attendance at the Queen's Hall, it was impossible to ignore, and extensive reports appeared in both the *Chronicle* and the *Jewish World*.[67] The latter was especially eager to highlight the unsettling nature of the League's outlook and noted a "kinship with Dr [Karl] Lueger [mayor of Vienna], the notorious antisemite." "Is not," it asked, "every member of the League a Leaguer (Lueger)?": "We would suggest to the British Brothers that they should continue the alliteration and call themselves the "British Brothers Broom" for sweeping England. But one thing we would like to know, and that is where are the British Brothers Brains?"[68]

The *World* challenged the League in other ways, including a statistical analysis of the foreign demographics of East London, which refuted the BBL notion that the area was swamped with Jews.[69] In a story about a Jewish Lads' Brigade concert held in Her Majesty's Theatre in the West End, the *World* threw further incisive light on the mode of agitation the BBL promoted against "the hard-working, industrious, wealth-producing alien": "With all our insular pride in this country we may still learn a great deal from those who come from other quarters.[. . .] This was rammed home on Sunday when the sturdy little fellows of the Jewish Lads Brigade, 75 per cent the sons of alien immigrants, showed that they know how to handle arms for the development of their bodies, and are available, when they grow older, for the defence of the commonwealth."[70] This head-on, uncompromising response, which refuted a range of antisemitic allusions, characterized aspects of Jewish East London's challenge to the BBL, where the atmosphere undoubtedly was troubled.

There is some evidence, for example, that relations in the East End were turning violent (though, as already noted, it was hardly an area unknown for its brutal associations). But there were individual cases that revealed the increasingly strained dealings between Jew and gentile. In October 1901, for example, a letter from an "Englishman" to the *East London Observer* reported on an assault on a "number of foreigners," who were about to take possession of some houses in St. George's. They were attacked by "a number of Englishmen," their "furniture was broken and windows were smashed, and a crowd of many hundreds witnessed the scene." "As a Briton," the correspondent wrote, "I detest violence. All we want is a fair field and no favour."[71] The Queen's Hall meeting had produced its own tensions, and in its wake Jews were "chased in Mile End Road" and Jewish shops were attacked.[72] It certainly inspired one newspaper correspondent to threaten that the British Brothers would "make it so hot for the Jews, that the aliens will be glad to ask mercy of Russia or Romania."[73] Several months later, in April 1902, the *East London Observer* recorded an incident in Whitechapel:

A number of respectable Jews were perambulating High Street, White-chapel, [when] one of them unintentionally pushed up against an English labourer who was passing by. The latter immediately turned round and dealt the Jew a violent blow, at the same time using a copious supply of un-parliamentary language, in which he threatened to "kill every Jew present." Within a minute a crowd of over 300 persons, nearly all Jews, assembled, the labourer assuming a menacing attitude, and exclaiming he would "kick the foreign liver" out. Several young Englishmen went to support him and offered to fight any "of the foreign swine." The Jews, however, remained passive, offering an apology and explaining that no offence was intended. The workers pushed themselves further into the crowd and were joined by others, who urged them to use their "lifters" [?] and "murder them." Quite an exciting scene then occurred, but fortunately the police arrived, and forcibly removed the workmen, who left threatening to "do for the Jews." Scrim-mages in Old Montague Street are of frequent occurrence.[74]

Whether or not this incident took place cannot be determined and, indeed, the depiction of Jews as stereotypically passive may give cause for some doubt. But another incident, which again revealed the strained atmosphere in East London, presented the Jewish response in a different light. On this occasion, in November 1901, a member of the League, a newsagent, was attacked for displaying a copy of the BBL's manifesto in his shop window.[75] The identity of those attacking the shopkeeper was designated simply as "foreign," as were those involved in the episode in St. George's. Thus, one cannot be certain that they were Jews.

Nevertheless, there were several levels at which Jewish protest against the League was registered. For instance, letters were sent to newspapers repudi-ating anti-alien accusations. In January 1902, ten days after the Queen's Hall meeting, a letter from "son of an alien" bitterly advised that local MPs could now "greet their new born child, antisemitism."[76] East End Jewish institutions also weighed in on the debate. In January 1902, the Poor Jews' Temporary Shel-ter, a key philanthropic body that provided assistance to immigrant Jews, issued a strong objection. It rejected any notion that immigrant Jews made demands on the "local rates" (that is, non-Jewish charity), that they were universally un-skilled, and that there were widespread health problems among new arrivals.[77] In the same combative vein, Stuart Samuel, MP for Whitechapel, vigorously took to task the BBL's antisemitic proclivities.[78] Samuel was also present at a face-to-face encounter with a prominent BBL and LCC member, A. T. Williams, at a meeting of the Whitechapel Costermongers Union.[79]

At this meeting, Williams was accused of including antisemitic remarks in his Queen's Hall speech. This reflected a burgeoning concern that the British Brothers League was deliberately and provocatively stirring up anti-Jewish feeling in East London. The *East London Observer*, originally sympathetic to the aims of the BBL, now described it as a "choleric and ill-defined body" and alleged that "lies [were] not conspicuous by their absence" in its alarmist propaganda: "To allege, as was alleged [at the Queen's Hall] that hooliganism [that is, crime] is a direct result of the alien settlement is not only unfair, it is a stupendous falsehood."[80] A few weeks later, it issued an excoriating editorial on the "shrieking brotherhood":

> We do not remember any agitation fostered by greater impropriety or one having had a quicker descent into the gutter [and one which] is more than half based on ignorance, bolstered up by prejudice and is justified only by selfishness. [. . .] Not withstanding suspicious protestations to the contrary, we believe anti-alienism is antisemitism, in both origin and conduct. [. . .] now in imitation of vile Continental practice, we are practically asked—agitators dare not say it publicly or the cause would be lost beyond redemption—to raise once more the cry of "Down with the Jews: kill! kill!" [. . .] Envy, hatred, malice and all uncharitableness are playing their unholy parts in this crusade; the very worst that is in human nature is being fanned into flame.[81]

This response, which evidently understood the precise orientation of the BBL and the threat it posed to Jewish-gentile relations in East London, was spurred in part by a propaganda faux pas from the president of the League, William Shaw.[82]

In late January 1902, Shaw, no doubt buoyed by the success of the Queen's Hall meeting, penned his own literary contribution to the alien debate in the form of a poem entitled "No English Need Apply." Published in the *East London Observer*, it is unnecessary to explore the poem in any detail, as its message was sufficiently reflected in its title, which concluded that English workmen were economically and socially excluded in the East End. The reason for that, of course, was immigration, though Jews were not explicitly mentioned. The *East London Observer* confessed to never having seen such a sign anywhere in East London and demanded that Shaw provide evidence.[83] His response was unconvincing, and in the columns of the same newspaper, he appealed "for assistance from [. . .] readers to enable him to make his statement good."[84] A month later, there had not been a single reply.[85] The following week, however, he repeated the claim, arguing that "thousands of Britons" knew the sign as a "common sight in East London."[86]

Perhaps this moment of foolishness was the reason that Shaw stepped down as president of the British Brothers League in April 1902.[87] No public explanation was given, though the League's annual report, published in August 1902, suggested that Shaw was overburdened with work and family responsibilities.[88] However, Shaw clearly carried residual bitterness toward his successors, not least as he continued to write regularly to the press, mostly to complain about the BBL and its activities.[89] A letter in July 1902 revealed that he was especially aggrieved by a BBL leaflet which contained the line: "If you or any of your friends have suffered by the alien Jews coming here, now is the time to say." This, he argued, was a "departure" from the League's previous policy. Perhaps, therefore, Shaw's exit was more to do with the overt antisemitism with which the League was increasingly associated. One cannot be absolutely certain, but there is no doubt that, following the Queen's Hall meeting, the League acquired some vehemently anti-Jewish advocates.[90] Supportive letters published by the *East London Observer* at the time of Shaw's resignation blatantly reaffirmed that "alien" meant "Jew." These extreme perspectives even included allegations of blood libel. One letter, from "Union Jack," observed: "Fancy using Christian blood for their ritual! These sweaters and wicked persons must be put down, and to do this it is necessary for the working man to rise. Stand up for right, and down with foreigners!"[91]

The timing of Shaw's resignation, however, was somewhat odd, as it occurred less than three weeks before the convening of the Royal Commission on Alien Immigration on April 24, 1902. Finally, the BBL got what it wanted, a full parliamentary investigation into the causes and impact of immigration, with legislation a likely possibility. Of course, the League was not directly responsible for the instigation of the Commission. It was not even name checked in a House of Commons' debate on immigration on January 29, 1902, just two weeks after the Queen's Hall meeting.[92] However, several MPs, who were linked at one point or another to the League, were involved in this debate and with the Royal Commission. The most notable was Evans-Gordon.[93] Still, it did not follow that pressure from the League's East End ranks was of any significance. Indeed, although one member of the League, J. W. Johnson, appeared with tendentious evidence before the Commission, this was not a sign that the BBL had acquired any kind of political legitimacy in the Palace of Westminster.[94] So wholly ineffective was the League that it singularly failed to take any advantage from the daily national spotlight cast on immigration throughout 1902 and 1903. Rather than gain publicity, the opposite was the case, and it faded from the limelight. Therefore, to count the convening of the Commission as an achievement for the League would be stretching things.[95] Internal dissension, controversy about its agenda, and its rabble-rousing tactics sealed the BBL's fate as a small-time outfit, whose impact was at best dubious, and at worst, directly responsible for encouraging and compounding British prejudice against the Jews. This, of course, is where the true significance of the League lies.

Politically, therefore, the League was an abject failure. At some level, the extreme views with which it increasingly became associated may account for this, but its ignominious fate was not linked exclusively to its antisemitism. In particular, its working-class orientation, combined with the fact that it was often operationally based in public houses, held rowdy meetings, and furnished the Queen's Hall with strapping stewards, surely diminished any middle- or upper-class desire to become involved. It is likely that the League's "beery," unruly, and violent character was far more disreputable than its antisemitic outlook, rendering its lack of success essentially a matter of class.[96] As for the political elite, a permanent association with the League simply was unnecessary. After all, Evans-Gordon and his fellow parliamentarians did not require the working-class vote to guarantee electoral triumph, and thus any groundswell of popular anti-immigrant opinion was useful only in the short term. Once the Royal Commission convened, it was no longer required. As for the working classes of the East End, the BBL's single-issue agenda limited their adherence, especially in an era when socialism and trades unions were growing, organizations that promised more meaningful, wholesale change, including the acquisition of universal suffrage.

Nevertheless, while the political failure of the BBL can be easily explained, this does not diminish the historical import that antisemitism carried in East London. Yes, political antisemitism was less significant in the British capital than in many other European cities in the period before the First World War. But in lieu of universal suffrage, there was no particular advantage to British politicians in embracing the kind of propaganda and agenda followed by, say, the Christian Social Party in Vienna. Nevertheless, this was not a sign that antisemitism was absent in other forms, political and otherwise. The case of the British Brothers League illustrates that anti-Jewish discourse was deeply embedded as a social and cultural phenomenon. Stereotypical characterizations were widespread, and as I have argued elsewhere, British representations had much in common with continental imaginings of "the Jew."[97] Occasionally, there were challenges to these views, but negative depictions of Jews were in the majority, and they were embraced by all classes. This was amply highlighted during the BBL's brief period in the spotlight. For instance, a regular respondent to the League's activities, and one of the nastiest letter writers to the *East London Observer*, also was a member of the Royal College of Surgeons. Even though he served the Jewish community, this physician was incapable of concealing his acute hatred for "the Jew." In several missives he described his contempt for "filthy Polish Jews" and how he "shuddered" as he "went amongst these people; their habits and characteristics are vile, and no wonder they are shunned and detested by all civilised people."[98] It was not, therefore, solely the working man, who could easily be dismissed as uneducated and ignorant, who peddled antisemitic animosity in the East End.[99] Thus, the ideology and propaganda of the BBL was not out of step with wider everyday discourse in East London. It may well have inspired the further spewing of antisemitic hate, in newspapers and on East London's streets, but it was hardly its originator. The British Brothers League was an East End progeny, an ugly, bitter child, given birth from deep-rooted and fundamental cultural assumptions about "the Jew." In this aspect, its claim to "Britishness" was not wholly unjustified.

ALISON ROSE

BIGAMY AND BIGOTRY
IN THE AUSTRIAN ALPS
ANTISEMITISM, GENDER,
AND THE "HERVAY AFFAIR"
OF 1904

... there was no doubt that the District Captain v. Hervay had
fallen victim to an impostor who held him captive with a kind
of suggestive power.
— Tagespost, *Graz, June 17, 1904*

An unprejudiced person who does not know the purpose of this
trial and attends an hour of it would have to believe that it
concerns an act of fraud or an offense against public morality,
but that it is hardly a bigamy trial. All this is so very little
mentioned.
— Die Zeit, *Vienna, October 30, 1904*

In 1904, Leontine von Hervay, wife of the district cap-
tain of Mürzzuschlag, a small resort town in Styria halfway between Vienna
and Graz, was arrested, tried, and convicted of bigamy and false registration.
In the days after his wife's arrest, the district captain, Franz von Hervay, committed suicide. Although the charges against Frau von Hervay centered on two
minor legal matters—namely, that her previous marriage was not dissolved
until shortly after her marriage to the district captain and that she had entered
a false date for her birth year on her arrival and registration in Mürzzuschlag—
her arrest and trial caused an international sensation. These events attracted
large crowds, as well as the attention of the press and of a wide range of fin-
de-siècle Vienna's most acute observers, including Karl Kraus, Sigmund Freud,
and Hermann Bahr.

Frau von Hervay's Jewish background and her failure to behave according
to accepted gender norms helped to fuel the controversy. Spurred on by the
public thirst for scandal, local, Viennese, and even international newspapers
closely followed Hervay's arrest in June and the trial that took place in late
October in the town of Leoben, in central Styria. In the following years, the
case continued to draw the attention of legal scholars, journalists, writers, and

psychologists, who used it to highlight a variety of issues, ranging from the relationship between Vienna and the provinces to the "witch hunt" mentality of the antisemitic press based in Vienna. This chapter will closely examine the arrest and trial of Leontine von Hervay, focusing on antisemitism and gender-based stereotypes, the local context of small-town Austria, and the dynamic relationship between the provinces and the capital city.

The Hervay case provides an opportunity to explore Austrian antisemitism on the local level. Viennese antisemitism has attracted much attention from scholars, who attribute its intense nature to the weakness of liberalism, the strength of Catholicism, the rise of nationalism, and the size and composition of Austrian Jewry. Politically, antisemitism manifested itself in the Austrian Pan-German Movement of Georg von Schönerer (1842–1921) and the Christian Social Party led by Karl Lueger (1844–1910).[1] Much less has been written about antisemitism in the core Austrian provinces (Styria, Carinthia, Upper and Lower Austria, and so on), where conditions differed significantly from those in Vienna. Jewish populations were small in the Austrian provinces, even in comparison with the rural areas of Germany. Relatively low levels of industrialization and immigration meant that the population was largely German and Catholic. The few Jews who did live in Austria's small towns and villages often experienced persecution, expulsion, and blood libel accusations. Even where they lived side by side with their Christian neighbors, Jews formed a distinct social group. Yet they lacked the strong institutional and community framework that was found in larger cities. This left Jews in provincial Austria vulnerable to the upsurge of modern political and cultural antisemitism that traversed Europe in the years around 1900.

This chapter uses the bigamy trial of Frau von Hervay to measure the intensity of antisemitism in provincial Austria. In his study of crime in pre-World War I Vienna, Daniel Vyleta demonstrated that only openly antisemitic newspapers such as the *Deutsches Volksblatt* and *Kikeriki* portrayed Jewish criminal defendants in an overtly racist antisemitic light. Even the *Deutsches Volksblatt* acknowledged the Jews as rational actors, focusing on Jewish defendants as schemers who sought to undermine justice and social norms rather than as biological enemies of the German race.[2] In my analysis of the newspaper coverage of the scandal and trial, I will likewise show that although local antisemitic papers expressed hostility toward Frau von Hervay in particular and toward Jews in general, they made few blatantly antisemitic statements. However, I also show that descriptions of her demeanor, appearance, and speech often betray antisemitic sentiments and embrace stereotypes commonly seen in fin-de-siècle depictions of Jewish women. In this way, this chapter argues that the local context, anxieties about gender roles, and a scandal-hungry press turned what should have been an unremarkable legal case into a spectacle. Furthermore, it provides insights into linkages between events in the provinces and the antisemitic discourse in the center. Small-town Austria may have had few Jews, yet what happened there mattered greatly for the Jewish population of the Austrian lands.

■   THE LOCAL CONTEXT
The "Hervay affair" began with hostility toward outsiders and women and ended with tragic results. The setting in which it unfolded, a small Austrian town, played an important role in the chain of events. Significantly, antisemitism in the province of Styria was widespread despite the scarcity of Jews. Long barred from settling in the province, Jews began to move there in significant numbers only after legal restrictions on Jewish settlement were lifted in 1867. The census of 1869 counted 566 Jews in Graz (84.48 percent of all Jews in Styria), but only 16 in Leoben and 13 each in Mürzzuschlag and Kindberg. By 1880, 1,782 Jews lived in Styria, and by 1910, 2,895 Jews lived in 47 localities within the province.[3] In Graz the Jewish community built a large synagogue and school, which were completed in 1892 and consecrated by the Emperor Franz Joseph in 1895. A gymnasium was later added to give Jews the opportunity to engage in sports, because they were excluded from all German athletic clubs.[4] Graz also had an Orthodox prayer house, as did Leoben and Judenburg.[5] At the turn of the century, 63.7 percent of Graz Jews had occupations in commerce and finance, three times the proportion of the general population, and 6.5 percent were university graduates compared to 1.4 percent for the wider population. However, because of the small size of the Graz Jewish community, the total number of Jewish professionals, merchants, and bankers was relatively low and unlikely a cause of local antisemitism. More important factors on the ground were foreign influences, the hostility of the Catholic Church, student nationalism, and newspapers such as the German national *Grazer Tagblatt* and the clerical *Grazer Volksblatt.*[6] Although political antisemitism met with little success in Graz, there was tacit discrimination against Jewish businesses on the part of the provincial government, and some cafés did not admit Jews.[7]

The Jewish population of the district of Mürzzuschlag was small, numbering 101 in 1910, of whom just 29 lived in the town of Mürzzuschlag itself.[8] Mürzzuschlag's population had increased more than five times across the nineteenth century; Jews, however, comprised just 1 percent of its inhabitants. Jews in Mürzzuschlag worked as lawyers, postmen, railway officials, merchants, physicians, and manufacturers. They did not develop communal institutions, although an article in the local antisemitic press entitled "Animal Cruelty" suggests that there may have been a kosher butcher.[9]

In Mürzzuschlag antisemitic articles and stereotypes could be found in two local papers: the *Obersteierblatt*, the official organ of Schönerer's Pan-German movement for Upper Styria, and the *Mürzzuschlager Wochenblatt*, a local paper with a similar political orientation. Schönerer himself visited Mürzzuschlag on several occasions. In 1885 he came to promote the Association of German Nationalists in Styria. According to reports in the local press, antisemitism played a vital role in the rhetoric surrounding these events. For example, the *Obersteierblatt* reported that the most formidable task for Pan-German nationalists was to give ethnic Germans in Austria a "German racial consciousness," adding that war must be waged against "liberals and their allies, the Jews."[10] The association adopted a resolution expressing contempt for the "Viennese Jewish press and its 'Jewified' branches in the provinces."[11] On November 16, 1885, nationalists in Mürzzuschlag smeared the signs of Jewish merchants with oil paint. In 1886 imperial officials prohibited a planned gathering on the topic of "antisemitism and the working class" on the basis that such a gathering would likely lead to violence.[12]

The *Mürzzuschlager Wochenblatt*, founded in 1899, was the second local antisemitic paper. This paper targeted Jewish merchants, attacked Jews for lacking German national consciousness, and warned that Jews were purchasing property at an alarming rate. It urged "Germans" to buy only from non-Jewish businesses, playing on fears of Jewish financial power. In 1903 the *Mürzzuschlager Wochenblatt* gave front-page coverage to Pan-German demands that the Austrian parliament reverse the emancipation of Jews by requiring them to live in ghettos and allowing them to stay outside only eight days per year (paragraph 4), prohibiting marriages between Jews and non-Jews (paragraph 5), excluding Jews from acquiring land (paragraph 6) and holding any public office (paragraph 8), barring Jews from primary, middle, and high schools (paragraph 11), and not allowing Jews to be medical doctors, lawyers, publishers, and newspaper editors (paragraphs 13–15). There would also be a ban of immigration to Austria (paragraph 16). The proposed law had the full consent of the *Mürzzuschlager Wochenblatt*, but it was not adopted.[13] In April 1904 the *Mürzzuschlager Wochenblatt* set the events of the "Hervay affair" in motion with the publication of an aggressive feuilleton, and the paper later provided detailed reports on Frau von Hervay's arrest, the district captain's funeral, and Frau von Hervay's incarceration while she was awaiting trial.[14]

Leoben, the setting of the trial, was a small mining town about ninety miles southeast of Vienna and about twenty-five miles north of Graz. Nineteenth-century industrialization and the expansion of the Leoben-Donawitz iron works had contributed to population growth, which included an influx of Jewish merchants who had set up their businesses in the town center. According to funeral records from 1891 to 1938, which list seventy-three deceased members of the Jewish community, the community comprised German-speaking Jews. The Leoben Jewish community organization was better developed than that of Mürzzuschlag, and it established a Jewish cemetery and an Israelite Women's Association. Although the community did not establish a Jewish school, it employed a cantor, who also served as a religious teacher and ritual slaughterer. Jewish families of Leoben did not play a major role in the social life of the city. According to historian Wolfgang Haid, "They were considered not so much as empowered members of their communities, but they held fast to their religious customs, and there was hardly a holiday according to their religion, which was not celebrated."[15]

Thus both the Hervays' marriage and the subsequent trial took place in locations in which Jews had made some inroads into public life but remained socially isolated. Jews were nonetheless conspicuous in populations that were more or less homogenous, in which Jews' distinct traditions and occupational structure lent themselves to antisemitic stereotyping. Under these conditions, it is not surprising that the local population would greet someone like Frau von Hervay with deep suspicion.

■   "THE HERVAY AFFAIR"

Elvira Leontine Bellachini was born on July 18, 1860, in Posen, Germany, to the Polish Jewish conjurer Samuel (Bellach) Bellachini and his wife, Helene Krüger.[16] Bellachini had tried several trades and traveled the world before devoting himself to conjuring and becoming a court entertainer for Germany's Emperor Wilhelm I. In 1882 Bellachini suffered an attack of apoplexy, which weakened his hands, and in the following year he lost his favorite son in a duel, after which he suffered a final stroke and died on January 25, 1885.[17] Bellachini and Helene also had another daughter, Clara, who was born in 1857, married a merchant, and was living in Würzberg at the time of the trial.[18] According to some reports, Leontine Bellachini had traveled to the United States and performed with her father when she was a girl.[19] Leontine attended a girls' secondary school, and at sixteen she became a chorus girl in the old Victoria Theater in Berlin. She converted to Protestantism on November 22, 1880, although she later denied her Jewish ancestry and claimed that she merely had been received in a Berlin Protestant church community on this date and had always been a Christian. On May 29, 1881, she married Wilhelm Kuntz, a wine agent, in Berlin. They divorced in February 1887. She married her second husband, Karl von Lützow, a German military officer, on April 24, 1888. They were divorced on May 5, 1894. Her next marriage, to Ernst von Schewe, took place in Naples on January 29, 1895, and ended in divorce on March 29, 1900. Her fourth marriage, to landowner Leo Meurin, took place in London on June 7, 1900. Meurin filed for divorce on June 21, 1902, and the divorce was pronounced on November 11, 1903. Her marriage to Franz von Hervay took place on August 9, 1903, three months before the divorce with Meurin was finalized.[20]

Her unusual lifestyle had already attracted attention before her arrival in Mürzzuschlag. The German writer Frieda von Bülow based her 1901 novel, *Im Hexenring* (In the Witches' Circle), on Frau von Hervay.[21] The main character of the novel, Frau Sufi von Tschirn, traveled under false names and courted déclassé nobles by telling them tales of large fortunes and high birth.[22] Von Bülow told reporters that she had met Frau von Hervay in the summer of 1898, when Hervay had lived with her husband Ernst von Schewe, a retired Prussian officer, and another inactive officer who posed as her brother. "That's how I met her and had the opportunity to observe her strange nature and goings on at close range," recalled von Bülow.[23]

Frau von Hervay arrived in Mürzzuschlag on May 15, 1903. She checked into a local hotel, the Schwarzer Adler, as Tamara Baronin Lützow from Nice. She arrived in the company of an officer, Lieutenant Bartl, who "was variously said to be her brother, cousin, and husband." She wore pearls, diamonds, and magnificent dresses, and she claimed to have large sums of money deposited in Vienna. According to one later account, "The gentlemen, who always have a passion for the exotic, were delighted, although in Mürzzuschlag there are a respectable number of very clever ladies who, even at this time, were curious to know who she really was."[24] As Frau von Hervay described it, she met Franz von Hervay, the district captain, by chance during a walk in the forest shortly after her arrival. He introduced himself and accompanied her back to town because she had lost her way. En route, he complained that his family was pressuring him to marry against his will. She in turn told incredible stories about her past and struck the district captain as brilliant and fascinating. Local women judged her to be at least ten years older than she claimed, and some friends of the district captain were skeptical of her claims about her past and her wealth. Despite rumors, gossip, her mysterious relationship with Bartl, and warnings from many acquaintances, the district captain swiftly fell in love with her. They were engaged on May 30, 1903, and married within three months.

Franz Hervay Edler von Kirchberg had been born in 1872 in Stübing, a

Styrian town between Graz and Leoben. He studied law at the University of Vienna, served as an official in Carinthia and Dalmatia, and came to the Ministry for Culture and Education in Vienna in 1897. He was friendly with the minister for culture and education, Wilhelm von Hartel, who helped Hervay in his career. Hervay received four promotions and on January 1, 1903, was appointed district captain of Mürzzuschlag. In this post he not only represented the imperial government, but also was responsible for the safety of Emperor Franz Joseph when he visited his hunting lodge in nearby Mürzsteg. In October 1903, when the Mürzsteg Reforms for Macedonia were drawn up, Hervay found himself responsible for the safety of both the Habsburg emperor and the Russian tsar. Reports describe him as "a handsome, slim, blond man, who looked especially splendid on festive occasions in his uniform, with three very beautiful medals," who was the envy of all in the town and an ideal marriage partner.[25]

The engagement ceremony was held on July 15, 1903, and the marriage took place on August 9, 1903, in the parish church of Mürzzuschlag. To forestall the gossip of the local population, it was a closed ceremony. Karl Prangl, the local Roman Catholic priest, performed the ceremony.[26] The ceremony was a "sham marriage," which he did not register, because the couple lacked the required documents. Hervay's family had vehemently opposed the marriage and later contributed to the heightened attention and controversy surrounding it. Following the marriage, the belief that Frau von Hervay had lied about and edited her personal, family, and financial circumstances grew stronger and stronger among the population of Mürzzuschlag.[27]

In April 1904, the *Mürzzuschlager Wochenblatt* published a feuilleton alluding to the Hervay case under the title "An Ancient Tale" ("Ein uraltes Märchen"). It suggested that Frau von Hervay was still married to her previous husband and raised questions about her background.[28] While not mentioning her by name, it was obvious that the article described the district captain's wife. The district captain himself read it and confronted her, after which she left for Vienna and collapsed in the Kärntnerstrasse. She claimed to have poisoned herself with sublimate and was taken to the hospital. On June 17, a Graz newspaper reported that Franz von Hervay "had fallen victim to an imposter who held him captive with a kind of suggestive power."[29] The district captain requested a holiday to take care of family matters. Within forty-eight hours von Hervay was asked to surrender his position and to take an extended vacation. On June 18, Frau von Hervay returned to Mürzzuschlag but was not permitted to enter the building of the district administration or her husband's apartment. On the morning of June 19, she went to the Mürzzuschlag station to catch the train back to Vienna, where shrill whistles and abusive shouts greeted her.[30]

Frau von Hervay was arrested in Vienna on June 21, 1904, on charges of fraud and bigamy.[31] She was brought to Leoben by train, where her arrival caused a sensation: "When it was announced on Wednesday that the detainee would be transported at 1:15 from Vienna to Leoben, a thousand-strong crowd of people rushed to the Südbahnhof for the train that arrives here at 8:19 to see the woman. The whole station square and the street far from the new town were densely crowded."[32] She was led from the station to the district court, where she walked with "head held high through the dense line of people." After half an hour the crowd dispersed. Frau Hervay was housed in a cell with a maid who was under investigation for theft.[33]

Reports of the arrest of his wife, the hostile behavior of the crowd, and the insult to his honor drove the district captain to take his own life.[34] He shot himself at approximately 9:00 A.M. on the morning of June 24, 1904. His funeral, accompanied by a male choir, numerous wreaths, and a guard of honor, took place in Peggau on June 25 in the pouring rain. The large crowd included representatives of the local government, corporations, and associations, as well as local families and guests from as far away as Vienna. In the meantime his widow was transferred to the Stephanie Hospital of Leoben. She suffered from respiratory ailments, a heart condition, and severe bleeding. She used her few possessions to help pay for the hospital costs.[35] The prison physician found that she had symptoms of severe hysteria, but the court in Graz would later deny that her mental state had a bearing on her trial.[36]

Opinion quickly turned against Frau von Hervay. The *Obersteirische Volkszeitung*, a local paper not known to be antisemitic, described District Captain Hervay as a victim of societal beliefs and of a demonic woman.[37] The bitterness against Frau von Hervay caused many people to overlook the responsibility of others, most notably the Catholic priest who had performed the marriage ceremony. Had the priest followed the law, the marriage would not have occurred. It was known that Frau von Hervay was a divorced woman and that her previous husband was still living. According to paragraph 62 of the Austrian Civil Code, she should have had to prove the dissolution of her previous marriage; according to paragraph 78, the priest was strictly forbidden to perform the ceremony until the proper documentation had been produced. Paragraph 80 stated that evidence of the marriage contract, including the "first and last name, age, address, marital statuses of the spouses, first and last name and status of the parents and witnesses, the day the marriage was decided, and finally the name of the priest" had to be entered into the wedding register before consent could be declared.[38] Furthermore, Franz von Hervay was Catholic, and Austrian law prohibited divorce and remarriage for Austrian Catholics and also recognized the *impedimentum catholicismi*, which does not allow a Catholic to marry some-one who has been divorced if his or her former spouse is living.[39] Therefore, the marriage was illegal under both Austrian and canon law.[40]

Frau von Hervay was put on trial nonetheless. She was officially charged with bigamy and false registration. But in reality she was on trial for the death of her husband and for breaking the conservative conventions of provincial Austria. Her trial was the most elaborate ever held in Leoben. It began at 9:30 in the morning on Saturday, October 29, 1904. The district court vice president, Dr. Labres, presided; Dr. Hermann Obermayer served as defense counsel; and Deputy Attorney Reimoser was the prosecutor. The prosecution laid the entire blame for the scandal and suicide on Frau von Hervay. The parish priest who had not required the proper documents, Karl Prangl, served only as a witness. Mayor Anton Werba, who had issued a document stating that the bride had rights of citizenship without listing the location of her home jurisdiction, was not held accountable. It was assumed that the district captain was not complicit because he had repeatedly indicated to his colleagues that he expected to im-prove his career through the marriage.[41]

The trial attracted enormous crowds as well as journalists representing some twenty newspapers. Only sixty people could squeeze into the courtroom. People filled the aisles, and two tables were reserved for reporters.[42] During the trial, the correspondent for Vienna's *Neue Freie Presse* reported that the "sensation-hungry public stood in large crowds outside the courtroom and heckled Hervay whenever she spoke."[43]

The trial opened with the reading of the indictment. It stated: "Elvira Leon-tine Bellachini, married name, Hervay von Kirchberg, born in 1860 in Posen, under the jurisdiction of Mürzzuschlag, Catholic, widow of Franz Hervay von Kirchberg, formerly District Captain of Mürzzuschlag, is accused of bigamy and false registration: of bigamy because her fourth marriage with the landowner Meurin was not yet dissolved when the fifth with Herr von Hervay took place; and of the latter offense because in Mürzzuschlag she falsely indicated the year 1877 as her year of birth."[44] As more than one newspaper later observed, these were relatively small, technical infractions.

Yet the trial was anything but small. Much of the testimony focused on Frau von Hervay's former life, which had no direct relevance to the charges against her. The first day thus began with the testimony of the defendant and focused on her family and background. When the chairman asked about her parents, she responded, "I cannot say because I do not know, because not a trace of love and affection passed between my so-called mother and me." Von Hervay claimed that her mother had written a letter on her deathbed, in which she stated that Frau von Hervay had in fact been adopted and given the birth certificate of a deceased daughter. When the chairman asked her if her birth certificate said she was Jewish, she answered that she had been raised in a Protestant Institute in Eberswalde and always attended Protestant lessons and the Protestant church. When asked if she had converted to Protestantism when she married Wilhelm Kunz in 1880, Frau von Hervay stated that she had obtained a certificate of entry into the German church in order to be married in Berlin. When asked if she had been happy in any of her marriages, she responded, "My last marriage showed me how one can be happy."[45] Questioned about her claims to be the daughter of the Russian grand duchess, she said that she had once been told this was the case and that she had a picture of the duchess, which showed a "fabulous resemblance." She denied having claimed that she was the daughter of Colonel von Lützow and in possession of enormous property and wealth.[46]

Seventeen witnesses appeared in court, and many others submitted statements. On the first day, Anton Werba, the mayor of Mürzzuschlag, testified about the relationship between the Hervays; the stationmaster of Mürzzuschlag spoke about Frau von Hervay's relationship to Lieutenant Bartl; and the district captain's parents spoke of their son and the questionable financial circumstances of Frau von Hervay. In the afternoon, the District Commissioner Dr. Montel testified that he was taken aback when Frau von Hervay told him about her origins, her wealth, and her jewels. Baron Franz Duka, employed in the governor's office, confirmed the defendant's account of how she met the district captain, who had said, "I have found a deer in the woods."[47] The key witness, the priest Karl Prangl, spoke about the circumstances leading to the wedding ceremony and the reasons for his participation. He testified that Frau von Hervay had called him to her hotel and the district captain had been present. She had mentioned only one previous marriage, to Lützow, and had told him that Lützow had been declared legally missing and was presumed dead, and that the marriage had not been consummated. She also had promised to deliver the missing documents after the ceremony. Prangl said that two distinct ceremonies, an engagement that was not legally valid and a marriage that was valid, then took place and that the district captain had said, "You have to trust us, otherwise we will trust another" and threatened to leave the Catholic Church if Prangl did not comply. Prangl then reluctantly performed the marriage ceremony.[48]

Several other witnesses touched on the motivations of the district captain. A Viennese lawyer testified that the district captain's brother, Lieutenant von Hervay, had asked him to investigate his sister-in-law's past, and in this way

Lieutenant von Hervay learned of all four previous marriages and shared this information with his brother. The defense counsel submitted letters written by Hervay to lawyers in Trier, Paris, and Berlin, requesting the acceleration of the divorce from Meurin, to prove that the district captain knew about the marriage. In one of the letters the district captain wrote that his future wife was in a miserable situation and needed "urgently the calm of family life, full of spiritual peace, because her health is suffering greatly from this situation from which she must be rescued as soon as possible."[49]

The relationship of Frau von Hervay to her companion Lieutenant Bartl was also brought up at the trial, despite Frau von Hervay's protests. The attendant at the hotel where Frau von Hervay lived in Mürzzuschlag testified that he saw the lieutenant go from his room to Frau von Hervay's room in "informal dress" three times. A tax official likewise testified that he had seen Lieutenant Bartl "in questionable toilet" in her room. Frau von Hervay repeatedly asked the president why he allowed this discussion, which had nothing to do with bigamy. At the end of the first day, Frau von Hervay stated: "All of Mürzzuschlag has beaten me about. There is nothing, Mr. President, not presented to my disadvantage here. Not one word has been benevolent to me."[50] Dr. Obermayer, her attorney, complained that he had not received access to the defendant's files or had the opportunity to speak with the defendant before the trial.[51]

The trial continued on Monday, October 31, with the testimony of Lieutenant von Hervay. He stated that he first met the defendant when his brother announced their engagement. She claimed variously to have been born a Lützow, to have married a Lützow, and to have studied at the Sacré-Coeur in Paris. She once said she had been born in Teltow and another time in St. Petersburg. The lieutenant testified: "All these contradictions give me the impression that she is a liar. Then the stories, where she was everywhere, in Japan, in the Boer War, with a column of the Red Cross; all these things have proven to me that she was more than a liar, that she was an imposter."[52] The Lieutenant concluded that his brother did not know of her past. He tried to warn his brother that she was a "marriage swindler," but she was always with the district captain and convinced him otherwise. He said the district captain had a good relationship with his family, before the "demonic" influence of the woman.[53]

The trial soon came to an end. In his closing, the prosecutor spoke about the civil and penal code and the nature of bigamy. He referred to the defendant as a creature of little credibility and reviewed the long register of tales she had told, contrasting them with the district captain's "perfect past and possession of the highest honors." He concluded by linking her nature ("the embodiment of falsehood and deceit") to the lies she had told about her previous marriages. The defense counsel's closing statement focused on the improper actions of the authorities that had been overlooked by the court: "Others are guilty of gross dereliction of duty and inaccuracies which have been passed over here quietly and silently." He then denounced the great attention given to Frau von Hervay's past: "I have no doubt that the past lives of many highly placed persons would not tolerate the probe that was applied to the private life of Frau von Hervay." He continued: "If one considers all the surrounding circumstances that accompany this case, one would think that it is a federal case, a crime whose name inspires horror. In my thirty years of experience, I've never seen prison imposed for bigamy. And of what specifically is the defendant charged in this particular case? Nothing other than that the formal decision about the divorce process with Meurin was reached a few weeks after her marriage. . . ."[54] In closing, the defense argued that Father Prangl and the district captain bore much responsibility for the crimes for which Frau von Hervay was accused.

In her final statement, Frau von Hervay claimed innocence. She said, "I beg you to believe that what I have stated is really the truth, that I did not know what my husband had agreed to with the priest, and that I never had the idea to harm my husband. I ask the high court to put an end to my ordeal." The court then deliberated for a half hour before returning a guilty verdict and sentencing her to four months in prison. The court stated that the ceremony on August 9, 1903, had followed all the regulations of the Catholic rituals; the negligence of the priest did not influence the validity of the marriage. Because the defendant was at that time still married to Meurin in a valid marriage, she was guilty of bigamy.[55]

On November 3, 1904, the Graz Court of Appeal released Frau von Hervay on a bail of four thousand crowns. After her release, she briefly lived in a hotel in Vienna. In an interview, she claimed that the affair had been caused by the jealousy of officials in Mürzzuschlag's district administration, who had considered Hervay a careerist, and by his family, who had wished to improve their rank through a rich marriage. Supporters held a benefit concert for Frau von Hervay on February 2, 1905.[56] In the same year, Frau von Hervay published her memoirs, in which she described her life and her relationship with the district captain.[57] She later lived in Leipzig and Munich. Nine years after the trial, Frau von Hervay, who now went by the name Tamara Ratzoch, presented an application for a retrial, and twelve years after this she requested a cancellation of the verdict. Both requests were denied.[58] She married two more times, but the details of these marriages and when and where she died are not known.[59]

■ GENDER AND ANTISEMITISM

Gender stereotypes and stereotypes about Jewish sexuality contributed to the negative reactions to Frau von Hervay and fed into the sensation caused by the "Hervay affair." Depictions of Jews possessing overabundant sexual drives and overlapping male and female qualities were commonplace in Austria, where Jews were condemned for their supposed victimization of women and their involvement with prostitution. Antisemites linked Jews to venereal diseases, especially syphilis, and to a corrupt sexual morality. Jews and women were believed to share physical and mental disabilities. Jewish women were targeted by negative stereotypes and attracted a great deal of attention in the popular imagination in Austria.[60] Many of these attacks played out in the press.

The local German nationalist weekly, the *Mürzzuschlager Wochenblatt*, was responsible for setting the entire affair in motion with its publication of "An Ancient Tale" on April 30, 1904. Drawing on stereotypes of the bejeweled and deceptive Jewess, the feuilleton described a string of pearls worn by the "princess" thought to be worth millions by the townspeople, but in reality made out of glass and "borrowed from old Jews."[61] The *Mürzzuschlager Wochenblatt* continued to incite antipathy toward Frau von Hervay in its articles. For example, an article on June 18 commented that on her arrival in Mürzzuschlag, she presented a document stating she was a divorced baroness, Tamara von Lützow, born on July 12, 1871, at Charlottenberg, near Berlin, but not including her maiden name, religion, or evidence of the disappearance of her husband. The article claimed that she inflamed the district captain's heart through her intrigues and that *she* was bigoted. It portrayed her as inventing sensational stories and lies to influence leaders and as possessing "a past life wrapped in mysterious darkness."[62] The article concluded by commenting on her Jewish background and making a reference to the unpopular Queen Draga of Serbia, who had been assassinated with her husband one year prior. "It is also noteworthy that the downfall of this adventuress, who incidentally should be a Jewess, almost coincides with the anniversary of the downfall of Draga."[63]

This local paper went much further. In a June 25 article following the district captain's suicide, it wrote: "It is clear that the deceased was glad to be freed from the viper who made his young and hopeful life a misery for a year," and, "One remembers with disgust the old monster that entangled him in her net and through her ability and manners snatched away the promising career of an excellent man."[64] An article in the Viennese *Die Zeit* noted that the entire population had boycotted the *Mürzzuschlager Wochenblatt* and that local vendors and postal subscribers had rejected the June 25 issue because of its attacks on District Captain von Hervay. Critics denounced the paper for printing the initial feuilleton and for continuing to print sensational items. The *Mürzzuschlager Wochenblatt* defended itself and claimed to have the support of most of the local population. It quoted one local woman who espoused the duty of the free press to protect the honor of the German house.[65]

What did locals think about Frau von Hervay? What seems clear is that gender stereotypes and preconceived notions about Jews shaped the negative attitudes of the local men and women toward Frau von Hervay. Her arrival in the small town of Mürzzuschlag attracted attention because of her unconventional behavior and adventurous past. She defied accepted gender norms, and as details of her background emerged, she appeared increasingly mysterious and threatening to many residents of small-town Styria. Reporters commented on men's fascination with the unusual summer visitor, which stood in sharp contrast to the suspicious reception that women gave Frau von Hervay.

The Hervay case played on the curiosity inspired by a female criminal and defendant. The view of women as criminal, duplicitous, and purely sexual was promoted by Otto Weininger's 1903 bestseller, *Sex and Character*. With her multiple marriages and mysterious past, Frau von Hervay seemed to support Weininger's arguments that women were by nature polygamous and predisposed to prostitution.[66]

Crimes by women also made for particularly riveting reading material. The interest in women as defendants can be seen in the detailed physical descriptions in the newspaper reports. Elaborate depictions of Frau von Hervay and constant references to her ability to manipulate the court through her overly dramatic gestures (loud weeping, howling, shrugging, and fainting) as well as references to her as a magician's daughter are found in even the most "objective" reports. One paper described her in this way: "She wore a black mourning dress with a long veil, was strikingly pale, looked very careworn, the indictment in her hand."[67] Another commented on her "barely medium size," "elegant appearance," and "foreign accent."[68] Her "transformational skills and her ability to deceive and to charm" were said to be inherited from her father, the magician Bellachini.[69]

Frau von Hervay's failure to conform to preconceived feminine roles was further accentuated by the provincial context in which the trial took place. One newspaper article noted how out of place Frau von Hervay and the crime of bigamy were: "This is an adventurous crime, and in the mountainous regions where simple minds thrive in strong air, one does not love adventure. No less of a rarity is the defendant. Just think: the daughter of a Jewish conjurer who had three religions and five husbands, who was in the Transvaal and in Cameroon, Helgoland and in Nice, and most recently in Mürzzuschlag. A man could not go so far around in the world without arousing suspicion, let alone a woman."[70] Given such views, it is not surprising that much of the provincial public viewed the Hervay case as a major scandal and focused its attention on the past life and actions of the defendant rather than on other factors. Provincial public opinion condemned Frau von Hervay and blamed her alone for the death of the district captain.

Antisemitism also dominated press coverage of the trial. To be sure, a number of newspapers defended Frau von Hervay. Her defenders noted the bigotry of the provincial population as a root cause of the tragedy and pointed to the flaws in the trial itself. On November 5, 1904, for example, the *Obersteirische Volkszeitung*, in its analysis of the outcome of the trial, concluded that state officials should be responsible for marriages in Austria as was the case in Germany. The "scandal of Mürzzuschlag," it wrote, demonstrated the way the present system could fall victim to popular agitation. Several irregularities in the case also indicated that the independence of the judiciary was not to be trusted. In the Hervay case, an order of the governor had been sufficient to arrest an unpopular person; the defense attorney had been denied the right to inspect files and to have access to the defendant; and a high bail was set for the release of an unwell defendant. The paper further noted that the trial had raised "intimate personal and family circumstances of the defendant that had nothing in the least to do with the accusation, only to put the accused in an unfavorable light, and to cloak the emptiness of the legally very dubious moral judgment."[71]

Although the liberal press shied away from antisemitic interpretations, it too leaned heavily on conventional ideas of women's behavior. For example, a feuilleton in Vienna's bourgeois-liberal daily paper, the *Neue Freie Presse*, painted the district captain as the victim, a young man with a promising career who was deceived by a trickster, the daughter of the magician Bellachini. The article called her "a daring impostor" and him "the victim of a huge bluff." She was "a trickster who worked her charms on men." "She juggled men's hearts, she played a daring game of catch with human fates, she had husbands like shiny balls in the air whirl one by another and caught them with her hands." The author pointed out that "swindlers" usually choose big cities where they will not attract as much attention, but she chose "a dangerous terrain": a small town in a "quiet valley with its strict morality." The age difference—she was forty-four and he was thirty-two—also played to the theme that he was the victim and she the villain. Her family bore the responsibility for her cunning: "She must have learned from her father, it cannot be explained otherwise. The dexterity of the magician has been replaced with her remarkable ability to ensnare men's hearts." She had lost the ability to distinguish between truth and fiction, something else the paper blamed on her father.[72]

In contrast, the antisemitic press based in Vienna focused almost exclusively on the defendant's Jewish background, calling her a "depraved Jewess" and condemning the "liberal Jewish press" for coming to her rescue.[73] The German-nationalist *Deutsches Volksblatt*, a Viennese newspaper, described Frau von Hervay as dishonest, insincere in her religious conversions, and greedy. Under the headline, "Driven to His Death by a Jewess," it claimed that the "Jew-press" had concealed the true origins of the district captain's wife.[74] In the next issue, it described her as a "Jewish monster," "Jewish adventuress," and a "devilish Jewish woman" in league with the "whole Jewish press." It compared the Hervay affair to the Dreyfus affair, in which the *"Neue Freie Presse* and of course all other Jewish papers went through thick and thin for the traitor Dreyfus."[75] To the *Deutsches Volksblatt*, the trial's significance lay "in the victory of truth and justice over the boundless dissimulations, lies, and hidden schemes of the Jew-press."[76]

Kikeriki, a Viennese antisemitic satirical paper notorious for its poems and cartoons, also interpreted the Hervay affair solely as a Jewish scandal. An article entitled "The 'Rumor' from Mürzzuschlag" begins: "A woman from society is arrested. Frau von Hervay-Kirchberg-Belanchini-Lützow-Ballach-Singer by name. Singer is finally enough to determine the type, Jewess, who in the circles of K.K. state officials plays the role of Circe, turning men into pigs." The article targets the coverage of what it called the "intellectual press," specifically the Arbeiter-Zeitung, the Austrian Social Democratic paper, for claiming that "gossip" had created the scandal. It concluded: "That was the gossip of Mürzzuschlag, that so annoyed the social-democratic disguised Jews of the Arbeiter-Zeitung. Not us. We look forward to the moral force of the German Volk of green Styria."[77] On July 7, a cartoon depicted a woman with a sash reading "Hervay-Bloch" surrounded by men reaching for her, as two devils with stereotypical Jewish features look on. The title read "Die Jüdin," and underneath the image appeared the following:

> What she achieved in ignominious glory,
> The Jews achieve every day
> And lure with gold and false glass
> Many poor Christians in the morass.[78]

On November 4, another poem appeared on the trial. It included these two stanzas:

Who nothing but lies has woven
With truly a Jew's mind for crookery
All agree in Leoben
That she is a con artist certainly

Elsewhere people doubt and gripe
In circles namely where
Smart Yids sit and cunningly guide
The public's opinion, go here, go there.[79]

The first poem portrays Frau von Hervay as an alluring Jewess while the second describes her behavior as criminal, linking it to the Jews' "cunning nature." The themes of Jewish dishonesty and dissimulation and the dangers of femininity found in these poems permeated the antisemitic press.

The weekly *Wiener Caricaturen* also featured two cartoons based on the Hervay affair. The first cartoon showed two prostitutes. The first says to her colleague, "Already ten men have been ruined by me; from four I've divorced, one actually went mad!" The other responds, "That's nothing! I've even had the good fortune that one has shot himself to death for me. The likes of us do not experience that every day!"[80] On November 6, a front-page cartoon showed two men looking at a well-dressed woman. The title reads "A dangerous woman," and the caption is a dialogue of onlookers.

Take a look at this lady, baron. The most interesting woman who has ever crossed my life.

Four times she was already married, finally one has accused her of bigamy. Guess what she is today?

Well, I'm curious, Herr Doctor!

The wife of the prosecutor who has indicted her.[81]

Both of these cartoons play on antisemitic stereotypes of Jews' and Jewish women's sexuality, by linking Jews to prostitution and immorality and by portraying Frau von Hervay as a dangerous, seductive Jewess who takes pleasure in exploiting men.

Interpretations of the Hervay affair reversed the common charge that Jews were engaged in the "white slave trade." "White slavery" became a "mainstay of antisemitic rhetoric in the 1890s." The Styrian chaplain Johann Seidl's *Der Jude des Neunzehnten Jahrhunderts* was first published in Graz in 1899. The president of the Austrian League to Combat Traffic in Women, Josef Schrank, published his study of "white slavery" in 1904, the year of the Hervay affair. According to Schrank, Jews lured their victims into prostitution through their "devilish cun-

Die Jüdin, in *Kikeriki*, July 7, 1904. Courtesy of the Austrian National Library.

ning," communicated with clever codes, used disguises and false names, and switched identities to evade the law.[82] As Keely Stauter-Halsted has shown in her article about the 1892 L'viv White Slavery Trial, white slavery trials placed sole responsibility for society's moral ills on the Jewish defendants, overlooking other factors that contributed to trafficking in women.[83] The rhetoric used to describe the "white slave" traders is remarkably similar to the rhetoric used in the case against Frau von Hervay. Newspapers thus reported that Frau von Hervay was a "lithe woman" who knew how to "lure men into her net."[84] Her many marriages and uncertain origins only strengthened this supposed connection.

Antisemitic coverage of the trial did not go unnoticed. Karl Kraus wrote three articles about the Hervay affair in his newspaper, *Die Fackel* (The Torch), in which he roundly criticized the antisemitic press's coverage of the case.[85] Kraus's articles described the trial as a "witch hunt." He mocked "the *Volksblatt*'s attempts to turn 'Mrs. Von Hervay [into] a missionary of the Alliance Israelite sent to that quiet valley in the Alps.'"[86] Kraus noted that the overzealous public was eager to blame Frau von Hervay and that the antisemitic press treated her as a "woman possessed," a "modern vampire," and a "Jew-woman of a devilish nature."[87] Kraus used the Hervay case to showcase the intrusion of prejudice into the most intimate social space, the sexual sphere.[88] In this he received the endorsement of Sigmund Freud, who wrote to Kraus: "A reader who cannot be your supporter all that often, congratulates you on the penetration, the courage, and the ability to recognize the large in the small as shown by your article on the Hervay case."[89]

The Hervay affair thus inspired a widespread preoccupation, fascination, and moral panic. Journalists' narratives contributed to the sensational nature of the trial. To many observers, the trial revealed problems at the heart of Austrian society, even as it hinted at their causes and solutions. While on the local level in provincial Austria, press coverage and attitudes about the Hervay trial focused primarily on gender issues and hostility toward one perceived as a dangerous outsider; in the antisemitic press of Vienna, the case became yet another example of "typical" Jewish danger.

■   CONCLUSION

In 1909 the Austrian writer Hermann Bahr published *Drut*, a novel based on the Hervay case.[90] In the folklore of Upper Austria, a "drut" was an evil witch who visits people in the night, sits on their chests, and suffocates them. The novel tells of a young, ambitious civil servant named Baron Klemens Furnian, who is chosen as the district captain of Ischl, a spa town in Upper

Austria that was the favorite summer retreat of Emperor Franz Joseph. The district captain works to the best of his abilities, but encounters the distrust of the local population. He meets a Prussian baroness, Gertrude Sharrn, on a walk in the woods and falls in love with her, despite her dark and mysterious past. She becomes pregnant, and Klemens uses his influence to pressure the local parish priest to perform a ceremony without the required documents. When an anonymous article appears in the local tabloid, Klemens's colleagues use the scandal to discredit him. Gertrude is arrested for bigamy, and Klemens commits suicide in disgrace. An angry mob stones Gertrude to death on her way to the trial, blaming her for Klemens's death. In the end, Bahr places the most blame for the tragic events neither on Gertrude (Frau Hervay) nor the provincial population, but on the unforgiving culture of the Austrian bureaucracy. Klemens's attempt to break from the restrictive code demanded of him by his career as a civil servant and pursue happiness through his relationship with Gertrude brings about his downfall.[91]

Few provincial Austrians, it appears, shared Bahr's interpretation of events. The Hervay affair demonstrates how local tensions played out when an outsider appeared and pushed at social boundaries. Even though Frau von Hervay was unconventional and displayed questionable behavior, the overblown reaction of the local population, marked by hypocrisy and a sensational trial, reveals that distorted notions of Jews and gender were well entrenched in the culture of rural Austria.

The scandal had repercussions beyond the local setting. Frau von Hervay's arrest (which took place in Vienna) and her trial attracted the attention of newspapers in Vienna and beyond. Each paper offered its own perspective on the Hervay affair and the lessons it contained. While the antisemitic press interpreted the Hervay affair as evidence that Jews were sexually perverse, immoral, dishonest, and criminal, and that Jewesses possessed supernatural powers over men, some commentators viewed Frau Hervay's actions as a result of mental illness and a denial of her Jewish family and past. Still others defended Frau von Hervay, focusing attention on other factors that contributed to the tragic outcome, such as the provincial mentality of the local population; the improper actions taken by the parish priest, the mayor, and the district captain himself; and the flawed culture of the Austrian bureaucracy. Kraus viewed the Hervay affair as evidence of the dangers of the antisemitic press and its witch-hunt mentality, and he used the case to illustrate the hypocrisy of Austrian society, which confused "immorality" with "criminality."[92]

The case also reveals wider antisemitic influences at work in rural Austria. Antisemites were quick to connect aspects of the trial to the Dreyfus affair, the

"Jewish" press, and white slavery trials. They also drew on stereotypes of Jews and women that had little to do with provincial Austria. In this way, interpretations of the trial contributed to the development of a transnational antisemitism and gender stereotypes in Europe before the First World War. They also showed the power of events in the provincial towns examined here to shape antisemitism in the state capital. In an era of mass media and mass politics, the anger and antisemitism caused by a small-town bigamy trial could reverberate far and wide.

THE BLOOD LIBEL
ON GREEK ISLANDS
IN THE NINETEENTH
CENTURY

The present study focuses on blood libels that took place during the nineteenth century on three Greek islands: Rhodes, Chios, and Corfu. In particular, this chapter examines the role that tensions born of financial competition and perceived ethnic differences (defined in this context by language, religion, and culture) between Greek Orthodox and Jewish populations played in exacerbating older religious stereotypes. The blood libel of Rhodes in 1840 is especially important, since it functioned as the first major blood libel among Greek populations in the nineteenth century. The blood libel of Chios in 1892 is a typical example of ethnic rivalry and tension. Finally, the 1891 blood libel of Corfu is the most widely known ritual murder case in Greece, as well as one of the most tragic incidents of antisemitism in the country.

By examining particular aspects of these three blood libels, it becomes apparent that economic conflicts, together with broader ethnic and cultural tensions, led Greek Orthodox residents of the islands to revive medieval stereotypes about Jews.[1] For Christians, these accusations served as a means of "revenge" for perceived wrongs and to marginalize local Jews economically and ethnoculturally. Such anti-Jewish movements strengthened at the end of the nineteenth century, an era of rapid state and nation building in southeastern Europe.[2] The construction of a homogenizing national ideology and of an imagined community[3] solidified the idea in many states that a similar religion (and language)[4] was a sine qua non for political unity and social cohesion.[5] With the establishment of a Greek state, many thinkers asserted the need for a single religion, language, and "race," so that modern Greece would avoid the religious, linguistic, and racial fragmentation that was held to be responsible for the downfall of ancient Greece. Constantinos Paparrigopoulos, the forceful advocate of the historical continuity of "Greekness," which linked ancient Greece, Byzantium, and modern Greece, thus claimed: "Polytheism was succeeded by Christianity; diversity of dialects by linguistic unity; racial diversity by national unity, and yet the Greek folk, fortified by this triple armor, is struggling to repossess its political unity."[6] Within this ideological framework, such assertions sharpened emotions and justified practices against all those deemed foreigners; no space was left for religious minorities, including the Jewish one.[7] When combined with local tensions, this exclusive nationalist ideology strengthened antisemitism in the Greek islands across the nineteenth century.[8]

■   BLOOD LIBELS IN GREEK HISTORIOGRAPHY

Accusations of the Jewish blood libel, host desecration, and well poisoning blossomed in Europe during the Middle Ages.[9] The record of the blood libel charge started in 1144 in the English town of Norwich, with the supposed kidnapping by Jews of a twelve-year-old Christian boy named William and, subsequently, his murder by crucifixion for dark, magical purposes.[10] William's elevation to the status of martyr transformed him into a local miracle worker and his alleged perpetrators into Satanists. The first formulated accusation against Jews of ritualized child murder, allegedly carried out for the preparation of matzoth for the Jewish Passover with the blood of their young victims, occurred nearly a century later in the German town of Fulda in 1235.[11] The narrative regarding the ritual murder of children as a symbolic reiteration of the killing of Christ and as a potential source of blood, primarily for the satisfaction of Jewish religious and ritual needs, proved particularly resilient throughout the ages.[12] Indeed, it appeared in a new guise in the second half of the nineteenth century and continued well into the twentieth century.[13] Of particular importance was the sensational case of the blood libel of Damascus in 1840, which signaled new anti-Jewish antagonism within the wider European and Mediterranean context.[14]

For a long time, Greek historiography systematically ignored the presence of Jews in the Greek state.[15] Scholarly interest in Jews began with a series of conferences[16] and with works on Jewish intracommunal affairs and on relationships between Orthodox Greeks and local Jewish communities, primarily that of Salonica, which had the largest Jewish population in the Balkans.[17] Research on the Jews in Greece has highlighted many issues relevant to wider Greek historiography.[18] It has brought to light aspects of fruitful cooperation and support between Greek Christians and Jews,[19] as well as evidence of an often problematic coexistence.[20] Such was the recurring blood libel against the Jews that echoed among the Greek population.

Until recently, Greek scholars had produced little research on the subject of ritual murder accusations in the second half of the nineteenth and the first decades of the twentieth centuries. The work of Abraham Galanté (1873–1961) provides the richest historical data of the phenomenon among Greek populations. Galanté was an Ottoman Jewish academic and politician, who initially worked as a middle-school teacher and later as a supervisor of public schools in the Dodecanese.[21] Drawing on Ottoman and Jewish records, newspapers, and oral testimonies, Galanté wrote about the financial and social history of the Jewish communities of the Ottoman Empire. His works therefore constitute a valuable historical source "from within," despite the fact that his perceptions were undoubtedly influenced by the ambivalence that characterized relations between Jews and Orthodox Greeks at the time he was writing. Galanté demonstrated that financial and ethnocultural antagonisms often were related to blood libel accusations.

More recently, scholars have examined blood libels that took place on Rhodes (1840), in Alexandria, Egypt (1881), on Corfu (1891), and in Kavala (1894). With the exception of Corfu, these ritual murder accusations were made by Greek Orthodox populations that did not reside in lands under direct Greek rule; rather, they unfolded in the Ottoman Empire. According to historian Yitzhak Kerem, significant Greek-Jewish commercial antagonism provides an important interpretive context for analyzing the blood libel in Rhodes.[22] Commercial and financial rivalries between Greeks and Jews also intensified in Alexandria at the end of the nineteenth century, when the disappearance of a young boy who was found dead by drowning a few days later sparked a blood libel accusation.[23] Indeed, the Greek mercantile elite of Alexandria often considered Jews (and not the Ottoman authorities) to be its primary antagonists. These views spread to the lower social strata of the Greek Orthodox population. New sources of tension arrived with Jews who had fled Russia in the wake of the 1881 pogroms. That the blood libel appeared in the same year in Alexandria cannot be disconnected from these wider factors.[24] Despite the fragile balance in Alexandria and despite the resilience of old antisemiticprejudices, calm eventually prevailed. The blood libel charge was rejected, and relations between Alexandrine Greeks and Jews did improve, contributing to the city's commercial well-being.

Similarly, in the case of Corfu in 1891, historian Eftychia Liata mentions, among other factors, the financial aspects of the event. Accusing Jews of working for lower pay, Greek laborers encouraged anti-Jewish violence in order to expel the Jews from the island. At the same time, Greek politicians charged Jews with voting as a unified bloc and thereby unduly influencing election outcomes.[25]

Vasilis Ritzaleos studied the blood libel of 1894 in Kavala, then an Ottoman city and today in northeastern Greece. Ritzaleos argued that economic factors both helped lead the Greek population to make the blood libel accusation and, at the same time, encouraged the maintenance of good Greek-Jewish relations, which were necessary for the commercial life of the city. According to Rizaleos, the blood libel accusation against a wealthy tobacco dealer who worked for Allatini Brothers, one of the biggest tobacco companies, aimed to weaken the Jewish commercial role in Kavala. Jews were particularly active in tobacco sales in the city and exports from its port. Indeed, by the end of the nineteenth century, Jewish-owned companies such as Allatini Brothers and Herzog and Company controlled at least 70 percent of the sale, processing, and export of eastern tobacco. They pushed aside the Greek tobacco sellers who had dominated the market until the 1880s. However, despite antisemitic sentiments among the lower social strata, the Greek commercial elite understood the significant role of Jewish tobacco sellers and the importance of their capital, expertise, and international connections. The common class interests of the Greek Orthodox and Jewish elites overcame a long history of stereotypes and intercommunal disputes, allowing them to dampen ethnic, cultural, and religious tensions.[26]

In sum, scholarship on the Greek blood libels has demonstrated the importance of economic, ethnocultural, and political contexts. They show that, depending on local circumstances and wider antisemitic perceptions, ritual murder accusations sometimes can be rebutted or ignored, especially when this facilitates the financial and social interests of the local society or, at least, of some social groups on the ground. But the increase in blood libels among the Greek populations in southeastern Europe and the eastern Mediterranean during the second half of the nineteenth and the first part of the twentieth centuries also reveals how the interplay of wider ideologies and local circumstances continued to fuel antisemitism in this region.[27]

■   THE BEGINNING: RHODES (1840)

A ritual murder accusation was made in 1840 on the island of Rhodes, "the rose of the Aegean," which was then under Ottoman control.[28] This marks the beginning of a series of blood libels among Greek Orthodox populations.[29] Even if the majority of blood libels did not break through the borders of local society (the case of Corfu is the clear exception), they did reflect wider economic and cultural tensions throughout the region.[30]

Rhodes had a long-established Jewish population. Its presence is attested at least from the second century BCE. Jews numbered approximately "400 souls," according to the Spanish rabbi and traveler Benjamin of Tudela, who visited the island in the twelfth century.[31] The Jews of Rhodes faced diverse reactions from the adherents of the other religions on the island. During the period of the Knights of Rhodes (1309–1522), even though the Jewish population suffered significant oppression and many restrictions, it made notable advances in both commerce and the crafts.[32] It was only after the island's occupation by Suleiman the Magnificent and the Ottomans in 1522 that the Jewish community began to flourish.[33] The middle and lower social classes of the Jewish community declined during the seventeenth century;[34] however, the eighteenth century found the Jewish community of Rhodes with notable accomplishments in the spiritual, commercial, and economic domains. The presence of renowned rabbis on the island and the successful engagement of Jews in local and international commerce constituted the basic pillars of the Jewish community. Their economic success came from numerous sources. Some Jews collected rental taxes on behalf of the Ottoman administration (a familiar pursuit of Sephardic Jews within the Ottoman Empire). Jews were prominent in viticulture, weaving, and the sale of ready-made garments. Some Jews participated in the spice trade, not only within the local Rhodes market but also on the international markets of Asia Minor and Syria. Rhodes Jews also traded in silk and silken wares, an activity whose roots stretched back to the sixteenth century.[35]

The nineteenth century saw an even greater financial and demographic rise in the Jewish community on Rhodes, one that paralleled increasing conflict between Jews and Greek Orthodox Christians. The roughly one thousand Jews on the island at the beginning of the century grew to about fifteen hundred in the middle of the century and exceeded thirty-five hundred by its end.[36] As a result, some Jews left Rhodes for other Aegean destinations as well as for Egypt, Asia Minor, and later, America and Africa.[37] Jews remained a distinct minority on Rhodes. The earl of Carlisle, during his visit to the island just after the middle of the nineteenth century, estimated the existence of some one thousand Jews among twenty thousand Orthodox Greeks and six thousand Muslims, while approximately two hundred Roman Catholics constituted the smallest numerical population.[38] The traveler Albert Berg, who visited the island around the same time, noted the exact same numbers of Christians, Muslims, and Jews. Berg observed that about fifty-five hundred Ottomans and one thousand Jews lived together in the Castle, which was closed after sundown to Christians living in the surrounding suburbs.[39]

Later travelers also recognized the island's religious divisions. In the 1880s, the young German Byzantine scholar, Karl Krumbacher (1856–1909), visited Rhodes. He described the island's main city, also called Rhodes. He wrote of a dirty road that led ten minutes on foot from the fortress of Rhodes, where fifteen hundred Ottoman and five hundred Jewish families lived, to nearby Christian settlements with their "dark and gloomy" features. The Christian houses were surrounded by walls of ten to twelve feet, intended as protection from their enemies, the Muslims. As an additional security measure, Christians used small lamps at night. These lamps emitted only a dim light, which reinforced the town's gloomy picture, and gave Krumbacher the impression that he was wandering in "a town abandoned by its inhabitants."[40] Krumbacher character-ized the Jewish district and its inhabitants as disgusting, filthy, and noisy. On the Sabbath, the Jewish day of rest, he saw men, women, and children in fes-tive attire sitting in front of their houses and reading sacred scripture. Only then would "godly quietude" reign in these usually clamorous alleyways.[41]

Economic tensions sharpened religious differences. During the first quar-ter of the nineteenth century, Jewish merchants founded many commercial establishments, and some Jews became important players in the island's cof-fee trade.[42] Other prominent Jews staffed local consulates and subconsulates, which increased the social prestige of the local Jewish community.[43] Through-out the entire nineteenth century, however, the Jews of Rhodes struggled to maintain, alongside Armenian and especially Greek merchants, their position in the realm of import-export commerce in the eastern Mediterranean.[44] This economic competition, reinforced by ethnic hostility, rekindled intercommunal rivalries between the Greek Orthodox and the Jews.

Greek collective perceptions added fuel to the fire. Rhodian Greeks ac-cused Jews of working for the Ottoman authorities as spies and of making ter-rible accusations that both ordinary Christians and Muslims feared.[45] In the Greek collective memory, Jews had collaborated with the Ottomans during the struggle for independence.[46] In particular, Greeks accused Jews of participating in the 1821 desecration of the corpse of the Greek Orthodox Patriarch Gregory V in Constantinople.[47] This assault on the body of the patriarch was viewed as a direct attack on Greek Orthodoxy itself. In response, rebellious Greeks had killed, without distinction, some five thousand Ottomans and Jews in Tripolis on the Peloponnese.[48]

These violent events constitute the first important outbreak of Greek anti-semitism[49] and shaped collective memory in the Greek diaspora throughout the nineteenth century. The rising anti-Jewish sentiment among Greek popu-lations was part of a much wider matrix of religious and ethnic disputes and conflicts within the new Greek state and the Ottoman Empire. For example, the Tanzimat, the period of reform within the Ottoman Empire (1839–1876), had offered some hope to Jews. The Ottoman reforms promised that all subjects of the empire, no matter what their religion, could participate in all administrative, judicial, and military bodies. Further opportunities for Jews came with changes in their educational system, thanks to the later work of the Alliance Israélite

Universelle, which was also active in Rhodes. But such changes often upset the traditional social equilibrium of the Ottoman Empire, thereby creating problems for minority groups such as Jews.

One final factor on Rhodes deserves mention. During the nineteenth century, sponge fishing and trading developed rapidly in the Dodecanese. For this reason, the area attracted local traders as well as merchants from across Europe. However, the expansion of Jewish traders' interests in commercial sponge activities in the neighboring Aegean Islands, their access to substantial capital from the commercial and banking institutions of their coreligionists, and their important links with key urban centers across the Mediterranean, singled out Jewish merchants as feared competitors in the eyes of Greek traders, whose presence was also of pivotal significance for the sponging business of the Dodecanese.[50] Such economic fears were easily projected onto other spheres of life.

These manifold tensions formed the background to the blood libel of Rhodes in 1840. According to Galanté's detailed description, on the eve of Purim in 1840, an itinerant Jewish egg seller, Eliskim Léon Stambouli, was accused of kidnapping a Christian child in fulfillment of Jewish rituals. A commercial representative by the name of Calomiti, a non-Rhodes Jew, had recently visited the island in order to engage in sponging activities. The intrusion of a Jew and, moreover, a "foreign" one, had incited the jealousy of Greek and Catholic traders, who had exercised a monopoly over the sponge business and who now came to regard it as being under threat. Prime instigators in this campaign were a Greek by the name of Stephanakis and the consuls of western European countries in Rhodes, primarily the English Consul Nicolson, one of his interpreters by the name of Comelly, and the French consul. The participation of Abdella, a Jewish convert to Christianity, seemingly lent credence to the campaign, as it brought with it the weight of proof "from within."[51]

The Greek clergy and the consul body united to exert pressure on the island's governor, Youssouf Pacha, to barricade the Jewish part of town, as well as to imprison and torture Chief Rabbi Michael Jacob Israel and other members of the Jewish elite. The Rhodes Jewish population reacted both individually and collectively to the unjust accusation. The wife of the chief rabbi approached the mufti. The latter, accompanied by the military commander, pressured the governor to liberate the prisoners given the lack of evidence and to transfer the case to Constantinople. At the same time, the Jewish community appealed directly to the Ottoman authorities in Constantinople for help, making known the prevailing circumstances on Rhodes and formulating complaints against the unjust treatment it had received. The grand vezir's decree, addressed to the governor of the island, was explicit. It called on him to extend protection to

Jews and to form a mixed delegation, comprising three Jews and three Greeks, to resolve the case. The discovery of the missing child a few days later on the island of Syros confirmed that the ritual murder accusation had been without foundation. Sultan Abdul Medjid, who reigned from 1839 to 1861, issued a firman declaring null and void the Rhodes blood libel. However, the recurrence of ritual murder charges led Sultan Abdu'l-Aziz, who ruled from 1861 to 1876, to issue a new firman condemning blood libels.[52]

■   BLOOD LIBEL ON CHIOS (1892)
    Another blood libel took place on the neighboring island of Chios in the last decade of the century. Here too, Greek-Jewish intercommunal relations experienced phases of particular turbulence as explained in the following brief historical review. Although the exact date of the arrival of Jews on the island is unknown, the nineteenth-century French historian Numa Denis believed that Jews were present on Chios as early as 12 BCE.[53] Benjamin of Tudela mentions that some four hundred Jews were resident on Chios when he visited in 1147. During the Genoese presence and until the island's final occupation by the Ottomans in 1694, Jews were obliged to wear a distinguishing mark and were forbidden to move freely.[54] In 1840 the Greek historian and physician Alexandros Vlastos published a multivolume history of the island, in which he described Christian anti-Jewish prejudices: "Jews were always regarded as repulsive beings and so much religious hatred was nurtured by all the peoples (and this continues in our days) against the wretches that the Justinians had prevented them from leaving their homes between Maundy Thursday and Easter Monday so they would not be torn apart [by Christians] in some way desiring to avenge Christ's crucifixion. One could say that 'the fathers have eaten sour grapes, and the children's teeth are set on edge.'"[55] Vlastos's last line cites Jeremiah 31:29. Biblical quotations, often used in publications of the era, were commonly employed to lend an air of legitimacy to blood libel charges.
    The role of Orthodox Christianity among the Greeks requires careful consideration. Scholars have long noted that a small but politically articulate minority existed that had studied in western universities, absorbed the values of the Enlightenment and of the pre-Christian Hellenic past, and called for the establishment of a secular nation-state. This minority viewed the attitudes of the Church as obstacles to realizing this goal.[56] The majority of Greek revolutionaries and later citizens, however, had strong ties to the Church and to its traditions.[57] With the declaration of the autocephaly of the Greek Orthodox Church in 1833 and the severing of its relations with the Patriarchate of Constantinople (which was perceived as Turkophile), the Greek Church submitted

to the newly organized Greek state.[58] The Church continued to wield significant power within Greece and in particular toward religious minorities. Like
the Greek state it served, the Greek Orthodox Church officially supported the
tolerance of Judaism.[59] At the Synod of Constantinople in 1872, for example,
the Orthodox Church denounced prejudice against Jews, and two decades later,
the Holy Synod of Greece, using as pretext the widespread anti-Jewish practice
of burning an effigy of Judas on Good Friday and Easter Sunday, issued a circular that condemned this tradition.[60] Greek Orthodox priests often participated
in the anti-Jewish popular culture of the villages and small towns despite this
ban. In this period, the Greek Orthodox hymnal for Easter Week repeatedly referred to Jews as envious, impious, Christ-killing, lawless, defiled murderers.[61]
All this exacerbated the already tense Jewish-Christian relations.

But let us return to Chios. Only under Ottoman rule were the Jews of Chios
freed from the more degrading restrictions. During the Greek uprising on
Chios against the Ottomans in 1822, only sixty to seventy Jews had lived on
the island, among the Ottomans in the fortress.[62] Their lengthy coexistence
with Muslims and the protection the latter extended to the Jews further intensified the Greeks' fear and hostility. An accidental occurrence in 1822 during
the Greek rebellion against the Ottomans confirmed the Greeks' negative perceptions of the Jews. Early on in the revolution, a group of Greeks had secretly
tried to enter the Ottoman fortress at night. A Jewish woman by the name of
Seniora, having finished the week's baking, reportedly left the burning-hot tool
she had used against a wall. It happened to be the same wall that the rebelling
Greeks had filled with explosives, which soon ignited. The alarm was immediately sounded, and the Greek uprising on Chios was crushed. To make matters worse (from the Greek perspective), the Ottoman administration rewarded
Seniora generously, released local Jews from the obligation of paying certain
taxes, and granted them an additional cemetery for burying their dead.[63]

The atrocities inflicted by the Ottomans on the island's Christian population
proved difficult to forget.[64] The sultan's decree for the island demanded "fire,
iron, slavery." All men above the age of twelve, women above forty, and children above two were to be put to death, while the rest were sold as slaves.[65] It
was said that in the nearby markets of Smyrna, forty thousand Greeks were put
up for sale. The average sale price per head was 300 piastres.[66] Even though it
is difficult to calculate accurately the total number of people murdered or en-
slaved, contemporary estimates range from fifteen thousand[67] to thirty thousand dead.[68] Still other sources claim that forty-eight thousand people were
imprisoned and forty thousand saved, most of whom became refugees; some
were forced to convert to Islam.[69] In his memoirs, Andreas Mamoukas, an eye-

witness to the destruction of Chios, mourned: "The happy Chiotes deserted the brilliant and rich island, which had glowed in the Greek sea, like the blue sky and the morning star; and which had been the best [island] for commerce, industry, and music."[70]

In the eyes of Christian observers (and not just Greek ones), local Jews were closely linked to Ottoman brutality. According to French diplomat François Pouqueville, those who played a prominent role in selling Chiotes in the slave markets of the Orient, including that of Smyrna, were "the Jews, a filthy race; the Armenians accustomed to selling even their own children; the Turks, strangers to every human emotion."[71] The Parisian newspaper *La Gazette de France* claimed the massacre on Chios reached such proportions that the Ottomans had to bring Jews from Smyrna to throw corpses into the sea.[72] Andreas Mamoukas wrote that after the destruction of Chios, the Ottoman authorities had forced the "ever willing"[73] Jews to fling the corpses of Christians into the sea, ostensibly for reasons of hygiene but in violation of all "burial and religious customs."[74] According to Mamoukas, as soon as news of the arrival of the Ottoman armada spread in Chios, Jews readily offered "armed assistance from Smyrna and other places, against [the Christian Chiotes] for whom, of course, they have implacable hatred."[75] Mamoukas also claimed Jews later demanded that no Christian be spared and that the Ottoman administration hand over to them the island's Greek Orthodox metropolitan "to treat him, as they wanted."[76] Pouqueville wrote that Jews threw the corpse of Archbishop Platon into the sea, recalling to Greeks the desecration of the patriarch's corpse the previous year in Constantinople.[77] When the Ottomans, with "a bestial, avenging rage," left corpses hanging from trees as a lesson to the rebels, it fell to the Jews to take them down and heave them into the sea. Mamoukas asserted that the Jews readily blasphemed Christianity and tore up Christian corpses "as meat at the slaughterhouse." Jews had crucified "the Lord of glory himself" with much greater cruelty and would only humiliate and insult those who worshipped him.[78]

This event and the memory of it reinforced the image of Jews as Ottoman collaborators and as enemies of the Greek struggle for independence.[79] Jewish observers charged that Greeks had retaliated with the same violence. Near the New Monastery on Chios, Christian villagers seized Muslims and Jews. They killed the former and they crucified the latter upon trees, in "revenge" for the crucifixion of their God.[80] Local Greeks obviously attached very different meanings to such acts of violence. What lodged in the Greek collective memory was the Jews' use of violence, their collaboration with the Ottomans, and their role as spies—that is, as an invisible, internal enemy.[81]

When Greek Orthodox returned to Chios later in the nineteenth century, a financial rivalry soon developed between Christian and Jewish merchants. This too had deep roots. In the eighteenth century, both groups had bought imported textiles from European merchants and resold them mainly, but not exclusively, in the island's local markets. On Rhodes, Jewish merchants had encroached on an activity traditionally dominated by Greek Orthodox merchants; on Chios, in contrast, Greek merchants started engaging more intensively with financial and speculative commercial ventures that for centuries had been regarded as a Jewish domain. According to the French vice consul on Chios, the island had become one of the wealthiest in the Aegean, but it was easy for Orthodox merchants to feel insecure about the position they had achieved. Greek Orthodox and Jewish merchant communities increasingly competed in the same commercial and speculative financial activities, including currency exchange, the buying and selling of promissory notes, and lending money at interest.[82]

Long-standing religious, historical, and economic rivalries between the Greek and Jewish populations of Chios continued through the end of the nineteenth century. The appearance of the blood libel—and its widespread acceptance among Greek Christians—must be considered against this background. In 1892 a Greek Orthodox child disappeared, and Jews were held responsible for his disappearance. As local Greeks began to attack Jews, the administration recognized the danger and made every effort to control the situation and investigate the case. A few days later, the missing boy was found in a sewer into which he had accidentally fallen while at play, again proving the false and baseless nature of such accusations.[83] A few years later in 1900, a rumor began to circulate that "fate" demanded the disappearance of a Christian. So when two Christian boys who had wandered into a Jewish neighborhood to buy pumpkins went missing, their parents quickly accused the Jews. For their unjust accusations, however, they were severely punished by the Ottoman authorities.[84]

The Greek reaction to Jews in 1897, the year of the Greco-Turkish War, deserves a brief mention. During the war, relations between Christians and Jews were again upset because of the latter's seeming adherence to the Ottomans. The Christians on Chios reacted with a widespread economic boycott, ceasing to purchase all products from itinerant Jewish traders. As a result, the latter were forced to seek out financial assistance from other Jewish communities until tensions had subsided.[85]

To summarize the case of Chios, we note the potent interaction of traditional religious animosity with sharp economic competition. To this must be added the collective memory of Greeks regarding the role of Jews during their war of independence. For Greeks, the extreme violence and (initial) failure of this struggle strengthened the search for scapegoats. These factors helped produce an environment on Chios in which the existing status quo and the seemingly even flow of everyday life could be overthrown. In this case, as on Rhodes, the Ottoman administration had acted quickly to maintain order. What would happen, however, when a ritual murder accusation was made on an island under Greek rule?

■   BLOOD LIBEL ON CORFU (1891)

In 1891, off the western coast of Greece, the fiercest Greek blood libel of the nineteenth century occurred on the island of Corfu, leading to the effective disintegration of what had been the largest Jewish community in the Ionian Islands.[86] The Jewish presence on Corfu, which Benjamin of Tudela observed in 1147, endured through the oppressive rule of the Angevins (1267–1386) and then of the Venetians (1386–1797).[87] The latter often demanded financial and military assistance from the Jewish population.[88] The external pressures imposed on Jews by their conquerors were compounded by tensions between the island's established Jews, the Greek-speaking Romaniotes, and newly arrived Spanish- and Italian-speaking Jews, who had been expelled from Spain in 1492 and from Italy in 1540.[89] Corfu's Jews enjoyed equal political rights during two brief periods of French sovereignty (1797–1799 and 1806–1814). English control (1815–1864), however, again pushed Jews to the margins of social and political life.[90] To this official harassment was added the everyday mistrust of the Orthodox population, who saw Jews as Christ killers. On Corfu, Greek Orthodox believers developed the tradition of throwing crockery out of the windows and into the street "onto the heads of the Jews," in reenactment of the stoning of Judas.[91] Furthermore, it was mostly (but not only) the island's Greek rural populace, incited by its priests, who participated in occasional antisemitic violence.[92] To this anti-Jewish religious agitation were added the stereotypes of Jews as usurers and wealthy merchants.[93] In 1864 the incorporation of Corfu and the Ionian Islands into the Greek state meant that legally, the political equality of Jews was a fact. Despite this, Jews continued to live for a number of decades at the margins of Greek political life without securing any significant positions in the country's administration.[94]

The Jewish community of Corfu, which numbered an estimated five to six thousand shortly before the union with Greece, constituted the most important Jewish population in the Ionian Sea, both in terms of numbers and resources.[95] Yet Jews remained a clear minority among the island's Christian population, which at the end of the eighteenth century numbered 82,853.[96]

This important Jewish presence was violently interrupted by the 1891 blood libel. The spark was the April 1 murder of an eight-year-old Jewish girl (and not, as was usually the case, a boy) named Rubina Sarda. The fact that the girl's father, Vita Sarda, was caught with other Jews carrying the bloody sack containing his daughter's corpse in the middle of the night guaranteed that the event would cause a sensation. Corfu's police added fuel to the fire by spreading the rumor that the perpetrator was a Jew and his victim a Christian; therefore, this incident was really a fresh example of Jewish ritual murder in fulfillment of their religion's supposed requirements. The first forensic examination of the body seemed to confirm police suspicions of ritual murder. In contrast, the cautious attitude of some of the island's authorities, headed by the prosecutor Theagenis Kefalas, who noted the lack of convincing, incriminating evidence, divided Corfu's officials.

Local Christians had no doubts about the Jews' collective guilt. They took the law into their own hands, meting out the "justice" the state would not. Many Christians believed that the judges, prosecutors, and military authorities had been blackmailed into freeing the Jewish ritual murderers in order to gain the goodwill of Jewish voters in the coming municipal elections.[97] After Christians attacked the Jewish quarter in the city of Corfu, the prefect L. Vlachos ordered that a Greek military force be deployed to uphold law and order and prevent further violence. His actions only reinforced the conviction among the island's Christian population that the authorities were biased in favor of the Jews.[98] Meanwhile, additional military reinforcements arrived from nearby Patras.[99] The Greek prime minister, Theodoros Deliyannis, took a personal interest in the case and closely monitored developments. He conveyed instructions for safeguarding the peace to the island's new prefect, G. Bouklakos (his predecessor, L. Vlachos, had resigned suddenly for reasons of health).[100]

The police, however, not only tolerated but also encouraged the continued spread of false rumors against Jews. First among them was the rumor about the identity of the dead girl, widely thought to be a Christian. A story circulated of an orphan girl from Ioannina, Maria Desylla, who reportedly had come as a child to work in the home of the Jew Vita Sarda and was sacrificed for ritual purposes. This story spread widely among the Christian population of the island and was reproduced in the local and Athenian press.[101] The publication of several documents by the chief rabbi of Corfu that confirmed the Jewish identity of the dead girl, Rubina Sarda, failed to assuage the violent anti-Jewish feelings of the Christian population.[102] Angry mobs attacked Jewish shops and residences. When the police proved incapable or unwilling to prevent the violence, the authorities ordered troops to intervene. The resulting fighting left several dead and hundreds wounded.

Most important, a small but influential number of Corfu politicians and other elites took a strongly antisemitic tone in their words, deeds, and positions. Foremost was Iakovos Polylas, a writer, literary critic, and publisher of the national poet of Greece, Dionysios Solomos. Polylas had been active in politics since the time of the British occupation of the Ionian Islands and had struggled in favor of the island's union with the Greek state. Between 1869 and 1879, Polylas, at the time a member of the Liberal Party of Greek Prime Minister Charilaos Trikoupis, served four times as Corfu's member of parliament. In 1884, after disagreements with the Liberal Party, Polyas joined the conservatives under Theodoros Deliyannis. He withdrew his conservative party membership in 1890.[103] Polyas remained influential on Corfu. He published attacks on the Jews in his political newspaper *Rigas Fereos* (named after an eighteenth-century Greek national hero) and in the satirical *Kodon*.

Polylas accused Jews of not being real Greeks, not working in favor of Greece's financial interests, behaving arrogantly toward Christians, and trying to influence politics for selfish purposes.[104] Remarkably, he held the Jews responsible both for the ritual murder and for the charges of barbarism and medievalism leveled by mainland Greeks and Europeans against the Christian population of Corfu in the wake of the anti-Jewish violence.[105] Polylas protested specifically against statements that Ioannis Gennadios, the Greek ambassador in London, made to the British newspaper the *Daily News*. Gennadios condemned the antisemitic violence on Corfu in order to lessen the European outcry against Greece.[106]

As Polylas recognized, some Christian elites rose in defense of the Jews, rejecting the ritual murder accusation as the product of anti-Jewish stereotypes[107] and irrational behavior.[108] A similar division could be found in the Greek Orthodox Church. Many lower clergy had long encouraged anti-Jewish behaviors and attitudes: for example, by the tradition of burning an effigy of Judas in the churchyard.[109] Some priests in the upper ecclesiastical ranks supported the antisemitic movement, while others denounced antisemitic agitation.[110] An excellent example of the latter is Dionysios Latas, the archbishop of Zante from 1884 to 1894. Latas praised the great contributions of the Jewish people to world civilization and attested to their peaceful presence in Greece. In so doing, he effectively declared blood libels to be entirely unsubstantiated and untenable.[111]

The rural population of Corfu nonetheless nursed strong antisemitic sentiments. In the absence of savings banks or other credit institutions, rural dwellers often turned to Jewish moneylenders so they could rent olive groves from wealthy Christian landowners. In years of poor harvests, however, Christian farmers often were unable to pay both the lease and the high interest on their loans, and thus ended up in debt and often in prison. The brutal conditions of imprisonment intensified the Christian farmers' hatred for those deemed responsible for their misfortune: the wealthy Christian landowners on the one hand and the Jewish moneylenders on the other.[112]

Jews occupied a complex position in the local economy. At the time of the blood libel, a contemporary Jewish physician stressed the Jews' lack of wealth, claiming that Jews did not own property in the town of Corfu, with the exception of some decrepit houses in the Jewish quarter, did not possess many banking establishments, were not leaders of industry, and were not involved in the profitable trade of grain and wine. He stressed that most Jews were unskilled laborers who worked under the supervision of Christians and that merchants involved in the import and transit trade did not succeed in scaling the financial heights because foreign merchandise was sold cheaply in Corfu.[113] According to the electoral list of 1865, Jews in Corfu town constituted 40 percent of the registered merchants, 27.5 percent of the retailers (mainly peddlers, spirit sellers, and wine sellers, but also grocers, butchers and bakers), and 22 percent of the craftsmen (mainly tailors, but also tinsmiths, tanners, soap makers, mattress fitters, glassblowers, coppersmiths, and goldsmiths). Nearly half (47 percent) of all registered laborers were Jewish, mainly porters, but also olive oil workers, water carriers, and builders. In addition, twenty-three industrialists, fourteen brokers, three public brokers, seven advocates, and five physicians were registered. In other words, alongside the significant percentage of Jewish manual laborers, there was an equally important group of Jews who were merchants, sellers, and craftsmen. This was not unusual for the eastern Mediterranean. Some Christians, however, accused Jews of unfairly monopolizing the market in olive oil, a profitable commodity. They also accused Jews of unfair business practices and, in particular, of buying products cheaply from indebted Christian farmers and then selling them elsewhere on the most profitable terms.[114]

Political tensions on Corfu also influenced the meanings that locals attached to the blood libel. Corfu's Jewish community had long supported the opposition Liberal Party. But its leader was a Corfu native, Georgios Theotokis, who, like Iakovos Polylas, began to take an increasingly antisemitic stance. His was an isolated but important voice in the Greek political world.[115] The ritual murder accusation came at a moment when some Corfu Jews had begun to orient themselves toward Deliyannis's Conservative Party, which also happened to be the incumbent party.[116] During the violence, Georgios Theotokis's brother, Michael Theotokis, who was Corfu's mayor, led attacks against Jews and encouraged Jews to leave the island.[117] Thus it is not surprising that when Michael Theotokis again stood for office in the municipal elections, planned to take place on July 7, 1891, he was not supported by the island's Jews, who instead united in support of Constantinos Vassilakis, the mayoral candidate from Deliyannis's Conservative Party.[118]

The electoral victory of Michael Theotokis to the office of mayor and the emigration of two to three thousand Jews (out of a total of five thousand Jews) to various destinations in mainland Greece, the Ottoman Empire, and western Europe, marked the beginning of the rapid decline of the Jewish community on Corfu. Its violent end came during the Second World War.[119]

The blood libel accusation and subsequent violence on Corfu led to an international Jewish boycott of etrogs—a yellow citrus fruit similar to the lemon—from the island. Already in the late seventeenth century, kosher etrogs from Corfu were in great demand by Jewish communities abroad for use during the holiday of Sukkot, the Feast of Booths. At the beginning of the nineteenth century, however, several European rabbis accused Corfu's Christian planters of grafting their trees with the common citrus, resulting in fruit that could no longer be regarded as kosher.[120] Those rabbinic accusations were not entirely unfounded, for nonkosher etrogs were imported into Corfu from other Ottoman territories. These etrogs were then falsely certified by Corfu's rabbi who, for his personal financial gain, resold the fruit as kosher to Jewish markets in Europe. The tensions surrounding the Corfiote etrog worsened during the last quarter of the nineteenth century, when Christian landowners and merchants sharply raised the price of etrogs from the island. First the Lithuanian and then the Polish Jewish communities stopped importing etrogs from Corfu. The English Jewish community turned to the Moroccan market. Even though these measures brought about a steady decline in the sales of the Corfiote etrog, Corfu's Greek planters and merchants remained unyielding and did not lower the price of their product. The climax of this dispute between the Christian cartel of etrog growers who would raise the prices and the rabbinic certifiers who were opposed to these price hikes was a meeting of the latter in 1882 in Trieste, the hub of etrog commerce. At this meeting the decision was taken to seek etrog suppliers other than Corfu. Faced with this dramatic turn of events, Corfu's Christian planters and merchants grudgingly lowered their prices.[121] In the years that followed, they regained some of the market share they had lost. But the blood libel and violence in 1891 raised protests from all of Europe's Jewish communities, which again shunned Corfu's etrog. The boycott, combined with the increased production and successful promotion of the Palestinian etrog, spelled the end of the etrog on Corfu—and with it, the end of an important point of contact between Christians and Jews.[122]

As with the other cases examined here, the blood libel on Corfu set off an antisemitic chain reaction. This reached its peak on the neighboring Ionian island of Zante, which had an important and long-established Jewish presence.[123] On April 19, 1891, during the traditional Good Friday procession, in which seven to eight thousand Christians participated, riots broke out as some Christians attempted to force their way into the Jewish district. In the ensuing panic, the responsible military commander ordered troops to open fire, which caused the death of five Christian civilians. The instigators of this "abominable vandalism" were thought to be, first, persons from the political party of the opposition (Georgios Theotokis's party), and second, "local thieves and robbers and to a lesser extent pious persons who were driven by foolishness and without fully understanding what they were doing."[124] Thus religious tensions constituted only the surface of anti-Jewish practices, which in this and the other cases examined here were fed by political factors, local economic interests, and collective memories.

■ CONCLUSION

Blood libels flourished during the second half of the nineteenth century among the Christian population of Greece, including the Greek islands. The first case occurred on Rhodes in 1840 when a Jew, originally from Constantinople, was accused of kidnapping a Christian child for ritual murder. It was more than prejudice and negative stereotyping of Jews by the Christian population that propelled the island's Christian population and European consuls to formulate and lend credence to ritual murder accusations. Economic factors were also important. The Jewish community, which already had a strong presence in local and wider Mediterranean commerce, had started to "intrude" in the particularly profitable area of sponge fishing and sponge trading, which until then "belonged" exclusively to Christian traders (Greek Orthodox and Western Catholics). However, the flourishing Jewish community of the island reacted assertively to the ritual murder accusation, appealing for help to the local Ottoman authorities and directly to the Sultan Abdul Medjid himself. In this way, it successfully defended itself against the accusations of blood libel. The Sultan even issued a firman that condemned similar accusations.

A similar scenario took place on the adjacent island of Chios a half-century later. Here a blood libel unfolded in 1892, sparked by the disappearance of a Greek Orthodox boy. On Chios, too, financial controversies between Christians and Jews found fertile ground. The same was true of the local Christian population, which "remembered" the unwillingness of the Jews to support the liberation struggle against the Ottomans in 1821. Long afterward, local Greeks still considered Jews to have been close collaborators of the Ottomans in the Christian massacre and in the enslavement of many Christians that followed.

The most important blood libel on the Greek islands took place on the Ionian island of Corfu. This was initiated by the discovery of the body of a murdered Jewish girl, who was rumored to be the adopted Christian daughter or Christian maid of a local Jewish family. The hostility of much of the Orthodox population to civic equality for Jews — guaranteed after the union of the Ionian Islands to Greece in 1864 — and the visible role that Jews played in the island's economy are both crucial to understanding this case. The presence on Corfu of Georgios Theotokis, a future prime minister of Greece, and his brother Michael Theotokis, mayor of Corfu town, along with the politician Iakovos Polylas, ensured that antisemitic charges found a sympathetic hearing on the highest levels. These three figures played a primary role in fostering an antisemitic atmosphere on Corfu. Unlike the events on Rhodes and Chios, the blood libel on Corfu received wide attention in the Athenian and European press.

From the above synopses, the multiple factors that contributed to the construction of the three blood libels can be seen. The traditional religious understanding of Jews as "Christ killers" played an important role. The uneducated lower clergy of the Greek Orthodox Church wholly endorsed this view. With some noteworthy exceptions, leaders of the Orthodox Church did little to counter antisemitic ideas and practices. The rising sense of nationalism, which equated Orthodoxy and "Greekness," likewise facilitated the exclusion of Jews. "Orthodox" and "Greek" were tautological and interchangeable terms; one could not have complete meaning without the other. In this context, to be a "Greek Jew" was a contradiction in terms. In addition, the construction of the Jews in the collective Greek imagination and memory as Ottoman collaborators, vehemently opposed to the long struggle of Greek independence and to the expansion of the newly established Greek state, strengthened the negative feelings of many educated Greeks against Jews. Jews were considered a dangerous presence in the midst of the national community. Furthermore, the financial and commercial activities of Jews often brought them into conflict with Orthodox Greeks, since both groups increasingly competed in the same commercial markets of the eastern Mediterranean.

Greek elites of the period had paid little attention to the small Jewish communities scattered throughout the Greek islands. This made them slow to react when the blood libel reared its head. This indifference stemmed from the fact that the old Jewish communities of the Peloponnese, the core of the newly established Greek state, had been decimated by Greek rebels in the 1820s (the largest mainland Jewish community in the region, that of Salonica, would not be incorporated into the Greek state until 1912). On Corfu, moreover, influential local politicians developed an intense antisemitic discourse, which based its arguments on the supposed financial dominance attributed to the Jews of Greece, as well as on Jews' incomplete assimilation and lack of service to the state in which they resided.

The blood libel emerged in Greece at a fraught moment. The Greek national community seemingly did not have space for religious, ethnic, and cultural otherness, particularly when the "other" seemed to have significant financial influence. This apparent "threat" to the majority group helped put several mechanisms of demonization and marginalization into action. One of these was shaped by the medieval repertoire of anti-Jewish persecutions, including that of blood libel. Ritual murder accusations were tried and tested with dismaying frequency and seriousness during the second half of the nineteenth and first half of the twentieth centuries in many areas of Europe and the Middle East. The content of this old category was reshaped in new forms and took on new dynamics. Even if such accusations proved again and again to be insubstantial and full of lies, and even if the authorities condemned them and punished those responsible for them, blood libels proved to be very resilient, demonstrating the strength of the national imagination used to marginalize and demonize groups perceived of as dangerous others.

PART 4

REVOLUTION AND WAR

"HORRIBLE WERE THE AVENGERS, BUT THE JEWS WERE HORRIBLE, TOO"
ANTI-JEWISH RIOTS IN RURAL LITHUANIA IN 1905

A wave of violence and social unrest broke across the western provinces of the Russian Empire in 1905, at the most intensive stage of the Russian Revolution. While violence was aimed mainly at the authorities and the nobility, a significant part of it was directed toward Jews, resulting in pogroms, more violent than any witnessed thus far, throughout Bessarabia, Ukraine, Poland, and Belarus. Lithuania, however, for the most part was spared large-scale anti-Jewish violence, which was more likely to spread in industrialized cities than in the rural areas that dominated the Kovno and Vil'na gubernias. Yet in spring 1905, a town by the name of Dusetos, located in what today is eastern Lithuania, became the scene of large-scale riots against the Jewish population.

In this chapter, I present the Dusetos riots in their local context, while at the same time keeping in mind the empire-wide revolution of 1905–06 and its wave of pogroms. Moving from a grassroots level to a more general analysis, I include the perspectives of multiple actors, including local officials, the public prosecutors, the Catholic clergy, and the Lithuanian intelligentsia. Taking the representations of these groups into account, I draw conclusions regarding the practice of anti-Jewish violence exerted by the peasants. My approach thus employs the method of "thick description,"[1] which has proven to be particularly fruitful in research on pogroms.[2] Another focus here is on the place of action. The small town (the Yiddish *shtetl*, Russian *mestečko*, and Lithuanian *miestelis*) of Dusetos bore characteristic traits that make it both unique and at the same time comparable to a multitude of other towns in the Pale of Settlement. Moreover, Dusetos will be treated not as a static place, but as a site experiencing dramatic transformations at the moment that the riots took place. Jewish-Christian relations, economic life, and settlement patterns in Dusetos, as in many towns in Lithuania, were undergoing marked changes in the early twentieth century.

Simon Dubnow's interpretation of pogroms as having been instigated by Russian officials and soldiers dominated the narrative of the history of post–World War I historiography on the Jews of the Russian Empire.[3] Later, scholars challenged this interpretation, arguing that Russian officials, although often sympathetic with the rioters, saw pogroms as a threat to public order.[4] Lithuanian émigré historians, such as Bronius Kviklys and Pranas Čepėnas, drew on Dubnow's model in their efforts to explain the Dusetos pogrom; however, they did not develop their interpretations by using a broad base of primary sources.[5] Building on this foundation, this chapter will revisit the Dusetos pogrom by concentrating on the relationship between the Tsarist administration and the local population. Because of its relatively small scale, anti-Jewish violence in Lithuania has not been researched systematically. The claim of Lithuanian and non-Lithuanian historians that "Lithuania remained a sort of peaceful island in the surrounding hostile, antisemitic, violent ocean"[6] before World War I has prevented anti-Jewish violence from becoming an object for sustained historical research. Detailed studies incorporating the perspectives of different actors have been written regarding only the first pogrom wave of 1881–1884 in Lithuania[7] and for the years preceding the revolution of 1905.[8]

For a number of reasons, the Dusetos pogrom is a good starting point for research on anti-Jewish violence in Lithuania, as it displays traditional and, at the same time, distinctly modern features. Although it took place in one of the most rural and "backward" regions of Lithuania, its eruption would not have been possible without the situation created by the revolution of 1905. It thus requires a multiperspective approach, integrating how the Russian administration, which in spring 1905 was under enormous pressure to regain control of the vast empire, viewed the pogrom and what meaning educated Lithuanians attached to it. In the absence of first-person accounts from peasants, the view of state officials and Lithuanian elites will be contrasted with a detailed description of the peasants' behavior, which focuses on the meaning inherent in their actions and social practices. I will also examine concepts that were of significance for the peasants' everyday lives, such as arson allegations and conceptions of morality and law, which often clashed with the policies of the Russian authorities.

■ PROTOCOL OF A POGROM

Dusetos was a rather typical *shtetl* of just 1,301 inhabitants in 1897. The town was serenely located at the picturesque southern shore of the long Lake Sartai and on the banks of the Šventoji River in the hilly east of Lithuania. Jews made up nearly 90 percent of the population of Dusetos (Yiddish: *Dusiat*; Polish: *Dusiaty*), which was high even by Lithuanian standards. It was a remote and sleepy place in the remote and sleepy district of Novoaleksandrovsk, more than 30 kilometers from the small district center by the same name (today Zarasai) and nearly 150 kilometers from the gubernia centers of Kovno and Vil'na. With its location at the center of a triangle made up of the small trading towns Utena, Rokiškis, and Zarasai, it served the function of a modest economic center. Christian peasants from the surrounding villages frequently came to Dusetos to sell their goods to Jewish merchants and to visit the stone church with its detached white bell tower near the bridge across the Šventoji. The economic situation of Dusetos, however, had long since been in sharp decline, as it relied heavily on the cultivation and trade of flax,[9] and the demand for flax had been shrinking for decades.[10] Moreover, Dusetos had not benefited from the expansion of railroads into Lithuania, being equally distant from the Dvinsk-Panevėžys railway and the Dvisnk-Vil'na line.

On April 24, 1905, the office of the public prosecutor in Vil'na received a detailed account of a "pogrom against Jews involving acts of pillaging" in Dusetos, in the course of which one person was killed and four more wounded.[11] Prior to the riots, the report stated, a fire had ravaged the town. It had broken out on the night of April 16–17 on Miller Street in the center of Dusetos and burned down twelve residential buildings and eighteen other buildings, most of them kilns and threshing floors owned by Christian peasants.[12] According to police reports, the fire had started in two separate threshing floors, which were situated around three hundred meters away from each other.[13] As a result of a strong wind, the fire spread quickly. However, it spared the town's Christian shops. Two Jewish houses also fell victim to the fire.[14] April 16 and 17 were not normal working days—they were Easter Sunday and Easter Monday. When the fire started on the evening of April 16, Easter Mass was being held, attended by the few Christian inhabitants of Dusetos and many Lithuanian-speaking peasants from the surrounding villages and hamlets. The police reports sent to the public prosecutor mentioned rumors that immediately spread among the peasants after the fire had been extinguished: namely, that the Jews had started it in order to settle old scores.[15] Consequently, the next morning peasants demanded that the Jews take an oath that they neither had started the fire nor knew whom the arsonist was.[16] The Jewish population of Dusetos gathered in the synagogue and took the oath in the presence of the town constable.[17]

Even more peasants from the hinterland came flooding into the town, and on April 18, after the morning mass, rumors spread that some peasants had decided in a conspiratorial meeting to wreak vengeance on the Jews.[18] Around noon, an estimated one thousand peasants—Dusetos's entire population numbered only slightly more than thirteen hundred—began destroying and looting Jewish houses and shops.[19] The report particularly emphasized the speed with which destruction was visited on Jewish properties: within just four hours, twenty-five houses and forty-six commercial buildings had been damaged and looted.[20] Many of the peasants had consumed considerable amounts of alcohol and equipped themselves with iron bars and other weapons from the first shops they had plundered. Remarkably, no one was harmed, at least initially.[21] Many Jews had hidden in backyards and attics. However, at some point during the day, a few Jews decided to protect their possessions by force of arms. Shots were fired, and the rioters then began to direct their attacks not only against property but against people. Two drunken peasants rang the church bell in order to attract more peasants into town.[22] After some time, the shooting ceased without any rioters being hurt. The rioters then stormed the house from which the shots had been fired.[23] Upstairs they encountered the brothers Itzak and Leyb Baron. Although Leyb managed to escape, Itzak was injured first by the blow of an axe and then by stumbling over the railing of the balcony and dropping onto the street,[24] where he was fatally wounded by the blows of peasants.[25]

After the death of Itzak Baron, the violence subsided, and the peasants began to return to the surrounding villages.[26] When the district police chief arrived with fifteen Cossacks in the early morning of the next day, he encountered a "crowd of weeping Jews, the square and the streets were covered with torn pillows, in the proximity of a shop lay a pile of diverse trade goods, the window frames, doors, and furniture of several houses had been demolished."[27]

The arrival of the district police chief did not calm Jewish-Lithuanian relations in Dusetos. The report states that the Jewish population was in a condition of fear and hostility toward everyone.[28] The next day, the police had to close down the market square, as Jews attacked a Lithuanian peasant who had drawn a knife.[29] The peasants, however, feared reprisals, as Jews from other towns came to Dusetos to help their brethren repair what had been damaged.[30] Yet violence did not break out again. The district police chief, who had conducted talks with representatives of the opposing camps, was vaguely pessimistic: "Although the population has calmed down and taken up their usual activities after these measures, the resentment and bitterness gives me no reason to be optimistic that this conflict between peasants and Jews will not repeat itself."[31]

Investigations established that in the course of the pogrom fifty-nine persons had suffered losses totaling 76,357 rubles. Some of the plundered goods were found in peasants' houses in Dusetos,[32] which led to the temporary arrest of fourteen persons.[33] However, only one of those under investigation admitted to having taken goods from Jewish houses; all the other suspects claimed that the Jews had hidden the things in their houses. Moreover, there was no concrete evidence indicating which individual or individuals had inflicted the lethal injuries on Itzak Baron.[34] According to a report of the public prosecutor in Kaunas, only three persons were under arrest at the end of April, although at first a total of forty-six persons were suspected to have been involved as perpetrators in the pogrom.[35] In September, another person was arrested, before the investigations against Lithuanian peasants were finally dropped.[36] Legal proceedings began only in the course of 1906. Some fifty-eight persons were accused of participation in the pogrom, twenty-one of whom were convicted and on September 17, 1906, sentenced to terms of between eight and eighteen months. Among those receiving the most severe sentences were Juozas Viena-žindis, whose house had been the meeting place for peasants prior to the outbreak of the pogrom; Jurgis Savickas, who was strongly suspected of having killed Itzak Baron;[37] and Ignotas Barzda, a Christian shop owner in Dusetos. Norbertas Bražis, the owner of one of the threshing floors that had burned down, and Ignotas Namaniūnas, a minor police official, were also convicted.[38]

■   THE 1905 REVOLUTION AND POGROMS

The Russian chief of the district police was particularly alarmed because of the wave of pogroms with hundreds of fatalities that was sweeping through the Pale of Settlement. Right after the deadly pogrom in Kishinev in 1903, the governor of Kovno had issued a circular that reminded officials to be particularly sensitive to all signs of impending anti-Jewish mass violence.[39] To emphasize the urgency of the incident, the police chief applied the term "pogrom" to what had happened in Dusetos, thus marking it as a manifestation of the violence that the administration, though often sympathetic with the perpetrators, was desperately trying to get under control.[40]

Prior to 1905, there had already been significant revolutionary activity in the Russian Empire. This period had started as early as the turn of the century and was perceived by contemporaries as an upsurge "of revolutionary disturbances and a proceeding erosion of state authority."[41] Peasants in the years before the 1905 revolution, one scholar has written, "took advantage of the government being in crisis to see what they could get away with."[42] In Lithuania a streak of anti-Jewish violence had marked the years after the turn of the century, and it was linked inextricably to the growing weakness of the authorities and the ensuing feeling that crimes committed went unpunished. In the summer of 1900, for example, a series of anti-Jewish disturbances had broken out in the north of Lithuania (in the Šavli and Ponevež districts). The riots had borne traditional characteristics: the violence broke out in the marketplace; peasants smashed the windows of Jewish houses and shops but did not hurt the Jews themselves; and rumors swirled of the ritual murder of a Christian girl.[43] Several features of these riots, however, indicate that they were also stamped by the revolutionary situation. First, the police proved unable to stop the riots, which was not from lack of trying, but because the rioters felt confident in their sheer superiority in number. In Žagarė, on June 29, 1900, a peasant boldly told the governor, who had come all the way from Kovno to see that order was restored: "Today you are here, but tomorrow the-hell-knows-where, and then we will beat the Jews, just as we have beaten them already."[44] The crowd in Žagarė would not disperse until a unit of 150 Cossacks on horseback brutally drove into it.[45] In many instances, lower-ranking policemen, most of them of Christian origin, refused to follow the orders of their superiors and sided with the rioters. In Girbutkiai, on June 18, 1900, a Lithuanian *desyatnik*, an assistant policeman recruited from the local peasantry, took off his badge of office and actively participated in anti-Jewish riots.[46] In Vabalninkas, on August 1, a *desyatnik* spread rumors that "revenge actions" against Jews were permitted by the authorities. He later told a police officer that it was impossible to protect the Jews "because of the peasants there are thousands."[47]

In the years 1901 and 1902, only sporadic incidents of anti-Jewish violence occurred in Lithuania. In 1903, however, against the backdrop of the large-scale pogrom in Kishinev, the police in Lithuania grew extremely cautious, as large crowds of Lithuanian Jews gathered to mourn their Bessarabian brethren. This time, the officials feared the Jews more than the Lithuanian peasants. The police took significantly less notice when Jews reported frequent anti-Jewish rumors of impending pogroms among the Christian population than they did of the gatherings of Jews who aimed to prevent the outbreak of anti-Jewish violence.[48] The police superintendent (*pristav*) of Vilnius reported on the high degree of determination among Jews to strike back against pogromists even beyond the limits of their own *shtetls*. On May 25, 1903, for instance, he encountered a crowd of more than five hundred Jews who wanted to make their way to nearby Vileyka (today in Belarus), where allegedly there had been rumors of an impending pogrom. The superintendent dispersed the crowd with the aid of mounted policemen.[49] With such measures, the police reinforced the conviction among peasants that the tacit rules of anti-Jewish riots excluded the possibility of Jewish resistance. This is well illustrated by an incident in Šiauliai, where on June 22, 1903, two Jewish cobblers actively resisted three drunk and aggressive Lithuanian peasants who had threatened them. In the course of a short brawl, one of the cobblers injured a peasant with a knife. Quickly, rumors sprang up that Jews had killed a Christian, which led to a strong, aggressively anti-Jewish mood in Šiauliai. This was strengthened by the behavior of the police, who arrested the cobbler but let the peasants go.[50]

The attitude of Tsarist officials toward Jews and Christian peasants varied wildly. It is not possible to distinguish a systematic pattern of behavior. The direct participation of officials in pogroms seemed to restrict itself to the lower ranks of the police, who were recruited from the local population and had conflicted loyalties to the state and to their village communities. Higher-ranking police officials rarely sided openly with the pogromists; however, they often blamed the Jews for provoking violence through their immoral and "parasitic" behavior. This was the case in Dusetos as well, as illustrated by a dispute between the public prosecutors of the Lithuanian governorates. Aleksandr Freze, the governor general of Vil'na, Kovno, and Grodno, admonished the public prosecutor of Kovno, Nikolay Demčinskiy, that he had not taken into account the fact that the Jews had behaved "in an extremely provocative fashion against the Christians" and were trying to prolong the investigations in order to cause the greatest harm possible to the families of the detainees. Freze urged Demčinskiy to investigate whether there was an "exclusive responsibility of the Christians" for the pogrom, thus hinting at the Jews' potential responsibility for the violence.[51] Demčinskiy refuted Freze's claims[52] and did not answer the latter allegation directly, but apparently willfully misunderstood Freze's formulation: "The circumstances mentioned in your letter, that 'exclusively Christians are being held to account regarding the pogrom' is due to the fact that we did not assume that persons of non-Christian faith could have participated in the pogrom, and we cannot assume it now, because—with the exception of the Jews—there are no such people living in the localities in the vicinity of Dusetos."[53]

As has been shown, the concept of "pogroms" was well established in Lithuania in 1905. Russian authorities feared them mainly for two reasons. First, they seemed increasingly difficult to contain, as violence-prone peasants were numerically far superior to the Tsarist police and—to make things worse—increasingly aware of their own power. Second, it seemed difficult to find a common agreement on how to act *among* the authorities, as lower-ranking policemen often sided with the rioters and even high-ranking state officials quietly sympathized with the attackers.

■   ARSON AND BACKWARDNESS

During the revolution of 1905, the determination of Jews to resist rioters in the Pale of Settlement was at times successful,[54] but in a number of cases it also served as an "alibi for murder"[55] for rioters and facilitated an escalation of violence. By choosing to resist, Jews forsook the "historic pattern of anti-Jewish violence" that "demanded submission, huddling in houses, a passive acceptance of the script of a ritual drama."[56] In some cases, self-defense units even seemed to have intimidated peasants, especially those units organized by the revolutionary socialist "Bund," whose members had the reputation of being young and unpredictable hotheads. During the revolution, they held frequent and sizeable meetings on peasant lands, as in Kupiškis in summer 1905.[57] In other cases, Bundists fired shots into the air, intimidating the rural populace.[58] The police chief of the district of Kupiškis noticed that the "provocative behavior" of the Bundists had led to tensions that might erupt into "a pogrom on the houses of the Jews, as the peasants know that there are no troops stationed in this place."[59] In 1905 the ubiquitous possession and use of firearms became a serious problem, often contributing to the escalation of violence, as the state lost its gun monopoly and did not manage to regain it until 1906.[60]

However, more important for our case was the general fear of arson. Peasants in Lithuania mostly lived in wooden huts, which—unlike in other regions in the western part of the Russian Empire—rarely were separated into individual farmsteads, but instead were crammed along the roadside. This was particularly true for the east of Lithuania. Land reforms in the late nineteenth century, which accelerated following the agrarian reforms initiated by Pyotr Stolypin after the 1905 revolution, had divided up roughly half of the villages in northern Lithuania into individual farmsteads. In eastern Lithuania, however, more than two-thirds (in some regions almost 90 percent) of all farms remained in nucleated villages, with houses clustered densely on both sides of a road.[61] Once a fire broke out, it could easily spread to adjacent buildings, often destroying whole villages.[62] During the spring and summer of 1905, fires and arson were ubiquitous tragedies, as revolutionaries set outbuildings, estate buildings, and sometimes entire towns and villages ablaze.

In Lithuania, arson frequently was attributed to Jews. The police chief of Vil'komir district reported in June 1905 that "the local population has been intimidated by Jewish youngsters belonging to the 'Bund' party, and now they fear arson attacks."[63] The arson allegation was not new: for years it had been used by Lithuanian intellectuals who wanted to strengthen Christian peasants-turned-merchants vis-à-vis Jewish merchants.[64] Arson always implied a battle in the shadowy, clandestine sphere, which intellectuals and priests depicted as a Jewish realm, as opposed to the open, honest, moral, and up-front behavior of Christian peasants.[65] Like the ritual murder allegation, which around the turn of the century still sprang up frequently in Lithuania,[66] arson allegations most likely were made by non-Jews in order to cover up their own guilt, as the vast majority of conflagrations were caused by negligent or careless behavior.[67]

Moreover, like ritual murder allegations and other popular, recurring rumors, arson allegations must have made sense to listeners when they were uttered.

It thus comes as no surprise that many contemporaries considered the fire in Dusetos to be much more important than the subsequent riots. After all, a total of twenty-five houses had been destroyed, and the fire exhibited the characteristics of arson: it had started in the night, began in outbuildings, and only later spread to residential quarters. The interpretations of the Lithuanian press differed significantly from what the chief of the district police reported—not only regarding the course of events, but also by the use of words.

The liberal camp did not even mention the riots at first. More than two weeks after Easter, the liberal newspaper *Vilnius News* (*Vilniaus žinios*) merely reported that a fire had broken out in Dusetos. It concluded with the statement: "Who carries the guilt? As of yet, there is no real information."[68] *Vilnius News* maintained this position in the following weeks and months. Correspondent and famous Lithuanian cultural activist Mečislovas Davainis-Silvestraitis wrote extensively on the streak of fires that ravaged towns throughout all of Lithuania in the early summer of 1905 and mentioned Dusetos among them.[69] In several cases, he noted, rumors had spread regarding the culprits, but "it turned out that there were many lies in this gossip."[70] One thing we have to take into account, however, is that Dusetos in general did not attract a lot of coverage from liberal papers. Dusetos's geographic isolation and poverty contributed to this state of affairs. The peasantry of this district was also considered extremely conservative and backward, partly because of their active resistance to the agricultural reforms of Stolypin. Peasants in this area committed acts of sabotage against land surveyors, thereby frustrating the conversion of villages into individual farmsteads[71]—and also effectively obstructing efforts to develop agriculture in the region through the drainage of swampland.[72] Moreover, the "Lithuanian" character of the region frequently was disputed. A contact zone between the Lithuanian and Belarusian populations,[73] Novoaleksandrovsk often was described as a lost cause.[74] Although Lithuanian nationalists regarded Belarusians as having no national consciousness and as hardly more than the little brothers of the Lithuanians, they feared their sheer numbers[75] as well as their cultural and linguistic influence on the ethnographic Lithuanian territory, which allegedly was amplified by the authorities' Russification policies.[76] Lithuanian newspaper circulation in the region was particularly low, and in the eastern parts of the district, peasants spoke Slavic more than Lithuanian.[77] The cultural, historical, and ethnic belonging of the region, in short, was a matter of discussion among Lithuanian liberal politicians.

Liberals saw Dusetos as a backwater and in the firm grasp of the Catholic Church. They complained that the Catholic movement of Dusetos was made up of "uneducated peasants and hypocrites."[78] While Lithuanian clubs and societies were in a desperate condition, the only thriving industry was alcohol: "On weekends and even on church holidays, all the taverns are [. . .] bursting with people: with young and old, rich and poor, even with women."[79] Only one and a half years later, when the verdicts against twenty-one participants in the riots were passed, did the liberal press mention the riots at all, stating that they had been "triggered by the false rumors that the fire had been a work of arson, committed by the Jews."[80]

■   "REVENGE" FOR AN ACT OF SABOTAGE

While the editors of *Vilnius News* looked disparagingly on the provincial town, the Catholic movement knew better what was happening in the neglected rural and poor regions of Lithuania. The liberals' information network could not compete with that of the Catholics. The well-established system of parishes allowed for dense communication among priests and with the local population. Thus, the Catholic weekly *Lithuanian Newspaper* (*Lietuvos laikraštis*), edited in distant St. Petersburg but publishing mainly articles written by priests in Lithuania, understood well the reality of life for the Lithuanian peasants in the countryside, far away from the administrative centers.

For the Catholic camp, strengthening Catholicism and "Lithuanianness" among peasants meant empowering them economically. Intellectuals hoped to improve the nation's situation not in opposition to the state, but by working on a grassroots level to further education and foster economic growth; like the priests, they wanted the peasants to enter the middle class. This strategy was heavily indebted to the concept of "organic work," which was developed in Poland in the aftermath of the failed Polish uprising of 1863. Conceiving of society and nation as "organic," it gave attention to increasing levels of wealth, education, and organization among all strata of society and thus represented an alternative strategy to the failed revolutions.[81] This meant peasants would have to be encouraged to become artisans and merchants and get involved in the trade of commodities, leading them inevitably toward conflict with the Jewish population, which already was concentrated in these professions. The vast majority of merchants in Lithuania were Jews, and because the Russian administration did not permit Jews to purchase land, trade was the only profession that many of them could practice. This attempt at social engineering, which aimed at preventing Jews from "harming" the peasantry, became particularly severe after the introduction of the May Laws in the aftermath of the assassination of Tsar Alexander II and the ensuing pogrom wave in the early 1880s. At first introduced as provisional laws, the May Laws remained in effect until the collapse of the Russian Empire.[82]

Particularly in the months prior to the outbreak of the 1905 revolution, a large number of Lithuanian shops had been founded in the towns and villages, and several cooperatives commenced operation,[83] the majority of them headed by Catholic priests.[84] Dusetos itself hosted four Christian shops at the time that the pogrom broke out; they were, however, situated in unfavorable locations on the shores of Lake Sartai and the Šventoji River and thus not in the immediate vicinity of the marketplace.[85] Not until 1908 did a Christian consumer cooperative open directly in the marketplace.[86]

Long before 1905, the theme of "Jewish revenge" had been widespread among proponents of this economic empowerment. Jews, they said, would do anything to prevent Lithuanians from becoming involved in trade, including, of course, arson. Already in 1885, Lithuanian novelist Juozas Andziulaitis-Kalnėnas had written about a case in which Jewish merchants allegedly had set fire to the house of a peasant who had opened a shop and thus entered into competition with the local Jews: "The blackbeards were blind with rage. But that was not enough. One night, with the town in a deep slumber, we hear a noise from the street. Everybody is running outside: The hut of our merchant is aflame! Barely did he survive, his tuft scorched, as the door had been barricaded by the sons of Israel [. . .]. It is arduous for the Lithuanian to wrest the trade from the blackbeards' dirty claws — try it, and you and all your belongings will go up in flames."[87]

The ethnic character that economic competition between Lithuanians and Jews had attained, the antisemitic rhetoric of priests and the cooperative movement, and the fear that economic rivalry might turn into violence have to be considered when analyzing the reactions of the Catholic press to the riots. Before the liberal press even reacted, the *Lithuanian Newspaper* already had reported on the events in Dusetos, stating that only peasant homes had been struck by the fire, which in turn had led the peasants to conclude that the Jews were the culprits. Anger and desperation had then led to riots, in the course of which "a number of Jews were also pummeled."[88]

Three months later, at the end of July, Antanas Macijauskas, a factory inspector and engineer residing in Riga,[89] published his account of the Dusetos event in the *Lithuanian Newspaper*. He explained that it had taken him so long to bring forward his views because he had first offered his article to liberal newspapers, all of which had refused to publish it. "The Revenge of the People from Dusetos" was its title. "Towns burn from time to time," Macijauskas wrote in the introduction, "but the cause for this fire was something else, revenge"[90] — revenge of the Jews by sabotaging the economic empowerment of the Lithuanian peasants.

According to Macijauskas, the rumors of Jewish arson were proven to be true by the fact that the fire had started on the threshing floor of a peasant called Bražis. Dusetos did not have a Christian consumer-cooperative shop,[91] but there was a shop run by a Christian Lithuanian merchant by the name of Gaulia, who, according to Macijauskas, was very successful and immensely popular among the Christian population. The Jews, Macijauskas stated, had threatened Gaulia and other Lithuanians several times in the past and now had made good on their threats to burn down Christian homes. Another peasant named Barzda, whose son was later convicted as a main perpetrator of the pogrom,[92] allegedly had been a victim of Jewish arson three times in the past, and according to Macijauskas, the Jews of Dusetos frequently threatened the Christians by saying: "You will be treated like Barzda."[93]

Macijauskas enumerated a number of pieces of evidence to support his theory. Witnesses allegedly had seen a Jew making a drawing of the threshing floor shortly before it went up in flames. Peasants had seen Jews running away from the building. A Lithuanian who could speak Yiddish had overheard a Jew mention that his fellow Jews had set the fire. Jews reportedly had warned some people, who had wanted to cross the bridge over the Šventoji River, not to enter the town center, as it would "get ugly this night in Dusetos."[94] According to Macijauskas, it was only by sheer luck—the wind had turned—that the Christian shops were spared and two Jewish huts burned down instead. All these facts, he wrote, "confirmed the people's suspicions that Jews were responsible for the fire; there was no other plausible reason and neither is there any today."[95] Why, however, had the Jews not set fire directly to the shop of their new competitor Gaulia? The Jews, Macijauskas explained, also had wanted to exact revenge on Bražis, the owner of the threshing floor, who had let another Lithuanian merchant live there.[96] This, however, is contradicted by the results of the investigation conducted by the chief of the district police, which concluded that there was no evidence that Bražis's threshing floor had been inhabited prior to the fire; on the contrary, it had not been used for a long time because of the long and severe winter (when the riots took place in April, Lake Sartai was still frozen).[97]

What ultimately sparked the riots was the Jews' refusal to confess to the arson, Macijauskas stated. This refusal to admit to a crime that had already been proven and the reluctance on behalf of the Russian constable to side unequivocally with the Lithuanians had so enraged the peasants, Macijauskas explained, that they had decided to seek justice on their own. However, it never had been the people's intention to hurt or to kill people or even to plunder houses. On the contrary, according to Macijauskas, the detention of several rioters, in whose houses stolen goods had been found, was the result of slander: the Jews had denounced as anti-Jewish violence what in fact had been a justified act of revenge.[98]

Macijauskas devoted hardly any lines to the violence itself, which apparently was not a central issue to him. Rather, he described in detail how Jews allegedly had continued to threaten the Lithuanians: the Jews were going to take murderous revenge; the Jews were going to set fire to any shop a Lithuanian would open; the Jews were planning to kill the priest. In the end, the atmosphere of daily life had been poisoned: "The Jews and the Lithuanians have now calmed down, but there is no old friendship left. The people are afraid of buying from the Jews and thus acquiring something the Jews would afterwards have their houses searched for. The people have heard that the whole community will have to pay for the damages incurred by the Jews and are thus not buying anything from them, because otherwise the Jews would become even richer through their revenge and would choke the Christians even more."[99] This interpretation is telling in many ways, as it links the pogrom to the emancipatory issues considered central to the project of strengthening "Lithuanianness." This concept, which became a bone of contention between the Lithuanian secular intelligentsia and Catholic activists after the turn of the century,[100] drew heavily on ideas and strategies to empower the peasantry across eastern Europe. Authors, priests, and political activists such as Jan Jeleński in Warsaw[101] or Stanisław Stojałowski in Galicia[102] called for solidarity among peasants, the boycott of Jews, and the organization of the peasants into agrarian circles and trade cooperatives.[103] This strategy to attach meaning to anti-Jewish violence was thus much in line with similar efforts in the regions of the former Polish-Lithuanian Commonwealth and in the whole Pale of Settlement.

■ MORALITY, LAW, AND CRIME

Although biased and completely out of line with the police reports, Macijauskas's report on the peasants' behavior is revealing. Macijauskas's claim that the peasants had decided to seek "revenge" on their own, because they had no support from the authorities against the Jews, is in line with the Christian peasants' concept of justice. The presence in rural Lithuania of the state authorities was—as in most parts of the empire—rather low. Most judicial matters fell to the village council; only the most significant crimes were handled by the *volost'* courts.[104] Attempts to strengthen legal state authority in the Lithuanian countryside ran contrary to the peasants' belief that the elders of the village were responsible for maintaining order in the vicinity,[105] which also may have been a result of the fact that a self-governance of the *zemstvo* type was never introduced to Lithuania.[106] Some government officials were particularly unpopular because of their (often arbitrary) interference in village issues. This included the land captain (*Zemskiy Načal'nik*), a post introduced in 1903 as a counterbalance to the *zemstvo*.[107] However, since there were no *zemstvo* in Lithuania, the land captains remained largely unchecked and were said to "bring people to prison merely because they did not take their hats off."[108] Moreover, land captains were recruited from the local landowning gentry, which did not help their popularity. Among the Lithuanian intelligentsia, the police superintendents (*pristavy*) also were unpopular,[109] although less so than among the peasants. John Klier has emphasized that despite the introduction of these representatives of state power at the local level "Russia was notoriously under-policed, and the authorities often had little choice or flexibility in dealing with street disorders."[110] This certainly was the case in 1905, when the state authorities were on the brink of losing their grip on the empire.

Jews maintained contact with government officials much more frequently than did peasants, because of their economic functions and because Jews and officials both lived and worked in towns. For this reason, the Lithuanian intelligentsia and Catholics often accused Jews of collaborating with the Tsarist regime (and with the Polish noblemen): "The Jews are an element in our fatherland, on which we cannot rely for our rebirth [. . .], because in such regards they have never helped anyone, but rather always sided with the victors and oppressors."[111] This sentiment — in addition to the armed resistance coming from their house — may also have served to direct violence against the Baron family. Relations between the Jews of Dusetos and the local authorities apparently had been harmonious, and the family of Itzak Baron in particular had the reputation of maintaining good relations with the Russian officials in Dusetos.[112]

Moreover, Itzak's brother, Šmuel Baron, ran an illegal tavern. As such, at least among Christians, he was a man of the lowest reputation. The sobriety movement in Lithuania was strong and decidedly anti-Jewish,[113] and Jewish tavern keepers were the most frequent target of Catholic anti-Jewish rhetoric. Taverns not only were said to ruin the peasants' health and economy, but also had the reputation of being criminal spaces.[114] Tavern owners themselves often became victims of criminal and even lethal violence,[115] but as often were suspected of robbing their customers. One month before the riots in Dusetos, Šmuel Baron was arrested by the police. A Lithuanian from Dusetos had accused him of conducting criminal activities in his tavern and insinuated that he was acting hand in glove with the village constable Berezovskiy. The Lithuanian told the police clerk that he had had a drink with Berezovskiy, and an argument had led to him being pushed out of the room "into the dark corridor, where a drunk, unknown person attacked me, and, together with the accused Baron, mauled and booted me, and wrenched bills and money from my pockets."[116] According to the police report, a Jewish woman from Dusetos also was involved in the mugging.[117]

This may help explain why the Baron family became a target for the rioters. But the relations of the Baron family to the Russian officials also help rebut claims made in subsequent Lithuanian historiography regarding the pogrom. In the interwar period, Lithuanian historians claimed that the village constable Berezovskiy had been responsible for the 1905 pogrom in Dusetos. These scholars claimed that Berezovskiy had "spread the lie that Jews had set fire to the town,"[118] that he had "used a couple of coarse blockheads,"[119] and that subsequently he had led the violent mob against the Jews. Official sources refute these allegations. The village constable had "taken up all possible measures in order to end the pogrom," but himself had become a victim of the rioters: "The crowd attacked him, struck him to the ground and threatened to kill him if he did not disappear."[120] Moreover, even Macijauskas, who wrote in the most sympathetic way possible about the peasants' behavior, did not mention any involvement of the village constable.

If we investigate the riots against the background of the revolution of 1905, when uprisings against Tsarist rule sprang up all over the empire, and Russian officials were expelled or killed,[121] it seems far more credible that the village constable suffered a serious loss of authority. It appears unlikely that he led the peasants against the Jews. If we take into account the peasants' concepts of morality and laws and the stereotype of cooperation between Jews and officials, it is plausible that the peasants felt obliged to act on their own and to take "revenge" because they suspected the Russian officials of siding with the Jews anyway, and because they felt that the Russian authorities were weakened. The importance of the revolution for the pogrom in Dusetos becomes all the more apparent if we take into account that in the following years several fires broke out in Dusetos. In 1910 even the Christian cooperative shop was destroyed two times by fire.[122] In none of these cases did riots ensue.

CONCLUSION

The riots in Dusetos need to be interpreted against the background of at least two violent phenomena, both of which were intertwined and of empire-wide relevance: the revolution of 1905–06 as well as the pogrom wave that lasted from 1903 to 1906. While the most lethal pogroms were a distinctly urban phenomenon, more recent research has shown that anti-Jewish riots were happening both in the cities and in the countryside.[123] In this regard, Lithuania cannot be seen as a "peaceful island" around which pogroms raged.[124] Rather, the absence of extreme violence can be attributed to the absence of larger, industrialized cities (the only larger cities, Vilnius and Kaunas, remained trade cities). Lithuania was shaken by anti-Jewish riots (on a relatively modest scale) from 1900 until 1905, however, with the riots in Dusetos forming the most violent example. Another reason to view Dusetos as part of the pogrom activity in the Pale of Settlement is that the Russian officials viewed it as a pogrom and applied the same (rather unsuccessful) strategies as elsewhere in the empire to suppress it and displayed the same ambivalence about the Jewish victims as their colleagues in Ukraine did.

Thus, although the violence in Dusetos retained several features of "traditional violence" (it occurred during the Easter holidays, for example), it also bore features that were decidedly modern. The riots took place at a time when the traditional conflict between Jews and peasants experienced a modernization and intensification, as priests urged peasants to "emancipate" themselves from the Jewish merchants and tavern keepers, to boycott them, and to compete with them. This model stopped viewing cohabitation or economic "symbiosis" as the core of Christian-Jewish relations, advocating instead the supersession of Jews in all spheres of life. The riots in Dusetos, the Lithuanian press claimed, were a misguided, but ultimately morally justified manifestation of this struggle, used to achieve a clear objective: to prevent the Jews from forestalling the efforts of the peasants to organize and "emancipate" themselves.

DUTY AND AMBIVALENCE
THE RUSSIAN ARMY AND POGROMS,
1903-1906

On October 23, 1905, the mayor of the central Ukrainian town of Chernigov (Chernihiv) held a patriotic demonstration of support and gratitude to the imperial ruler for granting the Manifesto of October 17.[1] Similar celebrations were held in many Russian towns after the announcement of the manifesto, and in many of them, as in Chernigov, the demonstration gave way to threats against Jews (who comprised 32 percent of the town)[2] and then to open violence against Jewish persons and property. Chernigov Governor Khvostov organized the demonstration and, along with the local police, apparently abetted its turn toward anti-Jewish violence.

However, the resistance to the pogrom was more concerted and effective than that offered in most other towns. An organized self-defense force intimidated the rioters and drove them off a key street, denying them access to half the city. That self-defense force of 150 Jews and Christians included members of the normally rivalrous Jewish Bund, Zionist Socialists, and Russian Socialist Revolutionary Party. The city's duma opposed the governor's stance by appealing to Prime Minister Witte for aid, organizing a fund to aid pogrom victims, and threatening to form an emergency governing authority. Although troops did not arrive until the next day, they immediately took the situation in hand, denied would-be peasant looters access to the city, and decisively ended the pogrom. All told, the pogrom lasted only six or seven hours and cost the Jewish community 45,000 rubles, a relatively small amount compared to other urban pogroms.[3]

In a season of inflamed prejudice, violence, and tragedy, the events in Chernigov show what was sometimes possible when positive forces and feelings were properly aligned. They put on display all the key actors in the making and unmaking of pogroms: the provincial representatives of the central authorities—whether governor, governor-general, city prefect, or *gradonachal'nik* (police prefect)—the local police, the rioters and looters, organized self-defense, civil society (usually acting through the city duma), and army troops. The success or failure of these forces to act in time or in coordination with one another is what allowed tiny minorities of the worst elements of urban Russia to terrorize Russia's Jews and to hold a great plurality of the Russian population hostage with varying degrees of violence and hooliganism for weeks during the fall of 1905. In Chernigov, as elsewhere, the last and decisive act was performed by military force that, once unsheathed, exposed the cowardice and opportunism of the anti-Jewish rioters and ended their rampages. The decisiveness of their role in Chernigov begs the questions of why they were not as prompt and decisive in so many other instances and why army troops frequently even encouraged and participated in pogroms.

Russia's pogroms were an organic and inseparable part of the 1905 revolution. They caused the greatest loss of life and property at the hands of anti-Jewish rioters in its history up to that time.[4] The scale of losses and suffering of Russia's Jews was commensurate with the scale and magnitude of the revolt against the Russian autocracy—the greatest since the Time of Troubles—and with the magnitude of the resulting upheavals in the structure and beliefs of Russian society. The lawlessness and savagery of the attacks on Jews and other victims of Russia's thugs and jingoists dampened civic pride and enthusiasm for the reforms promised in the October Manifesto and worsened Russia's already tarnished international reputation.

Most existing studies have dealt well with the historical and political circumstances that underlay the pogroms, but some important aspects have not been carefully examined, among them, the role of army troops in both preventing and provoking anti-Jewish violence. In the tumultuous events of 1905, army troops were widely used to restore and maintain order. In the numerous strikes, marches, and demonstrations, small, local police forces often were overwhelmed, and in October this became so widespread as to cause dysfunction in major urban centers. City and provincial governing authorities turned to the military for reinforcements as a matter of course, and in October such requests strained even the army's resources. Army troops were better armed and disciplined than the police (or any other armed force for that matter), and they did most of the shooting and accounted for a major part, if not the majority, of the casualties suffered in the pogroms. Hence, the lion's share of physical harm done to Jews and others, and therefore the most tragic and reprehensible part of pogrom violence, may be attributed to the actions of army troops. Understanding their part in the events is a crucial and neglected part of understanding the nature of revolutionary violence generally and anti-Jewish violence in particular. At the same time, troop presence alone was often enough to moderate violence or forestall its outbreak, and all the large-scale pogroms ended once orders were given to take decisive action against pogromists, usually by army troops and usually only after major damage already had been done to life and property.

Two principal questions are posed by the army's participation in the pogroms: why did it not act sooner and more expeditiously to prevent the widespread rioting and destruction, and how did it happen that the army both promoted and prevented the violence? The first question I have already addressed elsewhere,[5] and this chapter is intended to continue that inquiry as well as to address the second question. It will explore answers to these questions in the Russian/Ukrainian pogroms of October 1905, especially in provincial capitals and smaller towns.[6] It seeks the reasons for the troops' mixed behavior in both defending and attacking Jews and both pacifying pogrom violence and participating in it. Why were armed troops able to stop the pogroms almost everywhere they were deployed, even as soldiers often could be seen among the pogromists, sometimes in the same riots?

Investigating the role of the military is also an attempt to look beyond interethnic relations in the way we view pogroms.[7] Because the violence occurred along ethnic lines and its perpetrators targeted a specific ethnic group, perhaps 90 percent of the time, it has been natural to seek its causes within the relationship of Jews and gentiles or Russians.[8] As a result, the historiography of pogroms has been dominated by the most obvious interethnic issue involved, the endemic antisemitism of the Russian population. Antisemitism was indeed widespread in the Russian Empire, reaching from the most ignorant street thug to the tsar himself, from the most impoverished and envious peasant to the upper reaches of the government bureaucracy and parts of the intelligentsia. Soldiers were no less and no more subject to antisemitic prejudice than other Russians, although their predominantly peasant origins indicate that their anti-Jewish preconceptions were of a rural variety. Ethnic tension and rivalry between Russians and Jews was chronic and was worsening in the late nineteenth century (as it was everywhere in Europe). Yet, for most years and for long decades, antisemitic views and feelings were compatible with widespread cohabitation, commercial cooperation, and even friendship in thousands of towns and villages throughout the empire and throughout the Pale of Settlement.[9] A historical explanation of the massive pogrom violence witnessed from 1881 to 1882, 1903 to 1906, and 1918 to 1920 needs to go beyond affect and ideology to take account of the complex circumstances, among them the role of the army, which made them possible and determined their outbreak and outcome precisely at those times.[10]

From their earliest occurrence, a strong belief arose that troop behavior was determined by orders from the Tsarist government, which was thought to have orchestrated the pogroms for political reasons. Although this view is no longer accepted,[11] attributing the pogroms to the central government had the virtue of accounting for several circumstances that have since gone unexplained: the large number and near simultaneity of anti-Jewish riots following the Manifesto of October 17, the delay by the police and local authorities in responding to widespread lawlessness, and the frequently observed cooperation of soldiers and police with the rioters and even, at times, their direct participation in the riots.[12] These are all features common to many of the most frequently reported pogroms, and they remain largely unaccounted for.

Within this larger framework, the particular circumstances that this chapter addresses are the duties, procedures, needs, and shortcomings of Russian military forces in engaging the threat and the actuality of pogroms in 1905 and how troop participation affected their outcome and the behavior of participants on both sides.

■   TROOPS UNDER ORDERS

The behavior of troops during the pogroms depended, in the first instance, on whether they were serving under orders and direct supervision or not. Although revolts and indiscipline in the Russian army played their part in the disorders of 1905, the troops' overall loyalty to the regime proved decisive to its fate.[13] The same assumption about the behavior of soldiers and officers in their duties policing domestic riots can also be made. When clearly ordered to stop the pogroms, troops usually did so with dispatch and with nearly instantaneous success. There is no evidence that army troops were ever ordered to protect Jews, even though putting a stop to looting and rioting usually had that effect; and there is little evidence that they were ever ordered to attack Jews, although their forays against antigovernment meetings and demonstrations often had that effect. Hence Russian troops both protected and attacked Jews, and the reasons for this lie in the nature of the orders under which they served, whether and how they were executed, and how they behaved when not under orders. What then *were* the kinds of orders under which the troops served?

Two examples will help to frame the general circumstances under which troops responded to civil disorders. The first is an August 20, 1905, order by the commander of the Kiev military district, General V. A. Sukhomlinov, specifying conditions for the defense of Kiev by defining the kinds, strengths, and deployment of troops. He ordered that troops be deployed solely to guard strategic civic and state property and personnel, such as the water, gas, and electricity works; train stations; bridges; liquor and arms warehouses; the military flour mill; and the home of the military district commander.[14] The order was designed to guard state property and the locales and facilities needed for the maintenance and mobility of the military itself against the possibility of an organized attempt to conquer the city by revolutionary forces. We shall return to this document subsequently.

The other example comes from the commander of the Warsaw military district, Adjutant General Prince Imeretinskii, instructing his troops on their conduct during civil disorders.[15] The general's instructions crudely distinguish between unruly crowds that offer no resistance to the arrival of troops and crowds that do offer resistance, as though the difference would be immediately and unambiguously apparent. In the former case, the crowd should be surrounded, herded together, and warned that the "slightest display of violence" on its part would result in being detained and turned over to the civil authorities. In the case of resistance in the form of shooting or throwing sticks and stones, the troop commander was authorized to resort to deadly force (*pristupit' k deistviiu oruzhiem*) and to apply it at his discretion and without responsibility for the consequences.

The loose and general nature of these instructions cannot explain troop behavior in any particular situation, as they left so much room for interpretation and invention to the actual commanders on the ground, normally lieutenants and noncommissioned officers (NCOs), both in deciding what constituted an unruly or "insubordinate" crowd and in what amounted to the "slightest display of violence" or "any kind of actions against the troops" (*kakiia-libo deistviia protiv voisk*) that might lead to troops firing on crowds of civilians. Given the threat that could be felt by a small unit of soldiers when vastly outnumbered by the massive, excited crowds frequently encountered in 1905, the type of order General Imeretinskii issued left open the possibility of great violence against civilians, especially during the October Days of 1905.

While it cannot be proven that his order was representative of those given by other commanders in other military districts, it does reflect the general preference of Russian military men when called on to perform police work among Russian civilians. Domestic security work was widely resented by military leaders, who felt such duty misused their troops and distracted them from their normal military duties, training, and readiness to face foreign enemies. Nonetheless, as military men they were bound to follow orders; and in the autocratic state, the military was subordinated to and at the disposal of civilian authorities.[16] Many commanders felt that their troops should be called on only when their chief purpose was needed: the management and application of deadly force, their principal raison d'etre; all else in the management of civil disorder should be left to the civilian authorities. This spirit is reflected in Imeretinskii's order and likely characterized the attitudes and orders of most other senior commanders.[17]

This disposition did not necessarily lead troops engaged in riot control duties to use excessive force, though an ambivalent tension existed at all levels of command. Evidence of actual troop behavior in the face of large crowds in 1905 reflects the same distinction of duties that was voiced at command levels: cooperation between military and civil agencies and personnel was seriously limited by resentment at carrying out unfamiliar duties under ultimate civilian authority and by the sharp and unambiguous boundaries of duty and account-ability characteristic of military culture. The need for both large- and small-unit officers to maintain their authority and unity of command at every level further strengthened their determination to adhere to the letter of the law in execut-ing their orders.[18]

Returning to General Sukhomlinov's August 1905 directive on the defense of Kiev, the military's priorities in preparation for anticipated disorders are clearly spelled out. Restricting troop deployment to the protection of state property, geographically strategic choke points, and sites of importance to the military itself had the virtue (for the military) of putting the troops of the Kiev Garrison under military orders in advance, prior to the outbreak of disorders. The tasks involved troops in routines they were trained for such as patrol and guard duties, and the preexisting orders would give the garrison commander, subject to the authority of Kiev's civilian authority, some leverage in preserving the integrity of his troop units against demands to draw troops into policing dis-orders. That Sukhomlinov's directive actually was implemented is borne out by a report on the military's role during the October Days of 1905 in Kiev, which pleaded the numerical inadequacy of troops because of competing military rou-tines and duties as the reason they were unable to prevent or interdict pogrom rioting, despite the deceptively large number of troops in Kiev.[19]

Indeed, the report's findings appear to be accurate. When the pogrom struck in Kiev in the early evening of October 18 and for the two days following, troops that were stationed at various strategic points in the city (in Sukhomli-nov's reckoning) did prove inadequate to the task of preventing the murder, arson, and robbery that ensued. Adding to the shortage of troops in Kiev was an October 13 order from Interior Minister D. F. Trepov requesting that the Kiev Military District immediately send troops to Khar'kov Province, where the res-toration of railroad communications and local troop shortages demanded re-inforcements.[20]

Sukhomlinov's order had occasioned a revealing correspondence between General Kleigel's, governor general of Kiev, Podolia, and Volhynia, and General A. I. Karass, temporary commander of the Kiev Military District, who was charged with implementing Sukhomlinov's order. Kleigel's insisted that not only the state bank but also private banks be guarded by army troops. Although they eventually agreed to this, the generals' correspondence reveals an unresolved ambiguity in the relations of civil and military authorities and in the improvised nature of civil-military coordination in an emergency situation, as the military was normally subordinated to civilian authority.[21]

Given the priorities of the military command and their civilian superiors, how much farther from the thinking and intentions of either must the protection of Jewish life and property have been? Did the behavior of the troops in riot situations reflect these guidelines set by the military command? Actually, the performance of the officers and troops who dealt directly with the strikes and riots, while operating within the parameters of these orders, was far more complex, diverse, and difficult to summarize. It is remarkable that the officers and men facing violent demonstrations and other disorders in 1905 displayed as much restraint and economy of violence as they did, not resorting more frequently to the right to shoot given in General Imeretinskii's order. In his correspondence with Kleigel's, General Karass described the situations they often faced:

The summoning of armed force, in the opinion of the police, prevents street disorders; [but] from the viewpoint of the troops they are only [passive] witnesses of unpunished disobedience and the disruption of [law and] order by an unruly crowd; in such situations various nasty remarks, mockeries, and even spitting are directed at the troops.

These unpunished public gatherings have a demoralizing influence on the troops, [so that] the summons of troops not for suppressing or halting disorders, but only for such [crowd intimidation], places them in a [helplessly] unaccountable (neotvetstvennoe) and extremely onerous position.[22]

The military commanders' priorities notwithstanding, the viewpoint of "the police" was correct, as there is ample evidence that the approach or presence of troops (or the police) in riot situations did prevent violence by unruly crowds and individuals, including those threatening Jews and Jewish property.[23] In fact, given the military's priorities and preferences, placing troops under civil control was the logical way to increase the population's security, including that of Jews. Civil leaders, despite frequent malfunctions, had legal authorization and were familiar with the ways to preserve public order, and the military was not.

Army troops were not under the control of superiors at all times, and their behavior was not always directly subject to authority and discipline. Individual soldiers might be off duty, working in the barracks, or at work in the civilian economy earning money. Soldiers of the Russian army were responsible for providing many of their daily, soldierly needs such as boots, uniforms, and blankets. In addition, they were responsible for part of their regiment's financial upkeep. Hence, they were routinely sent to farms and workshops outside their camp to earn money for these needs. As much as half a regiment's complement might be engaged in such *"vol'nye raboty"* (outside work) off the military base. In addition, while in camp, they were required to perform errands or tasks for superior officers or to work as tailors, cobblers, and repairmen, making and maintaining equipment and clothing.[24]

These practices, holdovers from the prereform army of serf-soldiers, compromised the professionalism and military readiness of the army and affected its performance during pogroms. Soldiers' "domestic" duties limited the number of soldiers available for actual military duty, compared to the formal complement of a platoon, company, or regiment. Discussion of this particular consequence, along with other factors limiting troop availability, will be resumed subsequently.

The point is that soldiers working off the base or those left on the base to perform maintenance work, along with those completely off duty, were free to engage in the meetings, demonstrations, and pogrom crowds that frequently occurred in the more highly populated locales where soldiers were most likely to be deployed in 1905. These facts of Russian military life go a long way toward accounting for soldiers, in and out of uniform, being present in pogrom crowds and participating in other unlawful behavior that burst forth in 1905. Off-duty soldiers and those not under direct supervision easily reverted to the ways of the young, male peasants that most of them were, and this sometimes led to drinking, fighting, and rioting.[25] The relative freedom from direct supervision provided an opportunity not only to relax and enjoy themselves, but also to release and act out feelings normally held under externally imposed restraint, including resentments against their restricted, exploited, and oppressive military life; against the material injustices of imperial Russian society generally; and yes, at times against what many of them regarded as the actual and symbolic agents of their social oppression, the Jews.[26]

Soldiers' involvement in anti-Jewish violence sometimes resulted from direct altercations with Jews. In August 1905, for instance, five soldiers caught stealing apples and rolls in the bazaar (market) of Orsha (Mogilev province) were stoned by nearby Jewish smiths and butchers, who wounded one of them. In this case, the Jews escaped before the police arrived, while the soldiers were caught and sent to their regiment to be disciplined; no pogrom followed, and order was maintained.[27] Bazaars and markets were the places where pogroms often began, as conflicts between Jewish merchants and Christian consumers, including soldiers, were common. The 1903 Gomel pogrom, for instance, began with such an incident in the bazaar.[28]

When it came to anti-Jewish violence, the most volatile military elements in the 1905 pogroms were not soldiers, but half-soldiers, freshly mobilized recruits or reservists, caught in the usually regretful transition from civilian to military life. They often engaged in what have been called "mobilization pogroms,"[29] when anxious recruits, not yet subjected to military discipline, exercised their last freedom as civilians by rioting, often victimizing Jews in the process. Because the recruits usually were brought under control by regular troops, these incidents also can be considered intramilitary conflicts in which Jews got caught in the middle. Such occurrences also stressed the wide gap in soldierly behavior between disciplined and undisciplined troops.

An example of this occurred in the small town of Miropolia (Volyn Province) at the height of political tensions in October, when a soldier-recruit broke a clay pot in a Jewish-owned shop and was set upon by the shopkeeper and other Jews. In retaliation, bystanders and other soldiers attacked the Jews and then turned their indignation against the Jewish community as a whole. Troops called in were able to end the looting of Jewish shops and homes the same night.[30] The Okhrana of Ekaterinoslav reported another altercation leading to a pogrom, when the induction of reservists in September 1904 brought a large number of recruits and their relatives to town. The otval'naia's (farewell parties) occasioned a lot of drinking, yet the liquor stores were closed; the only source of vodka was, reportedly, from Jews selling it illegally at inflated prices. Although it was bought and consumed, resentment and drunkenness mounted, and by the third day, about fifty reservists destroyed several stalls selling the illegal vodka. Local idlers and some workers joined in, and later that day an entire liquor store was destroyed and several restaurants and hotels vandalized. The police and a half-company of Cossacks on duty had to be reinforced by additional troops, but even then order could not be restored until the following day.[31]

Another wilder and lengthier example of such a riot occurred in Cherkassy (Kiev Province) in June 1905. This one is worth recounting in greater detail because of the close interaction with events and authorities in the town, showing how anti-Jewish rioting could combine both military and civilian dynamics.

On June 19, the day before the arrival of the first mobilized reservists, a fight over a bazaar transaction between a Jewish merchant and two soldiers nearly resulted in an attack on Jewish merchants. Earlier tensions over the widely believed provocative behavior of young Jews had recently roused the town's Christian population to talk of revenge. Hence, a setting ripe for a pogrom already existed in Cherkassy, although in this instance quick action by the police prevented the bazaar incident from escalating. The actual arrival of reservists from Poltava and Kiev on the twentieth was uneventful. A third contingent, arriving in Cherkassy on the twenty-second, brought a wild and insubordinate bunch to town, half of whom were drunk, some sitting and even dancing on top of the train cars. While most of them were successfully herded to camp, a number made their way into town, intending to avenge themselves on the Jewish population. The police document gives three reasons for this intention: resentment of the Jews for avoiding military induction; an encounter with "Jewish" agitators urging the reservists to refuse to go to war and to disobey their commanders; and local newspaper reports stating that "Jews" had thrown sulfuric acid in the faces of an assistant police chief and the director of a local prison.[32] The reservists' attacks on Jews had not gone very far when, toward evening, "mill workers, bums and teenagers (*bosiaki i podrostki*)" appeared on the streets, and the attacks on the Jews increased, compelling the district police superintendent (*Uezdnyi Ispravnik*) to call in troop reinforcements. Even so, he was unable to control the pogrom crowd, and when violence spread to the Old Bazaar, he asked the troop commander to prepare the troops to shoot. At the drum roll signaling the firing of a volley, the crowd dispersed. A cat-and-mouse game then ensued, with the crowd fleeing before the troops, only to resume its violence and vandalism on a neighboring street, to which the troops then moved in pursuit. The superintendent prevented the destruction of homes as well as he could and in one instance saved several young Jews from being beaten for allegedly having fired a gun. On the whole, the crowds were dispersed by 9:00 P.M. Police and troops patrolled the town throughout the night to prevent further disorders, although attempts at robbery and destruction continued the next morning, when some of the reservists and bums challenged the military units. One of the platoons on duty finally fired on them, wounding the peasant worker Roman Gladun and the reservist Il'ia Kozlov; Kozlov later died in the hospital. Several others were wounded in the course of the disorders, including fifteen Jews, several of them seriously. A Jewish self-defense group was also active during the pogrom, and one of the reservists was seriously wounded by a Jew's revolver shot. Over forty persons were arrested; and ninety-six homes, twenty-seven shops, and fourteen property lockers were destroyed, totaling

23,082 rubles (by the victims' estimate, but considered by the report to be "ex-aggerated").[33]

The Cherkassy events illustrate how the volatility of recruits, embodying a mixture of motives, could ignite a pogrom among civilians who already bore resentment against the Jews for events and fears of local import, and how both groups "understood" that it was the Jews who should bear the brunt of their anger. These events also show how a well-intentioned police force could be overwhelmed by the magnitude of a riot.

■   AMBIGUITIES

Thus far, we have described a kind of pattern of troop behavior, ap-plying the dichotomy of being under orders or not under orders. Under orders, soldiers normally behaved like automatons and did what they were told within the wide parameters laid down by their commanding officers and executed by their immediate leaders. When not under orders, they were liable to engage in many different kinds of activities, such as drunkenness, fighting, attending meetings and demonstrations of the right or left, and even attacking police and other soldiers. Yet this pattern provides only the broadest framework for under-standing troop behavior in the presence of anti-Jewish violence. Several other variables should be accounted for, including the specific antisemitic ideology most prevalent and potent in 1905, the habits of the troops trained for combat, lack of discipline, and the discretion of the officers and NCOs in actual charge of the troops.

First, it is important to recall that, beginning with the massive mobilization of troops in St. Petersburg to block the workers' procession on January 9, 1905 (subsequently known as "Bloody Sunday"), the role of soldiers throughout the mounting unrest for the remainder of the revolutionary year was to combat strikers, demonstrators, illegal meetings, and political processions. Army troops became the prime force employed to counter the "revolution." For all the ob-jections the higher command harbored, this is the kind of duty the officers and men deployed within the empire were accustomed to, not only in 1905, but also in combating labor and political unrest in earlier years. Normally, the kinds of troops so employed were Cossacks, whose elite and ethnic subculture suited them to act without compunction against urban labor disorders, although other mounted and foot soldiers were similarly deployed, especially against peasant unrest, but in cities as well. Beginning in early October 1905, as the announced railroad strike gathered momentum and students opened the universities and higher schools to public meetings, the army's consciousness of its role as the au-tocracy's shield against disorder and sedition was correspondingly heightened.

The emotionally polarized character of civic life therefore had reached a kind of flood stage by October, and soldiers, along with police and other identifiable representatives and symbols of autocratic authority, underwent intensified abuse and violence from "revolutionary" crowds. Prior to October 17, barricades were built and troops were fired upon and bombed in Odessa, Ekaterinoslav, Bialystok, and other cities, killing and wounding soldiers and police.[34] The domestic police duty of the troops had begun to pose a mortal danger, and this affected every soldier's wariness and anxiety when confronting the newly militant citizenry.

A long-standing police stereotype, identifying Jews with radicalism and revolution,[35] was heightened in 1905 by more recent developments, which should be reviewed in order to grasp the position of army troops in the tumultuous revolutionary events. In the course of 1905, all the revolutionary parties were more visible, active, and effective in mobilizing increasingly sizeable parts of the population. Police forces in most towns were overstretched, discouraged, and even demoralized by unexpected and increasingly unmanageable antigovernment crowds. Troops sent to reinforce the police had their own belief in the identity of Jews and revolutionaries strengthened. The overerepresentation of Jews in revolutionary parties and the prominence of Jewish youths in public demonstrations and other oppositional activities, especially in the Pale provinces, lent a false facticity to the perception of the police and the troops that the political enemies they were combating had an ethnic face. The fact that a number of specifically Jewish parties had been organized since the late 1890s supplied the stereotype with further "proof" of its veracity. Finally, these same parties—the Bund, Poalei Zion, and the Zionist Socialists—also organized armed, self-defense groups to protect Jewish communities from the increasing violence against Jews by deterring would-be pogromists and, if necessary, combating them.[36] This belief and the false conclusions drawn from Jewish defensive responses to gentile hostility served as a lubricant, for soldiers and civilians alike, in the mental slide from suspiciousness of Jews toward fear and hostility—and finally to the acceptance of open violence against them.

In the pressurized months of heightened antigovernment activity, army troops functioned in a setting in which combating revolution was widely assumed to be synonymous with combating Jews. The same prejudice certainly affected their officers and senior commanders. This belief underlay their behavior both when under orders and when acting on their own initiative. In Bialystok (Grodno Province), where Jews made up 64 percent of the population,[37] a bomb exploded in the market on June 21, 1905, wounding several policemen and passersby, probably the work of anarchist terrorists. Troops were called in the next day by the police, who began sabering and shooting people in Surash-kaia Gasse and neighboring streets, a poor Jewish quarter of the city whence, it was claimed, the revolver shots had originated. Police and troops shot up this same neighborhood twice more, on June 27 and again on July 30, when they used rifle butts to break up gatherings of Jews. That tactic led to a soldier shooting an elderly Jew named Feinstein after he protested against the brutal treatment. Later that day a bomb killed several Jews and wounded many others, including two soldiers. In response, the police and troops began shooting into Jewish homes, indiscriminately killing men, women, and children. The shooting spread throughout the city and lasted over four hours, although both Jewish and Christian witnesses claimed that no shots were fired from the Jewish side.[38] Apparently, these troops readily shared the police assumption that the bombs were thrown by Jews and had no problem brutalizing and killing randomly encountered Jews in response, even taking the initiative to do so.

Nothing mobilized the emotions of combat in soldiers like being bombed and shot at, which happened frequently enough, in October especially, keeping troops on edge and prepared to view riot duty as a wartime scenario of "shoot or be shot." This helps to explain why responsible troop commanders would address themselves to the source of gunfire first and regard looting, vandalism, and even the brutalization of Jews as of secondary concern. In a civilian situation in which only the army and the police possessed and used firearms legally, any gunfire not emanating from them could be viewed as illegal at least and, in the tense days of October, as hostile and in need of suppression. Thus there were reports of troops firing into buildings and homes from which shooting came and in some cases when they merely were told that shooting had occurred.[39]

In a different configuration of events, the close connection between the control of "revolutionary" crowds and anti-Jewish violence also was illustrated in Kamenets-Podol'sk (Podol'sk Province) on October 18, when the governor ordered troops to use force against a pro-manifesto meeting crowd, once its speeches began to insult the imperial ruler. The crowd, described as consisting of Jews, gymnasium students, and a number of women, was subjected only to the soldiers' rifle butts, and injuries were minimal. The next day, however, a group of Christian townspeople who also had been upset by the anti-tsarist speeches beat up some Jews carrying a red flag, and another group announced a pogrom and attacked a meeting of Jews on Novyi Boulevard, breaking the windows of Jewish shops. More Jewish property was attacked that night, although no Jews were hurt.[40] The events in Kamenets illustrate the unquestioning and commonly made association by both the Podol'sk governor and the townspeople of pro-manifesto sentiment with anti-tsarist sedition—and of both with Jews. For alarmed tsar loyalists, little distinction was made among pro-manifesto demonstrators, opponents of the autocracy, and revolutionaries. The routine identification in police documents and other venues of "Jews" in antigovernment crowds, when the crowd composition was otherwise characterized by occupational, gender, and age groups and not by ethnic identity, underscores the potency of this stereotype.

Most references to soldiers directly taking part in anti-Jewish violence imply that they were off duty, such as the Cossacks and soldiers who looted Nota Pronin's shop in Ekaterinoslav on October 21,[41] or the troops and police who took part in a pogrom that same day in Klintsy (Chernigov Province) led by the police superintendent (pristav),[42] or even during the Kishinev pogrom of April 1903.[43] Such instances of voluntary participation by soldiers in pogroms usually involved looting, reflecting the criminal amorality of plunderers everywhere and the material indigence of large parts of the Russian population, including Russian soldiers. As prevalent as indiscipline and rioting by individual soldiers were, however, more harm against Jews was likely perpetrated by troops nominally and ostensibly disciplined and under orders. Let us consider several cases that do not provide a definitive explanation, but that take us closer to some of the realities at play.

The west Siberian city of Tomsk witnessed a bloody standoff between several hundred railroad administrative workers, backed by the town's duma and its armed militia, and an ugly and bloodthirsty crowd of "patriots" and pogromists. Despite the fact that its Jewish population was much smaller than that of most Pale towns, the attack of Tomsk's "patriots" voiced anti-Jewish rhetoric from the beginning of their disputations with the town's progressives, and on the second day they turned their spite against Jewish homes and businesses. The case of Tomsk also illustrates the broader political animus and anxiety that lay behind all pogroms in 1905, which, in regions of denser Jewish settlement, focused almost exclusively on Jews. In Tomsk, a mutual civic enmity had been nurtured, on the one side by the antigovernment agitation of Tomsk's progressive citizens, their support of the railroaders, and their desire to replace Tomsk's police force. On the other side, the "patriots" had conceived a heated resentment against the railroad employees, whose general strike had caused them material hardship, and against "the Jews" (progressive forces), who they said were taking over the city. On the morning of October 20, the town's militia exchanged fire with a "patriot" crowd, some of whom had already not only vilified Jews, students, and railroad employees, but even assaulted some of them. Troops were summoned, and the militiamen then refused to agree to the demand of the colonel in charge to surrender their arms and instead retreated into the railroaders' building, already filled with some three hundred railroad employees, who had come to collect their salaries. The angry crowd tried to pursue the militiamen into the building, but the doors were barred, and the crowd had to satisfy themselves with shooting at those inside the building and brutalizing those outside whom they counted as belonging to "the unpatriotic." Later, the crowd set fire to the building, then prevented the fire brigade from extinguishing it. Throughout these events, the troops did not act to discipline the crowd or interdict its lawless behavior. Even the governor and the archbishop failed to dissuade the crowd from its attack on the railroad building. Nonetheless, the troops were able to allow the removal of the wounded on army stretchers, and soldiers helped rescue another group of employees, trapped by the "patriots" in an adjacent building.[44]

The Tomsk events illustrate a situation in which troop units, under the control of commanders who sought to maintain order and minimize violence, could be overwhelmed by the size, anger, and militancy of the "patriot" crowd. That being the case, the events in Tomsk also offer further insight into the interaction of army troops with a crowd of self-styled "patriots." Troop conduct presents different possible explanations: at worst, they were merely in sympathy with the "patriot" crowd and deliberately let them have their way; at best, troop behavior reflected the reluctance of their top commanders to take sides in the political standoff being enacted.[45] The formally correct behavior of those in charge at the scene, however, suggests a third reason, that they felt they could not control the crowd without shooting, which they were not willing to do. The great anger and numbers of the attacking crowd gave it the upper hand, and the troops' leaders may have felt they were in no position to take it on. It is also possible that the officers did not believe that an order to attack Russian, Christian commoners would be carried out by the troops or that the officers themselves did not want to give such an order.[46]

In Orsha, Mogilev Province, one encountered a completely different situation: one of those "patriotic processions" assembled on the occasion of the October Manifesto that often preceded attacks on Jews, led by District Police Superintendent (*Uezdnyi Ispravnik*) Vysotskii. As the principal police officer in town, he commanded the troops present, and he ordered them to accompany the procession. Ostensibly intended to protect the patriotic procession from attack by radicals, Vysotskii and his troops simultaneously lent the stamp of government approval to what began as a celebration of the tsar's "gift" of the manifesto, but degenerated into a mobile pogrom crowd, bent on avenging itself against the imagined enemies of the imperial ruler. The superintendent turned a blind eye to the anti-Jewish violence that some in the procession engaged in, and at one point he and most of the procession stood by while some of the crowd and the troops shot at and then attacked and plundered the homes of three Jewish families in a single compound, killing eight Jews in the process. A Captain Baranov reportedly participated fully in the slaughter and ransacking, along with his troops.[47]

The Orsha events also dramatize the decisive role the immediate troop commanders could play in pogroms. At one point, Vysotskii's procession encountered Army Captain Esipov leading another company of troops. Vysotskii put the captain in charge of the procession, while he sent his own troops to be fed. When the crowd again began to stone Jewish houses, Esipov immediately made it clear that he would not tolerate such behavior and threatened to shoot violators. Later he used his troops to rescue a Jewish couple, besieged by a mob in their home.[48] The contrast of Vysotskii's (or Baranov's) and Esipov's leadership highlights the crucial role of the officer in charge at the scene where the pogroms occurred. It suggests that inquiries into troop behavior should focus at least as much on the nature and quality of their direct leadership as on standing orders or the beliefs and qualities of the troops themselves.

Cases of overt indiscipline, that is, troops under orders but openly defying them, were fairly frequent in 1905, as John Bushnell's study documents. However, instances of indiscipline directed against Jews were probably rarer than violations of the loose discipline that governed off-duty behavior that was seen in the run-ins of off-duty soldiers with Jews cited earlier.[49] One example of clear-cut indiscipline occurred sometime during the October railroad strike, when a large crowd at the Razdel'naia station near Odessa began attacking Jews packed in one of the cars of an idled train, believing they had heard them yelling that they would "cut up the Russians and kill Russian children." Soldiers guarding the station joined the crowd, breaking the windows of the Jewish car with rifle butts, throwing Jews out of the car, and beating them. The soldier in charge, one Talimonov, was unable to regain control of his troops and stop the violence, as neither his security detail nor the train's engineer would assist him.[50] Finally, the stationmaster helped him by moving the train forward, presumably beyond the reach of the crowd, and Talimonov was able to reassert control.[51] This example of troop indiscipline illustrates a break in the chain of command that also might be attributable to faulty leadership.[52]

A hint that such indiscipline may have been more widespread than this single example indicates occurred in Ekaterinoslav's October pogrom, where an Okhrana report stated: "The soldiers, and especially the Cossacks, very reluctantly carried out the officers' commands to restore order and apparently sympathized with those who began the pogrom."[53] In the particularly vicious Orsha pogrom, Vysotskii's outrageous conduct led the provincial government to quickly replace him, even before the pogrom ended. The new superintendent came upon some troops watching a crowd attack shops in Orsha's bazaar. He asked the officer in charge to engage the rioters, but the latter refused, saying "that he could not take decisive measures because he was certain that the soldiers, [so] hostile toward the Jews, would not carry out his orders."[54] Whether this was from fear of losing his authority by giving an order that would be disobeyed or only the officer's excuse for his own reluctance to act is not clear from the document. Either possibility is equally plausible.

■   CONCLUSION

These examples illustrate much of the complexity of accounting for troop behavior prior to and during anti-Jewish riots. As a first approximation, we have established that troops under orders were not charged with protecting Jewish life, but with protecting government property and with disciplining unruly crowds during the intense civic activism that reached a high point in 1905 as a whole and boiled over in October. Generally speaking, it appears that soldiers under orders, while not tasked to protect Jews, were not ordered to attack them either. Evidence of troops openly disobeying orders in order to attack Jews is rare, the case of Razdel'naia Station being the exception that proves the case, or at least illuminates this conclusion. The possibility that individual officers ignored their charge to keep order and instead used their authority to permit soldiers to participate in pogroms, illustrated by the case of Orsha, seems a more common and likely possibility. The action of troops in Tomsk is most revealing of all, as it suggests that in a case of perfect discipline among the troops and officers, they failed to use force against a lawless and destructive mob because their commanders (in this case, including the governor himself) most likely felt in some sense unequal to the task, even though they clearly opposed the crowd's violence. The commanders limited themselves to dissuading the crowd from its excesses and used troops only to remove the wounded and to rescue some of the besieged.

The occurrence of shooting in the course of clashes with political oppositionists and during pogroms seems to have placed troops and their commanders in situations that triggered responses they were trained to make in combat situations. Unfamiliar and uncomfortable as they were with policing civilians, when the troops were shot at, they felt for a change that "they knew what to do": return fire and eliminate the source of mortal danger.

An examination of altercations of Jews with off-duty soldiers, that is, troops not under orders or direct supervision, indicated that soldiers, part of Russia's indigent underclasses, often got in fights with Jewish merchants which at times led to wider anti-Jewish violence. The frequent reports of soldiers present at pogroms most likely involved off-duty soldiers acting as individuals or those not under close supervision. Off-duty soldiers were as likely to get in fights with each other and with the police as with Jews or political opponents. A case of ambiguous duty and discipline occurred in the case of recruitment pogroms, where the heightened anxiety of inductees could give way to large-scale indiscipline, including attacks on Jews, as the examples of Ekaterinoslav and Cherkassy illustrated.

The cases of Orsha and Tomsk, where troops under the command of officers used deadly fire against Jews and other civilians in one case, and permitted mayhem through inaction in another, illustrate that, by commission or omission, troops under orders could do more violence than occurred through the voluntary participation or indiscipline of individual soldiers. The soldiers who harassed Jews and shot up a Jewish quarter in Bialystok on three occasions in June and July 1905 probably did so under the orders of commanders attempting to stop the terrorist violence that allegedly had been directed against them and, acting on prevailing prejudice, were probably seeking to avenge themselves on the imagined perpetrators.

These examples of troop interaction with the civilian and Jewish populations, mainly but not exclusively in the Pale of Settlement, highlight three features of the pogroms with which we may conclude: first, and most tentatively, the examples cited here suggest that for the most part disciplined troops, despite very likely causing more Jewish casualties than undisciplined troops or pogromists, did function as the machine-like instruments they were designed to be. Following orders and obeying one's superiors being the "default" position of military machines, they probably did more to avoid greater pogrom violence and destruction precisely because of that structure and function. This judgment certainly includes many ambiguous situations when troops, acting within the parameters of orders, actually were doing the bidding of pogromists, such as firing at the windows of houses from which shooting came or reportedly had come. Several of the examples cited in the previous paragraph suggest the opposite conclusion, of course; yet they are offset by many other incidents in which troops, present at or summoned to the site of rioting, acted to curtail it (see note 20). This contention also suggests that despite the misuse of troop units by commanders willing to do violence to Jews, the majority of them observed discipline and acted to maintain and restore order.

This study of troop behavior also reinforces broader observations, such as the fact that the 1905 revolution witnessed a great deal more violence than its compromised, constitutional outcome might imply, more than its moderate defenders expected, a violence that emanated from both revolutionaries and counterrevolutionaries. Although troops, police, and *pogromshchiki* (participants in pogroms) perpetrated the great bulk of the violence, Jews were not simply passive victims. Insofar as Jews played a disproportionately large role in the revolutionary movement, and even more so in the Pale, they also contributed to the violence, directly in a small way and indirectly through the indignant and exaggerated responses that their oppositionist activities provoked. The actions of armed Jewish self-defense groups and shooting by individual Jewish property owners defending their homes and businesses fueled the mistaken but nonetheless widespread public fear that all Jews were an armed, hostile danger to society. Significant and highly visible parts of Jewish communities were righteously opposed to the autocracy and favored the aims of the liberation movement, while even normally conservative property owners sometimes offered armed resistance to pogromists, even though it was illegal for most citizens to possess and use firearms. This militant and courageous response by Jews contrasts with the relative unpreparedness and absence of self-defense during the 1881–1882 pogroms,[55] and it marked the Russian Jewish community's great advance toward social and political modernity. Nevertheless, it also contributed to the overall level of violence in the 1905 era pogroms, given the political polarization and "great fear" that circulated. The chief student of the 1905 pogroms noted that the pogrom at Gomel was "more a fight than a pogrom" while "in Zhitomir there was no pogrom but a war."[56] Although these were two of the 1903–1906 pogroms in which Jews acquitted themselves well, the frequency and seriousness of determined resistance to the bullying of thugs and hooligans—and the heightened violence it occasioned—were unique to the 1903–1906 pogrom wave.

The final observation is that, from the viewpoint of the army, soldiers and officers alike, their behavior in the pogroms was dictated largely by the belief that they were defending the state against its enemies, which is the purpose of all legitimate military forces. That in Russia this led to a reluctance to defend Jews and a tendency to avoid harming their attackers bespeaks the strength of the belief that Jew and revolutionary were synonymous and interchangeable terms. In this sense, counterrevolutionary ideology and antisemitism comprised a seamless belief system that drew the military, willingly and unwillingly, because of a predictable sympathy for the government's jingoist defenders, onto the side of the *pogromshchiki*, whose actions enjoyed the shelter and support of that inactive majority in "patriot" pogrom crowds.

The practice of military forces killing innocent civilians in pursuit of the enemy is not new, nor has it disappeared in the present age of cyberwarfare. This chapter reveals the possibility of comparing Russian army troops shooting Jews during 1905's pogroms to more recent examples of troops shooting and bombing civilian bystanders in pursuit of the "terrorist" enemy, with as little actual prejudice toward the enemy's national identity and culture, or as much.

■   APPENDIX 1: BRIEF DEFINITION OF *POGROM*

A brief and admittedly inadequate definition of "pogrom" may at least help to illuminate those pogroms discussed here. Pogroms may be thought of as counterrevolutionary outbursts, the largest number of whose supporters believes that they are defending tsar, country, and sometimes religion by attacking their enemies, most commonly interpreted as Jews, but including others. It was jingoism blended with antisemitism that inspired the largest number of pogromists in the 1905 era. It has been said, and I have found, that pogromists may be separated into three strata: those who perpetrate the violence by vandalizing homes and shops and by injuring and murdering Jews (and others) and whom I have named *pogromshchiki*; those interested mainly in the plunder thus made available, the looters; and those who normally do not engage in either murder or plunder, but who swell the pogrom crowds that follow the *pogromshchiki* and whose presence lends indispensable support and encouragement to the latter. I have used the undeservedly neutral term "patriots" to refer to this group. The interaction of the first and last groups may be compared to that of a lynch mob, which contains both active lynchers and passive witnesses, in whose interest to a large degree the social ritual of the lynching is performed. "Pogromist" is used to refer to all participants, irrespective of motive.

■   APPENDIX 2: EXCERPTS FROM AN INSTRUCTION
    TO THE TROOPS ON HANDLING POPULAR UNREST

Paragraph 5: "If, with the approach of troops to an insubordinate (*nepovinuiushcheisia*) crowd engaged in no action of any kind harmful to the troops (threats, shooting, stones, sticks, etc.), then, without resorting to arms (*ne pribegaia k deistviiu oruzhiem*), the troops will quickly surround members of the crowd, force them into a compact mass, and warn them that in case of

Appendix 2 From an order of General Imeretinskii, Commander of the Warsaw Military District (c. 1905), RGVIA, 13140/1/780,11. 65–66, "Instruktsiia voiskam, vyzvannym dlia sodeistviia Grazhdanskim vlastiam v preduprezhdenii ili prekrashchenii narodnyx bezporiadkov i volnenii."

the slightest display of violent action, the crowd will be subdued (*istreblena*), then conveyed to a place designated by the civilian authorities or beyond the city where the insubordinate [crowd] will be turned over to the Civil or Judicial authorities.

■ Paragraph 7: "If, with the approach of troops to an insubordinate crowd, any kind of action against the troops is shown upon being surrounded, such as shooting, throwing sticks and stones, threats by any kind of weapon, or, [upon] disobedience to a given order, the troop commander, applying sections 17 and 18 of the second appendix to the Order on Garrison Service, will order resort to arms (*pristupit' k deistviiu oruzhiem*), [and] the latter action, without responsibility for its consequences, may be carried out at his discretion either until the complete defeat of the crowd, or [may be] suspended once he concludes that any further attempts at resistance to the troops by the insubordinate crowd is no longer possible."

REFUGEES AND ANTISEMITISM IN HUNGARY DURING THE FIRST WORLD WAR

By the summer of 1918, Austria-Hungary had endured four long years of war. More than a million of its soldiers had died; the specter of defeat and disintegration haunted its leaders. Accusations and recriminations grew louder and louder. It was in this context that an angry debate broke out in the city council of Nagyvárad, a city in the eastern part of the Hungarian kingdom (the city today is called Oradea and is in Romania). At an otherwise routine meeting, a handful of city councilors suddenly asserted that Nagyvárad had too many "Galicians," a pointed reference to the refugees, many of them Jewish, who had arrived in Nagyvárad in the first years of the war. The councilors insisted that the refugees be evicted and their apartments given to Hungarians.[1] In response, the police investigated the matter. The police found evidence of only fifty-three Galician families in the city, of whom seventeen had already left, five had reasons why they could not leave, ten had residence permits from the Hungarian Ministry of the Interior, and twelve had secured permits from the local housing office. This left only nine families living illegally in a city whose wartime population had grown by ten thousand. At a subsequent meeting, one city councilor nevertheless demanded that the police immediately evict the nine families and urged the city to request that the Ministry of the Interior revoke the permits it had granted to the ten families. "I consider it necessary," he said, "not just to remove the Galicians, but because of the current food supply and state of war, to deal with all the foreigners."[2] That the Galicians were war refugees and had come from the Austrian half of the monarchy did not matter.

At this point the long-serving mayor of Nagyvárad lost his patience. In office since 1902, Károly Rimler was a moderate, a liberal, and a Lutheran. His angry words revealed what this debate had always been about: the presence in Nagyvárad of Rabbi Yisroel Hager, a Hassidic rabbi who had arrived in Nagyvárad early in 1915. Addressing his opponents, the mayor stated: "Concerning the oft-mentioned Vizhnitzer Rabbi, I would like to inform the honorable member of the city council that [Rabbi Hager] and his family, in addition to his

236

followers, are in Nagyvárad on the order of the Hungarian Ministry of the Interior at the request of the Austrian Ministry of the Interior." The mayor angrily concluded by reminding the council that "[w]e live in a state of law! That is how this matter will be handled. It cannot be handled in a brutal, violent manner." The motion to evict the rabbi was tabled, and he and his followers remained in Hungary until the end of the war.

By focusing on the unfortunate Rabbi Hager, this chapter examines how the residents of one Hungarian city responded to the arrival of Jewish refugees during the First World War. The competing responses to these outsiders, this chapter argues, allow us to chart the strength and intensity of antisemitism in Hungary over the course of the war. At its most basic level, this study joins recent work that has attempted to shift scholars' attention away from the battlefronts of western Europe and instead explores one of the First World War's "other fronts." We still know surprisingly little about the civilian experiences of the war in much of eastern and southeastern Europe. With its emphasis on refugees, this study also joins a growing literature on the movement and involuntary displacement of millions of civilians during the war.[3] Historians have begun to connect the experience of refugees in Belgium and France in 1914 to later events in Galicia, Serbia, the Ottoman Empire, and elsewhere. Finally, in examining antisemitism, this chapter takes seriously historian Omer Bartov's claim that the First World War set in motion a "fundamental transformation" of the categories of "foe and friend, victim and perpetrator" in many European states.[4] It examines how, in the context of war, neighbors and fellow townspeople could be seen as enemies no less perilous than those at the front.

The present study builds upon important recent work on Hungarian antisemitism. Over the past decade, scholars such as Péter Bihari, Paul Hanebrink, and Rebekah Klein-Pejšová have done much to illuminate how the war radicalized and reinforced Hungarian antisemitism.[5] This scholarship adds to earlier research by Péter Pastor, Gábor Vermes, and others on the Hungarian home front.[6] Yet such work almost always takes as its starting point the state apparatus and the capital city of Budapest; the war's effects on the provinces, where the bulk of the population lived, is still not well understood. Nor have scholars fully explored the impact of refugees on places far removed from the capital city and the front lines.

A key assumption behind this chapter is that local studies can help us understand the sharpening of antisemitism in Hungary. This chapter thus examines how the arrival of Jewish refugees in one provincial town triggered a wide range of responses from key players, including the city government, local press, middle-class spokesmen, and the Jewish community. This activity mattered for at least three reasons. First, the war held the potential for radically new and ever changeable conceptions of the local community. The arrival and enduring presence of refugees, in other words, forced locals to reevaluate their conceptions of "us" and "them." Second, these responses mattered not only because they shaped wartime attitudes and exposed social tensions, but also because definitions of who "belonged" mattered in material ways and directly influenced the wartime distribution of food, charity, housing, and residence permits. Last, how people responded to strangers—and the extent to which they recognized these outsiders as fellow citizens engaged in a common struggle—can shed light on how people in the provinces understood the meaning of the war: that is, what they were fighting for, what they were fighting against, what the war had changed, and why the war was being lost. To pursue these arguments, the chapter first describes Nagyvárad at the start of the war. It then analyzes the arrival of the Hasidic refugees and the first attacks on them in the local press. Finally, it outlines the ways in which antisemitism breached the bastions of liberal Hungary (the city council, the press, associations) in Nagyvárad in the last years of the war.

■   THE FIRST REFUGEES

Before the war, a song named "... Nach Grosswardein" had been popular in the cabarets of Budapest. Aimed at Jewish audiences, it humorously described several Budapest Jews who planned to visit Grosswardein (the German and Yiddish name for Nagyvárad), a city of more than sixty thousand residents some 160 miles east of Budapest, at the eastern edge of the Hungarian Great Plain. The song celebrated Grosswardein for its beautiful women, lively markets, and colorful local figures:

> When it's market day in Grosswardein
> One sees the Jews, tall and short
> Merchants, beggars and hawkers with their goods
> Little thieves and all sorts of ruffians.[7]

The song had some basis in fact: nearly one in four residents of Nagyvárad was Jewish, and Jews played an active role in the city's political, economic, and cultural life. There were Jewish city councilors, medical officials, and policemen (although few Jews served in the upper reaches of the courts and county administration). "Jews raised the city out of provincialism," wrote the poet Endre Ady, who worked there as a journalist.[8] Indeed, the prominence of Jews in Nagyvárad led some observers to overestimate their share of the population.[9] A more careful examination reveals a diverse population, one that included wealthy

"A very pretty, pleasant little metropolis" reads an early twentieth-century postcard, whose author has helpfully identified the imposing Orthodox synagogue on the right riverbank. The smokestacks in the distance testify to the city's industrial growth, just as the buildings in the foreground hint at its commercial activity.

merchants and celebrated distillers as well as poor peddlers and marginal craftsmen. Better-off Jews lived in Nagyvárad's newer neighborhoods and Secessionist apartment buildings; poorer Jews lived in one-story houses in the crowded older districts. The former were likely to attend the imposing Neolog (moderate reform) synagogue, the latter the more modest Orthodox synagogue. The song ". . . Nach Grosswardein" had it right: one could see Jews of all kinds in Nagyvárad.[10]

Antisemitism also dwelled in Nagyvárad, as well as in the surrounding countryside, where Christians often saw Jews as an alien and unwelcome presence. In the city, antisemitism was more muted, revealing itself in subtle forms of segregation and prejudice. Historical sources that otherwise praise prewar Christian-Jewish relations reveal that some social clubs admitted only Christians and that city doctors routinely refused to treat poor Jews.[11] Importantly, Nagyvárad had a large Roman Catholic population, with its dense network of Catholic schools, charities, reading circles, and newspapers. From the 1890s onward, Catholics across Hungary had proven increasingly receptive to antisemitic messages. A fierce struggle over the introduction of civil marriage had alienated many Catholics from the Hungarian state, even as it spurred Catholic political activism and social mobilization. In Nagyvárad, Catholics could take pride in their long history and close connection to Saint László (Ladislas), the revered medieval Hungarian king who was later canonized and buried there. But Nagyvárad's Catholics could also feel besieged: although the city itself had a slim plurality of Catholics, the surrounding countryside was largely populated by Calvinists, Greek Catholics, and Eastern Orthodox.

Antisemitism nonetheless remained marginal in Nagyvárad before 1914. It ran counter to the town leaders' strong local patriotism, which held that Nagyvárad's many religious and ethnic groups had always lived in peace and come together during moments of crisis. The mayor's remarks quoted previously also give evidence of the broad liberalism of local elites, which had certain limits (especially when it came to socialists or Romanians) but did help to minimize the influence of antisemitism in public affairs before the war. So too did their firm commitment to public order, which they backed up with thousands of soldiers garrisoned in the city.

War would change this and much else. Almost overnight, the war changed patterns of mobility, as well as the meanings attached to different movements of people. The residents of this region, of course, had been highly mobile before 1914. Economic motives had set many people in motion, including highlanders who went to the plains to work in the summer and peasants who left their villages for distant cities in Hungary and North America. The outbreak of war in July 1914 pushed the residents of Nagyvárad and the surrounding countryside in new directions and militarized their movements. This process began with mobilization in the late summer of 1914, as villagers from across the region streamed into Nagyvárad to get uniforms, guns, and a bit of last-minute training before setting out for the front. The wounded, prisoners of war, and soldiers on leave soon made this trip in reverse. Women traveled great distances to visit family members in hospitals, and they also came to Nagyvárad to work in the growing munitions industry. As a result, the population of Nagyvárad grew during wartime, but it also shifted: there were fewer men of military age and more newcomers. These sudden changes must have been unsettling for many residents.

This mixture of movement and disorientation can be seen in the war memoirs of Pál Szabó, a poor day laborer from a small village near Nagyvárad. Szabó was constantly in motion until the army called him up. He was lucky to have a bicycle, which he used to go from one estate to another, planting, weeding, and harvesting crops; he and a friend later poached fish, rode an hour to Nagyvárad, and sold them to restaurants. In Nagyvárad, Szabó marveled at the city's soldiers, movies, and women's orchestra. But for Szabó, the cumulative effect of the war, with its constant movement and new experiences, was destructive and dislocating: "Our old lives finally disappeared along with our old, kindly, dear village; what now existed in the village was no longer ours."[12] What he found in Nagyvárad was equally unsettling. Yet Szabó was young and possessed what we might call local knowledge. What about refugees, who did not have such resources?

The first months of the war were a military disaster for Austria-Hungary. Russia quickly occupied large parts of Galicia and Bucovina, two provinces in the Austrian half of the monarchy, as well as parts of northeastern Hungary. When Russian troops entered Habsburg territory, tens of thousands of civilians fled ahead of them. Because the Carpathian Mountains covered much of this region of Hungary, contemporaries often spoke of "Carpathian" refugees. For the most part, the refugees respected the monarchy's administrative divisions and followed its railroad lines, with the result that the "Austrian" refugees headed to Vienna and its hinterlands and the "Hungarian" refugees went to Budapest and other cities across Hungary. Crucially, Jews and Ukrainians (or Ruthenians, as they were then called) comprised the lion's share of these refugees.

The first refugees began to reach Nagyvárad in early October 1914. They arrived at a time when the population's short war illusions were rapidly dissipating, but its commitment to solidarity and sacrifice held firm. The refugees thus encountered men and women who had recently showered departing soldiers with alcohol and food and who would soon sacrifice their wedding bands and church bells, strip copper from their churches and synagogues, observe smoke- and meat-free days, and support many other charitable undertakings. Women played an important role in this work: without their labor, the hastily improvised hospitals, soup kitchens, nurseries, and food distribution programs could not have functioned.

The Jewish population of Nagyvárad threw itself into the war effort. Individuals subscribed to war loans and made donations to soldiers on the front. Working together, the Neolog and Orthodox communities established a military hospital, an orphanage, and a soup kitchen, which in October 1914 was feeding 450 people. In December, Nagyvárad Jews also launched a standing committee to help "Jewish Austrian citizens," promising to provide them with housing, clothes, food, and heating.[13] As Marsha Rozenblit has observed of Vienna, Jews had multiple reasons to aid the refugees, including humanitarianism, patriotism, and Jewish solidarity.[14]

In Nagyvárad in 1914, what counted most was that the Carpathian refugees were understood to be Hungarian citizens. Because most refugees were Jews and Ukrainians, "Hungarian" in this context was defined in a territorial rather than an ethnic or linguistic sense. In Nagyvárad, the local press carried stories about the refugees' dignity and patriotism, thereby emphasizing the wartime unity of all Hungarians (if not Austro-Hungarians!).

The Hungarian government, in contrast, saw the refugees as a danger to morale and a burden on public finances. To the authorities, the refugees' stories—and indeed, their very presence in the hinterland—threatened to undermine rather than bolster civilian morale.[15] From the start, the Hungarian government had taken the position that all Austrian refugees should be removed from Hungarian territory and demanded financial compensation from Vienna for those who stayed.[16] The government also urged the return of all Hungarian refugees to their home villages as soon as possible. In June 1915 the Hungarian minister of the interior outlined a plan to facilitate the return of the Carpathian refugees to Hungarian counties now cleared of Russian troops.[17] He promised an orderly return, in which the state would provide assistance to individuals and communities alike. The aim was to reunite families, restore local administration, and reopen schools. Of course, the Hungarian officials hoped to do all this cheaply, and they did not want to encourage the return of refugees who had already found work elsewhere in Hungary. They also made exceptions for wealthy individuals and, more grudgingly, for the elderly and ill.[18]

This was a bold plan. Its success rested on a set of assumptions about the future conduct of the war, none of which would be borne out: continued military success, economic stability, and governmental control over the movement of people. For now, the plan won the backing not just of most refugees, who were anxious to return to their homes, but of ordinary men and women across Hungary, who donated large sums of money to help rebuild ruined Carpathian villages. In Nagyvárad, the county administration alone donated 120,000 crowns to the cause. Small towns also pitched in: the nearby village of Bagamér, which had just over twenty-five hundred residents and few refugees, pledged 1,000 crowns to help rebuild villages, organized a door-to-door collection, and called on the local Calvinist and Greek Catholic priests to encourage their followers to make donations.[19]

Not all residents of the region were so generous. Already in 1914, some Nagyvárad newspapers grumbled that none of the refugees had actually seen Russians. A year later, indifference to the plight of the refugees had grown more widespread. In a small town near Nagyvárad, which earlier had donated five thousand crowns to rebuild Carpathian villages, the local newspaper decried the apathy of the town's leading men and women toward this "patriotic and cultural" cause.[20] The paper did not explain the source of the elites' indifference, but it was certainly not unique. Apathy took many forms as the war ground on: thinner crowds at train stations when wounded soldiers arrived, fewer visits to the military hospitals, lower subscriptions to war bonds, and less attention paid to the government's exhortations and directives. The larger issue was the population's growing fatigue with the war and the sense that people on the home front, more so than the soldiers in the trenches and the displaced refugees, were the real victims of the conflict.

The refugees, moreover, never fully shed their status as outsiders and, by extension, as a threat to the wider population. Like all combatants in the war, Austria-Hungary closely monitored foreign nationals of enemy states on its territory. There were few of them in Nagyvárad at the start of the war—thirty by one count—and these French tutors, English governesses, and Russian theater directors posed little threat to public security (Nagyvárad was hundreds of miles from the front).[21] The local authorities instead instructed the population to be on its guard against outsiders more generally. To this end, innkeepers were required to report all out-of-town guests and ordinary citizens to report all downed airplanes (never mind that it would take a very misdirected Russian or Serbian pilot to reach Nagyvárad!). Not even the countryside was safe: in June 1915 county authorities circulated a confidential report warning that Hungary's enemies would use all means possible to weaken it, including economic sabotage. It thus called on local officials to be on the lookout for "malicious foreign elements" who might try to burn fields of ripe grain.[22] Such fears were often projected onto refugees. Soon after their arrival, the liberal paper *Nagyvárad* warned that there might be "spies and traitors" among them and cautioned locals not to speak about military matters in the street or on trains and streetcars.[23] The point to be emphasized is that from very early in the war, "outsiders" proved to be a capacious category, and one that could encompass foreigners and refugees alike.

Still, little that happened in Nagyvárad in 1914 was unusual. The mixture of solidarity and fear that defined public life was typical of Europe in the first year of the war. In his study of Russian refugees, Peter Gatrell has documented the hardships faced by refugees, the resourcefulness of local officials, and the generosity of individual citizens, all of which sat uneasily alongside the suspicions of military authorities and the wariness of the settled population in the interior.[24] For the Jewish population of Nagyvárad the war had brought dramatic changes, as men marched toward the front and women organized unprecedented charitable work. This charity provided the main link between Jews and refugees, who had been largely welcomed in Nagyvárad and other towns and villages in the region. In retrospect, we can see worrisome signs: the government's overly optimistic plans to return the refugees to their devastated villages, the growing indifference of the wider public toward this cause, and the association of refugees with spying and sabotage. In the first year of the war, however, most refugees had been greeted as "loyal Hungarians." But what would happen when a small but visible group of new refugees—Hasidic Jews from Austrian territory—arrived in Nagyvárad?

■   THE VIZHNITZER REBBE

In military terms, the second year of the war was a good one for Austria-Hungary and the Central Powers, who pushed Russia out of Poland, held off the Entente in the Dardanelles, and overran Serbia in late 1915. These victories provided a distraction from the stalemate on the Western Front. For Austria-Hungary, whose armies were already stretched thin, Italy's entrance into the war in April 1915 added a deadly new front. Yet Italy's "betrayal" of its former allies enraged public opinion in Austria-Hungary and renewed the commitment of both citizens and soldiers to the war.

The population of Nagyvárad closely followed these events. The front pages of local newspapers contained updates from all fronts, diplomatic reports, military maps, and stories about the bravery of local soldiers. The papers' inner pages documented the war's heavy toll. Here the war meant military hospitals, funerals, quarantines, inflation, war loans, corruption, and shortages. Few of these issues directly involved refugees. To a handful of antisemitic writers in Nagyvárad, however, refugees were essential to understanding some of the most important issues that people on the home front faced: military service, public health, and the food supply. In the hands of antisemites, refugees became scapegoats for the ills visited on the home front, as well as surrogates for the entire Jewish community of Nagyvárad. The presence of a small but visible group of refugees fueled these attacks.

Rabbi Yisroel Hager arrived in Nagyvárad in early 1915. Hager was from Vizhnitz, a small village in Bucovina, then part of the Austrian half of the monarchy (today the town is called Vyzhnytsya and is in Ukraine). As the third Vizhnitzer Rebbe, Hager was a charismatic Hasidic leader with thousands of followers, including many in northeastern Hungary. When Vizhnitz fell to the Russians in 1914, he and seventy of his closest followers fled to neutral Romania and from there to Hungary.[25] The Hungarian Minister of the Interior granted them permission to settle in Nagyvárad, where they arrived by train in February 1915. The town's small Hasidic community welcomed Rabbi Hager, and a local merchant lent a building to house the refugees and serve as a makeshift synagogue. But the town's Orthodox and Neolog Jewish leaders regarded Hager warily, as they did the Hasidic movement as a whole.[26] Hager in turn conspicuously refused to eat meat until he had inspected the knives used by local Jewish ritual slaughterers. When the president of the Orthodox community at first told the butchers to ignore the request, Hager threatened to leave Nagyvárad. Through the intercession of an Orthodox rabbi from a nearby town, Hager and the local Jewish leaders eventually reached an understanding, according to which Hager and his followers promised to respect the ritual practices of the large Orthodox synagogue (which they sometimes attended) and the leadership of the yeshiva, as well as to refrain from charitable collections that would compete with the Jewish community's own fundraising campaigns. In return, Hager asked only to be left alone (and for the *mikvah* to be heated each morning!).[27]

In Jewish histories of Nagyvárad, the arrival of the Hasidic refugees was a defining moment: never before had the Hasidim been so numerous or so visible. Jewish memoirists and historians have used the episode to illuminate the enduring goodwill, deep religiosity, and mutual respect of the town's Jewish leaders. Once settled in Nagyvárad, Rabbi Hager often visited the Orthodox Rabbi Benjámin Fuchs to pay his respects, a favor Fuchs graciously returned. Furthermore, as one historian noted, Hager's presence increased the number of visitors to Nagyvárad and thus provided some economic benefits as well. The history of the Jewish community of Margitta (today Marghita in Romania), a small town close to Nagyvárad, tells a similar story of the war bringing an unprecedented number of Hasidic refugees. The apprehension of local Jews, it tells us, soon proved groundless: "The Hasidim adapted to the life of the village and earnestly took part in the social work of the community."[28] Seen in this light, the war seemed to increase feelings of Jewish solidarity and self-sufficiency.

Most people in Nagyvárad, it seems safe to say, probably took little notice of Rabbi Hager and his followers. By 1915 the number of refugees in Nagyvárad had declined, and at least one newspaper pointed out that the remainder included skilled workers who could help ease the local labor shortage.[29] Yet a number of locals saw things differently, and they increasingly raised their voices against the Jewish refugees. One barometer of wider opinion was Nagyvárad's Catholic newspaper, *Tiszántúl* (Beyond the Tisza). The paper appeared daily and reached readers of all social classes in the city and the surrounding countryside. In late 1915 it published an article that described Rabbi Hager's household.[30] The unnamed reporter emphasized the foreignness of the Hasidim's appearance and habits, including Hager's silk caftan and gold tableware, his followers' ceaseless study of Hebrew texts, and the many pilgrims who had come to Nagyvárad to seek the Vizhnitzer Rebbe's advice. The article condemned the Hasidim's living conditions: "They are loyal to their Bucovinian customs," it read, and "the filth in which they live is simply disgusting." It suggested that many people in Nagyvárad shared this revulsion, claiming, "Numerous complaints have arrived against them; there are far too many problems with them because their nature does not at all accept the requirements of hygiene and cleanliness. The dirtiness, which spreads all around them, is simply unbelievable." Such words tapped deep-rooted associations between "Eastern" Jews and contagion and summoned fears of the epidemic diseases that coursed through Europe during the war. To the author of this article, the solution was obvious: "Their departure would cause wide rejoicing in Nagyvárad, and in Jewish circles as well." In this analysis, then, refugees are seen as wholly different from and (because dirt equals disease, and disease equals death) a mortal threat to the local community; such logic inexorably leads to talk of their disappearance or removal. The logic is as familiar as it is frightening.

Opposition to Rabbi Hager—and to Jewish refugees more generally—in the second year of the war went far beyond questions of public health. It is ironic that Rabbi Hager, by all accounts a gentle man, ensconced in cramped quarters, surrounded by books, and presumably dreaming of a small town in Bucovina, became a touchstone in local debates about military service. Starting in 1915 and continuing to the end of the war, the Hungarian press began to discuss, sometimes openly and sometimes indirectly, the military contribution (or lack thereof) of different ethnic and religious groups and different regions within Austria-Hungary. The Austrian half of the monarchy was often the target of Hungarian anger. An editorial from a Nagyvárad paper in 1917 was typical: "Hungary has shed more blood than Austria," it read, and it accused Austrians of downplaying Hungarian losses.[31] But complaints about "shirking" also had local targets, and in Nagyvárad a number of antisemitic writers used Jewish refugees to suggest that Jews as a whole avoided serving on the front lines. The accusations started with individuals and anecdotes. For example, the article in the local Catholic paper mentioned previously reported that the police had called on Hager to remind him that some of his young followers had to serve in the army. Hager had apparently agreed and sent the authorities a letter with the names of three young men who had not yet performed military service. But when the police came to find the young men, they were nowhere to be found.

The arrival of Rabbi Hager triggered verbal attacks on Jews in another key area: the food supply. The connection between Hager and food was again tenuous: the Hasidim were not involved in the production, distribution, or sale of food in any significant way. What mattered was that Hager was foreign and Jewish, two qualities that antisemites linked to illegal economic activity on the home front. In histories of World War I, Hungary is often characterized as reasonably well supplied with food, particularly in comparison with Austria and especially Vienna, whose residents in turn accused Hungarians of withholding food.[32] Local histories of Nagyvárad take pride in the relative success of local authorities in keeping the city fed, noting that it was among the first cities in Hungary to introduce flour and bread coupons and that its city-run milk exchange and orchards helped ensure that the urban population received food.[33] Yet the city did not avoid rationing, shortages, food lines, angry letters to the authorities, and conflicts in the marketplace, most of them started by women.

In Nagyvárad, the question of food focused antisemitic attacks not just on refugees, but on the Jewish community as a whole. When local leaders took steps in early 1915 to enforce maximum prices and ensure a fair distribution of food, they made it clear that food would not be given to nonresidents (idegenek), who presumably had to rely on charity or the black market.[34] When these measures proved insufficient, locals called for action. Led by the Feminist Association, middle-class men and women in Nagyvárad attempted to organize a consumers' alliance, which had as its goal the tighter supervision of markets and prices. Although the alliance, in the words of one of its leaders, "did not want to accuse or be aggressive," in practice it allowed and even encouraged violent rhetoric. At its founding meeting, one speaker compared usurers to Cain and declared their activities treasonous.[35] The press likewise began to call for decisive action against outsiders who allegedly manipulated prices and hoarded goods. As the Catholic paper wrote: "Brokers, peddlers, middlemen, itinerant vendors. Where did they come from? Where do they live?"[36] It was all too easy to point fingers at the Jewish refugees, who were highly visible but largely defenseless.

From 1915 onward, accusations against "outsiders" and "foreigners" often expanded to include local Jews. The immediate cause was a series of trials against a number of Nagyvárad merchants, on the grounds that they had supplied the army and local markets with substandard goods. The most spectacular trial involved Sándor Ullmann, a respected local merchant, bibliophile, and for the past sixteen years, the president of the Orthodox community.[37] Ullmann was ultimately acquitted of charges that his firm had defrauded the army, but the trial left him a broken man and he died in 1919 at the age of forty-two. For one antisemitic writer, the fact that the Orthodox community had stood by their president was evidence of Jews' distinct behavior (különérzés) and "clannishness"; for the Catholic paper, the fact that many of the defendants in these trials were Jews did not just reflect the distinct occupational profile of Hungarian Jewry, but was evidence that for Jews, "money was the god."[38] In such attacks, the distinction between the Austrian, Hassidic refugees and the Hungarian, resident Jewish community disappeared: all were "Jews" and all were suspect.

In closing this section, it is worthwhile to contrast the vitriol directed against Rabbi Hager and other Jews in Nagyvárad with the treatment of an even larger group of refugees. In August 1916, Romania abandoned its neutrality and invaded Transylvania. Austria-Hungary had feared this attack since 1914, yet it was caught unprepared. Tens of thousands of refugees, most of them Hungarian-speaking, Roman Catholic Szeklers, streamed into Nagyvárad, which soon had fifteen thousand refugees, about one-quarter of the town's prewar population. Local charities and officials worked overtime to find them housing and food. But the city's resources were limited, and within a month, the mayor issued a statement urging the refugees to leave town for designated places of internment. Large numbers of Transylvanian refugees nonetheless remained in the city for the remainder of the war. Some writers used their presence to return to the Jewish refugees. The title of an article in the Catholic paper made the comparison plain: "Transylvanians—Galicians. Munitions Work—Usury."[39] The body of the article praised the Transylvanian refugees for rapidly accepting work in munitions factories. They stood in sharp contrast to the thousands of "Austrian refugees" or "Galicians," who allegedly engaged in speculation and cheating: "The sidelocks (pajesz) stay here, swimming in front of us, their caftans float, making food expensive in their wake. That is their war work." The conclusion here is obvious: refugees are not the problem, Jews are. By 1916, then, the Catholic press—and presumably some of its readers and other residents of Nagyvárad—had come to see Jews as the source of many of the economic, military, and material costs of the war.

■ "A SUBMARINE IN THE OPEN SEA"
   The final years of the war revealed the surprising resilience of the Hungarian home front, which endured shortages in the cities and military requisitions of food in the countryside. Nagyvárad and other towns in the region continued to subscribe to war bonds long after the hope of victory had been extinguished. Women's charitable work also continued unabated: in 1918, for example, a small town near Nagyvárad sent the army a huge donation, including 2,700 towels, 1,800 men's shirts, 597 sheets, and 251 pillow covers. The entire shipment weighed nearly 2,500 kilograms.[40]

   But clothes and linens were a poor defense against growing discontent and political polarization. In Nagyvárad, the statewide campaign for universal suffrage in 1917 created great excitement and large demonstrations, particularly among the middle classes. Workers in munitions plants, many of them women, also grew increasingly restive, and strikes punctuated the spring and summer of 1918. Ordinary people grumbled about local officials, whom they accused of incompetence and corruption.[41] Even while this was happening, however, state and local authorities embarked on an aggressive campaign against socialists and ethnic Romanians in the region. Officials who had once praised the loyalty of local Romanians now saw them as "internal enemies," and the crackdown on them would continue through the end of the war.

Antisemitism too moved from the margins to the mainstream. A key figure in this process was Péter Ágoston, a teacher at the Catholic law school. Ágoston was a curious figure: a socialist, materialist, journalist, and Freemason. He had been involved in left-wing politics in Nagyvárad since the turn of the century, which had brought him into contact with like-minded Jews. From the start, Ágoston had opposed the world war, which he blamed on German militarism. Citing his egalitarian principles, Ágoston had volunteered for the army (he was forty in 1914) but was soon dismissed, disillusioned with the stupidity of the officers and the military as a whole. He then devoted himself to writing, teaching, and a number of charitable organizations (his wife was a leading member of the Feminist Association). In early 1917 Ágoston published *A zsidók utja* (The Jews' Path), which promised its readers a disinterested examination of the "Jewish Question" in Hungary, but instead presented a familiar catalogue of antisemitic stereotypes under the guise of a pseudo–social-scientific methodology. Historian János Gyurgyák, who finds Ágoston somewhat interesting for being a left-wing antisemite, has accurately described *A zsidók utja* as full of "faulty logic, false historical facts, and baseless generalizations."[42] However flawed, the book struck a chord in 1917, and its attacks on Jews reverberated across Hungary. Although scholars have looked closely at debates surrounding his book in Budapest — Oszkár Jászi's journal, *Huszadik Század* (Twentieth Century), devoted an entire issue to it — little attention has been paid to its origins and reception in Nagyvárad.

Many of the ideas presented in *A zsidók utja* drew on Ágoston's wartime experiences in Nagyvárad. Although Ágoston later claimed that he had wanted to write a book about the "Jewish question" even before 1914, his experience of the war decisively shaped his thinking about Jews. Ágoston's wartime diary contained numerous observations — all of them negative — about the city's Jewish population, including their alleged refusal to serve in the army, ill-gotten gains from trade, and defense of war profiteers. Ágoston was obsessed with "Galician" Jews: a typical diary entry describes an incident, obviously heard secondhand, in which the son of an unidentified Galician rabbi promised to volunteer for the army but, according to Ágoston, clearly had no intention of fulfilling his promise and going to war.[43] Ágoston also used his diary to denounce local merchants whose sons avoided military service by starving themselves before their army medical examinations and the local Jewish hospital that allowed wounded Jewish soldiers to stay indefinitely and thus avoid returning to the front.[44] By mid-1915, such episodes had confirmed Ágoston's view that Jews had closed ranks against the rest of the population and that they had financial motivations to support the war. A few months later, when a local newspaper refused to publish an appeal from a Catholic charitable association led by Ágoston and days later published an appeal from the Jewish women's association, Ágoston responded bitterly in his journal: "Jews have closed themselves off from Hungarian society and are meanwhile winking at the Germans. For me the wartime experience has been horrible because now there is nobody on whom I can rely. Still, if I had to choose, I would fight against the Jews for the survival of the Hungarians. Some had predicted that a time would come when I would be against the Jews and it looks as though they were right."[45] *A zsidók utja* was thus the product of Ágoston's decision to "fight against the Jews." The book used sociological language and dealt in generalizations, and it did not mention events in Nagyvárad. But the problems it claimed to diagnose and the solutions it proposed had an obvious bearing on the Jewish community in Ágoston's hometown.

Refugees formed an implicit but important part of Ágoston's thinking. The association of Jews with mobility is central to *A zsidók utja*, which repeatedly asserts that Jews are "an immigrant people" (*bevándorló nép*) who live among "receiving peoples" (*fogadó népek*). Ágoston conceded that over the course of the nineteenth century some Jews had partially assimilated into Hungarian society, and he considered the mass conversion of Jews to Christianity one possible solution to the "Jewish Question." But to Ágoston, the continued immigration of "Eastern" Jews — with Rabbi Hager and his followers as but the latest wave — ensured that the "Jewish Question" would not go away. To Ágoston, these Eastern Jews were by definition unassimilible and as such posed a direct threat to Hungarian culture and to the prospects for democracy in Hungary. They served, moreover, as mementos of what assimilated Hungarian Jews once had been and, because of the clannishness exhibited by Jews during the war, as a warning of what they might again become as "foreign elements" came to dominate Hungarian Jewry. There are two points to make here. First, in Ágoston's writing, Galician Jews (if not Jews as a whole) are no longer just scapegoats for the misery caused by the war: they instead represent an existential threat to the Hungarian people and the Hungarian state. Second, it is plain that for Ágoston, Jews from Bucovina and Galicia simply have no place in Hungary; by Ágoston's logic, their removal is a necessary precondition for the successful assimilation of Hungarian Jews. *A zsidók utja*, in short, articulates what historian Maureen Healy has called "expulsion fantasies" — the desire to expel

physically outsiders from the community—and identified as one of main lega-
cies of the war.[46]

Ágoston's book did not go unchallenged in Nagyvárad. Local newspapers
uniformly criticized Ágoston for stirring up religious tensions during the war,
even if they differed widely in how vigorously they disputed his allegations
about Jews. Antal Sándor, a local Jewish journalist, sculptor, and like Ágoston,
a socialist, used a series of newspaper articles to demonstrate Ágoston's many
errors and ignorance of Judaism; these articles were later published as a pamphlet.[47] Another local Jewish writer, János Székely, also issued a pamphlet to
refute Ágoston.[48] Both Sándor and Székely agreed that Ágoston's book threatened Hungary's wartime unity: in Székely's strained metaphor, the book was "a
submarine in the open sea of Hungarian life," which had "torpedoed the boat in
which rowed the soldiers building the future Hungary." Both also agreed that
Hungary faced more dire social problems (wounded soldiers, workers' rights,
and popular education) than the "Jewish Question." Interestingly, the two differed in their discussion of Jewish refugees. Székely defended them by stating
that the influx of Jews from Galicia and Bucovina posed no threat to the strong
cultural and patriotic attachments Hungarian Jews felt toward their homeland; he added that Ágoston's attacks on the "dirty" traditional Jews revealed a
profound ignorance of Jewish law, with its emphasis on cleanliness. Sándor in
contrast held the Jewish refugees at arm's length. "The [Christian] orphans of
those volunteers who died heroic deaths for the Hungarian homeland are much
closer to my heart than Jews who have fled from Bucovina." He grimly concluded that the refugees should be handed a hoe and told to work in the fields;
but "if they do not want to work, then we will immediately send them back to
their homes." In Sándor's words, one hears hints that some Jews in Nagyvárad
no longer welcomed the refugees.

Ágoston's book soon led to the eruption of what was by all accounts a
"heated debate" in the Nagyvárad city council. In the past, the city council had
prided itself on collegiality and consensus. In July 1917, several months after the
appearance of A zsidók utja, the council took up the issue of whether it should
provide funding to a Catholic charitable organization for children led by Ágoston. Such requests for funding usually were approved without discussion, but
not in this case. Jakab Gábel, a highly respected school principal and influential member of the Orthodox Jewish community, angrily stated that he could
not support an association whose president preached humanism but "with his
deeds incited the deepest hatred and wanted to tear Hungarian society into
pieces."[49] Another Jewish councilor added that "he would not vote one cent for
someone who insulted him, his grandfather, father, and descendants because

of their religion."[50] Ágoston was not present to speak, but several other councilors responded to the allegations against him, with a number suggesting that the city council chambers "were not the place for confessionalization [*felekeze-tisesség*]." They would have preferred to avoid the subject altogether.

The fiction that the local authorities could—or would—ignore refugees and antisemitism could not be sustained indefinitely. The tenor of politics across Hungary was changing. In late 1917 and early 1918 the Hungarian minister of the interior repeatedly ordered that all "Austrian" refugees leave Hungarian territory.[51] In August 1918, in a well-publicized speech in the Upper House of the Hungarian Parliament, the Roman Catholic Bishop Ottokár Prohászka attacked socialists, radicals, and "Galicians" for endangering Hungary at a crucial juncture in the war. József Patai, the editor of an early Zionist periodical, helped unlock the meaning of the bishop's words: "[W]hen the Jew haters speak or write about *Galicians*, they do not mean the few hundred stranded 'Galician' refugees, but in fact the children and grandchildren of yesterday's 'Galicians,' that is the entire Hungarian Jewry. . . ."[52] For radicalized antisemites, the expulsion of refugees would not be the ending, but only the beginning of their solution to what Ágoston had called the "Jewish Question."

Like few events before it, the First World War had set people in motion. It had created a new landscape, one populated with soldiers, prisoners of war, munitions workers, refugees, and parentless children. In Nagyvárad and elsewhere, the arrival of strangers had unleashed powerful emotions, including profound feelings of solidarity and compassion, which found expression in an outpouring of charitable works and in cemeteries with soldiers from all regions and religions. At the same time, the war also summoned xenophobia from the depths, resulting in a heightened fear of real and imagined enemies: spies, speculators, saboteurs, ethnic minorities, foreigners, and outsiders more generally. Fear dissolved social ties and undermined trust. In Nagyvárad, the Neolog Rabbi Lipót Kecskeméti sadly observed in September 1918 that the war had destroyed people's sense of fellow humanity. Instead of uniting people, he said, the war had driven them apart: ". . . we [Jews] were among those who sacrificed the most; and those with whom we sacrificed together. . . . [now] deny what they lived through, and they direct lies at us and menace us with their hatred."[53]

■   CONCLUSION

In late 1918, Nagyvárad stood on the brink of postwar revolution, occupation, and incorporation into Romania. These events brought profound changes to the city and its population. They also created a new wave of refugees—this time *from* Nagyvárad, as thousands of ethnic Hungarians, many of them local landowners and state officials, abandoned the newly expanded Kingdom of Romania. We can only imagine what went through the mind of Rabbi Hager as he watched some of his former accusers hurriedly pack their belongings and dash across the border into Hungary. Hager remained in the city, now known as Oradea-Mare, surrounded by his family and followers. In his memoirs, Elie Wiesel vividly describes the rabbi's visit to his Romanian hometown and the sad but accurate prophecy Rabbi Hager made about the eight-year-old Elie: Hager said that the boy would "become a *gadol b'Israel*, a great man in Israel," but added that neither he nor Elie's mother would live to see that day.[54] Hager died in Oradea-Mare in 1936.

In Hungarian and Romanian historiography, the dramatic postwar events too often have obscured our view of the war itself. As I have attempted to show here, the war had a profound effect on places such as Nagyvárad, located far from the front lines. Several points seem especially salient. First, in thinking about the extremes of solidarity and xenophobia caused by the war, we need to pay close attention to how locals defined the "wartime community." In Nagyvárad, the "Spirit of 1914" united all "loyal Hungarians," which created a place, in theory if not always in practice, for refugees from northeastern Hungary, even if they were Jewish and did not speak the Hungarian language. But the subsequent redefinition of these refugees as "strangers" or "foreigners" undermined their position in the local community. The reception given to Rabbi Hager, doubly "foreign" as an Austrian and a Hassidic Jew, revealed another truth: namely, that not all forms of wartime solidarity were seen as acceptable by the majority population. Just as the authorities in Nagyvárad denounced socialism and Romanian nationalism as a betrayal of the war effort, antisemites saw Jewish solidarity—shown most plainly in the Jewish community's reception of refugees—as evidence not of patriotism or charity, but as a sign of Jews' purported "separatism" or "clannishness." How locals defined the "wartime community" mattered, since it directly influenced who received food, housing, and residence permits. The boundaries of the local community, in other words, determined who enjoyed basic human rights and who did not.

Where and how locals debated who belonged in the local community is also meaningful. Antisemitism had been present in prewar Nagyvárad, but other social, religious, political, and national tensions had as well. The experience of total war sharpened all these conflicts. If antisemitism stood out, it was not only for the volume and shrillness of antisemitic attacks, but also because they now sounded loudly in places where earlier they had been muted or not heard at all. Antisemitic rumors thus swirled around marketplaces, warehouses, and recruiting stations. At the same time, antisemitic leaders proved expert in using the institutions of formal and informal politics (associations, newspapers, city hall, and the courts) to broadcast their messages. The war had given these institutions greater power than they had ever possessed. Historian Omer Bartov has observed that across Europe, the war "strengthened the state's ability to identify, control, and supervise its population to an unprecedented degree."[55] This case study offers a reminder that struggles over state resources and power often played out on the local level, not just in parliaments and capital cities, and that what happened in the realm of informal politics often influenced formal political institutions.

Finally, it is important to recognize that the events described here had many parallels across Europe. When antisemites in Nagyvárad accused Jewish refugees of endangering public health, shirking military service, and threatening the food supply, they were moving in lockstep with antisemites in wartime Vienna, Berlin, and other cities. Even during wartime, wider, transnational forces were at work in Nagyvárad. Refugees fleeing enemy armies were the most visible proof of this, but ideas too skipped across borders. The Catholic press, which was central to wartime antisemitism in Nagyvárad, had long been a conduit to antisemitic movements elsewhere in Central Europe, and it continued to serve this function during the war. The world war brought a large measure of isolation and anomie to urban Europe, but it also enlivened some transnational connections and networks, a point antisemites understood very well.

Refugees mattered greatly, even in places far from the front lines. In Nagyvárad, the arrival of refugees helped some residents attach meaning to a world war that was otherwise disorienting, disruptive, and distant. Global anxieties and fears could be projected onto refugees glimpsed in the streets and described in the local newspaper. More than a century ago, the sociologist Georg Simmel observed that when faced with strangers, "the consciousness of having only the absolutely general in common has exactly the effect of putting a special emphasis on what is not common."[56] In this town in Hungary, the bonds that held many residents to the war refugees — a sense of participating in a common cause — dissolved all too quickly. What remained was a profound sense of difference, a strong current of fear, and a growing wave of antisemitism.

AFTERWORD
EUROPEAN ANTISEMITISM—
THE SEARCH FOR A PATTERN

Riots in Galicia, anti-Jewish violence in Habsburg Croatia, a publishing campaign by self-identified Catholics in France, the writings of a Catholic newspaper in Milan, a village uprising in Romania, political protest and anti-Jewish violence in Moravia, an anti-immigrant association in the East End of London, a trial for bigamy in Leoben, reverberations of the blood libel on the Greek isles, violence and social unrest in rural Lithuania, the intervention of the Russian army in the 1903–1906 pogroms, and a campaign against Jewish refugees in Nagyvárad, Hungary, during the last years of the First World War: the essays before us open up manifestations of hostility, conflict, and violence that are both numerous and varied. While their chronological scope is confined to the last decades of the nineteenth century and the first decades of the twentieth, their field of vision is wide. It encompasses speech, the dissemination of the written word, criminal litigation, economic boycott, political protest, and finally, acts of physical violence.

The reader of our volume might ask if the field of vision is, in fact, too vast? Are there too many manifestations of antagonism, exclusion, and hostility to consider? Our contributors have worked to delineate the many sites of antisemitic agitation and violence in modern Europe. But what generalizations emerge? Are we dealing with a coherent phenomenon? Can we now find pattern in all of the detail?

One way, I think, to start to build a unified picture of modern European antisemitism, one that is both comprehensive and coherent, is to revisit the framing questions and observations laid out in our book's introduction. Robert Nemes's and Daniel Unowsky's opening claim, that the decades around 1900 witness a striking upsurge in manifestations of antisemitic aggression of all kinds, is clearly borne out by the evidence presented in our volume's individual contributions. From this perspective, variety in form does nothing to dilute the overall impression that one is dealing here with a phenomenon that achieved explosive force during this particular conjunction of time and space. Relations between Jewish Europeans and their non-Jewish neighbors—and between Jews and state institutions—were disrupted in ways that point to a shattering of the status quo in a variety of political and geographic settings and which raise fundamental questions about Jewish citizenship and belonging. For many of our authors, the first question to be addressed was what broke the existing social balance?

By social balance I do not wish to suggest that we ought to be looking for a dividing line separating friendship and enmity or pro-Jewish and anti-Jewish attitudes and behaviors. Indeed, as Gerald Surh rightly observes, negative attitudes toward Jews were rampant in Imperial Russia, extending from the most impoverished peasant to the upper echelons of the government (and, of course, to the tsar himself). Ethnic tensions and rivalries between Russians and Jews were more or less chronic, while worsening during the last decades of the nineteenth century. "Yet, for most years and for long decades, antisemitic views and feelings were compatible with widespread cohabitation, commercial cooperation, and even friendship in thousands of towns and villages throughout the Pale of Settlement." This observation could easily be applied to the towns and villages of Galicia, Moravia, Hungary, and Romania, to say nothing of Paris, Milan, or London. Clearly, the question before us is not whether non-Jewish Europeans liked their Jewish neighbors—this, in fact, is beside the point: we are not required to approve of, or like, our fellow citizens. Antisemitism is not a discourse of emotional preferences, and the study of modern antisemitism cannot produce satisfying answers if it focuses mainly on attitudes or even hostile speech. The key question, as articulated in our book's introduction and several contributions, has to do with the distortion and shattering of social institutions and with their eventual remapping.

From this perspective, the editors' insistence on awarding primary agency to place, to the thick description of local circumstances, offers the book's contributors the opportunity to explore, in varying settings, the crucial question of the production of disorder. It is only when day-to-day social structures and practices are carefully reconstructed that one can locate where, when, and under what circumstances they fall apart. Thus we learn that in the *shtetls* of Galicia in the summer of 1898, major incidents tended to follow a certain pattern, commencing in towns that were flooded with visitors from surrounding areas during market days, Sundays, Catholic holidays, or newly invented national festivals. Following confrontations with the military or the police, rioters would fan out into the countryside, attacking homes, taverns, and stores owned by Jews as they made their way home. It was in part the festive presence of outsiders—in this case, peasants—in the towns that worked to alter the stable structure of social relations, although the actual agitators and organizers of local violent incidents tended to be known and respected householders. At the same time, the very act of joining in—haranguing crowds, spreading rumors of imperial permission, looting shops—helped to establish a certain esprit among the rioters. Catholic peasants and small-town residents, we learn, acted to create a temporary community defined by both the violence in which they were swept up and the violence against the Jewish "other." In another essay, Michal Frankl explains that, for the Jewish and non-Jewish condominium in the Moravian towns to be shattered in October 1899, a combination of local, regional, and national ingredients—and actors—was required. Genuine political crisis in the form of the revocation of the Badeni language ordinances, local protest meetings, the Hilsner ritual murder trial, and targeted outside agitation produced the combustible brew that overturned long-standing, if delicate, structures of coexistence in this Austrian province. Occasionally the most mundane of events, such as the eviction of an inebriated customer from a Jewish-owned tavern, sufficed to spark a violent confrontation between communities.

The behavior of the regular army, army reservists, the police, and other state actors has been highlighted in a number of essays. In Galicia, newspapers reported on unruly crowds being dispersed by the military, while illustrators depicted Jews being rescued by gendarmes; outnumbered policemen fired live ammunition at rioters in Moravia; district captains in the Habsburg lands and governors in Imperial Russia responded to popular disturbances with determination, sometimes with cowardice, and occasionally with malice against Jewish victims. In the Ukrainian town of Chernigov in 1905, it was the imperial governor himself who organized patriotic demonstrations and then, with the collusion of the local police, directed violent action against the local Jewish population. The city's duma, in contrast, opposed the governor's tactics, appealed to the prime minister for assistance, and organized a fund to aid pogrom victims. Klaus Richter reports, in the context of the 1905 pogrom in Dusetos, in eastern Lithuania, that it is not possible to distinguish a systematic pattern of behavior on the part of tsarist officials toward Jews and Christian peasants. The direct participation of officials in pogroms seems to have been restricted to the lower ranks of the police, who were recruited from the local population and had conflicting loyalties to the state and to their village communities. Higher-ranking police officials rarely sided openly with the pogromists, but they often blamed the Jews for provoking violence through their unethical and "parasitic" behavior.

Gerald Surh notes, in his study of the role of the Russian army in the pogroms that accompanied the democratic revolution of 1905, that many contemporary observers—including the great historian Simon Dubnow—believed that the Russian government had orchestrated the violence against the Jews. Most recent historical writing rejects this view, although it had the virtue, at least, of accounting for the fact that the police and local authorities had delayed in responding to the riots and that some soldiers and police appeared to be taking part in the disturbances rather than acting to quell them. The army, of course, was better armed and trained than the police, was more disciplined, and had many more personnel. Remarkably it was responsible both for preventing and for instigating violence against Jews—and also against the rioters. The army simply did the most shooting and, as a result, was responsible for most of the pogrom violence. In those places where troops were acting under direct orders to stop the pogroms, they usually did so. It is doubtful that soldiers were ever given specific orders to protect Jews, but putting a stop to the looting and rioting usually had the same effect. When, on the other hand, they were commanded to move against antigovernment meetings and demonstrations, their actions could result in the deaths of many, including Jews. Soldiers who were off duty, travelling, or visiting their hometowns often mingled with the rioting crowds and took part in the violent festivities. Finally, the most volatile elements of the military appear to have been either freshly mobilized recruits or reservists, caught in the transition from civilian to military life—not yet subject to military discipline and, perhaps, rioting as a last gasp of civilian freedom.

In light of the emphasis in much historical writing on the role of ideology and rhetoric in modern European antisemitism, the close attention paid in our volume to relations on the ground, and in specific localities, has generated some surprising observations. For many of the rioters in Galicia and in Moravia, for example, the ideational cluster of modern antisemitism does not appear to have been a central motivating factor. Some rioters took part in the disturbances already armed with criminal records for assault and other violent crimes. Some joined the crowds in pursuit of free alcohol or to engage in opportunistic looting of homes and businesses. Some were inebriated to begin with. In the Galician case, what seems to have been most important in the minds of the rioters were the quickly spreading and persistent rumors of official permission, according to which violence against Jews had received the blessing of the highest authorities. Similar rumors accompanied pogroms in Imperial Russia from 1881 to 1882 and again in 1905. In Moravia many of the disturbances had been organized as protests against government nationality policies before veering off into anti-Jewish violence. When debates broke out in the city council of Nagyvárad, Hungary, in the summer of 1918 over the presence of Galician refugees, the agitation had as much to do with competition over increasingly scarce resources as with conventional antisemitism. Admittedly, the combined effects of long years of war, material deprivation, and a worsening military situation led the residents of this city to reconsider notions of belonging and "outsiderness"—eventually to redefine the nature of citizenship—but this transformation in political understanding was as much a product of local circumstances as of emerging political ideology.

Our insistence on reconstructing social conflict from the ground up in local settings has had the salutary effect of reminding us of the importance of social structures, material interests, mundane interpersonal relations, and contingency in the production of heightened hostility or violence. It is remarkable how infrequently local actors articulated, or even referred to, formal antisemitic ideology in framing or in justifying their actions. This silence is particularly surprising in light of the virtual explosion in antisemitic writing since the 1870s. Our authors have noted much of this production: Rohling's *The Talmud Jew* (1871), Drumont's *Jewish France* (1886), Jeż's *Jewish Secrets* (1898), *The Protocols of the Elders of Zion* (1903), to name only some of the works that were published and sold. One might add to the list of books and pamphlets the numerous newspapers from the turn of the century that promoted antisemitism as part of their political agenda: *Deutsches Volksblatt* (Vienna), *Staatsbürger Zeitung* (Berlin), *Libre Parole* (Paris), *L'Osservatore Cattolico* (Milan), and others. With so much writing on the so-called "Jewish Question," which sought to redress the recently achieved political emancipation or to block social integration through novel interpretations of Jewish danger, why do we hear only faint echoes of these ideas in places of face-to-face conflict? What role do ideology and rhetoric play in modern antisemitism?

To begin to address these questions, let us first consider the creative power of ideas in the transition to a *modern* antisemitism. Here we face a paradox of sorts. The very originality of antisemitism as a political ideology of the late nineteenth century rested on the newness of its rhetoric, on an epistemological shift from an understanding of Jews and Jewish culture in theological terms to a new form of knowledge based on an awareness of radical social, cultural, and racial difference. Pre-Enlightenment discussions of the place of Jews in society had derived from understandings of Judaism as both Christianity's precursor and its mirror opposite, the two engaged in mutually incompatible pursuits of truth and salvation. Nineteenth-century writers offered significantly new readings of the politics of identity, even if their work sometimes continued to betray religious underpinnings. The message, nevertheless, was new: the liberal order was corrupt and in danger of disintegration by virtue of a social mixing, which, while superficially succeeding, was ultimately impossible. The fact that this message may have been delivered by clerics, or in the defense of Christian society, does not mean that it comprised traditional, religious teaching. Finally, antisemitism presented a cluster of ideas (and a call for mobilization) that challenged the social, political, and economic order of an urbanizing and industri-alizing Europe.

And yet antisemitism's power, it turns out, does not rest in the coherence of its ideas—which is not very strong—but in its own sense of urgency and in the emotions that it is able to produce in others. It is a language of symbols and allusions, which lends itself more fruitfully to symbolic, discourse analysis than to intellectual history. The ideas in themselves are not that interesting, but their social and cultural reverberations are. Thus when anti-immigrant spokespeople expressed alarm at the influx of "Galicians" into Nagyvárad, they transmitted a code that was rich in meanings and allusions stretching back to the emer-gence of political antisemitism in Hungary in the 1870s, recalling the rhetoric surrounding the Tiszaeszlár ritual murder trial in 1883, and paying homage to the agitations for the "defense of Christian Hungary" that first emerged in the 1890s. The handwritten flyer that was posted on houses in a Galician village in 1898 offers another example of how antisemitic tropes were refracted in local settings. When the poster warned, "You have shed the blood of our savior and you have shed our blood. You have degraded our country, you rob our people, and you grow rich from our work. You are everywhere," it was recapitulating a repertoire of themes and associations—not carefully articulated ideas—in the form of catchphrases and slogans cloaked in common wisdom: a little ritual murder theory, a little economic critique, a little political analysis, a little tradi-tional Christian anti-Judaism—nothing too serious. What was taken seriously was the overall sentiment: it was right and appropriate to punish the Jews.

The second point worth noting is that, in the end, it is very difficult to know what impact ideas have on action, or put another way, how ideas get translated into collective or individual behavior. At a minimum, the evidence collected in our volume suggests that the relationship between ideas and praxis is not a linear one, nor is it one-directional. Antisemitic writers and publicists dissemi-nated their messages into a bustling, chaotic, and transnational marketplace to be picked up, sampled, and sometimes discarded by distracted consumers with other things on their minds. If I might extend the metaphor a little fur-ther, the shoppers themselves could also act as sellers, leaving behind theories and arguments for others to buy. From Daniel Unowsky's chapter, we learn that during the months of trials that followed the riots in Galicia, the rioters—now defendants—produced their own discursive understandings of the events in question. In this they were joined by witnesses, defense attorneys, and even the prosecution in the production of a narrative of "Catholic victimhood and Jewish provocation." Thus the episodes of rioting were followed by a struggle to interpret the violence, which led to the further institutionalization of discourses of incompatibility and difference. In the aftermath of the Moravian disturbances of 1899, Czech nationalist politicians rose to address the Austrian Reichsrat to denounce the tactics of the police, deny any fundamentally anti-semitic motives on the part of the rioters, and reduce expressions of anti-Jewish sentiment on the part of Czechs to a by-product of the nationality struggle in the Bohemian Lands. Antisemitism, in this reading of Czech politics, did not exist except as a function of the Czech and German nationality conflict, caused in part by the historical association of Jews with German culture and hege-mony. This disciplining of antisemitism to the narrative requirements of Czech national liberalism has in fact dominated Czech historiography until recent decades.

The tension in our volume between discourse and action leads to another sig-nificant observation. One cannot help but notice that the sites of the most pro-digious antisemitic writing in this period—Paris, Berlin, Vienna, and Milan—do *not* correspond, for the most part, to the locations in which riots and pogroms occurred. Why should that have been the case? Vicki Caron deftly illustrates the interweaving of anticapitalist, antirepublican, religious, and racial themes in the writings of Edouard Drumont, Joseph Lémann, Henri Desportes, and others in the 1880s and 1890s in France; the fevered discussions of Jewish "ritual murder" that a number of these works featured (in the absence of any formal trials); and the effects of this rhetorical agitation on popular attitudes in France as the Dreyfus affair was about to unfold. The rhetoric of this campaign may have been shrill, the language, at times, suggesting violence; but what was produced in the end was discourse—a protest against the modern, liberal, and secular order; a figurative call to arms, which left the physical battle to others. The court-martial of Alfred Dreyfus in 1894 and his unsuccessful retrial in 1899 justifiably caused alarm in the French Jewish community, but the Third Repub-lic ultimately emerged strengthened from the affair, and Jewish integration into French society continued unabated until the country's defeat in 1940.

Ulrich Wyrwa's chapter explores the peculiar career of the Italian newspaper *L'Osservatore Cattolico*, published in the northern Italian city of Milan, the capital of Lombardy. A number of oddities marked this paper's editorial policy: it agitated for an uncompromising Catholicism in a region where the Church historically had opposed Habsburg rule and where numerous priests had sup-ported the liberal revolutionary tradition. *L'Osservatore Cattolico* earned a reputation for being one of the most virulent antisemitic publications of the late nineteenth and early twentieth centuries, yet it issued from a city that had about three hundred Jews when the paper was founded, 0.1 percent of the city's population. From this isolated perch, the paper not only railed against the liberal order but, more importantly, came to specialize in the accusation of Jewish ritual murder, reporting on every rumor that passed through its doors as well as the major trials of the 1880s and 1890s. To the French and Italian cases of ineffectual antisemitic speech, one might well add the political-cultural campaigns in Berlin from around 1879 to the eve of the First World War, spearheaded by such individuals as Wilhelm Marr, Eugen Dühring, Adolf Stoecker, and Heinrich von Treitschke (and which Fritz Stern aptly labeled "the politics of cultural despair").

What we have in all three sites is cultural production as social and political critique issued from the margins of liberal society. It is a kind of sniper fire, threatening in tone, able to inflict some real damage here and there, but *not*, ultimately, a threat to the social, economic, political, and legal institutions at which it is taking aim. Antisemitism in these settings constitutes a discourse of protest, an effort to mobilize opinion and limited political action, but neither a revolutionary movement nor violent resistance. Most antisemitic speech is compatible with, and can be contained by, the legal, political, and social institutions of the liberal state. In a sense, liberalism produces the kind of antisemitism that is conducive to its political and legal structures. Hence, there were vile speeches and writing in England, France, Germany, and Italy and periods of riots and pogroms in parts (but not all) of Austria, Hungary, Romania, and Russia. When the liberal state is transformed into a revolutionary state, and constitutions succumb to direct political action, a serious opportunity opens up for rhetorical antisemitism to become institutionalized in practice. Then all bets are off.

In closing, I would like to move away from the binary oppositions that I have signaled thus far—local versus national and transnational, rhetoric versus violent action, religious versus secular, and modern versus traditional—to suggest another level of analysis. A call for future research might challenge the conventional wisdom that "all politics is local" by asking scholars to locate the specific pathways by which a transnational market in ideas alters the ways in which communities understand their own social institutions, or discover how a general environment of revolutionary instability overturns long-established patterns of coexistence and whether (to borrow from the insights of David Nirenberg, applied to a much earlier time period) after the settling of scores and infliction of punishment, the sites of riots and violent attacks settle down to reinscribe previous social arrangements. Antisemitic violence, in this reading, would not be understood as "exclusionary" as much as "corrective," functioning to shore up social hierarchies rather than to remove Jews from the social contract. With regard both to the relationship between ideas and praxis and to structural understandings of antisemitic protest, general appeals to "context" or to the availability of antisemitic writings are not very satisfying. What is needed is a painstaking reconstruction of the methods by which structure imposes itself on social dynamics and the articulations of activist writers manage to be picked up, digested, and revised in concrete settings.

My sense is that this kind of hard, fingernail-dirtying labor will renew the argument for the distinctiveness of antisemitism in modern Europe: not by ignoring historical precursors or eliding over contingent factors and circumstances, but by demonstrating antisemitism's profound intertwining with—and fundamental response to—the conditions of European modernity.

NOTES

Introduction

1. Sholom Aleichem, *The Old Country*, trans. Julius and Frances Butwin (New York: Crown, 1946), 260–264.

2. Sholom Aleichem, *Old Country Tales*, ed. and trans. Curt Leviant (New York: G. P. Putnam's Sons, 1966), 102.

3. Sholom Aleichem, *Old Country Tales*, 98–135.

4. For urbanization levels across Europe, see Andrew Lees and Lynn Hollen Lees, *Cities and the Making of Modern Europe* (Cambridge: Cambridge University Press, 2007), 133, which estimates that in 1910 only 41 percent of the European population lived in cities with more than five thousand inhabitants. Also see Peter Clark, *European Cities and Towns, 400–2000* (Oxford: Oxford University Press, 2009), 229–235.

5. For recent discussions of the nineteenth-century roots of the Holocaust, see Helmut Walser Smith, "Where the *Sonderweg* Debate Left Us," in *Imperial Germany Revisited*, ed. Sven Oliver Müller and Cornelius Torp (New York: Berghahn, 2011), 21–36; Donald Bloxham, "Europe, The Final Solution and the Dynamics of Intent," *Patterns of Prejudice* 44, no. 4 (2010): 317–335. For reasons of space, we have limited our footnotes to English-language sources. The case studies that follow cite important scholarship in nearly a dozen European languages.

6. On emigration, see John Doyle Klier, *Russians, Jews and the Pogroms of 1881–1882* (Cambridge: Cambridge University Press, 2011); on Jewish politics, see Ezra Mendelsohn, *On Modern Jewish Politics* (Oxford: Oxford University Press, 1993; Joshua Zimmerman, *Poles, Jews, and the Politics of Nationality: The Bund and the Polish Socialist Party in Late Czarist Russia, 1892–1914* (Madison: University of Wisconsin Press, 2003); Theodore R. Weeks, *From Assimilation to Antisemitism: The "Jewish Question" in Poland, 1850–1914* (DeKalb: Northern Illinois University Press, 2006); Joshua Shanes, *Diaspora Nationalism and Jewish Identity in Habsburg Galicia* (Cambridge: Cambridge University Press, 2012).

7. The classic work is Shulamit Volkov, "Antisemitism as a Cultural Code: Reflections on the History and Historiography of Antisemitism in Imperial Germany," *Leo Baeck Institute Year Book* 23 (1978): 25–46.

8. See Hillel Levine, *Economic Origins of Antisemitism: Poland and Its Jews in the Early Modern Period* (New Haven: Yale University Press, 1991); Derek J. Penslar, *Shylock's Children: Economics and Jewish Identity in Modern Europe* (Berkeley: University of California Press, 2001); Viktor Karady, *The Jews of Europe in the Modern Era: A Socio-Historical Outline*, trans. Tim Wilkinson (Budapest: Central European University Press, 2004).

9. Helmut Walser Smith, *The Butcher's Tale: Murder and Anti-Semitism in a German Town* (New York: Norton, 2002), 21.

10. See, for example, Jakab Katz, *From Prejudice to Destruction: Antisemitism, 1700–1933* (Cambridge: Harvard University Press, 1980); Robert Wistrich, *Antisemitism: The Longest*

Hatred (New York: Pantheon Books, 1991); Albert S. Lindemann, *Esau's Tears: Modern Anti-Semitism and the Rise of the Jews* (Cambridge: Cambridge University Press, 1997).

11. See especially Hillel Kieval, "The Importance of Place: Comparative Aspects of the Ritual Murder Trial in Modern Central Europe," in *Comparing Jewish Societies*, ed. Todd M. Endelman (Ann Arbor: University of Michigan Press, 1997), 135–65, as well as the essays in the following: Christhard Hoffmann, Werner Bergmann, and Helmut Walser Smith, eds., *Exclusionary Violence: Antisemitic Riots in Modern German History* (Ann Arbor: University of Michigan Press, 2002); Robert Blobaum, ed., *Antisemitism and Its Opponents in Modern Poland* (Ithaca: Cornell University Press, 2005); Jonathan Dekel-Chen et al., eds., *Anti-Jewish Violence: Rethinking the Pogrom in East European History* (Bloomington: Indiana University Press, 2010); Werner Bergmann and Ulrich Wyrwa, eds., *The Making of Antisemitism as a Political Movement: Political History as Cultural History (1879–1914)* in *Quest: Issues in Contemporary Jewish History* 3 (2012), http://www.quest-cdecjournal.it.

12. On the need for disaggregation, see Alison Frank, *Oil Empire: Visions of Prosperity in Austrian Galicia* (Cambridge: Harvard University Press, 2005), 253.

13. Oded Heilbronner, "From Antisemitic Peripheries to Antisemitic Centres: The Place of Antisemitism in Modern German History," *Journal of Contemporary History* 35, no. 4 (2000): 561.

14. Clifford Geertz, "Thick Description: Toward an Interpretative Theory of Culture," in Clifford Geertz, *The Interpretations of Cultures: Selected Essays* (New York: Basic Books, 1973), 5. On the wider influence of the pogroms and the Dreyfus affair, see Klier, *Russians, Jews and the Pogroms of 1881–1882*, esp. pt. 3; Sam Johnson, *Pogroms, Peasants, Jews: Britain and Europe's "Jewish Question," 1867–1925* (New York: Palgrave Macmillan, 2011); Louis Begley, *Why the Dreyfus Affair Matters* (New Haven: Yale University Press, 2009).

15. Stephen Eric Bronner, *A Rumor about the Jews* (New York: St. Martin's Press, 2000), 99–128.

16. On the wider influence of the pogroms and the Dreyfus affair, see Klier, *Russians, Jews and the Pogroms of 1881–1882*, esp. pt. 3; Sam Johnson, *Pogroms, Peasants, Jews: Britain and Europe's "Jewish Question," 1867–1925* (New York: Palgrave Macmillan, 2011); Louis Begley, *Why the Dreyfus Affair Matters* (New Haven: Yale University Press, 2009).

17. Brian Porter, "Anti-Semitism and the Search for a Catholic Modernity," in Blobaum, *Antisemitism and Its Opponents in Modern Poland*, 119.

18. See in particular Hoffmann, Bergmann, and Walser Smith, *Exclusionary Violence*.

19. Charles King, "The Micropolitics of Social Violence," *World Politics* 56, no. 3 (2004): 434.

20. King, "The Micropolitics of Social Violence," 448.

21. In addition to the works cited above, see Donald L. Niewyk, "Solving the 'Jewish Problem': Continuity and Change in German Antisemitism, 1871–1945," *Leo Baeck Year Book* 35 (1990): 335–370; Peter Pulzer, "The Return of Old Hatreds" and "The Response to Antisemitism," in *German-Jewish History in Modern Times*, ed. Michael A. Meyer and Michael Brenner, vol. 3 (New York: Columbia University Press, 1997), 196–280; Richard S. Levy, "Political Antisemitism in Germany and Austria," in *Antisemitism: A History*, ed.

Albert S. Lindemann and Richard S. Levy (Oxford: Oxford University Press, 2010), 121–135.

22. Klier, *Russians, Jews and the Pogroms of 1881–1882*; Dekel-Chen et al., *Anti-Jewish Violence*.

23. Marsha L. Rozenblit, *Reconstructing a National Identity: The Jews of Habsburg Austria during World War I* (Oxford: Oxford University Press, 2001).

24. Stefan Zweig, *The World of Yesterday*, intro. by Harry Zorn (Lincoln: University of Nebraska Press, 1964), 65.

1. Local Violence, Regional Politics, and State Crisis

1. These figures are incomplete. As of January 5, 1899, 522 accused still awaited verdicts. The number of communities counted by the Ministry of Justice does not include those that experienced attacks before the last week of May or after June 30. The Central Archives of Historical Records in Warsaw (hereafter AGAD), C. K. Ministerstwo Sprawiedliwości, box 307: 93; 106; 135.

2. On issues related to scholarly approaches to "ethnic" violence, see Paul Brass, *Theft of an Idol: Text and Context in the Representation of Collective Violence* (Princeton: Princeton University Press, 1997); Brass, ed., *Riots and Pogroms* (London and New York: Macmillan and NYU Press, 1996). On violence against Jews in this period, see Christhard Hoffmann, Werner Bergmann, and Helmut Walser Smith, eds., *Exclusionary Violence: Antisemitic Riots in Modern German History* (Ann Arbor: University of Michigan Press, 2002); Jonathan Dekel-Chen et al., eds., *Anti-Jewish Violence: Rethinking the Pogrom in East European History* (Bloomington: Indiana University Press, 2010).

3. Rogers Brubaker, *Ethnicity without Groups* (Cambridge: Harvard University Press, 2004).

4. When I started looking into this wave of anti-Jewish riots, little more had been published on the events than two articles by Frank Golczewski: "Die Westgalizischen Bauernunruhen 1898," in Frank Golczewski, *Polnisch-Jüdische Beziehungen, 1881–1922* (Wiesbaden: Steiner, 1981), 60–84; "Rural Anti-Semitism in Galicia before World War I" in *The Jews in Poland*, eds. Chimen Abramsky, Majiej Jachimczyk, and Antony Polonsky (Oxford: Oxford University Press, 1986), 97–105. In the last few years, the 1898 events have drawn increasing interest. See Daniel Unowsky, "Peasant Political Mobilization and the 1898 Anti-Jewish Riots in Western Galicia," *European History Quarterly* 40, no. 3 (July 2010): 412–435; Marcin Soboń, *Polacy wobec Żydów w Galicji doby autonomicznej w latach 1868–1914* (Cracow: Wydawn. Verso, 2011); Tim Buchen, *Antisemitismus in Galizien: Agitation, Gewalt, und Politik gegen Juden in der Habsburgermonarchie um 1900* (Berlin: Metropol, 2012).

5. *Österreichische Statistik*, Band LXIII (Wien: K. K. Statistischen Zentralkommission, 1902), Tab. XXI, XXXIII. The census also counted small Armenian Catholic, Greek and Armenian Orthodox, Protestant (Lutheran and Calvinist), and other religious groups—including one Galician Muslim.

6. Andrzej Laskowski, *Jasło w dobie autonomii galicyjskiej* (Jasło: Tow. Nauk. Societas Vistulana, 2007).

7. The rising price for such leases and higher taxes drove those who held the subleases to open

yet more taprooms in the last decades of the nineteenth century. Bohdan Baranowski, *Polska Karczma. Restauracja. Kawiarnia* (Wrocław: Zakład Narodowy im. Ossolínskic, 1979).

8. On the Jewish tavern keeper in Polish literature and culture, see Magda Opalski, *The Jewish Tavern-Keeper and His Tavern in Nineteenth-Century Polish Literature* (Jerusalem: Zalman Shazar Center for the Furtherance of the Study of Jewish History, 1986).

9. Alison Frank, *Oil Empire: Visions of Prosperity in Austrian Galicia* (Harvard: Harvard University Press, 2005).

10. By the 1890s Jews owned approximately 15 percent of estate lands and leased over 50 percent of leased estates. Kai Struve, "Gentry, Jews, and Peasants: Jews as Others in the Formation of the Modern Polish Nation in Rural Galicia," in *Creating the Other: Ethnic Conflict and Nationalism in Habsburg Central Europe*, ed. Nancy M. Wingfield (New York: Berghahn, 2003), 114.

11. On the social, cultural, and economic divides between Jews and Catholics, see Rosa Lehmann, *Symbiosis and Ambivalence: Poles and Jews in a Small Galician Town* (New York: Berghahn, 2001).

12. Hillel Kieval, "Middleman Minorities and Blood: Is There a Natural Economy of the Ritual Murder Accusation in Europe?" in *Essential Outsiders: Chinese and Jews in the Modern Transformation of Southeast Asia and Central Europe*, ed. Anthony Reid and Daniel Chirot (Seattle: University of Washington Press, 1997), 208–233. Kieval considers the question of local knowledge in "Ritual Murder as Political Discourse" in Hillel J. Kieval, *Languages of Community: The Jewish Experience in the Czech Lands* (Berkeley: University of California Press, 2000), 181–197.

13. Joseph Margoshes, *A World Apart: A Memoir of Jewish Life in Nineteenth Century Galicia* (Boston: Academic Studies Press, 2008); Joachim Schonefeld, *Jewish Life in Galicia under the Austro-Hungarian Empire and in the Reborn Poland, 1898–1939* (Hoboken, N.J.: Ktav Publishing House, 1985).

14. For an excellent overview of the mythic image of the Jew as the alien and dangerous "Other" in the Polish-speaking regions of eastern Europe, see Joanna Beata Michlic, *Poland's Threatening Other: The Image of the Jew from 1880 to Present* (Lincoln: University of Nebraska Press, 2006).

15. Mateusz Jeż, *Tajemnice Żydowskie* (Cracow: Nakładem Autora, 1898).*

16. On Joseph Samuel Bloch's public humiliation of Rohling in 1882, see Robert Wistrich, *The Jews of Vienna in the Age of Franz Joseph* (Oxford: Oxford University Press, 1989) and Ian Reifowitz, *Imagining an Austrian Nation: Joseph Samuel Bloch and the Search for a Multiethnic Austrian Identity, 1846–1919* (Boulder, Colo.: East European Monographs, 2003).

17. AGAD, C. K. Ministerstwo Sprawiedliwości, box 309: 358. The Ministry of Religion and Education, prompted by the Austrian-Israelite Union in Vienna, wrote Governor Piniński to express concern about *Jewish Secrets*. Central State Historical Archive of Ukraine in Lviv (TSDIAL), 146/4/3117/15. For the promoters of Catholic antisemitism, the confiscation of *Jewish Secrets* only confirmed the truth of the pamphlet's arguments. *Prawda*, March 25 and June 5, 1898.

18. At the same time, the leadership held off efforts by the clergy to dominate the party and succeeded in keeping control in the hands of the wealthy peasantry.

19. Polish liberal democrats, including Henryk Rewakowicz, editor of *Kurjer Lwowski*, played a role in the organization of this party. Secular/nationalist-oriented radical Bolesław Wysłouch edited the main publication of the party, *Przyjaciel Ludu*. He and his wife Maria came to Lemberg in the 1880s to escape the censorship of Russian Poland. See Krzystof Dunin-Wąsowicz, *Jan Stapiński Trybun ludu wiejskiego* (Warsaw: Książka i Wiedza, 1969); Peter Brock, "Bolesław Wysłouch: Founder of the Polish Peasant Party," *Slavonic and East European Review* 30, no. 4 (1951): 139–174; Dunin-Wąsowicz, *Dzieje Stonnictwa Ludowego w Galicji* (Warsaw: Ludowa Spółdzielnia Wydawnicza, 1956).

20. On Stojałowski, see "Herrschaft in der Krise—der 'Demagoge in der Soutane' fordert die galizischen Allerheiligen" in *Imperiale Herrschaft in der Provinz: Repräsentationen politischer Macht im späten Zarenreich*, ed. Jörg Baberowski, David Feest, and Christoph Gumb (Frankfurt am Main: Campus, 2008), 331–355; Anna Staudacher, "Der Bauernaggitator Stanisław Stojałowski: Priester, Journalist und Abgeordneter zum Österreichischen Reichsrat," in *Römische historische Mitteilungen* 25 (1983): 165–203; Fr. Kacki, *Ks. Stanisław Stojałowski i jego działalność polityczna* (Lwów: Kasa im. Rektora J. Mianowskiego, Instytut Popierania Polskiej Twórczości Naukowej, 1937).

21. Antoni Gurnicz, *Kółka rolnicze w Galicji* (Warsaw: Ludowa Spółdzielnia Wyd., 1967).

22. On the political changes described here, see, above all, Harald Binder, *Galizien in Wien: Parteien, Wahlen, Fraktionen und Abgeordnete im Übergang zur Massenpolitik* (Vienna: Verlag der Österreichischen Akademie der Wissenschaften, 2005). Also, Kai Struve, *Bauern und Nation in Galizien: Über Zugehörigkeit und soziale Emanzipation im 19. Jahrhundert* (Göttingen: Vandenhoeck and Ruprecht, 2005).

23. *Naprzód*, February 10, 1898, p. 1.

24. *Dziennik Polski*, March 23, 1898, p. 1; *Dr. Bloch's Österreichische Wochenschrift*, May 27, 1898, p. 415; *Wieniec Polski*, April 1, 1898.

25. For these dramatic events, see *Kurjer Lwowski*, June 25, 1898, p. 1. On Stapiński, one of the most important and charismatic of the peasant politicians in the People's Party, see Dunin-Wąsowicz, *Jan Stapiński*.

26. *Pszczółka*, June 26, 1898, p. 1.

27. See, among others, Vicki Caron, "Catholic Political Mobilization and Antisemitic Violence in Fin de Siècle France: The Case of the Union Nationale," *Journal of Modern History* 81, no. 2 (2009): 294–346; Robert Michael, *A History of Catholic Antisemitism: The Dark Side of the Church* (New York: Palgrave Macmillan, 2008); David Kertzer, *The Popes Against the Jews: The Vatican's Role in the Rise of Modern Anti-Semitism* (New York: Alfred A. Knopf, 2001); Brian Porter-Szűcs, *Faith and Fatherland: Catholicism, Modernity, and Poland* (New York: Oxford University Press, 2011).

28. TSDIAL, 146/4/3126/45.

29. AGAD, C. K. Ministerstwo Sprawiedliwości, box 308: 297.

30. TSDIAL, 146/4/3126/40; AGAD, C. K. Ministerstwo Sprawiedliwości, box 309: 358.

31. For trial testimony, see *Kurjer Lwowski*, August 18, 1898, p. 2; *Głos Narodu*, August 17,

1898; *Dziennik Polski*, August 17, 1898, p. 2. Miras received a one-year term in prison for his leading role in the violence. The incident in Frysztak sparked several internal investigations and offered fodder for the political leaders of the peasant parties, who repeatedly pressured the Vienna government to take action against those responsible for the twelve deaths. TSDIAL, 146/4/3128: 26.

32. AGAD, C. K. Ministerstwo Sprawiedliwości, box 308: 242; *Kurjer Lwowski*, August 23, 1898.

33. AGAD, C. K. Ministerstwo Sprawiedliwości, box 309: 358.

34. *Głos Narodu*, August 11, 1898, p. 2; *Głos Narodu*, August 13, 1898, p. 2.

35. AGAD, C. K. Ministerstwo Sprawiedliwości, box 310: 54–56; TSDIAL, 146/4/3117/1–2; *Kurjer Lwowski*, March 20, 1898, p. 1. For the trial of those involved, see *Głos Narodu*, July 21, 1898.

36. Tim Buchen brought this double meaning of *żyd* to my attention.

37. TSDIAL, 146/4/3117/40–45; AGAD, C. K. Ministerstwo Sprawiedliwości, box 307: 3.

38. Newspaper reports and trial records locate the origin of this rumor in Pielgrzymka, a small village a few kilometers south of Jasło, just west of Nowy Żmigród. *Kurjer Lwowski*, June 19, 1898, p. 1; *Dziennik Polski*, June 21, 1898, p. 2; *Dziennik Polski*, August 23, 1898; AGAD, C. K. Ministerstwo Sprawiedliwości, box 308: 242.

39. *Słowo Polskie*, June 18, 1898 (poranny), p. 1; *Słowo Polskie*, June 28, 1898, p. 2; TSDIAL, 146/4/3124/67; *Związek Chłopski*, July 6, 1898, p. 156. This rumor, along with other such fantasies, was cited by Ignaz Daszyński and other politicians in speeches blaming the riots on the poor administration of the Galician elites. *Związek Chłopski*, December 1, 1898, pp. 269–271.

40. AGAD, C. K. Ministerstwo Sprawiedliwości, box 309: 518.

41. I discuss this in Daniel L. Unowsky, *The Pomp and Politics of Patriotism: Imperial Celebrations in Habsburg Austria, 1848–1916* (West Lafayette, Ind.: Purdue University Press, 2005).

42. These defenders can be identified today only because of the letters of praise and commendation sent by individual Jews and Jewish communities to the Galician authorities as examples of righteous people whose deeds should not go without recognition. TSDIAL, 146/4/3127/33.

43. Archiwum Panstwowe (National Archive), Oddział Nowy Sącz (Nowy Sącz branch), *Protocol Posiedzeń: Rada i wydz powiat w Nowym Sącz: 1898*, Wrp-ns 86, July 6, 1898.

44. *Związek Chłopski* denounced Stojałowski and his party for allegedly spreading false rumors and encouraging violence even as this organ of the Peasant Party Union placed all the blame on the Jews and called for systematic action against them. *Związek Chłopski*, July 1, 1898.

45. *Słowo Polskie*, June 18, 1898 (morning edition).

46. For newspaper reports on the events in Ulaszowice, see *Kurjer Lwowski*, June 14, 1898; *Czas*, June 16, 1898; *Die Welt*, June 17, 1898; *Drohobyczer Zeitung*, July 1898. On the trial of those who took part, see *Głos Narodu*, September 25, 1898. Many of those involved were described as "Gypsies" who had served long sentences in prison for previous vio-

lence offenses. For an example of an incident where the burning of Jewish property led to an uncontrollable fire that damaged nearby homes and a church, see *Słowo Polskie*, January 3, 1899.

47. Jan Madejczyk, *Wspomnienia* (Warsaw: Ludowa Spółdzielnia Wydawnicza, 1965), 53.

48. AGAD, C. K. Ministerstwo Sprawiedliwości, box 307: 35.

49. This effort was not without controversy. Byk insisted that any Jews accepting money from this fund had to pledge not to sue perpetrators for damages.

50. TSDIAL, 146/4/3124/145; TSDIAL, 146/4/3124/148.

51. AGAD, C. K. Ministerstwo Sprawiedliwości, box 308: 320. In this incident, Jews who fled Kołaczyce after the violence that erupted there on Corpus Christi were robbed as they sought refuge in Jasło. Jan Madejczyk describes witnessing a similar event in the same area.

52. See, for example, AGAD, C. K. Ministerstwo Sprawiedliwości, box 309: 452.

53. *Głos Narodu*, July 21, 1898; *Głos Narodu*, July 22, 1898; *Czas*, July 22, 1898.

54. TSDIAL, 146/4/3125/86.

55. *Nowa Reforma*, July 7, 1898, p. 3; *Głos Narodu*, July 6, 1898, p. 3; July 7, 1898, p. 3.

56. The antisemitic press reported on the outcome of this trial with glee, referring to Hagel as having the "usual appearance of the Galician type of fanatical Jew" with his sidelocks, black beard, and pale face. *Głos Rzeszowski*, July 10, 1898, p. 3; *Głos Narodu*, July 7, 1898, p. 3. The prosecutor claimed Hagel had to be convicted to prove that not only Poles were responsible for the violence. According to the prosecutor, Hagel, like the Jews in general, had acted provocatively and thus was himself to blame for the violence. *Neue Freie Presse*, July 6, 1898 (evening edition), p. 2.

57. TSDIAL, 146/4/3117/40.

58. In late May the gendarme commander organized a citizens' guard in Tłuste to protect the town from marauding rail construction workers. *Dr. Bloch's Österreichische Wochenschrift*, June 10, 1898, p. 439. The vice-mayor of Sanok organized some forty Jews into a city guard to protect the town from rioters. *Dr. Bloch's Österreichische Wochenschrift*, July 1, 1898, p. 494.

59. TSDIAL, 146/43122/28.

60. *Kurjer Lwowski*, June 19, 1898, p. 5.

61. Österreichisches Staatsarchiv, Allgemeine Verwaltungsarchiv (AVA), Ministerium des Innern, Präs. Sign. 22, Galizien, 1898, ct. 867 [Präs. Nr. 5590].

62. Among many others, *Głos Narodu*, August 3, 1898; *Slowo Polskie*, January 3, 1899, p. 4.

63. For a powerful example, see Governor Piniński's report to the Ministry of the Interior from July 28, which was presented to Emperor Franz Joseph. AVA, Ministerium des Innern, Präs. Sign. 22, Galizien, 1898, ct. 867 [Präs. Nr. 6345]. See also TSDIAL, 146/4/3117/40.

64. *Czas*, July 7, 1898; *Czas*, July 22, 1898.

65. The liberal *Słowo Polskie*, attacked for this by conservatives, invited Daszyński and Stojałowski to write about the riots. *Słowo Polskie*, July 13, 1898.

66. Democratic leaders organized a meeting of like-minded politicians and journalists in Lemberg on August 14 to send a delegation to Vienna to formally protest the ongoing

state of emergency. *Nowa Reforma*, August 17, 1898; *Kurjer Lwowski*, August 15, 1898, p. 1.

67. See, for example, Jan Stapiński's November 24 speech in the Reichsrat. *Przyjaciel Ludu*, December 1, 1898. Stapiński also minimizes the seriousness of the riots and blames the situation on the overreaction of the government and gendarmes.

68. *Neue Freie Presse*, November 25, 1898, p. 2.

69. *Związek Chłopski*, July 1, 1898, p. 146.

70. *Neue Freie Presse*, November 25, 1898, p. 2.

71. *Dr. Bloch's Österreichische Wochenschrift*, June 24, 1898, p. 486; *Dr. Bloch's Österreichische Wochenschrift*, July 15, 1898, p. 528.

72. *Głos Narodu*, July 30, 1898, p. 3.

73. For examples of such writing, see Larry Wolff, *Inventing Eastern Europe: The Map of Civilization on the Mind of the Enlightenment* (Stanford: Stanford University Press, 1994); Larry Wolff, *The Idea of Galicia: History and Fantasy in Habsburg Political Culture* (Stanford: Stanford University Press, 2010).

74. *Słowo Polskie*, June 25, 1898.

75. On the typical tensions and violence that took place where Jews and Catholics interacted in Galicia, see Joachim Schonfeld, *Shtetl Memoirs: Jewish Life in Galicia under the Austro-Hungarian Empire and the Reborn Poland, 1898–1939* (Hoboken, N.J.: Ktav Publishing House, 1985); Jan Słomka, *From Serfdom to Self-Government: Memoirs of a Polish Village Mayor 1842–1927*, intro. by Stanisław Kot (London: Minerva, 1941); Jan Madejczyk, *Wspomnienia* (Warsaw: Ludowa Spółdzielnia Wydawnicza, 1965).

76. *Prawda*, July 25, 1898, p. 1.

77. Franciszek Bujak, *Żmiąca: Wieś powiatu limanowskiego* (Cracow: G. Gebethner i spółka, 1903).

78. Alfred Nossig, ed., *Jüdische Statistik* (Berlin: Jiidischer Verlag, 1903). The antisemitic press commented on this survey with biting sarcasm. See *Głos Narodu*, July 11, 1898, p. 2.

79. The 1898 anti-Jewish riots clearly were an example of what Helmut Walser Smith and others have termed "exclusionary violence." See Hoffmann, Bergmann, Smith, *Exclusionary Violence*, introduction. Paul R. Brass makes this point in relation to communal violence in *Theft of an Idol: Text and Context in the Representation of Collective Violence* (Princeton: Princeton University Press, 1997).

80. As Paul Brass argues in *Theft of an Idol*, while communal violence may not be organized by any particular political movement, such violence often becomes part of a competitive effort to interpret the violence in ways that would attract potential voters to various political programs.

81. *Dziennik Polski*, August 19, 1898.

2. The Rhetoric of Antisemitic Violence in France

1. Research for this article was generously funded by the John Simon Guggenheim Memorial Foundation (2000–2001); the J. B. and Maurice C. Shapiro Senior Scholar-in-Residence Fellowship, Center for Advanced Holocaust Studies, U.S. Holocaust Memorial Museum

(2004–2005); the Radcliffe Institute for Advanced Study at Harvard University (2008–2009); and Cornell University. I would also like to thank the Columbia University Institute for Scholars at Reid Hall, Paris, for providing me with a scholarly home during the 2000–01 academic year. Finally, I am grateful to Sanford Gutman and Harriet Jackson, as well as Robert Nemes and Daniel Unowsky, for comments on earlier drafts of this chapter.

On Stoecker, see Paul Massing, *Rehearsal for Destruction* (New York: Harper, 1949), 21–59; Peter Pulzer, *The Rise of Political Antisemitism in Germany and Austria*, rev. ed. (Cambridge: Harvard University Press, 1964), 83–118; Uriel Tal, *Christians and Jews in Germany*, trans. Noah Jonathan Jacobs (Ithaca, N.Y.: Cornell University Press, 1975), 223–289; Hans Engelmann, *Kirche am Abgrund* (Berlin: Selbstverlag Institut Kirche und Judentum, 1984); Günter Brakelmann, et al., eds., *Protestantismus und Politik* (Hamburg: Christians, 1982); Hermann Greive, *Geschichte des Modernen Antisemitismus in Deutschland* (Darmstadt: Wissenschaftliche Buchgesellschaft, 1983), 59–64; Michael Burleigh, *Earthly Powers* (New York: HarperCollins, 2005), 416–421.

2. John W. Boyer, *Political Radicalism in Late Imperial Vienna* (Chicago: University of Chicago Press, 1981); John W. Boyer, *Culture and Political Crisis in Vienna* (Chicago: University of Chicago Press, 1995); John W. Boyer, "Karl Lueger and the Viennese Jews," *Leo Baeck Institute Year Book* 26 (1981): 125–141; Richard S. Geehr, *Karl Lueger* (Detroit: Wayne State University Press, 1990); Pulzer, *The Rise of Political Antisemitism*, 156–164; Laurence Cole, "The Counter-Reformation's Last Stand: Austria," in *Culture Wars*, ed. Christopher Clark and Wolfram Kaiser (Cambridge, U.K.: Cambridge University Press, 2003), 285–312; Bruce Pauley, *From Prejudice to Persecution* (Chapel Hill: University of North Carolina Press, 1992), 38–47.

3. Helmut Walser Smith, *German Nationalism and Religious Conflict* (Princeton: Princeton University Press, 1995); H. W. Smith, "The Learned and Popular Discourse of Anti-Semitism in the Catholic Milieu of the Kaiserreich," *Central European History* 27, no. 3 (Sept. 1994): 315–328; (Oxford: Berg, 2001), 49–65; Clark and Kaiser, eds., *Culture Wars*; Olaf Blaschke, *Katholizismus und Antisemitismus im Deutschen Kaiserreich* (Göttingen: Vandenhoeck and Ruprecht, 1997); Olaf Blaschke, "Wider die 'Herrschaft des modern-jüdischen Geistes,'" in *Deutscher Katholizismus im Umbruch zur Moderne*, ed. Wilifried Loth (Stuttgart: Kolhammer, 1991), 236–265; Wolfgang Altgeld, *Katholizismus, Protestantismus, Judentum* (Mainz: M.-Grünewald-Verlag, 1992); Wolfgang Altgeld, "Religion, Denomination and Nationalism in Nineteenth-Century Germany," in *Protestants, Catholics and Jews in Germany, 1800–1914*, ed. H. W. Smith (Oxford: Berg, 2001), 49–65; Tal, *Christians and Jews in Germany*; Ernst Heinen, "Antisemitische Strömungen im politischen Katholizismus während des Kulturkampfes," in *Geschichte in der Gegenwart*, ed. Ernst Heinen and Hans Julius Schoeps (Paderborn: Schöningh, 1972), 259–299.

4. On the continued virulence of Catholic antisemitism in Germany, see David Blackbourn, "Roman Catholics," in *Nationalist and Racialist Movements in Britain and Germany before 1914*, ed. Paul Kennedy and Anthony Nicholls (Oxford: Macmillan, 1981), 106–129; H. W. Smith, *The Butcher's Tale* (New York: W.W. Norton, 2002). On the Center Party

and antisemitism, see Blackbourn, "Roman Catholics"; Uwe Mazura, *Zentrumspartei und Judenfrage 1870/71–1933* (Mainz: Matthias-Grünewald-Verlag, 1994); Rudolf Lill, "Die deutschen Katholiken und die Juden in der Zeit von 1850 bis zur Machtübernahme Hitlers," in *Kirche und Synagoge*, ed. Karl H. Rengstorf and Siegfried von Kortzfleisch, 2 vols. (Stuttgart: Ernst Klett Verlag, 1968–1970), 2:370–420.

5. Doris L. Bergen, *Twisted Cross* (Chapel Hill: University of North Carolina Press, 1996); Richard Steigmann-Gall, *The Holy Reich* (Cambridge: Cambridge University Press, 2003); Robert P. Ericksen and Susannah Heschel, eds., *Betrayal* (Minneapolis, Minn.: Fortress Press, 1999), 1–128; Susannah Heschel, *The Aryan Jesus* (Princeton: Princeton University Press, 2008); Hermann Greive, *Theologie und Ideologie* (Heidelberg: L. Schneider, 1969); Hermann Greive, *Geschichte des Modernen Antisemitismus in Deutschland* (Darmstadt: Wissenschaftliche Buchgesellschaft, 1983); Hermann Greive, "Die Gesellschaftliche Bedeutung der Christlich-jüdischen Differenz zur Situation im Deutschen Katholizismus," in *Juden im Wilhelminischen Deutschland, 1890–1914*, ed. Werner E. Mosse and Arnold Paucker (Tübingen: Mohr, 1976), 349–388; Günther Brakelmann, "Nationalprotestantismus und Nationalsozialismus," in *Von der Aufgabe der Freiheit*, ed. Christian Jansen (Berlin: Akademie Verlag, 1995), 337–350; Robert P. Ericksen, *Theologians under Hitler* (New Haven: Yale University Press, 1985).

6. Tal, *Christians and Jews in Germany*, 223–289; Uriel Tal, "Religious and Anti-Religious Roots of Modern Antisemitism," *Leo Baeck Memorial Lecture*, no. 14 (New York: Leo Baeck Institute, 1971).

7. See especially Boyer, *Culture and Political Crisis in Vienna*.

8. Cited in *Cent ans d'histoire de "La Croix,"* ed. René Rémond and Émile Poulat (Paris: Le Centurion, 1988), 219.

9. Frederick Busi, *The Pope of Antisemitism* (Lanham, Md.: University Press of America, 1986), 68.

10. On Drumont see Grégoire Kauffmann, *Edouard Drumont* (Paris: Perrin, 2008); Robert F. Byrnes, *Antisemitism in Modern France* (New Brunswick, N.J.: Rutgers University Press, 1950), 137–155 and passim; Michel Winock, *Edouard Drumont et Cie* (Paris: Seuil, 1982); Michel Winock, *Nationalism, Anti-Semitism, and Fascism in France*, trans. Jane Marie Todd (Stanford: Stanford University Press, 1988), 85–102 and passim; Stephen Wilson, *Ideology and Experience* (Rutherford, N.J.: Fairleigh Dickinson University Press, 1982), 169–178 and passim; Busi, *The Pope of Antisemitism*; Jacob Katz, *From Prejudice to Destruction* (Cambridge: Harvard University Press, 1980), 292–300; Philip G. Nord, *Paris Shopkeepers and the Politics of Resentment* (Princeton: Princeton University Press, 1986), 372–408; Zeev Sternhell, *La Droite révolutionnaire, 1885–1914* (Paris: Seuil, 1978).

11. Kauffmann, *Edouard Drumont*, 205–214; Wilson, *Ideology and Experience*, 538; Paul Duclos, "Catholiques et Juifs autour de l'Affaire Dreyfus," *Revue d'histoire de l'église de France* 64 (1978): 39–53, esp. 43; Pierre Pierrard, *Juifs et Catholiques français* (Paris: Fayard, 1970), 46–47.

12. On the Ralliement, see Alexander Sedgwick, *The Ralliement in French Politics, 1890–1898* (Cambridge: Harvard University Press, 1965); Norman Ravitch, *The Catholic Church*

and the French Nation, 1589–1989 (London: Routledge, 1990), 94–96; Adrien Dansette, Religious History of Modern France, trans. John Dingle, vol. 2 (New York: Herder and Herder, 1961), 75–111; Kevin Passmore, The Right in France from the Third Republic to Vichy (Oxford: Oxford University Press, 2013), 73–100; Maurice Larkin, Religion, Politics and Preferment in France since 1890 (Cambridge: Cambridge University Press, 1995), 6–7, 53–68; Maurice Larkin, Church and State after the Dreyfus Affair (London: MacMillan, 1974), 37–43; Burleigh, Earthly Powers, 347–351; John McManners, Church and State in France, 1870–1914 (London: S.P.C.K. for the Church Historical Society, 1972), 64–73; Jacques Piou, Le Ralliement (Paris: Éditions "Spes," 1928).

13. Sternhell, La Droite révolutionnaire, 225, see also 152.

14. On the Third Republic's anticlerical campaign, see Dansette, Religious History of Modern France, 2: 7–9, 35–36, 40–57; Nicholas Atkin, "The Politics of Legality: The Religious Orders in France, 1901–45," in Religion, Society, and Politics, ed. Frank Tallett and Nicholas Atkin (London: The Hambledon Press, 1991), 149–166, esp. 151; Gérard Cholvy and Yves-Marie Hilaire, Histoire religieuse de la France, 1880–1914 (Toulouse: Privat, 2000), 18–19, 57–66; Burleigh, Earthly Powers, 344–345, 351–352, 356–364; McManners, Church and State; Larkin, Church and State, 22–28; Ralph Gibson, A Social History of French Catholicism, 1789–1914 (London: Routledge, 1989), 128–133; James R. Lehning, To Be a Citizen (Ithaca, N.Y.: Cornell University Press, 2001), 35–37; Sudhir Hazareesingh, Political Traditions in Modern France (Oxford: Oxford University Press, 1994), 98–123. On the long-term impact of anticlericalism, see Theodore Zeldin, France, 1848–1945, vol. 2 (Oxford: Clarendon Press, 1977), 983–1039.

15. See especially Stéphane Arnoulin, M. Edouard Drumont et les jésuites (Paris: Librairie des Deux-Mondes, 1902).

16. Years later Father du Lac complained to his superiors in Rome that Drumont had not heeded his suggestions. Duclos, "Catholiques et Juifs autour de l'Affaire Dreyfus," 39–53, esp. 40.

17. Ibid., 43–44; Larkin, Religion, Politics and Preferment in France, 16.

18. Kauffmann, Edouard Drumont, 104.

19. Sûreté générale rept., May 29, 1895, Archives Nationales, Paris (AN) F7 15951–2.

20. Sûreté générale repts., May 29, 1895 and June 1, 1895, both in AN F7 15951–2.

21. Edouard Drumont, "Le Mouvement littéraire," Le Livre V (1884): 139–144. See also Byrnes, Antisemitism in Modern France, 147.

22. This claim is reiterated in Edouard Drumont, La France juive, vol. 1 (Paris: C. Marpon and E. Flammarion, 1886), 294. See also Byrnes, Antisemitism in Modern France, 148.

23. Kauffmann, Edouard Drumont, 72. On the widespread use of racial terminology in the Civiltà cattolica as well as the Osservatore romano, see James F. Brennan, The Reflection of the Dreyfus Affair in the European Press, 1897–1899 (New York: P. Lang, 1998), 403, 405; David I. Kertzer, The Popes against the Jews (New York: Alfred A. Knopf, 2001), 133–151, 195–196. On the role of the Civiltà cattolica in disseminating the ritual murder accusation, see Francesco Crepaldi, "L'Omicidio rituale nella 'moderna' polemica antigiudaica di Civiltà Cattolica nella seconda metà del XIX Secolo," in Les Racines chrétiennes

*de l'antisémitisme politique (fin xix*e*-xx*e *siècle)*, ed. Catherine Brice and Giovanni Miccoli (Rome: École française de Rome, 2003), 61–78; Charlotte Klein, "Damascus to Kiev: *Civiltà Cattolica* on Ritual Murder," *Wiener Library Bulletin* 27 (1974): 18–25.

24. Cited in Robert Michael, *Holy Hatred* (New York: Palgrave MacMillan, 2006), 9.

25. Drumont, *La France juive*, 1: 9, 57, 58.

26. According to Jewish tradition, God delivered two laws to Moses at Mount Sinai: a written law (the Torah), and an oral law (*Torah shel baal pe*). During the first centuries CE, however, the oral law, together with the rabbinic commentary on it, came to be written down due to fear that it might otherwise be lost because of persecution. The Talmud consists of two main parts: the Mishnah, a law code fixed around 200 CE, and the Gemara, or completion, which consists of rabbinic interpretations and commentaries on these laws. The Gemara was fixed at the rabbinic academies in Jerusalem and Babylonia during the fifth and sixth centuries CE. The Mishnah and Gemara together constitute the Talmud.

27. Drumont, *La France juive*, 1: 20, 158–159, 162; 2: 405 n. 2.

28. Drumont, *La France juive*, 1: vi.

29. Ibid.

30. Drumont, *La France juive*, 1: 52; see also 1: 463. Drumont reiterated this charge in *Le Testament d'un antisémite* (Paris: E. Dentu, 1891), 358. There he declared: "When the French Kulturkampf began, the clergy did not know who their real enemies were, they could not explain to themselves the reasons for the relentless campaign directed against them. They had been told about the Freemasons, the unbelievers, the enemies of the Church, but no one had yet explained to them that it was the Jew who was behind it all." Cited in Wilson, *Ideology and Experience*, 555.

31. For Readclif's speech, see "Compte rendu des évènements politico-historiques survenus dans les dix dernières années," *Le Contemporain* LXXII (July 1, 1881), republished in "La Question juive: Le programme juif d'après un rabbin," *Les Questions actuelles* XV, no. 6 (Sept. 10, 1892), 170–175. For an English translation, see Norman Cohn, *Warrant for Genocide: The Myth of the Jewish World Conspiracy and the Protocols of the Elders of Zion* (1967; reprint, London: Serif, 1996), app. 1, 279–284. See also Raoul Girardet, *Mythes et mythologies politiques* (Paris: Seuil, 1986), 25–26; Ariane Chebel d'Appollonia, *L'Extrême droite en France* (Brussels: Éditions Complexe, 1996), 70–82. According to this account, which is clearly an early prototype of the Protocols of the Elders of Zion, a certain Sir John Readclif (also spelled "Readcliff" or "Retcliffe"), the alleged chief rabbi of international Jewry, recently had addressed a conclave of world Jewish leaders. The main point of Readclif's speech was to prove that although Jews seemed assimilated, in reality they were secretly plotting to conquer the world in order to avenge themselves on Christians, who had persecuted them for the past 1,800 years. For a fictionalized account of the origins of the Protocols in France, see Umberto Eco, *The Prague Cemetery*, trans. Richard Dixon (Boston: Houghton Mifflin Harcourt, 2011).

32. Quotations from this paragraph can be found in Drumont, *La France juive*, 1: 123–124, 463; 2: 5.

33. Drumont, *La France juive*, 2: 381. See also Wilson, *Ideology and Experience*, 553–554; Winock, *Nationalism, Anti-Semitism, and Fascism in France*, 91.

34. Drumont, *La France juive*, 1: 123.

35. On socialist antisemitism in France in the nineteenth century, see Wilson, *Ideology and Experience*, 319–378; Byrnes, *Antisemitism in Modern France*, 156–178; Nancy L. Green, "Socialist Antisemitism, Defense of a Bourgeois Jew and Discovery of the Jewish Proletariat," *International Review of Social History* 30 (Dec. 1, 1985): 374–399; George Lichtheim, "Socialism and the Jews," *Dissent* (July-Aug. 1968): 314–342; Katz, *From Prejudice to Destruction*, 119–128; Marc Angenot, *Ce que l'on dit des Juifs en 1889* (Montreal: Inter-university Centre for European Studies, 1984), 88–96.

36. Baron Alphonse de Claye [signed A. de Claye], *Le Monde*, April 26–27, 1886, p. 1; Pierre Pierrard, *Les Chrétiens et l'Affaire Dreyfus* (Paris: Les Éditions de l'Atelier, Les Éditions Ouvrières, 1996), 26.

37. Oscar Havard, "La France juive," 2 parts, *Le Monde*, May 5 and 6, 1886, pp. 1–2. For an extended version of this article, see O. Havard, *M. Ed. Drumont et La France juive* (Paris: F. Levé, 1886). See also Pierrard, *Juifs et Catholiques français*, 62.

38. Havard, *M. Ed. Drumont et La France juive*, 28.

39. Veuillot's emphasis. E. Veuillot, "France: Paris," *L'Univers*, Apr. 28, 1886, p. 1. See also Pierrard, *Juifs et Catholiques*, 62.

40. On the Boulanger movement, see William D. Irvine, *The Boulanger Affair Reconsidered* (New York: Oxford University Press, 1989); Bertrand Joly, *Nationalistes et conservateurs en France, 1885–1902* (Paris: Les Indes Savantes, 2008), 79–116; Nord, *Paris Shopkeepers*, 303–350; Michael Burns, *Rural Society and French Politics* (Princeton: Princeton University Press, 1984), 57–117; Sternhell, *La Droite révolutionnaire*; Lehning, *To Be a Citizen*, 155–181; Passmore, *The Right in France*, 45–72; Robert Lynn Fuller, *The Origins of the French Nationalist Movement, 1886–1914* (Jefferson, N.C.: McFarland, 2012), 30–71.

41. See, for example, A. Kannengieser, *Juifs et Catholiques en Autriche-Hongrie* (Paris: P. Lethielleux, s.d. [1896]) and the review of this book in the Jesuit periodical *Études*, suppl. to tomes 67–69 (1896), 451–454.

42. Abbé Joseph Lémann, *La Préponderance juive*, 2 vols. (Paris: V. Lecoffre, 1889–1894).

43. Lémann, *La Préponderance juive*, 1:27, 238. On Lémann, see Angenot, *Ce que l'on dit des Juifs en 1889*, 36; Paul Airiau, ed., *L'Antisémitisme catholique en France aux xixᵉ et xxᵉ siècles* (Paris: Berg, 2002), 111–116.

44. Auguste [sic] Rohling, *Le Juif-Talmudiste, résumé succinct des croyances et des pratiques dangereuses de la juiverie, présenté à la considération de tous les chrétiens, par M. l'abbé Auguste [sic] Rohling*, ed. and corrected by abbé Maximilien de Lamarque (Brussels: A. Vromant, 1888); Auguste [sic] Rohling, *Le Juif selon le Talmud*, ed. and augmented by A. Pontigny (Paris: A. Savine, 1889). Rohling was a professor of Catholic theology, and subsequently of semitic languages, at the German University of Prague. On Rohling's immense popularity throughout the Catholic world, see H. W. Smith, *The Butcher's Tale*, 91–135; H. W. Smith, "Konitz, 1900," in *Exclusionary Violence*, ed. Christhard Hoffmann,

Werner Bergmann, and H. W. Smith (Ann Arbor: University of Michigan Press, 2002), 93–122; H. W. Smith, "The Learned and Popular Discourse"; Greive, *Geschichte des Modernen Antisemitismus*, 52–57, 67; Greive, "Gesellschaftliche Bedeutung," 356–357, 373; Blaschke, *Katholizismus und Antisemitismus*, 31, 35, 49–51, 74–75, 89, 191, 268; Blaschke, "Wider die 'Herrschaft,'" 243–246; Mazura, *Zentrumspartei und Judenfrage 1870/71– 1933*, 28–29, 103–105; Katz, *From Prejudice to Destruction*, 219–220, 285–286; George Mosse, *Toward the Final Solution* (New York: H. Fertig, 1978), 138–141; Girardet, *Mythes et mythologies politiques*, 44–47.

45. H. W. Smith, "The Learned and Popular Discourse," 321; Entry on "The Talmud Jew," *Encyclopedia of Antisemitism: A Historical* Encyclopedia *of Prejudice and Persecution*, ed. Richard S. Levy (ABC-CLIO, 2005); Hillel J. Kieval, "The Importance of Place," in *Comparing Jewish Societies*, ed. Todd M. Endelman (Ann Arbor: University of Michigan Press, 1997), 135–166. On the medieval origins of the anti-Talmudic theme see Robert Chazan, *Medieval Stereotypes and Modern Antisemitism* (Berkeley: University of California Press, 1997), esp. 35–72, 102–109; Michael, *Holy Hatred*, 55–56.

46. According to Pontigny, since Rohling wanted the widest possible distribution for his book, he attached no conditions on amendments and corrections to foreign translations. Therefore, it was possible to take considerable liberties with this text.

47. Mosse, *Toward the Final Solution*, 139.

48. Drumont's preface to Rohling, *Le Juif selon le Talmud*, iv-v, ii, iii, vi.

49. The earlier works referred to here are: Jacob Brafman, *The Book of the Kahal* (Vilna, 1869); Achille Laurent, *Relation historique des affaires de Syrie depuis 1840 jusqu'en 1842*, 2 vols. (Paris: Gaume frères, 1846); and Henri Roger Gougenot des Mousseaux, *Le Juif, le judaisme et la judaïsation des peuples chrétiens* (Paris: Plon, 1869).

50. Rohling, *Le Juif selon le Talmud*, 7, 19, 26, 253, 260.

51. Although Desportes used the title "abbé," he apparently was never ordained. On Desportes, see Byrnes, *Antisemitism in Modern France*, 188–189; Wilson, *Ideology and Experience*, 528; Jeannine Verdès-Leroux, *Scandale financier et antisémitisme catholique* (Paris: Le Centurion, 1969), 71, 141, 367; Kertzer, *The Popes against the Jews*, 179, 214–218; Angenot, *Ce que l'on dit des Juifs*, 33–35; Marc Angenot, "Un Juif trahira: La préfiguration de l'Affaire Dreyfus entre 1886 et 1894," *Romantisme* 25, no. 87 (1995): 87–114, esp. 95, 97; Pierre Barrucand and François Teiletche, "Portrait: Un Aventurier ecclesiastique: Henri Desportes," *Politica hermetica* 8 (1994): 163–175.

52. The Italian title was *Il sangue cristiano nei riti [ebraica] della moderne sinagogua: revelazioni di neofito ex rabbino monaco greco per la prima volta pubblicate in itali versione del greco del professore* N.F.S. Prato, tipografia Giachetti, figlio e Ça. For the French translation of this text, see "Révélations faites par Néophyte, ancien Rabbin," *Les Questions actuelles* 15, no. 4 (Aug. 27, 1892): 111–124. On the publication of this text in 1883, see Isidore Cahen, "Chronique de la semaine," *Archives israélites* (AI), June 7, 1883, 181–182. For historical background on this text, see Kertzer, *The Popes against the Jews*, 91–105.

53. On JAB, see Angenot, *Ce que l'on dit des Juifs*, 35.

54. On the crash of the Union Générale, a Catholic banking house, see Verdès-Leroux, *Scandale financier*, and Frederick Brown, *For the Soul of France* (New York: Alfred A. Knopf, 2010), 59–80.

55. JAB, *Le Sang chrétien dans les rites de la synagogue moderne* (Paris: H. Gautier 1888), xiv, xxv, xxvii, xxx, xxxi.

56. Emphasis in the text. JAB, *Le Sang chrétien*, iii, 8, 210. For the section "Historical Documents," see pp. 63–379. See also L. Wogue, "Toi aussi, Brutus?" *Univers israélite* (Apr. 16, 1885): 467–471.

57. Henri Desportes, *Le Mystère du sang chez les Juifs de tous les temps* (Paris: A. Savine, 1889), i, ii, v, vi, vii, x, xi.

58. Desportes, *Le Mystère du sang*, 280.

59. Ibid., 365, 280–281.

60. "Notes of the Week," *Jewish Chronicle*, Dec. 6, 1889, pp. 5, 8; H. Prague, "Causerie," AI, Dec. 26, 1889, pp. 413–414. On the papal attitude toward ritual murder in the nineteenth century, see Kertzer, *The Popes against the Jews*, 127–128, 152–165, 232–234.

61. "Notes of the Week," *Jewish Chronicle*, Dec. 6, 1889, pp. 5, 8; H. Prague, "Causerie," AI, Dec. 26, 1889, pp. 413–414. On Cardinal Manning's subsequent intervention with the Vatican, see "Pope Leo XIII and the Jews," *Jewish Chronicle*, Feb. 7, 1890, p. 7; "Grand Rabbin et Cardinal," AI, Feb. 13, 1890, pp. 49–50.

62. Kertzer, *The Popes against the Jews*, 214–218; "Grand Rabbin et Cardinal," AI, Feb. 13, 1890, pp. 49–50. On the dispute between Isidore Cahen of the *Archives israélites* and Desportes over the circumstances that had led to Desportes's expulsion, see I. Cahen, "Simple Rapprochement," July 3, 1890, pp. 209–210; H. Prague, "L'Antisémitisme dans le Nord de la France," Aug. 28, 1890, pp. 273–274; Ben Israel, "Correspondances particuliers, Lille, 28 août 1890," Sept. 11, 1890, pp. 291–292; I. Cahen, "Un Ecclesiastique de fantaisie," Oct. 30, 1890, pp. 345–347; I. Cahen, "L'Audace de ces Messieurs," Dec. 11, 1890, pp. 393–394; Marc Lévy, "Critique religieuse: Essai sur la morale du Talmud," Apr. 2, 1891, pp. 110–111; "Les Mensonges antisémitiques," Aug. 25, 1892, 268–269, all in AI, as well as the prefaces by both Drumont and Desportes in Henri Desportes, *Tué par les Juifs* (Paris: A. Savine, 1890) and Édouard Drumont, *Le Testament d'un antisémite* (Paris: E. Dentu, 1891), 322–333.

63. Desportes, *Tué par les Juifs*, 13–18.

64. "Assassinat par les Juifs d'un enfant chrétien à Damas," *La Croix*, May 30, 1890, p. 1; I. Cahen, "Le nouvel incident de Damas, 1840–1890," AI, June 12, 1890, pp. 188–189.

65. In 1897, the Ligue antisémitique de France, founded by Drumont in 1889, was replaced by the Ligue antisémitique française, led by Guérin, although Drumont still served as honorary president. Here the initials LAF refer to the League throughout the 1890s, since the police referred to both groups as the Antisemitic League. See Wilson, *Ideology and Experience*, 179–186; Pierre Birnbaum, "Affaire Dreyfus, culture catholique et antisémitisme," in *Histoire de l'extrême droite en France*, ed. Michel Winock (Paris: Seuil, 1993), 83–123, esp. 90; Nord, *Paris Shopkeepers*, 374, 379–383; Joly, *Nationalistes et conserva-*

teurs en France, 253–299; Bertrand Joly, "Les antidreyfusards avant Dreyfus," *Revue d'histoire moderne et contemporaine* 39, no. 2 (1992): 198–221, esp. 201–202, 214; Sternhell, *La Droite révolutionnaire*, 221–230; Kauffmann, *Edouard Drumont*, 167–195.

66. H. Prague, "Causerie," AI, May 8, 1890, p. 145.

67. I. Cahen, "Le nouvel incident de Damas, 1840–1890," June 12, 1890, pp. 188–189; H. Prague, "Causerie," June 19, 1890, p. 194; "Nouvelles diverses," July 10, 1890, p. 223; I. Cahen, "Au journal *La Vraie France* de Lille," July 17, 1890, pp. 225–228; "Avérétés: Sur le chemin de Damas," July 31, 1890, p. 246; H. Prague, "Causerie," Aug. 21, 1890, pp. 266–267; H. Prague, "L'Antisémitisme dans le Nord de la France," Aug. 28, 1890, pp. 273–274, all in AI.

68. Desportes, *Tué par les Juifs*, 52, 59.

69. Ben Israel, "Correspondances particuliers, Lille, 28 aôut 1890," AI, Sept. 11, 1890, pp. 291–292.

70. In 1907 a French priest—the abbé Louis Marie Ollivier Duchesne, a prominent philologist and historian—publicly denounced "the stupid accusation of ritual murder" in his *Histoire ancienne de l'Église*, 3 vols. (Paris: Fontemoing, 1906, 1907, 1910–11). And in 1911, at the time of the Beiliss ritual murder trial in Russia, a French theologian, E. Vacanard, similarly railed against "stupid prejudices fed by popular hatred." See E. Vacanard, "La Question du meurtre rituel chez les Juifs," *Revue du clergé français*, 2 parts (Aug. 1 and Aug. 15, 1911): 301–320, 427–451, esp. 301, 306.

71. Dr. Martinez, *Le Juif: Voilà l'ennemi!* (Paris: A. Savine 1890), 10, 299.

72. Isidore Bertrand, *Un Monde fin de siècle*, 1st ed. (Paris: Bloud et Barral, 1891); 3rd ed. (Paris: Bloud et Barral, 1899), 121, 247, 360–361, 413. All citations are from the 3rd edition.

73. Bertrand, *Un Monde fin de siècle*, 413, 432, 444, 457–458.

74. Msgr. Léon Meurin, S.J., *La Franc-Maçonnerie: Synagogue de Satan* (Paris: V. Retaux et fils, 1893), 9, 188, 189.

75. This is a reference to Adriano Lemmi, the grand master of the Grand Orient in Rome.

76. Meurin, *La Franc-Maçonnerie*, 66, 157, 441.

77. Meurin, *La Franc-Maçonnerie*, 214, 468.

78. Other works by priests written for this contest include abbé A.-J. Jacquet, *Concours de "La Libre Parole" sur les moyens pratiques d'arriver à l'anéantissement de la puissance juive en France. République plébiscitaire, mémoire de M. A.-J. Jacquet* (Paris: Nouvelle Librairie nationale, 1897); abbé Jean Ansèlme Tilloy, *Le Péril judéo-maçonnique* (Paris: Librairie de la Libre Parole, 1897); Louis Vial, *Le Juif roi* (Paris: P. Lethielleux, 1899). Two other works by priests probably were written for this contest, but were not explicitly designated as entries: abbé Hippolyte Gayraud, *L'Antisémitisme de saint Thomas d'Aquin* (Paris: E. Dentu, 1896); and abbé Jules Cellier, *Pour et contre les Juifs* (Paris: Impr. catholique Saint-Joseph, 1896). On this essay contest, see Kauffmann, *Edouard Drumont*, 313–317; Byrnes, *Antisemitism in Modern France*, 257–258, 301; Pierrard, *Les Chrétiens et l'Affaire Dreyfus*, 27; Pierrard, *Juifs et Catholiques*, 65–67; Joly, "Les antidreyfusards avant Dreyfus," 205; Zeldin, *France, 1848–1945*, 2:1038; Puig, [abbé Baruteil-Puig], *Solution de la question juive* (Paris: Delhomme et Briguet, 1897), v-xi; E. Rouyer, pref. and "Rapport sur le concours," in A.-J. Jacquet, *Concours de "La Libre Parole,"* vii-xii, 1–58.

79. R. P. Constant, *Les Juifs devant l'Eglise et l'histoire* (Paris: Gaume, 1896), ii, 92. See also Kertzer, *The Popes against the Jews*, 165, 218.

80. Constant, *Les Juifs devant l'Eglise*, 41–43, 46–47.

81. Ibid., 47, 108.

82. Ibid., 36, 37.

83. Ibid., 47n. 1, 195, 216, 217.

84. Ibid., 24, 47, 53, 98, 113 n. 1; 284.

85. For biographical background on Puig, see Pierrard, *Juifs et Catholiques*, 68–70; Pierrard, *Les Chrétiens et l'Affaire Dreyfus*, 27; and Airiau, ed., *L'Antisémitisme catholique*, 81–85.

86. Puig, *Solution de la question juive*, 37, 38, 132, 187, 307.

87. Ibid., 63, 65, 71, 189.

88. Ibid., 164, 305, 310. On Sir John Readclif, see n. 31 in this chapter.

89. Puig, *Solution de la question juive*, 148, 156, 159, 163. Paul Airiau takes seriously Baruteil-Puig's claim that he believed in conversion. That claim is inconsistent with numerous other claims in the text, however. Airiau, ed., *L'Antisémitisme catholique*, 81–82.

90. Puig, *Solution de la question juive*, 123. This statement is a direct quote from Drumont, *La France juive* 1: 123.

91. A. Boué, review essay, *Études*, tome 73 (Nov. 5, 1897): 417–421. See also Pierrard, *Les Chrétiens et l'Affaire Dreyfus*, 27. All quotations in this paragraph and the next are from Boué.

92. Richard Millman has argued that the prominent role played by Jews in the anticlerical movement did elicit an antisemitic backlash. See Millman, "Jewish Anticlericalism and the Rise of Modern French Antisemitism," *History* 77, no. 250 (June 1992): 220–226.

93. Clark and Kaiser, ed., *Culture Wars*.

94. In *La France juive devant l'opinion* (Paris: C. Marpon et E. Flammarion, 1886), 7, Edouard Drumont wrote: "Parmi tant d'encouragements qui me sont arrivés de tous les coins de France, . . . ce qui m'a été le plus sensible, c'est l'allégresse de nos curés de campagne. . . . C'est en causant avec des curés de campagne, en lisant leurs lettres, que j'ai compris combien mon livre était utile." Cited in Pierrard, *Les Chrétiens et l'Affaire Dreyfus*, 26. See also Wilson, *Ideology and Experience*, 539.

95. "Lettre sur le devoir électoral," par S. G. Mgr. l'archevêque d'Aix [1893], AN F19 5619.

96. J.-M. Mayeur, "*La Croix* et la république," in *Cent ans d'histoire de "La Croix*," ed. Rémond and Poulat, 206–216, esp. 206–208.

97. See especially Anatole Leroy-Beaulieu, *Israël chez les nations* (1893; reprint, Paris: Calmann Lévy, 1983); A. Leroy-Beaulieu, *L'Antisémitisme* [pamphlet] (Paris: Calmann Lévy, 1897); A. Leroy-Beaulieu, *Les Doctrines de haine*, 3rd ed. (Paris: Calmann Lévy, s.d. [1902]).

98. See n. 70 in this chapter.

99. "*La Croix* et les Juifs," *La Croix*, Aug. 30, 1890, p. 1. See also Kertzer, *The Popes against the Jews*, 175; Burns, *Rural Society*, 131.

100. Pierrard, *Les Chrétiens et l'Affaire Dreyfus*, 42–50; Pierrard, *Juifs et Catholiques*, 88–89, 92–102; Claude Bellanger et al., eds., *Histoire générale de la presse française*, 5 vols. (Paris: Presses universitaires de France, 1969–76), 3:337; Pierre Sorlin, *"La Croix" et les Juifs, 1880–1899* (Paris: Bernard Grasset, 1967), 26–55; Kertzer, *The Popes against the Jews*, 166–

185; Burns, *Rural Society*, 131–133; Cholvy and Hilaire, *Histoire religieuse de la France*, 87; Wilson, *Ideology and Experience*, 207, 533; Byrnes, *Antisemitism in Modern France*, 194–198.

101. See, for example, the violent antisemitic speeches delivered by Auguste Roussel and Ernest Michel to the congress of Catholic jurists held in Angers, France, in October 1890. "Rapport présenté par M. Auguste Roussel, sur la presse juive" and "Rapport envoyé par M. Ernest Michel, sur la question juive," both in *Revue catholique des institutions et du droit*, ser. 2, 5, no. 12 (Dec. 1890): 510–525, 526–530, respectively.

102. Verdès-Leroux, *Scandale financier*.

103. Zadoc Kahn, Grand-Rabbin, "Lettre de M. Zadoc-Kahn," *Libre Parole*, July 8, 1892, clipped in Archives, Préfecture de police, Paris, BA 1301.

104. See especially Wilson, *Ideology and Experience*, 655–670. Basing his study on a number of indices, Wilson claims that antisemitism was strong in a large number of departments. Nevertheless, he asserts that it was strongest in the southwest and northeast, as well as on the peripheries, and in the four departments of the Paris basin. He also sees antisemitism primarily as an urban phenomenon, even in rural departments. Michael Burns, too, sees antisemitism as primarily urban and argues that peasants were largely indifferent to the Dreyfus affair. To the extent that they did react to it, he posits that they did so through the prism of local political concerns. Burns, *Rural Society*, 138–164. Finally, Nancy Fitch argues that although the Dreyfus affair was largely an urban concern, it did have a major impact in some rural areas. Ultimately, she suggests that the degree to which the local rural population reacted was linked to the strength of local conservatives, who frequently gravitated to antisemitism following the collapse of traditional conservative parties. By contrast, in areas where the left had a strong foothold, they frequently were able to combat this antisemitism. Nancy Fitch, "Mass Culture, Mass Parliamentary Politics, and Modern Anti-Semitism," *American Historical Review* 97, no. 1 (Feb. 1992): 55–95. For the countervailing view that antisemitism was strong throughout France, see Pierre Birnbaum, *The Antisemitic Moment*, trans. Jane Marie Todd (New York: Hill and Wang, 1998).

105. See especially Blaschke, *Katholizismus und Antisemitismus*; Blaschke, "Wider die 'Herrschaft'"; Michael Langer, *Zwischen Vorurteil und Aggression* (Freiburg: Herder, 1994); Brian A. Porter (Porter-Szucs), *Faith and Fatherland* (New York: Oxford University Press, 2011); Brian A. Porter, "Antisemitism and the Search for a Catholic Identity," in *Antisemitism and Its Opponents in Modern Poland*, ed. Robert Blobaum (Ithaca, N.Y.: Cornell University Press, 2005), 103–123; Paul A. Hanebrink, *In Defense of Christian Hungary* (Ithaca, N.Y.: Cornell University Press, 2006); Robert Michael, *A History of Catholic Antisemitism* (New York: Palgrave MacMillan, 2008).

106. In the 1890s, over 90 percent of the total French population of forty million was baptized Catholic, but only between 20 and 25 percent of the adult population was practicing Catholic (as measured by weekly attendance at mass), and most of these were women. Larkin, *Religion, Politics and Preferment in France*, 5; Dansette, *Religious History of Modern France*, 2:14.

107. Steven Englund, "Antisemitism, Judeophobia, and the Republic," in *The French Republic*, ed. Edward Berenson, Vincent Duclert, and Christophe Prochasson (Ithaca, N.Y.: Cornell University Press, 2011), 278–288.

108. On this debate, see Laurent Joly, "Mélanges: L'entrée de l'antisémitisme sur la scène parlementaire française," *Archives juives* 38, no. 1 (2005), 114–128. On the Catholic response, see "La Question juive a la Chambre: Discours de M. [Théodore] Denis," *La Croix*, May 28, 1895, pp. 1–3; "Les Juifs devant le parlement," *Les Questions actuelles* 29, no. 4 (June 1, 1895): 98–116; "Les Chambres: Chambre des deputés," *Le Monde*, May 28, 1895, p. 1; "Les Chambres: Sénat," *Le Monde*, May 29, 1895, p. 2.

109. Vicki Caron, "Catholic Political Mobilization and Antisemitic Violence in fin-de-siècle France," *Journal of Modern History* 81 (June, 2009): 294–347.

110. Nord, *Paris Shopkeepers*, 384; Birnbaum, "Affaire Dreyfus, culture catholique et antisémitisme," in Winock, ed., *Histoire de l'extrême droite en France*, 110–111; Wilson, *Ideology and Experience*, 113–114.

111. Caron, "Catholic Political Mobilization."

112. For recent works that distinguish theological anti-Judaism from modern secular antisemitism, see Frank J. Coppa, *The Papacy, the Jews, and the Holocaust* (Washington, D.C.: Catholic University Press, 2006); Chazan, *Medieval Stereotypes*, esp. 125–140; and Gavin I. Langmuir, *Toward a Definition of Antisemitism* (Berkeley: University of California Press, 1990).

113. See n. 31 in this chapter.

114. Msgr. Ernest Jouin, *Le Péril judéo-maçonnique* 1, *Les 'Protocoles' des Sages de Sion* (Paris: Revue internationale des sociétés secrètes, 1920).

115. Saul Friedlander, *Nazi Germany and the Jews* (New York: HarperCollins, 1997); Saul Friedlander, *The Years of Extermination* (New York: HarperCollins, 2007). On the role of Catholicism in Hitler's worldview, see Friedrich Heer, *Der Glaube des Adolf Hitler*, 2 vols. (Munich: Bechtle, 1998).

116. Cited in V. Caron, *Uneasy Asylum* (Stanford, Calif.: Stanford University Press, 1999), 270.

117. Michael R. Marrus and Robert O. Paxton, *Vichy France and the Jews* (New York: Basic Books, 1981), 93.

118. Ibid.

3. Antisemitic Propaganda in Milan

I would like to thank Steven Englund for his comments and critiques on a first draft of this chapter. Epigraph: Max Horkheimer and Theodor W. Adorno, *Dialektik der Aufklärung: Philosophische Fragmente* (Amsterdam: Querido, 1947), 208.

1. Martin Philippson, *Neueste Geschichte des jüdischen Volkes*, vol. 2 (Leipzig: Gustav Fock, 1910), 2.

2. Annalisa Di Fant, "'La Civiltà Cattolica' contro gli errori (e gli erranti) moderni," in *Gli Italiani in Guerra: Conflitti, identià, memorie dal Risorgimento ai nostri giorni*, vol. 2: *Le 'tre Italie': Dalla presa di Roma alla Settimana Rossa (1870–1914)*, ed. Mario Isnenghi (Turin: UTET, 2009), 80–89; Ruggero Taradel and Barbara Raggi, *La segregazione amichevole:*

'*La civiltà cattolica' e la questione ebraica (1850–1943)* (Rome: Riuniti, 2000); Josè David Lebovitch Dahl, "The Role of the Roman Catholic Church in the Formation of Modern Anti-Semitism: *La Civiltà Cattolica* 1850–1879," *Modern Judaism* 23, no. 2 (2003): 180–197; see also the apologetic Catholic position of *Civiltá cattolica*: Giovanni Sale, "Antigiudaismo o antisemitismo? Le accuse contro la Chiesa e la 'Civiltà Cattolica,'" *La Civiltà Cattolica* 152, no. 3647 (2002): 419–431.

3. On antisemitism as a "cultural code" for the conservative milieu in the German Kaiserreich, see Shulamit Volkov, "Antisemitism as a Cultural Code: Reflections on the History and Historiography of Antisemitism in Imperial Germany," *Leo Baeck Institute Year Book* 23 (1978): 25–46.

4. Roberto Paoluzzi, "Momenti, motivi e figure dell'antigiudaismo cattolico italiano (1848–1914): Il ruolo di don Davide Albertario e de l'Osservatore Cattolico" (Ph.D. diss., Università degli Studi di Roma La Sapienza, 2003).

5. On the development of Catholic antisemitism in Mantua, see Ulrich Wyrwa, "Antisemitic Agitation and the Emergence of Political Catholicism in Mantua around 1900," *Quest: Issues in Contemporary Jewish History* 3 (2012), http://www.quest-cdecjournal.it.

6. One example: there is no chapter on Italy in the massive volumes edited by Herbert A. Strauss, *Hostages of Modernization: Studies on Modern Antisemitism, 1870–1933/39*, 2 vols. (Berlin: W. de Gruyter, 1993).

7. Arnaldo Momigliano, review, in *La nuova Italia: Rassegna critica mensile della cultura italiana e straniera*, April 20, 1933, pp. 142–143, reprinted in *Pagine ebraiche*, ed. Silvia Berti (Turin: Einaudi, 1987), 237–239.

8. Antonio Gramsci, "Ebraismo e antisemitismo," in Antonio Gramsci, *Il Risorgimento* (Torino, 1949), 166–168. For current discussions of Momigliano's thesis, see Simon Levis Sullam, "Arnaldo Momigliano é la 'nazzionalizzazione parallela': autobiografia religione, storia," *Passato e Presente* 70 (2007): 59–82.

9. Andrew M. Canepa, "L'attegiamento degli ebrei italiani davanti alla loro seconda emancipazione: Premesse e analisi," *Rassegna Mensile di Israel* 43 (1977): 419–436; Andrew M. Canepa, "The Image of the Jew in the Folklore and Literature of the Postrisorgimento," *Journal of European Studies* 9 (1979): 260–273; Andrew M. Canepa, "Considerazioni sulla seconda emancipazione e le sue conseguenze," *Rassegna Mensile di Israel* 47 (1981): 45–89; Andrew M. Canepa., "Emancipation and Jewish Response in Mid-Nineteenth-Century Italy," *European History Quarterly* 16, no. 4 (1986): 403–439. In my own research regarding the emancipation of Jews in Tuscany, I have pointed out that this process was by no means so smooth and unproblematic as presented until now: see Ulrich Wyrwa, *Juden in der Toskana und in Preußen im Vergleich: Aufklärung und Emanzipation in Florenz, Livorno, Berlin und Königsberg i. Pr.* (Tübingen: Mohr Siebeck, 2003).

10. Andrew M. Canepa, "Emancipazione, integrazione e antisemitismo liberale in Italia: Il caso Pasqualigo," *Comunità: Rivista di informazione culturale* 29 (1975): 166–203; Andrew M. Canepa, "Reflections on Antisemitism in Liberal Italy," *Wiener Library Bulletin* 31 (1978): 104–111.

11. Collected in the volume: Mario Toscano, *Ebraismo e Antisemitismo in Italia: Dal 1848 alla guerra dei sei giorni* (Milan: F. Angeli, 2003).

12. Andrew M. Canepa, "Cattolici ed ebrei nell Italia liberale (1870–1915)," *Comunità: Rivista di informazione culturale* 32 (1978): 43–109.

13. I have pointed out this conflict as a basic prerequisite for the emergence of Italian anti-semitism in my study: Ulrich Wyrwa, "Der Antisemitismus und die Gesellschaft des Liberalen Italien 1861–1915," in *". . . denn in Italien haben sich die Dinge anders abgespielt." Judentum und Antisemitismus im modernen Italien*, ed. Gudrun Jäger and Liana Novelli-Glaab (Berlin: Trafo-Verlag, 2007), 87–106.

14. Simon Levis Sullam, "Per una storia dell'antisemitismo cattolico in Italia," in *Cristiani d'Italia. Chiese, società, Stato (1861–2011)*, ed. Alberto Melloni (Rome: Istituto della Enciclopedia Italiana, 2011), 1:461–470; David Bidussa and Simon Levis Sullam, "Alle origini dell'antisemitismo moderno," in *Storia della Shoah: La crisi dell'Europa, lo sterminio degli ebrei e la memoria del XX secolo*, ed. Marina Cattaruzza et al. (Turin: UTET, 2005), 1:69–95; Giovanni Miccoli, "Antiebraismo, antisemitismo: un nesso fluttuante," in *Les racines chrétiennes de l'antisémitisme politique*, ed. Catherine Brice (Rome: Ecole française de Rome, 2003), 3–23.

15. Domenico Sella and Carlo Capra, *Il Ducato di Milano 1535–1796, vol. 2: La grande storia di Milano: Dall'età dei Comuni all'unità d'Italia* (Torino: UTET, 2010); Carlo Zaghi, *L'Italia di Napoleone, vol. 3: La grande storia di Milano: Dall'età dei Comuni all'unità d'Italia* (Torino: UTET, 2010).

16. Marco Meriggi, *Il Regno Lombardo-Veneto, vol. 4: La grande storia di Milano: Dall'età dei Comuni all'unità d'Italia* (Torino: UTET, 2010); Cesare Mozzarelli and Rosanna Pavoni, eds., *Milano 1848–1898: Ascesa e trasformazione della Capitale morale*, 2 vols. (Milan: Marsilio, 2000); *Storia di Milano*, vol. 15: *Nell'unità Italiana (1859–1900)* (Milan: Fondazione Treccani degli Alfieri per la Storia di Milano, 1962).

17. Giovanni Miccoli, *Chiesa e società in Italia dal concilio Vaticano I (1870) al pontificato di Giovanni XXIII*, in *Storia d'Italia*, vol. 5, no. 1: *documenti* (Turin: Einaudi, 1973), 1497–1568; David I. Kertzer, *Prisoner of the Vatican: The Popes' Secret Plot to Capture Rome from the New Italian State* (Boston: Houghton Mifflin, 2004).

18. Jean Dominique Durand, "Die Kirche auf der Suche nach dem verlorenen Italien," in *Die Geschichte des Christentums: Religion, Politik, Kultur*, vol. 11: *Liberalismus, Industrialisierung, Expansion Europas (1830–1914)*, ed. Jean Marie Mayeur et al. (Freiburg: Herder, 1997), 595–620.

19. In "non expedit," pronounced in 1868, the Pope forbade Catholics from voting. Cesare Marongiu Buonaiuti, *Non expedit: Storia di una politica 1866–1919* (Milan: A. Giuffré, 1971).

20. Sullam, "Per una storia dell'antisemitismo cattolico in Italia." For Turin, see Michele Nani, *Ai confini della nazione: Stampa e razzismo nell'Italia di fine Ottocento* (Rome: Carocci, 2006) 157–230.

21. Angelo Majo, *Storia della Chiesa ambrosiana*, vol. 4: *Dal secondo Ottocento al card.*

A. C. *Ferrari* (Milano: NED, 1986); Giorgio Rumi, *Milano cattolica nell'Italia unita* (Milan: NED, 1980); Ada Ferrari, "Una religione feriale: aspetti e momenti del cattolicesimo ambrosiano dall'Unigtà agli anni Settanta," in *La Lombardia: Storia d'Italia: Le regioni dall'Unità a oggi*, ed. Marco Meriggi and Duccio Bigazzi (Turin: Einaudi, 2001), 431–477.

22. Klaus Kienzler, "Antonio Rosmini Serbati," in *Biographisch-bibliographisches Kirchenlexikon*, ed. Friedrich Wilhelm Bautz and Traugott Bautz (Hamm: Bautz, 1994), 8:707–714.

23. Giusppe Colombo, "La Società ecclesiastica in Milano," *Ricerche storiche sulla Chiesa ambrosiana* 2 (1971): 295–364.

24. Franco Fava, *Storia di Milano*, vol. 3: *Dalla morte dell' imperatore Giuseppe II d'Austria 1790 alla liberazione dal Nazi-Fascismo 1945* (Milan: Libreria Meravigli, 1982), 92; for the role of the Church in Milan, see A. Majo, *Storia della Chiesa ambrosiana*, vol. 4: *Dizionario della Chiesa ambrosiana*, ed. Angelo Majo, 6 vols. (Milan: NED, 1987–1994).

25. Marco Meriggi, *Milano borghese: Circoli ed èlites nell'Ottocento* (Venice: Marsilio, 1992); Marco Meriggi, "Lo spirito di associazione nella Milano dell'Ottocento (1815–1890)," *Quaderni Storici* 77, no. 2 (1991): 389–417.

26. F. Fava, *Storia di Milano*, 3:98.

27. John Pollard, *Catholicism in Modern Italy: Religion, Society and Politics since 1861* (London: Routledge, 2008), 52.

28. A. Canavero, *Albertario*, 19 f.

29. Ibid., 17, 24.

30. Angelo Majo, "Albertario giornalista e maestro del giornalismo," in Virginio Rognoni, Angelo Majo, and Giorgio Rumi, *Davide Albertario giornalista* (Milan: Nuove edizioni Duomo, 1981), 35–53, at 37.

31. The following sketch of Albertario refers especially to the study by Alfredo Canavero, *Albertario e "L'Osservatore Cattolico"* (Rome: Studium, 1988). Canavero carefully reconstructed the internal Catholic divisions into which Davide Albertario stepped, but he almost completely ignored the antisemitism of Albertario, mentioning Albertartio's antisemitic rhetoric just once, and as an aside . . . In his comprehensive appendix, Canavero published a selection of articles from *Osservatore Cattolico*, but included only one of the numerous antisemitic contributions from that paper.

32. Virginio Rognoni, "Un uomo libero e difficile," in Rognoni, Majo, and Rumi, *Davide Albertario giornalista*, 9–31; Annalisa Di Fant, "'Questione ebraica' e antisemitismo in alcune voci della stamoa cattolica italiana dopo l'Unità (1870–1893)" (Ph.D. diss., Università degli studi di Trieste, 2004), 47 f.

33. Scholars refer to Albertario as a "master of journalism" or even an "athlete of Catholic journalism." Giuseppe Pecora, *Don Davide Albertario, campione del giornalismo cattolico* (Turin: Società ed. internazionale, 1934).

34. *L'Osservatore Cattolico*, March 23–24 and April 14–15, 1876.

35. *L'Osservatore Cattolico*, April 11–12, 1876.

36. A. Canavero, *Albertario*, 49.

37. Shlomo Simonsohn, *The Jews in the Duchy of Milan (1387–1788,* 4 vols. (Jerusalem: Israel Academy of Sciences and Humanities, 1982–1986).

38. Germano Maifreda, "La 'rubrica degli Israeliti' dell'Archivio Storico Civico di Milano," *Rassegna Mensile di Israel* 60, no. 3 (1993): 24–66; Sara Sinigaglia, "Gli ebrei a Milano nella prima metà dell'ottocento: genesi di una comunità," *Storia in Lombardia: Quadrisemestrale dell'Istituto lombardo per la storia della Resistenza e dell' età contemporanea* (Milano) 19 (1999): n. 1, S. 37–71.

39. Sara Sinigaglia, "Gli ebrei a Milano nella prima metà dell'Ottocento: genesi di una comunità," (Tesi di laurea, University of Milan, 1994–95), 116.

40. Maifreda, "La 'rubrica degli Israeliti' dell'Archivio Storico Civico di Milano."

41. Germano Maifreda, *Gli ebrei e l'economia Milanese: L'Ottocento* (Milan: F. Angeli, 2000).

42. Vittorio Dell'Acqua, "Ebrei nella Milano dell'Ottocento: uno studio sulle dichiarazioni di successione (1862–1890)," (Tesi di laurea, University of Milan, 1993–94), 161–162.

43. Dell'Acqua, *"Ebrei nella Milano dell'Ottocento,"* 165–166.

44. Jonathan Morris, *The Political Economy of Shopkeeping in Milan (1886–1922)* (Cambridge: Cambridge University Press, 1993); Wyrwa, "Der Antisemitismus und die Gesellschaft des Liberalen Italien," 87–106, esp. 92–94.

45. Wyrwa, "Antisemitic Agitation and the Emergence of Political Catholicism in Mantua around 1900."

46. Albertario, *Dei cattolici e del liberalismo,* 58.

47. Albertario, *Un anno in carcere . . .*

48. Davide Albertario, *La questione sociale e la democrazia cristiana: Conferenza tenuta a cura del Fascio Democratico Cristiano Milanese il 17 Febbraio 1901* (Milan: A. Bertuelli, 1901).

49. Annalisa Di Fant, "Don Davide Albertario propagandista antiebraico. L'accusa di omicidio rituale," *Storicamente* 7 (2011), art. 21, http://www.storicamente.org/.

50. *L'Osservatore Cattolico* n. 24, 1891; reprinted in the antisemitic volume: Giuseppe Panonzi [Ponzian], *L'ebreo attraverso i secoli e nelle questioni della moderna società* (Treviso: Ist. Mander, 1898), 128–132.

51. Werner Bergmann and Ulrich Wyrwa, *Antisemitismus in Zentraleuropa: Deutschland, Österreich und die Schweiz,* vol. 18: *Jahrhundert bis zur Gegenwart im Vergleich* (Darmstadt: Wissenschaftliche Buchgesellschaft, 2011), 4.

52. *L'Osservatore Cattolico,* October 25–26, 1879.

53. *L'Osservatore Cattolico,* September 5–6, 1879.

54. *L'Osservatore Cattolico,* December 20–21, 1879.

55. *L'Osservatore Cattolico,* November 12–13, 1885.

56. *L'Osservatore Cattolico,* May 30–31, 1895.

57. Annalisa Di Fant examines this in *L'Affare Dreyfus nella stampa cattolica Italiana* (Trieste: Università di Trieste, 2002).

58. John W. Boyer, *Karl Lueger (1844–1910): Christlichsoziale Politik als Beruf: Eine Biografie* (Wien: Köln, 2010), 156.

59. *L'Osservatore Cattolico,* April 6–7, 1895.

60. *L'Osservatore Cattolico*, August 13–14, 1896.

61. *L'Osservatore Cattolico*, December 17–18, 1897.

62. Eugenio Righini, *Antisemitismo e semitismo nell'Italia politica moderna* (Milan: Sandron, 1901).

63. *Vessillo Israelitico* 48 (1900), 423. Also see Ulrich Wyrwa, "'Aber der Fortschritt wird sich Bahn brechen.' Der Antisemitismus in der Sicht des italienischen Judentums. Zur Berichterstattung der Zeitschrift Il Vessillo Israelitico (1879–1915)," in *Einspruch und Abwehr: Die Reaktion des europäischen Judentums auf die Entstehung des Antisemitismus (1879–1914)*, ed. Ulrich Wyrwa (Frankfurt am Main and New York: Campus, 2010), 131–149, at 138.

64. *L'Osservatore Cattolico*, January 11–12, 1901.

65. Louise A. Tilly, *Politics and Class in Milan 1881–1901* (New York and Oxford: Oxford University Press, 1992), 261–263.

66. *L'Osservatore Cattolico*, March 15–16, 1901.

67. Di Fant, "'Questione ebraica' e antisemitismo," 192–203; Di Fant, "Don Davide Albertario." On ritual murder, see Rainer Erb, ed., *Die Legende vom Ritualmord: Zur Geschichte der Blutbeschuldigung gegen Juden* (Berlin: Metropol, 1993); Rainer Erb, "Die Ritualmordlegende: Von den Anfängen bis ins 20. Jahrhundert," in *Ritualmord: Legenden in der europäischen Geschichte*, ed. Susanna Buttaroni and Stanisla Musial (Wien: Böhlau, 2003), 11–20.

68. Di Fant, "Don Davide Albertario."

69. In addition to the publications just mentioned, see also: Annalisa Di Fant, "Stampa cattolica italiana e antisemitismo alla fine dell'Ottocento," in Brice, *Les racines chrétiennes de l'antisémitisme politique*, 121–136; Di Fant, "Alcune considerazioni su polemica antiebraica e polemica anticlericale alla fine dell'Ottocento," in *Studi in onore di Giovanni Miccoli*, ed. Liliana Ferrari (Trieste: Università di Trieste, 2004), 329–345; Di Fant, "La polemica antiebraica nella stampa cattolica romana dopo la Breccia di Porta Pia," *Mondo Contemporaneo: Rivista di Storia* 3, no. 1 (2007): 87–118.

70. Di Fant, "Don Davide Albertario," 8.

71. *Jüdisches Lexikon: Ein enzyklopädisches Handbuch des jüdischen Wissens in vier Bänden*, vol. 1, sp. 1085 (Berlin: Jüdischer Verlag, 1927).

72. Edith Stern, *The Glorious Victory of Truth: The Tiszaeszlár Blood Libel Trial 1882–83. A Historical Legal Medical Research* (Jerusalem: Rubin Massachusetts, 1998).

73. Gerald Lamprecht, "'Allein der Antisemitismus ist heute nicht mehr eine bloße Idee ...': Strategien gegen den Antisemitismus in Österreich," in Wyrwa, *Einspruch und Abwehr*, 153–179; Tim Buchen, "'Herkules im antisemitischen Augiasstall': Joseph Samuel Bloch und Galizien in der Reaktion auf Antisemitismus in der Habsburgermonarchie," in Wyrwa, *Einspruch und Abwehr*, 193–214.

74. *L'Osservatore Cattolico*, February 27–28, March 5–6, 1889. This article was published one week after the court proceedings in which the accused was convicted. The judgment was not, however, carried out. Also Di Fant, "'Questione ebraica' e antisemitismo," 4.

75. For the difference between the traditional form of blood libels and their reinvention in

the nineteenth century, see Hillel J. Kieval, "Representation and Knowledge in Medieval and Modern Accounts of Jewish Ritual Murder," in *Jewish Social Studies* 1, no. 1 (1994): 52–72.

76. Max Liebermann von Sonnenberg, *Der Blutmord in Konitz* (Berlin: Deutschnationale Buchhandlung und Verlags-Anstalt, 1900), 3.

77. David I. Kertzer, *Die Päpste gegen die Juden*, 227, passim; Annalisa Di Fant, "'Questione ebraica' e antisemitismo in alcune voci della stamoa cattolica italiana dopo l'Unità (1870–1893)," (Ph.D. thesis, Università degli studi di Trieste, 2004), 202.

78. Carl Paasch, *Eine jüdisch-deutsche Gesandtschaft und ihre Helfer* (Leipzig: C. Minde, 1892), 91 f.; *Deutsch-sozialen Blätter*, July 6, 1890.

79. Roland Florence, *Blood Libel: The Damascus Affair of 1840* (Madison: University of Wisconsin Press, 2004); Jonathan Frankel, *The Damascus Affair: "Ritual Murder," Politics, and the Jews in 1840* (Cambridge: Cambridge University Press, 1997).

80. *L'Osservatore Cattolico*, May 14–15 and May 17–18, 1890.

81. *L'Osservatore Cattolico*, May 14–15, 1890.

82. *Jüdisches Lexikon*, vol. 1, sp. 1085; *L'Osservatore Cattolico*, May 22–23, 1890; Di Fant, "Don Davide Albertario," 3; Di Fant, "'Questione ebraica' e antisemitismo," 193.

83. Maria Margaroni, "Antisemitic Rumours and Violence in Corfu at the 19th Century, *Que*" *st: Issues in Contemporary Jewish History* 3 (2012), http://www.quest-cdecjournal.it.

84. Hermann L. Strack, *Der Blutaberglaube bei Christen und Juden* (Munich: C. H. Beck, 1891), ivf.

85. Christoph Jahr, "Staatsbürger-Zeitung (1865–1926)," in *Handbuch des Antisemitismus: Judenfeindschaft in Geschichte und Gegenwart*, vol. 6: *Publikationen*, ed. Wolfgang Benz (Berlin: De Gruyter Saur, 2013), 668–669.

86. *L'Osservatore Cattolico*, May 15–16, and May 19–20, 1891.

87. *L'Osservatore Cattolico*, September 24–25 and October 14–15, 1891; *L'Osservatore Cattolico*, January 28–29 and May 24–25, 1892; also see Di Fant, "Don Davide Albertario," 7.

88. See the foreword to Hermann L. Strack, *Der Blutaberglaube in der Menschheit: Blutmorde und Blutritus. Zugleich eine Antwort auf die Herausforderung des "Osservatore Cattolico,"* 4th rev. ed. (Munich: C. H. Beck, 1892). In his introduction, Strack discussed the background for this new edition. Also see Di Fant, "'Questione ebraica' e antisemitismo," 202.

89. Di Fant, "Don Davide Albertario," 8.

90. *L'Osservatore Cattolico*, July 13–14, 1892; also see Di Fant, "Don Davide Albertario," 12.

91. *Staatsbürger-Zeitung*, July 19, 1892.

92. August Rohling, *Der Talmudjude. Zur Beherzigung für Juden und Christen aller Stände* (Münster: Adolph Russell, 1871). In the same year, Theodor Kroner, the rabbi of Münster, debunked Rohling's claims. See Theodor Kroner, *Entstelltes, Unwahres und Erfundenes in dem "Talmudjuden" Professor Dr. August Rohling's* (Münster: Obertüschen, 1871). In the 1880s the Viennese Rabbi Josef Samuel Bloch initiated a sensational lawsuit against Rohling. See Lamprecht, "'Allein der Antisemitismus ist heute nicht mehr eine bloße Idee . . .'" and Buchen, "'Herkules im antisemitischen Augiasstall.'"

93. Strack, *Der Blutaberglaube in der Menschheit*, 109–135.

94. Johannes T. Groß, *Ritualmordbeschuldigungen gegen Juden im deutschen Kaiserreich (1871–1914)* (Berlin: Metropol, 2002).

95. *L'Osservatore Cattolico*, August 6–7, 1891; Di Fant, "'Questione ebraica' e antisemitismo," 197.

96. *L'Osservatore Cattolico*, September 24–25 and 25–26, 1891; Di Fant, "Don Davide Albertario," 7 f.

97. Di Fant, "Don Davide Albertario," 15.

98. *L'Osservatore Cattolico*, April 1–2, 1893; Di Fant, "Don Davide Albertario," 16.

99. This aspect, the short duration of this campaign, has not been considered by Annalisa Di Fant, nor has its connection with Church politics.

100. A. Canavero, *Albertario*, p. 76 ff.

101. Ibid., p. 77.

102. Horkheimer and Adorno, *Dialektik der Aufklärung*, 208.

103. Kieval, "Representation and Knowledge in Medieval and Modern Accounts of Jewish Ritual Murder."

4. The Brusturoasa Uprising in Romania

1. Carol Iancu, *Bleichroeder & Crémieux* (Bucharest: Hasefer, 2005); Carol Iancu, *Evreii din România (1866–1919): De la excludere la emancipare* (Bucharest: Hasefer, 2006); Victor Neumann, *Istoria evreilor din Romania: Studii documentare și teoretice* (Timisoara: Amarcord, 1996).

2. Mariana Hausleitner, "Antisemitism in Romania: Modes of Expression between 1866 and 2009," in *Antisemitism in Eastern Europe: History and Present in Comparison*, ed. Hans-Christian Petersen and Samuel Salzborn (Frankfurt am Main: Peter Lang, 2010), 199–226; Dietmar Müller, *Staatsbürger auf Wiederruf* (Wiesbaden: Harrassowitz, 2005); Raphael Vago, "The Tradition of Antisemitism in Romania," *Patterns of Prejudice* 27, no. 1 (1993): 107–119; Beate Welter, *Die Judenpolitik der rumänischen Regierung, 1866–1888* (Frankfurt am Main: Peter Lang, 1989).

3. As in 1885 the revolution of 1907 arose in part from the fact that most peasants owned little or no land, large landowners preferred to live in town and leased their estates, and leaseholders had to struggle to recover their investment and perhaps turn a profit, thereby earning the enmity of the peasants. The events of 1907 were much more widespread and violent, with estimates putting the death toll at around eleven thousand. Andrei Otetea, Ion Popescu-Puturi, and Augustin Deac, *Marea rascoala a taranilor din 1907* (Bucharest: Editura Academiei Republicii Socialiste România, 1967); Iancu, *Evreii din România*, 242–246.

4. Dumitru Vitcu, Dumitru Ivănescu, and Cătălin Turliuc, *Modernizare și construcție națională în România: Rolul alogenilor 1832–1918* (Iași: Junimea, 2002), 127; Mihai Bărbulescu et al., *Istoria României* (Bucharest: Corint, 2002), 323–325.

5. Vitcu, Ivănescu, and Turliuc, *Modernizare*, 127.

6. *The American Jewish Year Book* (Philadelphia: The Jewish Publication of America, 1914), 336–337.

7. Iancu, *Evreii din România*, 196.

8. Ibid., 200.

9. Constantin Nuțu, *România în anii neutralității 1914–1916* (Bucharest: Editura Științifică, 1972), 8.

10. Iancu, *Evreii din România*, 191; Constantin C. Giurescu, *Istoria românilor: Din cele mai vechi timpuri până la moartea regelui Ferdinand* (Bucharest: Humanitas, 2000), 277.

11. Iancu, *Evreii din România*, 192.

12. Elias Schwarzfeld, *Adevărul asupra revoltei de la Brusturoasa* (Bucharest: S. Mihalescu, 1885), 36; Elisabetha Mănescu, ed., *Dr. M. Gaster: Viața și opera sa* (Bucharest: Rotativa, 1940), 58.

13. *Fraternitatea*, no. 34–35, September 13, 1885.

14. Ibid.

15. Ibid.; Schwarzfeld, *Adevărul*, 4.

16. Schwarzfeld, *Adevărul*, iv.

17. Ibid.

18. Schwarzfeld, *Adevărul*, iv; *Fraternitatea*, September 6, 1885.

19. Schwarzfeld, *Adevărul*, iv.

20. Ibid., viii.

21. Ibid.

22. Ibid., ix.

23. *Fraternitatea*, September 13, 1885.

24. Schwarzfeld, *Adevărul*, ix.

25. Ibid., x.

26. Ibid., xi; *Fraternitatea*, September 6, 1885.

27. *Fraternitatea*, September 13, 1885.

28. Schwarzfeld, *Adevărul*, xii.

29. *Lupta*, no. 94, August 1, 1885.

30. *Fraternitatea*, September 20, 1885.

31. Ibid.

32. Iancu, *Evreii din România*, 242–261.

33. Arhivele Naționale ale României, Fond Direcția Generală a Poliției, File 2/1903, F. 10.

34. Schwarzfeld, *Adevărul*, xiii.

35. Ibid.

36. Ibid., ix.

37. *Fraternitatea*, September 13, 1885.

38. Arhivele Naționale ale României, collection "Liga pentru unitatea culturală a tuturor românilor," fila 28.

39. I was not granted access to the Orthodox Church archives. The only information I have about its position comes from the contemporary press.

40. Schwarzfeld, *Adevărul*, 29.

41. Iancu, *Evreii din România*, 237.

42. Schwarzfeld, *Adevărul*, 9–10.

43. Lupu Dichter, *Chestiunea evreiască: Caracterul și soluția ei* (Bucharest: Institutul de Arte Grafice "Eminescu," 1910), 15.

44. Mănescu, *Dr. M. Gaster*, 58.

45. The Law Against Foreigners from April 7, 1881, was published in the *Codul general al României*, vol. 2: *Legi uzuale 1860–1900*, ed. Constantin Hamangiu (Bucharest: "Vita romaneasca," 1907).

46. Lucia Wald, *Lingviști și filologi evrei* (Bucharest: Hasefer, 1996), 36.

47. Mănescu, *Dr. M. Gaster*, 54.

48. Edmond Sincerus, *Les Juifs en Roumanie: Depuis le Traité de Berlin (1878) jusqu'a ce jour. Les lois et leurs conséquences* (London: MacMillan, 1901), 161.

49. Andrei Oișteanu, *Imaginea evreului în cultura română: Studiu de imagologie în context est-central-european*, 3rd ed. (Bucharest: Polirom, 2012).

50. Schwarzfeld, *Adevărul*, 1.

51. During the interwar period, many well-known personalities sympathized with anti-semitic ideas. Among the best known are Emil Cioran and Mircea Eliade.

5. Moravian Anti-Jewish Violence of 1899

1. In order to avoid any nationalist connotations and following the German usage that differentiates between Czech in the ethnic sense and Bohemian in the territorial, I employ the expression "Bohemian Lands" rather than the more common "Czech Lands."

2. I. Michael Aronson, *Troubled Waters: The Origins of the 1881 Anti-Jewish Pogroms in Russia* (Pittsburgh: University of Pittsburgh Press, 1990); John Doyle Klier and Shlomo Lambroza, eds., *Pogroms: Anti-Jewish Violence in Modern Russian History* (Cambridge: Cambridge University Press, 1992); Jonathan L. Dekel-Chen et al., eds., *Anti-Jewish Violence: Rethinking the Pogrom in East European History* (Bloomington: Indiana University Press, 2011).

3. Helmut Walser Smith, ed., *Exclusionary Violence: Antisemitic Riots in Modern German History* (Ann Arbor: University of Michigan Press, 2002).

4. For instance, Zdeněk Fišer, *Poslední pogrom: Události v Holešově ve dnech 3. a 4. prosince 1918 a jejich historické pozadí* (Kroměříž: Katos, 1996); Helena Krejčová and Alena Míšková, "Anmerkungen zur Frage des Antisemitismus in den Böhmischen Ländern Ende des 19. Jahrhunderts," in *Judenemanzipation—Antisemitismus—Verfolgung in Deutschland, Österreich-Ungarn, den Böhmischen Ländern und in der Slowakei*, ed. Jörg K. Hoensch, Stanislav Biman, and Ľubomír Lipták (Essen: Klartext Verlag, 1998), 55–84.

5. Michael L. Miller, "Die Nationalgarde 1848: Grenzen der Emanzipation," in *Moravští židé v rakousko-uherské monarchii (1780–1918) / Mährische Juden in der österreichisch-ungarischen Monarchie (1780–1918)*, Mikulovské sympozium 26, ed. Emil Kordiovský (Brno: Státní okresní archiv Breclav, 2003), 151–159.

6. Michael Laurence Miller, *Rabbis and Revolution: The Jews of Moravia in the Age of Eman-

cipation, Stanford Series in Jewish History and Culture (Stanford: Stanford University Press, 2011), 279–287.

7. Michal Frankl, "'Silver!' Anti-Jewish Riots in Bohemia, 1866," *Judaica Bohemiae* 45, no. 1 (2010): 5–34.

8. Jiří Lapáček, "Protižidovské bouře v Kojetíně v roce 1887," in *Židé a Morava: Sborník příspěvků přednesených na konferenci konané 11. listopadu 1998 v Kroměříži*, ed. Petr Pálka (Kroměříž: Muzeum Kroměřížska, 1999), 3–16.

9. Krejčová and Míšková, "Anmerkungen zur Frage des Antisemitismus in den Böhmischen Ländern," 55–84.

10. Given the historically bilingual character of Moravia, all place names are reproduced in both Czech and German at first usage.

11. Moravský zemský archiv (Moravian Land Archives, MZA), B 13, box 348, report of the district captain of Přerov, October 18, 1899.

12. The synagogue was burnt and torn down shortly after the Nazi occupation of the Bohemian Lands in 1939. See Jiří Fiedler, ed., *Židovské památky v Čechách a na Moravě* (Praha: Sefer, 1992), http://www.holocaust.cz/cz/resources/jcom/fiedler/vsetin; Ladislav Baletka and Jaroslav Klenovský, "Osudy vsetínské synagogy," in *Židé a Morava: Sborník z konference konané v Muzeu Kroměřížska dne 3. listopadu 2004* (Kroměříž: Muzeum Kroměřížska, 2005), 164–170.

13. MZA, B 13, box 348, undated and unsigned report about the riots in Vsetín; "Czechische Demonstrationen und Excesse. Die Plünderungen in Wsetin," *Neue Freie Presse*, October 26, 1899, p. 8.

14. Central Archives for the History of the Jewish People, Jerusalem (CAHJP), Archiv der IKG Wien, 337, 3: undated report by Abraham Grätzer.

15. The speculation that this could have been a provocation by the agents of the government which was put forward in Czech historiography finds no support in the sources and would have made little sense from the government's point of view.

16. CAHJP, Archiv der IKG Wien, 339, see also Státní okresní archiv (State district archive, SOkA) Kroměříž, B-a2, inv. no 733.

17. See numerous reports of the district captain in Holešov in MZA, B 13, box 348–349; reports from Jewish citizens in CAHJP, Archiv der IKG Wien, 337, 3; "Jüdische Flüchtlinge aus Holleschau in Wien," *Neue Freie Presse*, October 25, 1899, pp. 8–9; see also Zdeněk Fišer, *Poslední pogrom: Události v Holešově ve dnech 3. a 4. prosince 1918 a jejich historické pozadí* (Kroměříž: Katos, 1996), 79–84; Inna Mirovská, *Den pěti světel: Svědectví o posledním protižidovském pogromu na Moravě* (Praha: Votobia Praha, 1998); Karel Bartošek, "Holešovské pogromy," *Holešovsko*, no. 16 (2010): 32; Karel Bartošek, "Holešovské pogromy (2)," *Holešovsko*, no. 17 (2010): 32; Karel Bartošek, "Holešovské pogromy (3)," *Holešovsko*, no. 18 (2010): 32; Karel Bartošek, "Holešovské pogromy (4)," *Holešovsko*, no. 19 (2010): 28; Petr Pálka, "Židovsko-křesťanské vztahy v Holešově na konci 19. století," *olam.cz*, n.d., http://olam.cz/aktuality/Prednaska_Holesov.html; Josef Svátek, "Pogromy v Holešově v letech 1774–1918," *Židovská ročenka* (1979–1980): 36–44; see also Erika Němcová, *Perzekuce Židů za druhé světové války v Holešově* (Brno: PF MU, 2007), 21–22;

František Čapka, "K historii židovské obce v Holešově," in *Moravští židé v rakousko-uherské monarchii (1780–1918)* / *Mährische Juden in der österreichisch-ungarischen Monarchie (1780–1918)*, Mikulovské sympozium 26, ed. Emil Kordiovský (Brno: Státní okresní archiv Breclav, 2003), 287–294.

18. MZA, B 13, box 348, report of the gendarmerie in Hovězí, November 3, 1899.

19. SOkA Kroměříž, District chieftain Holešov, inv. no. 593, box 183, reports of gendarmerie in Dřevohostice from December 12 and 31, 1899 and February 2, 1900; complaint by Edmund Fried dated December 11, 1899.

20. See, for example, "Wien, 23. October," *Neue Freie Presse*, October 24, 1899, pp. 1–2. See also "Zástupcům národa," *Českožidovské listy* 5, no. 21 (November 2, 1899): 1–2. For the attitudes of *Neue Freie Presse* to Czech antisemitism, see Steven Beller, "German Liberalism, Nationalism and the Jews: The *Neue Freie Presse* and the German-Czech Conflict in the Habsburg Monarchy 1900–1918," *Bohemia* 34, no. 1 (1993): 63–76.

21. Stenographisches Protokoll, Haus der Abgeordneten, 9. Sitzung der XVI, November 8, 1899, p. 518.

22. Arnošt Schneider, *Řeč poslance pana Arnošta Schneidra o výtržnostech v Holešově a o židovské otázce* (Prague: České zájmy, n. d.); Arnošt Schneider, *Židovstvo v Rakousku. Řeč, kterou v 12. sezení XVI. období říšské rady dne 10. listopadu pronesl říšský poslanec Arnošt Schneider* (Prague: Antonín Hrazánek, 1900).

23. Fišer, *Poslední pogrom*.

24. MZA, PM, box 348, gendarmerie report from Prostějov, October 15, 1899.

25. For a more detailed analysis, see Michal Frankl, *"Emancipace od židů": český antisemitismus na konci 19. století* (Prague: Paseka, 2007), 5–10.

26. "Stará písnička v novém vydání," *Brněnský drak* 7, no. 12 (June 20, 1892): 1.

27. Shulamit Volkov, "Antisemitismus als kultureller Code," in Shulamit Volkov, *Jüdisches Leben und Antisemitismus im 19. und 20. Jahrhundert: Zehn Essays* (Munich: C. H. Beck, 1990), 13–36.

28. Ines Koeltzsch, "Antijüdische Straßengewalt und die semantische Konstruktion des 'Anderen' im Prag der Ersten Republik," *Judaica Bohemiae* 46, no. 1 (2011): 73–99.

29. MZA, B 13, box 348, gendarmerie report from Velká Bíteš, November 10, 1899.

30. MZA, B 13, box 348, report of the district captain of Přerov, October 18, 1899.

31. David Engel, "What's in a Pogrom? European Jews in the Age of Violence," in *Anti-Jewish Violence. Rethinking the Pogrom in East European History*, ed. Jonathan L. Dekel-Chen et al. (Bloomington: Indiana University Press, 2011), 19–37.

32. Albert Lichtblau, "Die Debatten über die Ritualmordbeschuldigungen im österreichischen Abgeordnetenhaus am Ende des 19. Jahrhunderts," in *Die Legende vom Ritualmord: Zur Geschichte der Blutbeschuldigung gegen Juden*, ed. Rainer Erb (Berlin: Metropol, 1993), 267–293.

33. Klaus Holz, "Die antisemitische Konstruktion des 'Dritten' und die nationale Ordnung der Welt," in *Das "bewegliche" Vorurteil: Aspekte des internationalen Antisemitismus*, ed. Eva-Maria Ziege (Würzburg: Königshausen & Neumann, 2004), 43–61.

34. Representative of the rather extensive research on the Hilsner affair: Jiří Kovtun, *Tajuplná vražda: Případ Leopolda Hilsnera* (Praha: Sefer, 1994); Bohumil Černý, *Vražda v Polné* (Prague: Vydavatelství časopisů MNO, 1968); Daniel M. Vyleta, *Crime, Jews and News: Vienna 1895–1914* (New York: Berghahn Books, 2007).

35. Jan Hozák, "Hilsneriáda v českém tisku," in *Hilsneriáda (k 100. výročí 1899–1999)*, ed. Bohumil Černý (Polná: Linda–Jan Prchal, 1999), 157–186.

36. Tomáš G. Masaryk, *Nutnost revidovati proces polenský* (Prague: "Casu," 1899); Tomáš G. Masaryk, *Die Nothwendigkeit der Revision des Polnaer Processes* (Vienna: Verlag "Die Zeit," 1899).

37. SOkA Kroměříž, Okresní hejtmanství Holešov (District Captain Holešov), inv. no. 593, box 183: investigation of the participation of schoolteachers and students in the riots.

38. Fišer, *Poslední pogrom*, 80.

39. MZA, B 13, box 348, draft of a report to the Ministry of Interior, October 28, 1899.

40. Gustav Otruba, "Statistische Materialien zur Geschichte der Juden in den böhmischen Ländern seit dem Ausgang des 18. Jahrhunderts," in *Die Juden in den böhmischen Ländern: Vorträge der Tagung des Collegium Carolinum in Bad Wiessee vom 27–29. November 1981*, ed. Ferdinand Seibt, Bad Wiesseer Tagungen des Collegium Carolinum series (Munich: Oldenbourg, 1983), 326.

41. For an overview of Moravian Jewish history in the nineteenth century, see Miller, *Rabbis and Revolution*.

42. Emil Goldmann, "Die politischen Judengemeinden in Mähren," *Zeitschrift für Volkswirtschaft, Sozialpolitik und Verwaltung*, no. 7 (1898): 557–595.

43. Peter Urbanitsch, "Die politischen Judengemeinden in Mähren nach 1848," in *Moravští židé v rakousko-uherské monarchii (1780–1918) / Mährische Juden in der österreichisch-ungarischen Monarchie (1780–1918)*, Mikulovské sympozium 26, ed. Emil Kordiovský (Brno: Státní okresní archiv Breclav, 2003), 39–53.

44. Stenographisches Protokoll, Haus der Abgeordneten, 9. Sitzung der XVI, November 8, 1899, pp. 533–534.

45. Marie Dokoupilová, "Projevy antisemitismu v českých prostějovských novinách Hlasy z Hané," in *Židé a Morava. Sborník z konference konané 15. listopadu 2000 v Muzeu Kroměřížska*, ed. Petr Pálka (Kroměříž: Muzeum Kroměřížska, 2001), 120–139.

46. See, for instance, "Příčina hospodářského úpadku v Litovli," *Litovelské noviny* 4, no. 10 (May 24, 1894): 1; "Svůj k svému a náš venkov," *Vyškovské noviny* 3, no. 11 (June 1, 1894): 1.

47. "Poznámky k volbám do obch. komory," *Vyškovské noviny: List věnovaný potřebám pol. okresu vyškovského* 3, no. 1 (January 5, 1894): 2; "Seznam voličů druhého sboru při minulé obecní volbě v Prostějově," *Hlasy z Hané: List politický a národo-hospodářský* 1, no. 44 (November 23, 1882): 6 [supplement]; see also Michal Frankl, "'Jerusalem an der Haná.' Nationaler Konflikt, Gemeindewahlen und Antisemitismus in Mähren Ende des 19. Jahrhunderts," *Jahrbuch für Antisemitismusforschung* 15 (2006): 135–159.

48. Michal Frankl, "Obvinění z rituální vraždy v Kolíně," *Dějiny a současnost*, no. 6 (1998): 14–18.

49. Martin Markel, *Svoboda a demokracie v regionu rakouského impéria. Politika jihomorav-ských Němců v letech 1848–1919* (Brno: Matice moravská–Výzkumné středisko pro dějiny střední Evropy, 2010), 111–143.

50. Herman L. Strack, *Krev ve víře a v pověře lidstva* (Praha: Čas, 1902); Hermann L. Strack, *Das Blut im Glauben und Aberglauben der Menschheit* (Munich: Beck, 1900).

51. "Akciový křesťanský obchod v Kroměříži," *Žihadlo* 1, no. 22 (December 22, 1893): 170–171. Its name notwithstanding, the project probably was closer to a cooperative rather than a joint stock company.

52. "Živnostenský sjezd v Kroměříži," *Žihadlo* 2, no. 19 (October 10, 1894): 93–94.

53. "Lambert Klabusay," *Město Holešov*, July 31, 2013, http://www.holesov.cz/mesto-holesov /osobnosti-a-rodaci/lambert-klabusay; Pavel Marek, "K počátkům živnostenského hnutí na Kroměřížsku," *Archivní ročenka (Státní okresní archiv Kroměříž)* 2 (1996): 66.

54. August Rohling and J. Nebeský, *Mravouka židovská v Talmudu. Výňatky podle doktora Augusta Rohlinga, jenž přislíbil 1000 tolarů tomu, kdož by mu dokázal jen jediného nepravého dokladu v této mravouce obsaženého* (Holešov: Lambert Klabusay, 1896).

55. MZA, B 13, box 348, reports of the district captain of Litovel, October 25 and 30, 1899.

56. MZA, B 13, box 348, report of the gendarmerie in Prostějov, October 15, 1899.

57. SOkA Kroměříž, B-a2, inv. no 733: "Obyvatelstvu okresu Holešovského!"

58. "[. . .] der 'raffende Jude' erhielt durch die Aufforderungen zum Boykott bestimm-ter Geschäfte vor Ort einen Namen, ein Gesicht und eine Adresse." Hannah Ahlheim, *"Deutsche, kauft nicht bei Juden!" Antisemitismus und politischer Boykott in Deutschland 1924 bis 1935* (Göttingen: Wallstein, 2011), 204.

59. See mainly Fišer, *Poslední pogrom*; Mirovská, *Den pěti světel*; Svátek, "Pogromy v Hole-šově v letech 1774–1918"; Bartošek, "Holešovské pogromy (4)."

60. Fišer, *Poslední pogrom*, 97–98.

61. "Němci a židé v československé republice se zvláštním zřetelem k metropoli Slovače!," *Hanácká republika* 1, no. 30 (December 21, 1922): 3.

62. František Mezihorák, "Národopisný antisemitismus (zvláštní aspekt atmosféry holo-kaustu na jihovýchodní Moravě v letech 1938–1945)," in *Akce Nisko v historii "koneč-ného řešení židovské otázky" k 55. výročí první hromadné deportace evropských Židů*, ed. Ludmila Čermáková-Nesládková (Ostrava: Ostravská univerzita, Filozofická fakulta, 1995), 213–217.

63. Vladimír Ševela, "Malý český pogrom," *Týden*, no. 34 (January 16, 2012).

6. Anti-Jewish Violence in Habsburg Croatia

1. Krešimir Švarc, "Prilozi za povijest koprivničkih Židova," *Podravski zbornik* 17 (1991): 167–182; Ivan Pederin, "Židovsko pitanje u srednjoj Europi i Hrvatskoj u XIX. st.," *Croatica Christiana Periodica* 53 (2004): 125–147; Ljiljana Dobrovšak, "Židovi i njihov utjecaj na transformaciju naselja podravskog višegraničja krajem 19. i početkom 20. stoljeća," *Podra-vina* 3, no. 6 (2004): 22–43; Alej Budaj, *Vallis Judaea: Povijest požeške židovske zajednice* (Zagreb: D-Graf, 2007).

2. Hrvoje Klasić, "Antisemitizam u Sisku na prijelazu stoljeća (1897–1903): Prilog pruča-

vanja židovstva u gradu Sisku," in *Godišnjak Gradski Muzej Sisak* 2 (2001): 175–197; Ivo Goldstein, "Antisemitizam u Hrvatskoj," in *Zna li se? Antisemitizam, Holokaust, Antifašizam*, ed. Ognjen Kraus (Zagreb: Židovska općina, 1996), 12–63; Marija Vulesica, *Die Formierung des politischen Antisemitismus in den Kronländern Kroatien und Slawonien 1879–1906* (Berlin: Metropol, 2012).

3. Miroslava Despot, "Protužidovski izgredi u Zagorju i Zagrebu godine 1883," *Jevrejski almanah* (1957–1958): 75–85.

4. Ljiljana Dobrovšak, "Židovi u zbivanjima 1903–1904," *Časopis za suvremenu povijest* 37, no. 3 (2005): 635–652.

5. On the history of the Croatian lands, see Branka Magaš, *Croatia through History: The Making of a European State* (London: Saqi, 2007); Ludwig Steindorff, *Kroatien: Vom Mittelalter bis zur Gegenwart* (Regensburg: Pustet, 2007).

6. On 1848: Ljiljana Dobrovšak, "Židovi u hrvatskim zemljama 1848/1849," *Radovi* 30, no. 1 (1997): 77–89; Ljiljana Dobrovšak, "Razvoj židovskih zajednica u kraljevini Hrvatskoj i Slavoniji (1783–1873)" (Ph.D. diss., University of Zagreb, 2007), 207–245.

7. *Magyarization* was a contemporary term. Behind this lay the goal of securing the power of Hungarian politics. At the same time, this policy was supposed to promote the "integration" of non-Magyars into *one* political nation; however, non-Magyar peoples viewed this conception as a threat to their own national and cultural development and opposed it. It has also become an accepted term by scholars.

8. Mirjana Gross, *Počeci moderne Hrvatske* (Zagreb: Globus, 1985), 360–369; Ivo Goldstein, "Zagrebačka židovska općina od osnutka do 1941," in *Dva stoljeća povijesti i kulture Židova u Zagrebu i Hrvatskoj*, ed. Ognjen Kraus (Zagreb: Zidovska opcina, 1998), 12–18.

9. Ljiljana Dobrovšak, "Emancipacija Židova u Kraljevini Hrvatskoj, Slavoniji i Dalmaciji u 19. stoljeću," *Radovi* 37, no. 1 (2005): 125–143; Dobrovšak, "Razvoj židovskih zajednica," 386–392.

10. Agneza Szabo, "Židovi i proces modernizacije građanskog društva u Hrvatskoj između 1873. i 1914. godine," in Kraus, *Dva stoljeća*, 145 f.

11. *Židovska smotra*, August 1, 1912.

12. Mira Kolar-Dimitrijević, "Židovi u gospodarstvu sjeverne Hrvatska od 1873. do 1941. godine," in Kraus, *Dva stoljeća*, 129–136.

13. Mira Kolar-Dimitrijević, "Prvo dobrotvorno društvo Humanitätsverein u Zagrebu: u povodu stopedesete obljetnice 1846–1996," in Kraus, *Dva stoljeća*, 69–73; Vera Dojč, "100 godina organiziranog rada židovskih žena u Zagrebu," in *200 godina Židova u Zagrebu*, ed. Mirko Mirković (Zagreb: Jevrejska općina Zagreb, 1988), 53–61; Melita Švob, "Razvoj ženskih općih i židovskih dobrotvornih organizacija," in Kraus, *Dva stoljeća*, 268–282; *Dr. Blochs Österreichische Wochenschrift*, June 13, 1902.

14. *Statistički godišnjak zemalja Ugarske krune* (Budapest: Athenaeum, 1895), 358.

15. Wolfdieter Bihl, "Die Juden," in *Die Habsburgermonarchie 1848–1918*, ed. Adam Wandruszka and Peter Urbanitsch, vol. 3, pt. 2 (Vienna: VÖAW, 1980), 880–948, at 926.

16. Marija Vulesica, *Die Formierung des politischen Antisemitismus in den Kronländern Kroatien und Slawonien, 1879–1906* (Berlin: Metropol, 2012).

17. Paragraphs 56–61 of the Croatian-Hungarian Agreement made Croatian the sole language of administration in the crownland. See Tihomir Cipek and Stjepan Matković, eds., *Programatski dokumenti hrvatskih političkih stranaka i skupina 1842–1914* (Zagreb: Disput, 2006), 696.

18. Dragutin Pavličević, *Narodni pokret 1883. u Hrvatskoj* (Zagreb: Sveučilišna naklada Liber, 1980), 25–67.

19. This was also clear in the episode of the peasants breaking into and plundering a Jewish home in Bednja. During this incident, the perpetrators found a tobacco advertisement in the attic. They believed it was a Hungarian coat of arms, brought it to the street, and destroyed it in triumph. See Ivan Peršić, *1883–ća. Uspomene na predratni Zagreb povodom 50–godišnjice bune radi mađarskih grbova* (Zagreb: Tipografija, 1933), 27.

20. See the in-depth reporting of Vienna's *Neue Freie Presse* in August and September 1883.

21. Pavličević, *Narodni pokret 1883*, 126–131.

22. Ibid., 167.

23. The party and the newspapers were openly anti-Jewish up to and beyond the turn of the century. See Vulesica, *Die Formierung des politischen Antisemitismus*.

24. *Pozor*, August 28, 1883.

25. *Pozor*, August 31 and September 1, 1883.

26. *Pozor*, August 29, 1883.

27. *Pozor*, 2 August 9, 1883.

28. *Pozor*, September 7, 1883.

29. HDA, PRZV 1881–1883, doc. no. 3556, carton 182.

30. *Pozor*, September 7, 1883.

31. *Pozor*, September 9, 1883; Priester, Baumgärtner, and Wasserthal were famous Zagreb merchants. See Despot, *Protužidovski izgredi u Zagorju i Zagrebu godine 1883*, 80 f.

32. *Pozor*, September 9, 1883.

33. Ibid.

34. *Pozor*, September 10, 1883.

35. *Pozor*, September 27, 1883.

36. *Pozor*, September 27 and October 6, 1883.

37. Peršić, *1883–ća*, 87.

38. *Neue Freie Presse*, September 4, 1883.

39. HDA, PRZV 1881–1883, doc. ohne nummer, carton 182.

40. Rudolf Horvat, *Prije Khuena bana. Nemiri u Hrvatskoj god. 1883* (Zagreb: Hrvatsko Književno društvo Sv. Jeronima, 1934), 37 f.

41. HDA, UOZV, doc. no. 35.791, carton 723.

42. HDA, PRZV 1881–1883, doc. no. 3566, doc. no. 3476, carton 182.

43. HDA, UOZV, doc. no. 38.484, carton 724.

44. A telegram sent by a judge in Ivanec to the provincial government on September 4 confirmed the complete destruction of David Fritz's house. HDA, PRZV 1881–1883, doc. no. 3580, carton 181.

45. Horvat, *Prije Khuena bana*, 27.

46. HDA, PRZV 1881–1883, doc. no. 3872, carton 183.

47. Ibid.

48. Horvat, *Prije Khuena bana*, 28.

49. HDA, PRZV 1881–1883, doc. no. 3866, carton 183.

50. Despot, *Izgredi*, 80 f.

51. HDA, PRZV 1881–1883, doc. no. 4220, carton 183.

52. HDA, PRZV 1881. 1883, doc. no. 3517, carton 181.

53. HDA PRZV 1881–1883, doc. no. 3543, 3548 und 3565, carton 181.

54. HDA, PRZV 1881–1883, doc. no. 3543, carton 181. "Eszter" refers to Eszter Solymosi, the fourteen-year-old girl whose disappearance triggered the Tiszaeszlár blood libel. "Istóczy" refers to Győző Istóczy, the Hungarian MP who lent credence to the ritual murder charge and later organized an Antisemitic Party.

55. "Udri, udri in der Stadt, svim židovom štrik za vrat." This was an altered form of the slogan "Udri, udri in der Stadt, svim Magyarom štrik za vrat." This slogan retained "in der Stadt" in German in order to rhyme with the Croatian word for throat (*vrat*).

56. HDA, PRZV 1881–1883, doc. no. 3543, carton 181.

57. HDA, PRZV 1881–1883, doc. no. 4070, carton 183.

58. HDA, PRZV 1881–1883, doc. no. 4189, carton 183.

59. HDA, PRZV 1881–1883, doc. no. 4580, carton 183.

60. This paper, published in Budapest from 1882 to 1884, carried the subtitle: "The only anti-semitic humorous-satirical monthly published in the German language." "Ritter Jürgen" was listed as editor and Emerich Baltalits as publisher. The editions from November and December 1882 as well as January and July 1883 are held in the Croatian State Archives. They were confiscated by the police and sent to the provincial government in Zagreb.

61. HDA, PRZV 1881–1883, doc. no. 432, carton 179.

62. HDA, PRZV 1881–1883, doc. no. 416, carton 179.

63. HDA, PRZV 1881–1883, doc. no. 2693, carton 131.

64. HDA, PRZV 1881–1883, doc. no. 3476, carton 181.

65. *Katolički List*, October 4, 1883.

66. *Magyaron* was a derogatory term for a Croat who was thought to serve the Hungarians.

67. *Sriemski Hrvat*, September 8, 1883.

68. *Sloboda*, September 16, 1883.

69. Ibid.

70. *Narodne novine*, September 4, 1883.

71. Ibid.

72. *Neue Freie Presse*, September 4, 1883.

73. *Neue Freie Presse*, September 11, 1883.

74. *Allgemeine Zeitung des Judentums*, September 18 and 25, 1883.

75. *Allgemeine Zeitung der Judentums*, September 25, 1883.

76. Robert Nemes, "Hungary's Antisemitic Provinces: Violence and Ritual Murder in the 1880s," *Slavic Review* 66, no. 1 (2007): 20–44, at 38 f.

77. Mirjana Gross, "Narodni pokret u Hrvatskoj godine 1903," *Historijski pregled* 1, no. 1

(1954): 16–22; Agneza Szabo, "Uzroci i posljedice demonstracija 1903," *Časopis za suvremenu povijest* 37, no. 3 (2005): 597–608.

78. Stjepan Matković, *Čista stranka prava, 1895–1903* (Zagreb: Dom i svijet, 2001), 163–176; Izidor Kršnjavi, *Zapisci iza kulisa hrvatske politike*, ed. Ivan Krtalić, vol. 1 (Zagreb: Mladost, 1986), 239–243.

79. HDA, PRZV 1903–1905, doc. no. 2082, carton 680.

80. HDA, PRZV 1903–1904, doc. no. 2450, carton 680.

81. HDA, PRZV 1903–1905, doc. no. 2704, carton 680.

82. Kršnjavi, *Zapisci*, 1: 258.

83. HDA, PRZV 1903–1905, doc. no. 4432, carton 682.

84. *Die Drau*, May 12 and May 14, 1903.

85. Grga Tuškan (1845–1923) pursued a decidedly antisemitic political orientation from the mid-1890s. He produced numerous antisemitic publications. In 1897, in anticipation of the parliamentary elections, he and his press promoted openly antisemitic rhetoric. A great deal was written about Sisak in this period, because antisemites spread the story that the Jews of the town had baptized a cat in order to lampoon Christianity. See Vulesica, *Die Formierung des politischen Antisemitismus*.

86. Ljiljana Dobrovšak, "Židovi u zbivanjima 1903–1904," *Časopis za suvremenu povijest* 37, no. 3 (2005): 644–647.

87. Dobrovšak, "Židovi u zbivanjima," 643.

88. Marija Winter, *Iz povijesti Ludbrega i okolice* (Koprivnica: Nakladna kuća "Dr. Feletar," 2000), 156.

89. Vaso Bogdanov, *Hrvatski narodni pokret 1903/4* (Zagreb: Izd. zavod Jugoslavenske akademije znanosti i umjetnosti, 1961), 138, 149, 153.

90. Dobrovšak, "Židovi u zbivanjima," 648.

91. Vulesica, *Die Formierung des politischen Antisemitismus*, 173–230.

92. For more on Croatian Catholic antisemitism in this period, see Marija Vulesica, "How Antisemitic Was the Political Catholicism in Croatia-Slavonia around 1900?" *Quest: Issues in Contemporary Jewish History*, no. 3 (July 2012).

93. Ivo Banac, "'I Karlo je o'šo u komite.' Nemiri u sjevernoj Hrvatskoj u jesen 1918," *Časopis za suvremenu povijest* 24, no. 3 (1992): 23–43.

94. Banac, "Nemiri," 28 f.

95. *Židov*, no. 22 (1918), quoted in Goldstein, "Zagrebačka židovska," 51.

96. Banac, "Nemiri," 29.

97. *Židov*, December 1, 1918.

98. Ibid.

99. Goldstein, "Zagrebačka židovska, 48 f.

100. Banac, "Nemiri," 29.

101. *Židov*, December 1, 1918.

102. Banac, "Nemiri," 28.

103. *Židov*, December 1, 1918.

104. Werner Bergmann, "Exclusionary Riots: Some Theoretical Considerations," in *Exclu-*

sionary Violence: Antisemitic Riots in Modern German History, ed. Christhard Hoffmann, Werner Bergmann, and Helmut Walser Smith (Ann Arbor: University of Michigan Press, 2002), 161–184.

7. Anti-Jewish Sentiment in London's East End

1. See G. R. Searle, *The Quest for National Efficiency: A Study in British Politics and Political Thought, 1899–1914* (Oxford: Blackwell, 1971).

2. *Daily Mail*, January 15, 1902, p. 5.

3. See, for example, *Report from the Select Committee on Emigration and Immigration (Foreigners)* (London: Hansard & Sons, 1888).

4. The Board of Trade, which advised the government on a range of economic issues, published monthly statistics on immigration from the 1890s on; see Board of Trade (Alien immigration), *Reports on the Volume and Effects of Recent Immigration from Eastern Europe into the United Kingdom* (London: Eyre and Spottiswoode, 1894).

5. *Report of the Twenty-Eight Annual Trades Union Congress* (Manchester: Co-operative Printing Society Ltd., 1895).

6. *Royal Commission on Alien Immigration*, 4 vols. (London: HMSO, 1903). For discussion of the path to the Aliens Act, see Bernard Gainer, *The Alien Invasion: The Origins of the Aliens Act of 1905* (London: Heinemann, 1972); John A. Garrard, *The English and Immigration, 1880–1910* (London: Oxford University Press, 1971); Colin Holmes, *Antisemitism in British Society, 1876–1939* (London: Edward Arnold, 1979).

7. See Todd M. Endelman, *The Jews of Britain, 1656–2000* (Berkeley: University of California Press, 2002), 127. For further discussion, see Lloyd. P. Gartner, *The Jewish Immigrant in England, 1870–1914* (London: Vallentine Mitchell, 2001).

8. For discussion of the function of the image of the Irish in British national discourse, see Michael Willem de Nie, *The Eternal Paddy: Irish Identity and the British Press, 1798–1882* (Madison: University of Wisconsin Press, 2004).

9. *Hansard's Parliamentary Debates*, 4th ser., vol. 8 (London: Wyman & Sons, 1893), 163–164.

10. *East End News and London Shipping Chronicle* [henceforth *EENLSC*], February 12, 1901, p. 2.

11. See also *EENLSC*, February 12, 1901, p. 1, which referred to London as a "dumping" ground for continental Europe's "rubbish."

12. Endelman, *The Jews of Britain, 1656–2000*, 129.

13. Lord Bonham-Carter referred to the League as "proto-fascist"; see *The Official Report, House of Lords*, 5th ser., vol. 484 (London: HMSO, 1987), 131.

14. For a brief overview of the BBL, see Colin Holmes's entry in *Antisemitism: A Historical Encyclopaedia of Prejudice and Persecution*, ed. Richard S. Levy (Oxford: ABC-CLIO, 2005), 86.

15. For detailed East London census statistics from 1901, see *1901 Census of England and Wales, County Report*, http://www.visionofbritain.org.uk/census/.

16. Letter from "British Brother" to *East London Observer* [henceforth *ELO*], August 8, 1902, p. 2.

17. Gainer, *The Alien Invasion*; Garrard, *The English and Immigration*.

18. Anthony Julius, *T. S. Eliot: Antisemitism and Literary Form* (London: Thames & Hudson, 2003), 1.

19. The principal "fanatic" from this period is usually identified as Arnold White, who campaigned for legislation for many years. I would argue, however, that his rhetoric was part of a wider pattern of antisemitic discourse in the United Kingdom. See Sam Johnson, "'A Veritable Janus at the Gates of Jewry': British Jews and Mr. Arnold White," *Patterns of Prejudice*, 47, no. 1 (2013): 41–68.

20. The geographical limits of the East End remain debatable. The above-mentioned boroughs were created in 1900 and fell within the remit of the former Tower Division, a local government designation dating from the medieval period and encompassing many ancient parishes and hamlets. These included, among others, Limehouse, Isle of Dogs, parts of Mile End, St. George in the East, Bow, Whitechapel, Hoxton, and Haggerston.

21. Letter from "East Ender" to *EENLSC*, January 19, 1901, p. 8.

22. Michael Ball and David Sunderland, *An Economic History of London, 1800–1914* (London: Routledge, 2001), 223–226.

23. Charles Booth, *Life and Labour of the People* (London: Macmillan, 1889–1903). Volume I appeared in 1889, with subsequent editions appearing from 1892 to 1897 (nine volumes) and from 1902 to 1903 (seventeen volumes). Booth's poverty maps have been digitized and are available online via the archives of the London School of Economics, see http://booth.lse.ac.uk/.

24. For a discussion of the way Jews were described in Booth's study, see David Englander, "The Presentation of Jews and Judaism in 'Life and Labour of the People in London,'" *Victorian Studies*, 32, no. 4 (1989): 551–571.

25. There was regular reference to the East End ghetto in the British press. See, for example, the front-page images of "ghetto types" published by the *Jewish World* [henceforward *JW*], which included a *melamed* (teacher), *chazzan* (cantor), and a *yeshiva* student; *JW*, August 29, 1902; September 5, 1902; September 12, 1902. The term was used most notably by the Jewish playwright and author, Israel Zangwill. See his *Children of the Ghetto* (London: Heinemann, 1892) set in East London.

26. Endelman, *The Jews of Britain, 1656–2000*, 158.

27. The 1889 dock strike and the 1888 Match Girls' strike together are regarded as a watershed in British union history, especially in London. Subsequent years saw a growth in the new unions, whose members were unskilled and low-paid workers previously excluded from the traditional skilled "craft" unions. For discussion, see Louise Raw, *Striking a Light: The Bryant and May Matchwomen and Their Place in History* (London: Continuum, 2009).

28. Ibid., 160. Endelman erroneously claims that the League was founded by Major William Evans-Gordon, MP for Stepney (of which more follows). The reference probably alludes to the short-lived Londoners' League, founded in August 1901 by Evans-Gordon and other parliamentarians. Its single political act was to send a delegation to the home secretary and the president of the Board of Trade. There was no discernible outcome. See *ELO*, August 3, 1901, p. 5; *EENLSC*, August 9, 1901, p. 3.

29. *ELO*, May 11, 1901, p. 5.

30. *EENLSC*, May 14, 1901, p. 3; *ELO*, May 11, 1901, p. 5.

31. *ELO*, May 11, 1901, p. 5; *ELO*, June 1, 1901, p. 6. Evans-Gordon was the most renowned anti-immigrant MP in this period, and he regularly gave speeches in the House of Commons urging restrictive legislation. During a speech delivered in the same month as the BBL's biggest meeting (see the following), he spoke on the "danger and evil" of immigration. Unafraid of piquant imagery, he observed: "These foreigners congregate in certain quarters of certain towns [and] the effect of their coming is out of all proportion to the numbers who come. Ten grains of arsenic in 1,000 loaves would be unnoticeable and perfectly harmless, but the same amount if put into one loaf would kill the whole family that partook of it." See *Hansard's Parliamentary Debates*, 4th ser., vol. 101 (London: Wyman and Sons, 1902), 1272; 1274.

32. *ELO*, May 11, 1901, p. 5.

33. *EENLSC*, May 14, 1901, p. 3.

34. *ELO*, May 11, 1901, p. 5.

35. *EENLSC*, May 14, 1901, p. 3.

36. See: William J. Fishman, *East End Jewish Radicals, 1875–1914* (London: Duckworth, 1975).

37. Letter from "British Brother" to *ELO*, May 25, 1901, p. 6.

38. *ELO*, June 1, 1901, pp. 5–6.

39. *ELO*, June 1, 1901, p. 6.

40. *ELO*, June 8, 1901, p. 8.

41. *ELO*, June 8, 1901, p. 5; *East London Advertiser* [henceforward, *ELA*] June 29, 1901, p. 2.

42. *ELO*, June 29, 1901, p. 2.

43. *EENLSC*, June 7, 1901, p. 2; see also, *ELA*, June 22, 1901, p. 3.

44. *EENLSC*, June 14, 1901, p. 2.

45. *EENLSC*, June 11, 1901, p. 2; see also July 23, 1901, p. 2, with editorial on "aliens and housing."

46. *ELO*, October 26, 1901, p. 3.

47. *ELO*, November 16, 1901, p. 5; January 18, 1902, p. 2; February 22, 1902, p. 5; *EAHT*, November 23, 1901, p. 5; December 7, 1901, p. 3; March 15, 1902, p. 7.

48. *EAHT*, March 1, 1902, p. 5; see also: *ELO*, April 26, 1902, p. 6; *ELO*, May 3, 1902, p. 6, at which the "No 1 Bethnal Green" branch's flag was unfurled. As for badges, these were worn by the St. George's branch; see *EAHT*, March 15, 1902, p. 7.

49. I have found a single example of the recruitment of a "brother" beyond East London. This was Clarence Godfrey of Christ Church College, University of Oxford. I can find no biographical information about this individual. See *ELO*, November 16, 1901, p. 5.

50. *ELO*, September 27, 1902, p. 6. Endelman, *The Jews of Britain, 1656–2000*, 160, indicates a membership of twelve thousand, but furnishes no accompanying supportive evidence.

51. *ELO*, November 16, 1901, p. 5.

52. *EAHT*, December 14, 1901, p. 6.

53. *EAHT*, May 31, 1902, p. 3.

54. *EAHT*, February 15, 1902, p. 2.

55. *ELO*, May 3, 1902, p. 6.

56. See Anthony Kushner and Nadia Valman, eds., *Remembering Cable Street: Fascism and Anti-Fascism in British Society* (London: Vallentine Mitchell, 1999).

57. For a short history of the People's Palace, see the entry in Ben Weinreb and Christopher Hibbert, eds., *The London Encyclopaedia*, rev. ed. (London: Macmillan, 1992). The original building was destroyed by fire in 1931 and reopened in 1936.

58. *ELO*, December 28, 1901, p. 5; *ELO*, January 5, 1902, p. 2.

59. *EENLSC*, January 17, 1901, p. 2; *ELO*, January 18, 1901, p. 2; *EAHT*, January 18, 1902, p. 2.

60. *ELO*, January 18, 1901, p. 2.

61. *ELO*, January 11, 1902, p. 5.

62. *ELO*, January 18, 1901, p. 2.

63. *ELO*, January 18, 1901, p. 2.

64. *Daily Chronicle*, January 15, 1902, p. 6; *Times*, January 15, 1902, p. 3; *Daily Mail*, January 15, 1902, p. 3.

65. *JC*, May 17, 1901, p. 17; August 9, 1901, p. 13.

66. *JW*, April 5, 1901, p. 18.

67. *JC*, January 17, 1902, pp. 16–17, 20; *JW*, 17 January 17, 1901, pp. 289–290.

68. *JW*, February 14, 1902, p. 358.

69. *JW*, February 28, 1902, p. 392.

70. *JW*, January 24, 1902, p. 311; a report on this "striking display" also appeared in the *Daily Mail*, January 20, 1902, p. 3, under the headline "Athletic Alien Jews."

71. Letter from an "Englishman" to *ELO*, October 26, 1901, p. 3.

72. *ELO*, January 25, 1902, p. 2.

73. Letter from a "Citizen of no mean city," *ELO*, February 8, 1902, p. 6.

74. *ELO*, April 26, 1902, p. 6.

75. *ELO*, November 16, 1901, p. 5.

76. Letter from "Son of an alien" to *ELO*, January 25, 1902, p. 2; see also the letter from the "Hope of Israel" to *ELO*, April 12, 1902, p. 6.

77. *ELO*, January 4, 1902, p. 3.

78. Letter from Stuart Samuel to *ELO*, February 15, 1902, p. 6.

79. *JW*, February 14, 1902, p. 369; February 21, 1902, p. 378; a similarly combative meeting was hosted by the Federated Tailors' Union in Whitechapel, see *ELO*, September 20, 1902, p. 7.

80. *ELO*, January 18, 1902, p. 5.

81. *ELO*, March 1, 1902, p. 5.

82. Some members of the League were concerned about its burgeoning antisemitic reputation. Evans-Gordon and A. T. Williams attached their name to a poster, in English and Yiddish, that appeared in the East End and advised: "Do not be deceived by people who are trying to make you believe that 'alien' means 'Jew.' It does not!" See *JW*, February 28, 1902, p. 391.

83. *ELO*, January 25, 1902, p. 2.

84. *ELO*, February 15, 1902, p. 4; March 1, 1902, p. 2.

85. *ELO*, March 15, 1902, p. 5.

86. Letter from William Stanley Shaw to *ELO*, March 22, 1902, p. 6.

87. *ELO*, April 5, 1902, pp. 4–5.

88. *ELO*, August 16, 1902, p. 3.

89. *ELO*, June 7, 1902, p. 8. Following Shaw's resignation, the League elected Alderman J. L. Silver in June 1902 as president. Arnold White (see note 19) sought elevation to the presidency, but as with every other election in which he stood, was rejected.

90. *ELO*, July 5, 1902, p. 2.

91. Letter from "England for the English" to *ELO*, April 12, 1902, p. 6; letter from "Union Jack" to *ELO*, April 19, 1902, p. 5.

92. *Hansard's Parliamentary Debates*, 4th ser., vol. 101, 1269–1291; see also *ELO*, February 1, 1902, p. 6; *EENLSC*, February 4, 1902, p. 2.

93. *EAHT*, February 1, 1902, p. 8.

94. *Royal Commission on Alien Immigration*, vol. 3, 8553, 8612, 8614, 9699.

95. *ELO*, August 16, 1902, p. 6.

96. *ELO*, March 1, 1902, p. 5.

97. Sam Johnson, *Pogroms, Peasants, Jews: Britain and Eastern Europe's Jewish Question, 1867–1925* (London: Palgrave Macmillan, 2011), esp. chap. 7.

98. This was "M.R.C.S. [Member of the Royal College of Surgeons] Old Londoner": *ELO*, October 25, 1902, p. 7.

99. Other violently antisemitic letters were sent by "Citizen of no mean city": *ELO*, November 1, 1901, p. 6; November 23, 1901, p. 2; March 8, 1902, p. 6; his letter on March 22, 1902, p. 6, described immigrant Jews as "European offal." See also similar letters from Henry Davison, *ELO*, April 24, 1902, p. 6; March 22, 1902, p. 6.

8. Bigamy and Bigotry in the Austrian Alps

Epigraphs: "Eine Seltsame Affäre," Tagespost, June 17, 1904 (evening ed.), 1; "Gerichtssaal. Die Affäre Hervay," *Die Zeit*, October 30, 1904, 7.

1. See Peter Pulzer, *The Rise of Political Anti-Semitism in Germany and Austria*, rev. ed. (Cambridge: Harvard University Press, 1988); Robert Wistrich, *The Jews of Vienna in the Age of Franz Joseph* (New York: Oxford University Press, 1989); John W. Boyer, *Culture and Political Crisis in Vienna: Christian Socialism in Power, 1897–1918* (Chicago: University of Chicago Press, 1995); Richard Geehr, *Karl Lueger: Mayor of Fin de Siècle Vienna* (Detroit: Wayne State University Press, 1990); Andrew G. Whiteside, *The Socialism of Fools: Georg Ritter von Schönerer and Austrian Pan-Germanism* (Berkeley: University of California Press, 1975); Bruce Pauley, *From Prejudice to Persecution: A History of Austrian Anti-Semitism* (Chapel Hill: University of North Carolina Press, 1992); Ivar Oxaal, Michael Pollak, and Gerhard Botz, eds., *Jews, Antisemitism and Culture in Vienna* (London: Routledge & Kegan Paul, 1987); John Bunzl and Bernd Marin, *Antisemitism in Österreich: Sozialhistorische und soziologische Studien* (Innsbruck: Innsverlag, 1983).

2. Daniel M. Vyleta, *Crime, Jews and News: Vienna 1895–1914* (New York: Berghahn Books, 2007), 130–132.

3. Albert Lichtblau, ed., *Als hätten wir dazugehört: Österreichisch-jüdische Lebengeschichten aus der Habsburgermonarchie* (Vienna: Böhlau, 1999), 45.

4. Mosche Karl Schwarz, "The Jews of Styria," in *The Jews of Austria: Essays on Their Life, History and Destruction*, ed. Josef Fraenkel (London: Vallentine, 1967), 391–392.

5. Pierre Genée, *Synagogen in Österreich* (Vienna: Löcker Verlag, 1992), 102.

6. Gerd W. Salzer-Eibenstein, "Geschichte der Juden in Graz," in *Geschichte der Juden in Österreich: Ein Gedenkbuch*, ed. Hugo Gold (Tel Aviv: Olamenu, 1971), 15.

7. Salzer-Eibenstein, "Geschichte der Juden," 15; Schwarz, "The Jews of Styria," 392.

8. Heimo Halbrainer and Heimo Gruber, "Jüdisches Leben und Antisemitismus in Mürzzuschlag im 19/20 Jahrhundert," in *Zwei Tage Zeit: Herta Reich und die Spuren jüdischen Lebens in Mürzzuschlag*, ed. Heimo Halbrainer (Graz: Clio, 1998), 65.

9. "Thierquälerei," *Obersteierblatt*, May 11, 1890, p. 3, quoted in Halbrainer and Gruber, "Jüdisches Leben," 66–67.

10. "Zur Lage der deutschnationalen Partei," *Obersteierblatt*, November 12, 1885, p. 1, quoted in Halbrainer and Gruber, "Jüdisches Leben," 73.

11. *Obersteierblatt*, Rede des Herrn Ferdinand Krautmann über die Verderbtheit der Press; November 15, 1885, quoted in Halbrainer and Gruber, "Jüdisches Leben," 73.

12. Helmut Brenner, "Die Lage der Mürzzuschlager Arbeiterschaft und ihrer politischen Organisation 1862–1990," in *Im Schatten des Phönix. Höhen und Tiefen eines dominierenden Industriebetriebes und deren Auswirkungen auf die Region*, ed. Helmut Brenner, Wolfgang Nagele, and Andrea Pühringer (Graz: Weishaupt, 1993), 38, quoted in Halbrainer and Gruber, "Jüdisches Leben," 72–73.

13. *Mürzzuschlager Wochenblatt*, May 16, 1903, p. 1, quoted in Halbrainer and Gruber, "Jüdisches Leben," 75.

14. *Mürzzuschlager Wochenblatt*, April 30, 1904, pp. 1–2; June 18, 1904, p. 2; June 25, 1904, p. 2; July 2, 1904; July 9, 1904, pp. 3–4; July 30, 1904, p. 3.

15. Wolfgang Haid, "Geschichte der Juden in Leoben," in *Geschichte der Juden in Österreich: Ein Gedenkbuch*, ed. Hugo Gold (Tel Aviv: Olamenu, 1971), 51–52.

16. Barbara Pachler, "Der Fall Hervay: Die Rekonstruktion einer der grössten Bigamiefälle des 20. Jahrhunderts," (master's thesis, University of Graz, 2006), 6. Pachler's thesis provides a detailed account of the case based primarily on archival documents.

17. Hardin J. Burlingame, *Around the World with a Magician and a Juggler: Unique Experience in Many Lands* (Chicago: Clyde, 1891), 166–169. Also see "Wiener Neuigkeiten," *Die Zeit*, June 27, 1904, p. 3.

18. "Gerichtssaal. Die Affäre Hervay," *Die Zeit*, October 31, 1904, p. 3. According to Gerd Simon, the Nietzsche scholar and Nazi sympathizer Friedrich Würzbach was Clara's son. See "Chronologie Friedrich Würzbach," http://homepages.uni-tuebingen.de/gerd .simon/, 5, 7.

19. "A Magician's Daughter," *Star*, October 29, 1904, p. 6.

20. "Prozess Hervay," *Obersteirische Volkszeitung*, October 29, 1904, p. 7.

21. Otfried Hafner, "Zwei Kuriose Prozesse in Leoben im Jahr 1904. Zur Geistesgeschichte

der österreichisch-ungarischen Monarchie," *Der Leobener Strauss* 7 (1979): 178. Also see accounts such as "Wiener Neuigkeiten," *Die Zeit*, June 26, 1904, p. 5.

22. Frieda Bülow, *Im Hexenring*, vol. 4: *Engelhorns allgemeine Romanbibliothek* (Stuttgart: J. Engelhorn, 1901), as summarized in "Wiener Neuigkeiten: Frau Sufi," *Die Zeit*, June 28, 1904, p. 3.

23. "Die Affäre Hervay," *Die Zeit*, June 29, 1904, pp. 4–5.

24. "Wiener Neuigkeiten," *Die Zeit*, June 26, 1904, p. 5.

25. "Wiener Neuigkeiten," *Die Zeit*, June 26, 1904, p. 5.

26. Prangl was born in Gabersdorf, ordained in 1884, and served as a chaplain in Kirchberg an der Raab, St. Lorenzen Mürztal, and Liezen.

27. "Prozess Hervay," *Obersteirische Volkszeitung*, October 29, 1904, p. 7.

28. J. Durchschaudi, "Ein Uraltes Märchen," *Mürzzuschlager Wochenblatt*, April 30, 1904, pp. 1–2. The feuilleton depicts the district captain as a king and Frau von Hervay as a witch, who arrives by broomstick and is transformed into a beautiful princess in order to entice the king.

29. "Eine Seltsame Affäre," *Tagespost*, June 17, 1904, evening edition, p. 1.

30. *Mürzzuschlager Wochenblatt*, June 25, 1904, p. 2.

31. The charge of fraud was eventually dropped and replaced with the charge of false registration.

32. "Verhaftung der Frau von Hervay," *Obersteierliche Volkszeitung*, June 25, 1904, p. 6.

33. Ibid.

34. "Selbstmord der Bezirkshauptmannes v. Hervay," *Obersteierliche Volkszeitung*, June 25, 1904, p. 6.

35. "Wiener Neuigkeiten," *Die Zeit*, June 27, 1904, p. 3.

36. Pachler, "Der Fall Hervay," 19–20.

37. *Obersteierliche Volkszeitung*, June 25, 1904, p. 6, also mentioned by Hafner, "Zwei Kuriose Prozesse," 178.

38. "Die Affäre Hervay," *Die Zeit*, June 29, 1904, pp. 4–5.

39. Lennart Páisson, *Marriage in Comparative Conflict of Laws: Substantive Conditions* (Leiden, Sijthoff, 1981), 341.

40. For more on Austrian marriage law and the investigations conducted by the Viennese Fabian society concerning marriage and divorce law reform from 1904 to 1905, see John W. Boyer, "Freud, Marriage, and Late Viennese Liberalism: A Commentary from 1905," *Journal of Modern History* 50, no. 1 (1978): 84–91.

41. Pachler, "Der Fall Hervay," 21–23.

42. "Gerichtssaal: Die Affäre Hervay," *Die Zeit*, October 29, 1904, p. 7.

43. *Neue Freie Presse*, October 31, 1904, evening edition, p. 9, quoted in Vyleta, *Crime, Jews and News*, 134.

44. "Prozess Hervay," *Obersteirische Volkszeitung*, October 29, 1904, p. 7.

45. Ibid., 8.

46. Ibid., 9.

47. "Gerichtssaal: Die Affäre Hervay," *Die Zeit*, October 30, 1904, p. 7.

48. Ibid.

49. Ibid., 8.

50. "Prozess Hervay," *Innsbrucker Nachrichten*, October 31, 1904, pp. 6–8.

51. Ibid.

52. "Gerichtssaal. Die Affäre Hervay," *Die Zeit*, October 31, 1904, pp. 4–5.

53. Ibid.

54. Ibid.

55. "Gerichtssaal. Die Affäre Hervay. Frau Hervay verurteilt," *Die Zeit*, November 1, 1904, p. 7.

56. *Neues Wiener Tagblatt*, January 15, 29, and 31, 1905.

57. Tamara von Hervay, *Ihr Leben und Denken* (Vienna: Szelinski & Comp Verlag, 1905).

58. Pachler, "Der Fall Hervay," 75.

59. Hermann Bahr, *Tagebücher, Skizzenbücher, Notizhefte*, ed. Moritz Csáky, vol. 4 (Vienna: Böhlau, 1994): 301, 304–305, 318, 363, 375, 391, 396, 416.

60. Alison Rose, *Jewish Women in Fin de Siècle Vienna* (Austin: University of Texas Press, 2008), 142–147.

61. J. Durchschaudi, "Ein Uraltes Märchen," *Mürzzuschlager Wochenblatt*, April 30, 1904, pp. 1–2.

62. "Eine Skandalgeschichte ersten Ranges," *Mürzzuschlager Wochenblatt*, June 18, 1904, p. 2.

63. Ibid., p. 3.

64. *Mürzzuschlager Wochenblatt*, June 25, 1904, p. 2.

65. Die Affäre Hervay," *Die Zeit*, June 29, 1904, pp. 4–5; *Mürzzuschlager Wochenblatt*, June 18, 1904, p. 2.

66. For Weininger's influence on Kraus's view of the Hervay affair, see George Makari, *Revolution in Mind: The Creation of Psychoanalysis* (New York: HarperCollins, 2008), 146–147.

67. "Prozess Hervay," *Innsbrucker Nachrichten*, October 31, 1904, p. 6.

68. "Prozess Hervay," *Obersteirische Volkszeitung*, October 29, 1904, p. 7.

69. "Wiener Neuigkeiten," *Die Zeit*, June 27, 1904, p. 3.

70. "Gerichtssaal: Die Affäre Hervay," *Die Zeit*, October 31, 1904, p. 2.

71. *Obersteirische Volkszeitung*, November 5, 1904, p. 15.

72. *Neue Freie Presse*, June 26, 1904, morning edition, pp. 1–3.

73. Vyleta, *Crime, Jews and News*, 130–132.

74. *Deutsches Volksblatt*, October 29, 1904.

75. *Deutsches Volksblatt*, October 30, 1904, p. 1.

76. *Deutsches Volksblatt*, November 1, 1904, quoted and trans. in Vyleta, 132–133.

77. "Der 'Tratsess' von Mürzzuschlag," *Kikeriki*, June 26, 1904, p. 2.

78. "Die Jüdin," *Kikeriki*, July 7, 1904.

79. "Mir zu handeln," *Kikeriki*, November 6, 1904, p. 1, quoted and trans. in Vyleta, *Crime, Jews and News*, 133.

80. "Zur Hervay-Affaire," *Wiener Caricaturen*, July 3, 1904, p. 4.

81. "Eine Gefährliche Frau," *Wiener Caricaturen*, November 6, 1904.

82. Josef Schrank, *Der Mädchenhandel und seine Bekämpfung* (Vienna, 1904), quoted in Vyleta, *Crime, Jews and News*, 58–59; Edward J. Bristow, *Prostitution and Prejudice: The Jewish Fight against White Slavery: 1870–1939* (New York: Schocken Books, 1983).

83. Keely Stauter-Halsted, "'A Generation of Monsters': Jews, Prostitution, and Racial Purity in the 1892 L'viv White Slavery Trial," *Austrian History Yearbook* 38 (2007): 32.

84. "Die Ehetragödie in Mürzzuschlag," *Obersteirische Volkszeitung*, June 28, 1904, p. 3.

85. Karl Kraus, "Der Fall Hervay," "Der Hexenprozess von Leoben," and "Der Memoiren der Frau v. Hervay," *Die Fackel*, July, October, and November 1904. He included these articles in his 1908 collection, *Sittlichkeit und Kriminalität* (Frankfurt am Main: C. Wagenknecht, 1987).

86. Kraus, "Der Fall Hervay," *Die Fackel* (July 1904), 103, quoted in Vyleta, *Crime, Jews and News*, 134.

87. Edward Timms, *Karl Kraus: Apocalyptic Satirist: Culture and Catastrophe in Habsburg Vienna* (New Haven: Yale University Press, 1986), 63, 68.

88. Paul Reitter, *The Anti-Journalist: Karl Kraus and Jewish Self-Fashioning in Fin-de-Siècle Europe* (Chicago: University of Chicago Press, 2008), 177.

89. *Die Fackel*, 257–258, 40, quoted in Roberto Calasso, *The Forty-Nine Steps*, trans. John Sheply (Minneapolis: University of Minnesota Press, 2001), 284.

90. Hermann Bahr, *Drut* (Berlin: S. Fischer, 1909). Also published under the title *Die Hexe Drut: Roman* (Berlin: Sieben Stäben Verlag, 1929). (On the cover of this edition is a drawing of a witch on a broomstick.)

91. Nicolas Unger, "An Austrianism Beyond the Viennese: Reflections on the Role of Vienna in Herman Bahr's post-1900 novels" (paper presented at the Trans conference, 2011); *TRANS: Internet-Zeitschrift für Kulturwissenschaften* 18 (June 2011), http://www.inst.at/trans/.

92. Timms, *Karl Kraus*, 65.

9. The Blood Libel on Greek Islands

1. J. Dovidio, P. Glick, and L. Rudman, "Introduction: Reflecting on *The Nature of Prejudice*: Fifty Years after Allport," in *On the Nature of Prejudice: Fifty Years after Allport*, ed. J. F. Dovidio, P. Glick, and L. Rudman (Malden, Mass.: Blackwell Publishing, 2005), 1–15, at 14.

2. A. Kyriakidou-Nestoros, *I theoria tis ellinikis laografias: Kritiki analysi*, 3rd ed. (Athens: Association of Studies on Modern Greek Civilization and General Education, 1986), 32. Factors contributing to the construction of national identity during this period include the study of folklore and especially the many collections that started appearing at the end of the nineteenth century, such as those of Nikolaos Politis. See M. Margaroni, "Oi koinonikes anaparastaseis gia tous Evraious stis sylloges tou Nikolaou Politi kai oi apotyposeis tous sto synoliko ergo tou Costi Palama: michanismoi sygkrotisis ethnikis tautotitas kai stratigikes politismikou apokleismou," in *Praktika epistimonikou synedriou.*

Laikos politismos kai entechnos logos (poiisi—pezografia—theatro). Athina, 8–12 Decemvriou 2010 (Dimosieumata tou Kentrou Ereunis tis Ellinikis Laografias Athinon, 30), ed. C. Polymerou-Kamilaki and G. Vozikas, vol. 2 (Athens: Hellenic Folklore Research Centre of the Academy of Athens, 2013), 99–117.

3. B. Anderson, *Imagined Communities*, rev. ed. (London: Verso, 2006), 39–48; E. Skopetea, *To "protypo vasileio" kai i megali idea: Opseis tou ethnikou provlimatos stin Ellada (1830–1880)* (Athens: Polytypo, 1988).

4. M. Margaroni, "Evraioi, glossa kai tautotita: Zitimata eterotitas kai apokleismou sto neoelliniko kratos apo tin idrysi tou mechri kai to deutero pagkosmio polemo," in *Tautotites ston elliniko kosmo (apo to 1204 eos simera). Praktika. IV Europaiko Synedrio Neoellinikon Spoudon, Granada, 9–12 Septemvriou 2010*, ed. K. Dimadis, vol. 3 (Athens: European Society of Modern Greek Studies, 2011), 255–272.

5. Th. Veikos, *Ethnikismos kai ethniki tautotita* (Athens: Ellinika Gramata, 1999), 38–39.

6. C. Paparrigopoulos, *To teleutaion etos tis ellinikis eleutherias* (Athens: K. Antoniadou, 1844), 3–4.

7. P. Kitromilidis, "To elliniko kratos os ethniko kentro," in A. G. Tsaousis, *Ellinismos—Ellinikotita: ideologikoi kai viomatikoi axones tis neoellinikis koinonias* (Athens: Estia, 1983), 143–164.

8. W. Bohleber, "Ethnische Homogenität und Gewalt. Zur Psychoanalyse von Ethnozentrismus, Fremdenhass und Antisemitismus," in *Psychoanalyseheute: Klinische und kulturtheoretische Perspektiven*, ed. M. Leuzinger-Bohleber and R. Zwiebel (Opladen: Westdeutscher Verlag, 1996), 194–206.

9. J. Trachtenberg, *The Devil and the Jews: The Medieval Conception of the Jew and Its Relation to Modern Anti-Semitism* (Skokie, Ill.: Varda Books, [1943] 2001), 97–123; G. Langmuir, *History, Religion, and Antisemitism* (Berkeley: University of California Press, 1990), 298–303.

10. G. Langmuir, "Thomas of Monmouth: Detector of Ritual Murder," in *The Blood Libel Legend: A Casebook in Anti-Semitic Folklore*, ed. A. Dundes (Madison: The University of Wisconsin Press, 1991), 3–40; M. Rubin, "Making a Martyr: William of Norwich and the Jews," *History Today* 60, no. 6 (2010): 48–54. Regarding the stereotypical association of Jews to magic, see the classical work of J. Trachtenberg, *Jewish Magic and Superstition: A Study in Folk Religion* (Philadelphia: University of Pennsylvania Press, [1939] 2004).

11. R. Erb, "Die Ritualmordlegende: Von den Anfängen bis ins 20. Jahrhundert," in *Ritualmord: Legenden in der europäischen Geschichte*, ed. S. Buttaroni and S. Musiat (Wien: Böhlau, 2003), 9–16, at 14.

12. Cases illustrating religious ideas of sacrificing children and blood symbolism can be found in the excellent work of R. Po-Chia Hsia, *The Myth of Ritual Murder: Jews and Magic in Reformation Germany* (New Haven: Yale University Press, 1988). On magic and medicine, see Erb, "Die Ritualmordlegende," 9; and on the resilience of ritual murder, A. Cohen, "Ritual Murder Accusations Against the Jews during the Days of Suleiman the Magnificent," *Journal of Turkish Studies* 10 (1986): 73–78; Y. Ben-Naeh, *Jews in the Realm of the Sultans* (Tubingen: Mohr Siebeck, 2008), 131; Z. Guldon and J. Wijaczka, "The Accu-

sation of Ritual Murder in Poland, 1500–1800," *Polin* 10 (1997): 99–140; G. Hundert, *Jews in Poland-Lithuania in the Eighteenth Century: A Genealogy of Modernity* (Berkeley: University of California Press, 2004), 57–78.

13. H. Kieval, "Representation and Knowledge in Medieval and Modern Accounts of Jewish Ritual Murder," *Jewish Social Studies* 1, no. 1 (1994): 52–72; H. Walser Smith, *Die Geschichte des Schlachters: Mord und Antisemitismus in einer deutschen Kleinstadt* (Göttingen: Wallstein, 2004); S. Lehr, *Antisemitismus in Deutschland 1870–1914* (Munich: Kaiser, 1974), 239–243.

14. See J. Frankel, *The Damascus Affair: "Ritual Murder," Politics, and the Jews in 1840* (Cambridge: Cambridge University Press, 1997); J. Kalman, "Sensuality, Depravity, and Ritual Murder: The Damascus Blood Libel and Jews in France," *Jewish Social Studies* 13, no. 3 (2007): 35–58.

15. S. Marketos, "Ethnos choris Evraious: apopseis tis historiografikis kataskeuis tou ellinismou," *Sygchrona Themata* 52–53 (1994): 52–69.

16. E. Avdela and O. Varon-Vasar, eds., *Oi Evraioi ston elliniko choro: Zitimata istorias sti makra diarkeia. Praktika tou 1. symposiou Istorias (Thessaloniki, 23–24 Noemvriou 1991)* (Athens: Gavriilidis and Association of Studies on Jews in Greece, 1995); I. K. Hassiotis, ed., *The Jewish Communities of Southeastern Europe: From the Fifteenth Century to the End of World War II* (Salonica: Institute for Balkan Studies, 1997); R. Benveniste, ed., *Oi Evraioi tis Elladas stin katochi. Praktika tou 3. symposiou Istorias (Thessaloniki, 8 Noemvriou 1996)* (Salonica: Vanias and Association of Studies on Jews in Greece, 1998); M. Stephanopoulou, ed., *O Ellinikos Evraismos. Praktika Epistimonikou Symposiou (3–4 Apriliou 1998)* (Athens: Association of Studies on Greek Culture and General Education, 1999).

17. See P. Preschel, *The Jews of Corfu* (Ph.D. dissertation, New York University, 1984); R. Dalvin, *The Jews of Ioannina* (Philadelphia: Cadmus, 1990); R. Molho, *Oi Evraioi tis Thessalonikis, 1856–1919. Mia idiaiteri koinotita* (Athens: Themelio, 2001); V. Rizaleos, *Oi evraikes koinotites stin anatoliki Makedonia kai ti Thaki apo ta mesa tou 19ou aiona mechri to 2. Pagkosmio Polemo* (Ph.D. dissertation, Aristotle University of Salonica, 2006).

18. R. Benveniste, "Gia tin istoria ton Evraion tis Elladas," in *Praktika 4. Diethnous Synedriou Istorias: Istoriografia tis neoteris kai sygchronis Elladas 1833–2002 (29 Octovriou–3 Noemvriou 2002)*, ed. P. Kitromilidis and T. Sclavenitis, vol. 2 (Athens: Center of Modern Greek Research/National Research Foundation, 2004), 315–328.

19. See Ph. Konstantopoulou and Th. Veremis, *Documents on the History of the Greek Jews: Records from the Historical Archives of the Ministry of Foreign Affairs* (Athens: Kastaniotis, 1998).

20. M. Efthymiou, *Evraioi kai Christianoi sta tourkokratoumena nisia tou notioanatolikou Aigaiou: Oi dyskoles pleures mias gonimis synyparxis* (Athens: Trochalia, 1992); B. Pierron, *Juifs et Chrétiens de la Grèce moderne: Histoire des relations intercommunautaires de 1821 à 1945* (Paris: L'Harmattan, 1996); G. Margaritis, *Anepithymitoi sympatriotes. Stoicheia gia tin katastrofi meionotiton stin Ellada. Evraioi, Tsamides* (Athens: Vivliorama, 2005).

21. A. Kalderon, *Abraham Galanté: A Biography* (New York: Hermon, 1983).

22. Y. Kerem, "The 1840 Blood Libel in Rhodes," *Proceedings of the Twelfth World Congress of Jewish Studies*, div. B: *History of the Jewish People* (Jerusalem: World Union of Jewish Studies, 2000), 137–146.

23. Ch. Chatziiosiph, "Pascha stin Alexandreia: laikes prolipseis kai diakoinotikes diamaches stin Aigypto sta teli tou 19ou aiona," *Ta Istorika* 7, nos. 12–13 (1990): 121–148; D. Miccoli, "Moving Histories: The Jews and Modernity in Alexandria 1881–1919," *Quest: Issues in Contemporary Jewish History* 2 (2011), http://www.quest-cdecjournal.it.

24. F. Abatzopoulou, "'Dia ton fovon ton Ioudaion': paidoktonia, kanivalismos kai emfylos logos. Ena scenario gia ti Maria Michanidou," in *O logos tis parousias. Timitikos tomos gia ton Pan. Moulla*, ed. M. Mike, M. Pechlivanos, and L. Tsirimokou (Athens: Socolis, 2005), 25–43, at 29.

25. E. Liata, *I Kerkyra kai i Zakynthos ston kyklona tou antisimitismou. I "sykofantia gia to aima" tou 1891* (Athens: National Research Foundation, 2006), 35.

26. V. Rizaleos, "I ypothesi tou evraiou pragmatognomona kapnon Razon: sykofantia aimatos kai diacheirisi kriseon stin Kavala tou 1894," *Chronika* 213 (2008): 18–25.

27. Abatzopoulou, "'Dia ton fovon ton Ioudaion,'" 29.

28. L. Lacroix, *L'univers ou histoire et description de tous les peuples, de leurs religions, mœurs, coutumes, etc. Iles de la Grèce* (Paris: Firmin Didot Frères, 1881), 98.

29. Kerem, "The 1840 Blood Libel in Rhodes," 137–146; M. Margaroni, "I parousia tou evraikou stoicheiou stin christianiki Dodekaniso: kathimerinos vios, symviosi kai sygkrouseis," in *Glossiki kai koinotiki eterotita sti Dodekaniso tou 20ou aiona*, ed. K. Tsitselikis and M. Georgalidou (forthcoming).

30. Abraham Galanté was the first to give detailed documentation of the blood libel of Rhodes. According to Galanté, the blood libel did not only have religious causes, but also constituted the culmination of gradually rising economic antagonisms. A. Galanté, *Histoire des Juifs de Rhodes, Chio, Cos etc.* (Istanbul: Société Anonyme de Papeterie et d'Imprimerie, 1935), 89–99.

31. Efthymiou, *Evraioi kai Christianoi*, 19.

32. Lacroix, *L'univers ou histoire et description*, 148–182; E. Kollias, "To evraiko stoicheio tis Rodou kata to Mesaiona kai tin Tourkokratia," *Chronika* 188, no. 26 (2003), 6–11; C. Torr, *Rhodes in Modern Times* (Oxford: Archaeopress, [1887] 2003), 64–65.

33. M. Angel, *The Jews of Rhodes: The History of a Sephardic Community* (New York: Sepher-Hermon Press and the Union of Sephardic Congregations, 1978), 18; A. Shmuelevitz, *The Jews of the Ottoman Empire in the Late Fifteenth and the Sixteenth Centuries: Administrative, Legal and Social Relations as Reflected in the Responsa* (Leiden: Brill, 1984), 32; Efthymiou, *Evraioi kai Christianoi*, 34–41, 52–58.

34. Efthymiou, *Evraioi kai Christianoi*, 50–52.

35. On tax farming: L. Bernard, *The Jews of Islam* (Princeton: Princeton University Press, 1984), 132–133; M. Epstein, *The Ottoman Jewish Communities and Their Role in the Fifteenth and Sixteenth Centuries* (Freiburg: Schwarz, 1980), 125–128; on viticulture: A. van Egmont and J. Heyman, *Travels through Part of Europe, Asia Minor, the Islands of the*

Archipelago, Syria, Palestine, Egypt, Mount Sinai, etc., 2 vols. (London: Royal Society, 1759), 1:270; on garments: Galanté, *Histoire des Juifs de Rhodes, Chio, Cos*, 56–57; on spices: Shmuelevitz, *The Jews of the Ottoman Empire*, 134; on silk: Efthymiou, *Evraioi kai Christianoi*, 170–171.

36. Galanté, *Histoire des Juifs de Rhodes, Chio, Cos*, 79–82.

37. Y. Kerem, "The Migration of Rhodian Jews to Africa and the Americas from 1900 to 1914: The Beginning of New Sephardic Diasporic Communities," in *Patterns of Migration, 1850–1914*, ed. A. Newman and S. Massil (London: The Jewish Historical Society of England and the Institute of Jewish Studies, University College London, 1996), 321–334; Y. Kerem, "The Settlement of Rhodian and Other Sephardic Jews in Montgomery and Atlanta in the Twentieth Century," *American Jewish History* 85, no. 4 (1997): 373–391.

38. The Earl of Carlisle, *Diary in Turkish and Greek Waters*, ed. C. C. Felton (Boston: Hickling, Swan & Brown, 1855), 110.

39. A. Berg, *Die Insel Rhodus aus eigener Anschauung und nach den vorhandenen Quellen- historisch, geographisch, archäologisch, malerisch beschrieben und durch Originalradie- gungen und Holzschnitte nach eigenen Naturstudien und Zeichnungenillustriert* (Braunschweig: George Westermann, 1862), 27–28.

40. K. Krumbacher, *Griechische Reise. Blätter aus dem Tagebuche einer Reise in Griechenland und in der Türkei* (Berlin: August Hettler, 1886), 90, 93–94.

41. Ibid., 99–101.

42. Galanté, *Histoire des Juifs de Rhodes, Chio, Cos*, 60–61.

43. Efthymiou, *Evraioi kai Christianoi*, 190–194.

44. E. Benbassa and A. Rodrigue, *Die Geschichte der sephardischen Juden: Von Toledo bis Saloniki* (Bochum: Dr. Dieter Winker, 2005), 106.

45. Lacroix, *L'univers ou histoire et description*, 184.

46. Y. Kerem, "The Multicultural Background of Greek Jewry: Factors in Their Diversity and Integration in Modern Greece," in *Minorities religieuses de la Grèce contemporaine*, ed. G. Drettas (Paris: Herodotos, 2003), 57–79, at 67; D. Kokkinos, *I Elliniki Epanastasis (The Greek Revolution)*, 3rd ed., vol. 2 (Athens: Melissa, 1957), 317–318.

47. P. Argenti, *The Religious Minorities of Chios: Jews and Roman Catholics* (Cambridge: Cambridge University Press, 1970), 172.

48. Pierron, *Juifs et Chrétiens de la Grèce moderne*, 16.

49. G. Margaritis, "Ellinikos Antisimitismos: Mia periigisi, 1821, 1891, 1931," in *Epistimoniko symposio. O Ellinikos Evraismos. 3–4 Apriliou 1998*, ed. M. Stephanopoulou (Athens: Society for Studies on Modern Greek Civilization and General Education and Moraiti's Institution, 1999), 15–31.

50. Efthymiou, *Evraioi kai Christianoi*, 196–203.

51. Galanté, *Histoire des Juifs de Rhodes, Chio, Cos*, 91.

52. Ibid., 90–99.

53. N. D. Fustel de Coulanges, *Questions historiques: Revues et complétées d'après les notes de l'auteur par Camille Jullian* (Paris: Librairie Hachette, 1893), 324.

54. The first Ottoman occupation of the island came on April 17, 1566. Ottoman rule briefly was broken by the Florentines (1599) and then by the Venetians for one year in 1694–1695.

55. A. Vlastos, *Chiaka: Itoi istoria tis nisou Chiou apo ton archaiotaton chronon mechri tis etei 1822 genomenis katastrofis autis para ton Tourkon* (Ermoupoli: G. Polymeris, 1840), 48.

56. E. Voulgaris, *Schediasma peri tis anexithriskeias itoi peri tis anochis ton eterothriskon (eisagogi-simeioseis V. Lazaris)* (Athens: Stachy, 2001), 21–116.

57. C. A. Frazee, "Church and State in Greece," in *Greece in Transition: Essays in the History of Modern Greece 1821–1974*, ed. J. Koumoulides (London: Zeno, 1977), 128–152, at 128.

58. P. Matalas, *Ethnos kai orthodoxia. Oi peripeteies mias schesis: Apo to "Elladiko" sto Voulgariko Schisma* (Iraklio: University Press of Crete, 2002), 48–51.

59. C. A. Frazee, *Orthodoxos Ekklisia kai Elliniki Anexartisia 1821–1852* (*The Orthodox Church and Independent Greece 1821–1852*) (Athens: Domos, 1987), 69, 203.

60. It issued similar prohibitions in 1910 and 1918, suggesting that the practice had not stopped. I. Mourtzios, "To phenomeno tou antisimitismou kai i Elliniki Orthodoxi Ekklisia," *Chronica* 197 (May–June 2005), 3–7, at 4.

61. Ibid., 4.

62. S. Xenos, *Irois tis ellinikis epanastaseos, itoi skinai en Elladi, apo tou etous 1821–1828* (*Heroine of the Greek Revolution, or Scenes in Greece, from the Years 1821–1828*) (London: Press of the British Star, 1861), reprinted in "Scenes from Greece in 1821–1828: Chios and the Family of Mr Fragouli: Stephanou Xenou," *Chronika* 110, no. 13 (1990): 23. During the following decades of the nineteenth century, successive destructions on the island, such as the plague in 1865, the great fire in 1875, and the earthquake in 1881, contributed to the significant reduction of the Jewish population through an increase in deaths and migration. The Jewish population of the island, which numbered seventy families in 1881, dropped to forty in 1903, and these were gradually reduced until the complete disintegration of the community in 1933. *Evraiki Estia*, October 10, 1947, reprinted in Ch. Alchamanatis, "I istoria tis Israilinis Koinotitas Chiou," *Chronika* 206, no. 29 (2006): 20–21, at 20.

63. Galanté, *Histoire des Juifs de Rhodes, Chio, Cos*, 156–157.

64. Vlastos, *Chiaka*, 198–205; F. Pouqueville, *Histoire de la régénération de la Grèce: comprenant le précis des événements depuis 1740 jusqu'en 1824* (Paris: Firmin Didot, 1824), 441–523; N. Fustel de Coulanges, "Mémoire sur l'île de Chio, présenté par M. Fustel de Coulanges, membre de l'École française d'Athènes," in *Archives des missions scientifiques et littéraires. Choix de rapports et instructions publié sous les auspices du Ministère de l'Instruction Publique et des Culte*, vol. 5 (Paris: Imprimerie Impériale, 1856), 497–498, 639–641; Krumbacher, *Griechische Reise*, 229.

65. Lacroix, *L'univers ou histoire et description*, 283; Vlastos, *Chiaka*, 195; G. von Eckenbrecher, *Die Insel Chios* (Berlin: Bethge, 1845), 37, 39.

66. Pouqueville, *Histoire de la régénération de la Grèce*, 490.

67. *Courier*, May, 16/28, 1822, mentions a passage from a letter from Smyrna, dated April 5/17, 1822.

68. Vlastos, *Chiaka*, 204; Letter of A. Choumis from April 7, 1886, appears in "Tina peri Mitropolitou tis Chiou Platonos," *Evdomas*, April 20, 1886.

69. A. Mamoukas, "Paragrafos grafis enos Graikou A. pros ton filo tou N. peri tis katastrofis tis Chiou," in *Chiakon archeion* (Archeia tis Neoteras Ellinikis Istorias), ed. I. Vlachoyannis, vol. 1 (Athens: Sakellariou, 1924), 309. During the revolution, Mamoukas was secretary to the naval leader Constantinos Canaris, and later, member of parliament for Syros (1847–1853).

70. Vlastos, *Chiaka*, 205.

71. Pouqueville, *Histoire de la régénération de la Grèce*, 490.

72. *La Gazette de France*, May 5/17, 1822.

73. Vlastos, *Chiaka*, 205; See also the aforementioned letter of A. Choumis from April 7, 1886.

74. Mamoukas, "Paragrafos grafis enos Graikou A. pros ton filo tou N. peri tis katastrofis tis Chiou," 315.

75. Ibid., 307.

76. Ibid., 314.

77. Pouqueville, *Histoire de la régénération de la Grèce*, 486.

78. Mamoukas, "Paragrafos grafis enos Graikou A. pros ton filo tou N. peri tis katastrofis tis Chiou,", 315–316.

79. Pierron, *Juifs et Chrétiens de la Grèce moderne*, 18.

80. Mamoukas, "Paragrafos grafis enos Graikou A. pros ton filo tou N. peri tis katastrofis tis Chiou," 307.

81. On Jews as spies: the memoirs of Grigorios Photeinos, monk and later abbot of the New Monastery of Chios, contain the story of a monk named Serafim, who tried to board a Christian ship leaving for the neighboring island of Psara, in his efforts to escape impending death at the hands of the Ottomans. The other passengers, however, had judged him to be "a Jewish spy sent to deliver them to their destruction." His only salvation was the display of his nakedness, which proved he was uncircumcised and allowed him to board the ship and escape. See G. Photeinos, "Grigoriou Photeinou Apomnimoneumata," in *Archeia tis Neoteras Ellinikis Istorias*, ed. I. Vlachoyannis, vol. 1 (Athens: Sakellariou, 1924), 372.

82. E. Fragaki-Syrett, *Oi Chiotes emporoi stis diethneis synallages (1750–1850)* (Athens: Agricultural Bank of Greece, Department of Planning and Studies, 1995), 21–23, 27–29.

83. Galanté, *Histoire des Juifs de Rhodes, Chio, Cos*, 154.

84. Ibid., 154.

85. Argenti, *The Religious Minorities of Chios*, 176–177.

86. Liata, *I kerkyra kai i Zakynthos ston kyklona tou antisimitismou*; E. Liata, "The Anti-Semitic Disturbances on Corfu and Zakynthos in 1891 and Their Socio-political Consequences," *Historical Review/La Revue Historique* 4 (2007): 157–169; S. Gekas, "The Port Jews of Corfu and the 'Blood Libel' of 1891: A Tale of Many Centuries and of One Event," *Jewish Culture and History* 7, nos. 1–2 (2004): 171–196; M. Margaroni, "Antisemitic Rumours and Violence in Corfu at the End of 19th Century," *Quest: Issues in Contemporary Jewish History* 3 (2012), http://www.quest-cdecjournal.it.

87. P. Preschel, *The Jews of Corfu*, 12; I. Romanos, "I evraiki koinotita tis Kerkyras," *Kerky-*

raika Chronika 7, in *Ioannou Romanou Istorika Erga*, ed. K. Dafnis (Corfu: n.p., 1959), 388–391. The Sixth Earl of Orkney mentions that many decrees were promulgated in the Jews' favor; but their frequent repetition is also a proof of their general insufficiency. See G. W. H. Fitzmaurice, *Four Years in the Ionian Islands: Their Political and Social Condition, With a History of the British Protectorate*, ed. Viscount Kirkwall, vol. 2 (London: Chapman & Hall, 1864), 47.

88. Romanos, "I evraiki koinotita tis Kerkyras," 393–394.

89. K. E. Fleming, *Greece: A Jewish History* (Princeton: Princeton University Press, 2008), 34–41.

90. Pierron, *Juifs et Chrétiens de la Grèce moderne*, 28. For a more general overview of the English rule, see P. Chiotis, *I istoria tou Ioniou kratous apo tis systaseos autou mechri enoseos (eti 1815–1864)* (Athens: Karavia, [1874–1877] 1980). See also the work of the general inspector of army hospitals, J. Davy, *Notes and Observations on the Ionian Islands and Malta; with Some Remarks on Constantinople and Turkey, and on the System of Quarantine as at Present Conducted*, 2 vols. (London: Smith, Elder and Co, 1842); Fitzmaurice, *Four Years in the Ionian Islands*.

91. H. Pernot, ed., *Nosanciens à Corfou: souvenirs de l'aide-major Lamare-Picquot (1807–1814)* (Paris: F. Alcan, 1918), 80–81.

92. Fitzmaurice, *Four Years in the Ionian Islands*, 2: 47–48, 55.

93. S. Gekas, "Credit, Bankruptcy and Power in the Ionian Islands under British Rule, 1815," in *History of Insolvency and Bankruptcy from an International Perspective*, ed. K. Gratzer and D. Stiefel (Huddinge: Södertörn Academic Studies, 2008), 93–94; S. Gekas, "Business Culture and Entrepreneurship in the Ionian Islands under British Rule, 1815–1864," London School of Economics (LSE) Working Papers in Economic History, no. 89/05 (London: Department of Economic History, London School of Economics, 2005), http://eprints.lse.ac.uk/22332/1/WP89.pdf; S. Gekas, "Thesmoi kai exousia stin poli tis Kerkyras sta mesa tou 19ou aiona," *Istor* 15 (2009): 149–186, at 160.

94. G. Mavrogiannis, "I dithen isotis," *Estia*, February 26, 1895.

95. Gekas, "The Port Jews of Corfu and the 'Blood Libel' of 1891," 177.

96. *Government Gazette*, no. 313 (1889), as cited in A. Idromenos, *Synoptiki Istoria tis Kerkyras*, 2nd ed. (Corfu: S. Lantzas, 1930), 132.

97. Th. Kefalas, memorandum, December 15, 1891, *Ypomnima peri tis symperiforas kai energeias tis en Kerkyra astynomias kai ton filon autis kata ta evraika symvanta* (Memo Regarding the Behavior and Actions of the Corfu Police and Their Supporters during the Jewish Occurrences), Friends of the People Association (hereafter F.P.A.), Deliyannis Archive (hereafter D.A.), file BVI/106, doc. 1.

98. C. Dafnis, *Oi Israilites tis Kerkyras. Chroniko epta aionon* (Corfu: n.p., 1978), 19.

99. *Ephimeris*, May 2, 1891.

100. F.P.A., D.A., BVI/106, 3. Letter of May 2, 1891.

101. *Ephimeris*, April 9, 1891; N. Spandonis, "Anakriseis 'Akropoleos' epi ton Kerkyraikon tarachon. Meros B. Ai anakriseis tou Kerkyraikou laou," *Acropolis*, May 15, 1891.

102. M. Horovitz, Korfu. Vortrag, 28. Mai 1891 (Frankfurt am Main: Kauffmann, 1891), 13–15.

103. Y. Valetas, *Polylas: Apanta ta logotechnika kai critika*, 3rd ed. (Athens: Pigi, 1963).

104. N. Spandonis, "Synenteuxis meta tou k. Iakovou Polylas," *Acropolis*, May 13, 1891.

105. *Rigas Ferreos*, May 25, 1891.

106. Ibid., May 25, 1891.

107. P. Kassimatis, *Aima, Evraioi, Talmud, itoi apodeixeis thriskeutikai, istorikai kai dikasti-kai peri tis yparxeos ton anthropothysion par' Evraiois, epi ti vasei ton ergon pleiston syggrafeon kai idia tou syggrammatos tou Henri Desportes 'Le mystère du sang'* (Athens: A. Kollarakis and N. Triantafyllou, 1891).

108. G. Zavitsianos, *Aktis fotos. O katatregmos ton Evraion en ti istoria. Skepseis* (Corfu: N. Petsalis, 1891); S. Papageorgiou, *Sfazousin oi Evraioi Christianopaidas kai pinousin to aima ton?* (Athens: M. Saliveros, 1902).

109. E. Amilitou, "Erotas kai thanatos sto ghetto. I alli Zakynthos tou Gr. Xenopoulou," *Nea Estia* 150, no. 1738 (2001), 403–445, at 422–423; Anthimos, Bishop of Alexandroupoli, "To ethimo tou kapsimatos tou Iouda," *Chronica* 28, no. 197 (2005): 9–10. Belatedly, Greece's Holy Synod made a pro forma prohibition in one of its circulars without having the effective authority to abolish the said tradition. See "Egkyklios peri tou ouk exesti tois pistois pyrpolein omoioma tou Iouda en ti eorti tis lamproforou anastaseos tou Sotiros Iisou Christou," in *Syllogi Egkyklion Ieras Synodou* (Circulars' Collection of the Holy Synod), ed. S. Giannopoulos (Athens: A. Kallarakis, 1901), 405–406.

110. To the said Archmandrite, "as a steadfast fighter for truth," is dedicated the antisemitic work of P. Kassimatis. Martinos had passionately defended as true accusations regarding the human sacrifices of Christians by Jews.

111. D. Latas, *Drasis yper tou Israilitikou ethnous kai gnomai peri Ioudaismou diakekrime-nou Ierarchou tis Neoteras Ellinikis Ekklisias aoidimou archiepiskopou Zakynthou dia-typotheisai en to theio yp' autou kyrigmati kai en tois syggrammasi autou* (Zante, 1932).

112. K. Aroni-Tsichli, "To agrotiko zitima Kerkyras meta tin enosi tis Eptanisou mesa apo ta pafletia tis epochis," in *Epistimoniko Synedrio, I Enosi tis Eptanisou me tin Ellada, 1864–2004. Praktika*, ed. E. Gardika-Katsiadaki and E. Belia, vol. 1 (Athens: Greek Parliament, Academy of Athens/Research Centre for the Study of Modern Greek History, 2005), 593–607.

113. N. Spandonis, "Ti legoun kai oi Ioudaioi: Ouchi to symferon. Ouchi I politiki all' I prolips-sis. Synenteuxis meta tou iatrou B. de Semou," *Acropolis*, May 12, 1891.

114. Gekas, "The Port Jews of Corfu and the 'Blood Libel' of 1891," 179–182.

115. F.P.A., D.A., File BVI/106, doc. 1.

116. Liata, *I Kerkyra kai i Zakynthos ston kyklona tou antisimitismou*, 136–137.

117. F.P.A., D.A., File BVI/106, doc. 1.

118. Margaroni, "Antisemitic Rumours and Violence in Corfu."

119. Dafnis, *Oi Israilites tis Kerkyras*, 29.

120. Pertaining to a systematically repeated accusation of rabbinic argument till the beginning of the twentieth century, that to this "grafting with sapling of foreign texture" was attributed "the shining beauty" of the outer skin of this Corfiote fruit. See "In Angelegenheit der Palästina-Ethrogim," *Die Welt*, August 15, 1902, pp. 8–9, at 8.

121. Preschel, *The Jews of Corfu*, 97–115.

122. See the report of Dr. Arthur Ruppin from Jaffa to the Board of the Palestine Land Development Company in Berlin, entitled "Die Anlage von Pflanzungen in Palästina," *Palästina: Monatsschrift für die Erschliessung Palästinas*, vol. 8, nos. 1–2 (1911): 34–41 at 35.

123. See the detailed study of S. De Viazis, "I evraiki koinotis tis Zakynthou epi Enetokratias," *Parnassos* 14 (1892): 624–637, 662–670, 723–735.

124. F.P.A., D.A., BVI/106, 20, letter by an unknown sender to the Countess Aspasia Roma, April 23, 1891.

10. Anti-Jewish Riots in Rural Lithuania

1. As outlined in Clifford Geertz, "Thick Description: Toward an Interpretive Theory of Culture," in Clifford Geertz, *The Interpretation of Cultures: Selected Essays* (New York: Basic Books, 1973), 3–30.

2. See, for example, John D. Klier, *Russians, Jews, and the Pogroms of 1881–1882* (Cambridge: Cambridge University Press, 2011); Tim Buchen, *Antisemitismus in Galizien (1879–1914): Agitation, politische Praxis und Gewalt gegen Juden* (Berlin: Metropol, 2012); William Hagen, "The Moral Economy of Popular Violence: The Pogrom in Lwów, November 1918," in *Antisemitism and Its Opponents in Modern Poland*, ed. Robert Blobaum (Ithaca, N.Y.: Cornell University Press, 2005), 124–147; Stefan Wiese, "Die Große Angst in Žitomir: Zur Geschichte eines Judenpogroms und einer Selbstwehrgruppe im Zarenreich," *Transversal: Zeitschrift für jüdische Studien* 11, no. 1 (2010): 79–86.

3. See especially Simon Dubnow, *History of the Jews in Russia and Poland*, 3 vol. (Philadelphia: Jewish Publication Society of America, 1916–1920).

4. John D. Klier and Shlomo Lambroza, eds., *Pogroms: Anti-Jewish Violence in Modern Russian History* (Cambridge: Cambridge University Press, 1992); Klier, *Russians, Jews and the Pogroms*.

5. Pranas Čepėnas, *Naujųjų laikų Lietuvos istorija*, vol. 1 (Chicago: Kazio Griniaus fondas, 1977), 357; Bronius Kviklys, *Mūsų Lietuva: Krašto vietovių istoriniai, geografiniai, etnografiniai bruožiai*, vol. 4 (Boston: Lietuvių enciklopedijos leidykla, 1968), 587.

6. Mordechai Zalkin, "Antisemitism in Lithuania," in *Antisemitism in Eastern Europe: History and Present in Comparison*, ed. Hans-Christian Petersen and Samuel Salzborn (Frankfurt am Main: Peter Lang, 2010), 135–167, at 137.

7. Darius Staliūnas, "Anti-Jewish Disturbances in the North-Western Provinces in the Early 1880s," *East European Jewish Affairs* 34, no. 2 (2004): 119–138.

8. Klaus Richter, "Kišinev or Linkuva? Rumors and Threats against Jews in Lithuania in 1903," *Revista Româna de Studii Baltice și Nordice* 3, no. 1 (2011): 117–130; Vilma Žaltauskaitė, "Smurtas prieš žydus Šiaurės Lietuvoje 1900 metais Įvykiai ir interpretacijos," in *Kai ksenofobija virsta prievarta. Lietuvių ir žydų santykių dinamika XIX a.—XX a. pirmojoje pusėje*, ed. Darius Staliūnas and Vladas Sirutavičius (Vilnius: Lietuvos istorijos institutas, 2005), 79–98.

9. Angelė Vyšniauskaitė and Janina Laniauskaitė, eds., *Valstiečių lininkystė ir transportas* (Vilnius: Mokslas, 1977), 17.

10. The flax and linen industry suffered from the fact that it was difficult to process industrially. In Lithuania, flax cultivation suffered a heavy setback in the 1840s and again at the end of the nineteenth century, when areas of flax cultivation shrank across the whole Russian Empire. See Brenda Collins and Philip Ollerenshaw, "The European Linen Industry since the Middle Ages," in *The European Linen Industry in Historical Perspective*, ed. Brenda Collins and Philip Ollerenshaw (Oxford: Oxford University Press, 2003), 22, 29, 37; Martynas Jučas, *Baudžiavos irimas Lietuvoje* (Vilnius: Mintis, 1972), 277.

11. Lietuvos valstybės istorijos archyvas (Lithuanian Historical State Archive, hereafter LVIA), f. 446, op. 7, d. 657a, 2. Other sources mention up to seventy people injured. Such high numbers cannot be established using the relevant archival documents, nor is there confirmation for the participation of a high number of Belarusian peasants in the pogrom. On the contrary, most of the names of peasants arrested in connection with the pogrom are clearly of Lithuanian origin. See Berl Kagan, *Yidishe Shtet, Shtetlech und Dorfishe Yishuvim in Lite* (New York: B. Kohen, 1990), 70 f.

12. LVIA, f. 446, op. 7, d. 657a,1. 3.

13. LVIA, f. 378, op. 1905, d. 13,1. 37.

14. LVIA, f. 446, op. 7, d. 657a,1. 3.

15. Ibid., 4.

16. Ibid. According to an earlier police report, the Lithuanian inhabitants of Dusetos had demanded the extradition of the arsonist instead of an oath. LVIA, f. 378, op. 1905, d. 13,1. 37.

17. LVIA, f. 378, op. 1905, d. 13,1. 37.

18. LVIA, f. 446, op. 7, d. 657a, 4; LVIA, f. 378, op. 1905, d. 13,1. 37.

19. LVIA, f. 378, op. 1905, d. 13,1. 37.

20. LVIA, f. 446, op. 7, d. 657a,1. 4.

21. *Lietuvos laikraštis* 34 (1905): 485–487.

22. LVIA, f. 378, op. 1905, d. 13, 37; *Lietuvių laikraštis* 34 (1905): 485–487.

23. LVIA, f. 378, op. 1905, d. 13,1. 37.

24. LVIA, f. 378, op. 1905, d. 13,1. 37.

25. LVIA, f. 446, op. 7, d. 657a,1. 4.

26. LVIA, f. 378, op. 1905, d. 13,1. 37.

27. Ibid., 36. The detailed description of down feathers flying through the air in the course of riots and covering the streets in the aftermath bears a striking similarity to the reminiscences of Nikita Khrushchev, who as a child witnessed a pogrom in Yuzovka (today Donetsk) in 1905: "I saw watch-repair shops that had been smashed to bits, and a lot of down and feathers were blowing through the streets. When they looted the homes of the poor Jews they ripped open people's feather beds and feather comforters and dumped out the feathers." Nikita Khrushchev, *Memoirs of Nikita Khrushchev*, vol. 2: *Reformer (1945–1964)* (University Park, Pa.: Pennsylvania State University, 2006), 48. Similar reports of eyewitnesses to the illusion of snowfall exist in connection with the pogrom in Elizavetgrad (1881). See Klier, *Russians, Jews, and the Pogroms*, 26.

28. LVIA, f. 378, op. 1905, d. 13,1. 37 f.

29. Ibid., 38.

30. *Lietuvos laikraštis* 34 (1905), 486. Many of these Jews came from the neighboring town of Antalieptė, which had been ravaged by a fire in 1898. The Jews of Dusetos had helped rebuild the town. See *Encyclopedia of Jewish Communities in Lithuania*, s.v. "Antalieptė," http://www.jewishgen.org/yizkor/pinkas_lita/lit_00149.html.

31. LVIA, f. 378, op. 1905, d. 13,1. 38.

32. LVIA, f. 378, op. 1905, d. 13,1. 36.

33. Ibid., 37 f.

34. LVIA, f. 446, op. 7, d. 657a,1. 3.

35. LVIA, f. 378, PS, op. 1905, d. 13,1. 241–242.

36. LVIA, f. 446, op. 7, d. 657a,1. 5.

37. No tangible evidence was found against Savickas. According the Dusetian Jew Shayke Glick, Savickas later was killed by Itzak Baron's son Srulke, after the latter had found out that Savickas was his father's murderer. Sara Weiss-Slep, ed., *There Was a Shtetl in Lithuania: Dusiat Reflected in Reminiscences* (Tel Aviv: Society of Former Residents of Dusiat, 1989), http://www.jewishgen.org/Yizkor/Dusetos/dusetos.html#TOCo.

38. LVIA, f. 446, op. 7, d. 657a,1. 14.

39. Richter, "Kišinev or Linkuva?" 122 f.

40. Ibid., 127.

41. Malte Rolf, "1905: Revolution, Repression und Reform in Polen," in *Schlüsseljahre. Zentrale Konstellationen der mittel- und osteuropäischen Geschichte. Festschrift für Helmut Altrichter zum 65. Geburtstag*, ed. Matthias Stadelmann and Lilia Antipow (Stuttgart: Franz Steiner, 2011), 219–232, at 220.

42. Beryl Williams, "1905: The View from the Provinces," in *The Russian Revolution of 1905*, ed. Jonathan D. Smele and Anthony Heywood (London: Routledge, 2005), 34–54, at 37.

43. Vilma Žaltauskaitė, "Smurtas prieš žydus Šiaurės Lietuvoje 1900 metais. Įvykiai ir interpretacijos," in Sirutavičius and Staliūnas, *Kai ksenofobija virsta prievarta*, 79–98.

44. *Ūkininkas* 4 (1901), 27.

45. LVIA, f. 378, pol., ap. 208 (1900), b. 24,1. 10.

46. LVIA, f. 446, ap. 7, b. 460,1. 4–5.

47. LVIA, f. 446, ap. 7, b. 515,1. 2.

48. Richter, "Kišinev or Linkuva?" 124.

49. LVIA, f. 378, pol., ap. 1903, b. 52,1. 3.

50. Richter, "Kišinev or Linkuva?" 124–126.

51. LVIA, f. 446, op. 7, d. 657a, 1.

52. Ibid., 4.

53. Ibid., 6.

54. Regarding the case of Kharkov in 1905, Michael F. Hamm has shown that self-defense units actually could prevent pogroms, but only in cases when the local administration was willing to cooperate with them. Michael F. Hamm, "Jews and Revolution in Kharkiv: How One Ukrainian City Escaped a Pogrom in 1905," in Smele and Heywood, *The Russian Revolution of 1905*, 162, 171.

55. Helmut Walser Smith states that the appearance of self-defense units mainly was used as an "alibi for murder," because "the historic pattern of anti-Jewish violence demanded submission, huddling in houses, a passive acceptance of the script of a ritual drama." See Helmut Walser Smith, *The Continuities of German History: Nation, Religion, and Race across the Long Nineteenth Century* (Cambridge: Cambridge University Press, 2008), 155.

56. Ibid.

57. LVIA, f. 378, PS, ap. 1905, b. 13,1. 70.

58. *Darbas* ("Work") 5 (1905): 139–140.

59. LVIA, f. 378, PS, ap. 1905, b. 13,1. 70.

60. Rolf, "1905: Revolution, Repression und Reform in Polen," 227.

61. Pranė Dundulienė, *Žemdirbystė Lietuvoje: Nuo seniausių laikų iki 1917 metų* (Vilnius: Valstybinė politineės ir mokslineės literatūros leidykla, 1963), 70.

62. Cathy A. Frierson, *All Russia Is Burning! A Cultural History of Fire and Arson in Late Imperial Russia* (Seattle: University of Washington Press, 2002), esp. 40–48.

63. LVIA, f. 378, PS, ap. 1905, b. 13,1. 70–71.

64. See, for instance, *Tėynės sargas* 9 (1896): 20; *Tėynės sargas* 1 (1900): 30 f.; *Vilniaus žinios*, January 23, 1905, p. 3; *Viltis*, February 13, 1914, p. 3.

65. This phenomenon was not restricted to Lithuania, but has been observed regarding the Habsburg Crownland of Galicia as well, and may be characteristic for the rural regions of central eastern Europe in general. Lehmann, *Symbiosis*, 50 f.

66. The anti-Jewish riots in the summer of 1900 in Lithuania were, for instance, sparked by a ritual murder allegation made by a peasant girl who had wanted to give a plausible reason for her absence at work. See Richter, "Kišinev or Linkuva?" 119.

67. Negligent behavior such as throwing cigarettes to the ground or not properly extinguishing fireplaces accounted for more than half of the conflagrations in Lithuania. See, for example, *Lietuvos žinios*, June 7, 1910, p. 2; January 13, 1911, p. 3; March 23, 1914, p. 2; June 1, 1914, p. 3; April 18, 1914, p. 3; April 22, 1913, p. 2; April 30, 1914, p. 3; May 18, 1914, p. 2.

68. *Vilniaus žinios*, May 7, 1905, p. 3.

69. On May 15, a fire destroyed large parts of the town of Jonava. For the most part, Jewish houses were destroyed, and the Lithuanian population of Jonava apparently helped the Jews rebuild them. In the same month, fires destroyed houses in three villages around Jonava, in Žiežmariai, Žasliai, and in Kėdainiai. *Vilniaus žinios*, June 12, 1905, p. 3.

70. *Vilniaus žinios*, June 4, 1905, p. 3.

71. Gerhard Bauer and Manfred Klein, *Das alte Litauen: Dörfliches Leben zwischen 1861 und 1914* (Cologne: Böhlau, 1998), 45.

72. *Lietuvos žinios*, June 29, 1912, p. 3.

73. Only 8 percent of the population of Novoaleksandrovsk district was of Orthodox faith, while the figure was 5 percent in neighboring Vil'komir district and just 2 percent in Kovno district. I. E. Andreevskii, ed., *Enciklopedičeskiy slovar' Brokgauza i Efrona*, vol. 30 (St. Petersburg, 1890–1907), 525. Vytautas Merkys claims that Eastern Lithuania was populated by "many inhabitants with a very little pronounced national identity," who were mostly bi- or even trilingual. Vytautas Merkys, "Die nationale und soziale

Zusammensetzung der litauischen Stadtbevölkerung 1861–1914," *Archiv zur Sozialgeschichte* 34 (1994): 85–94, at 87.

74. In 1913 the nationalist newspaper "Hope" (*Viltis*) wrote about the east of Novoaleksandrovsk: "It is not long ago that this was a purely Lithuanian place [. . .]. The peasants are poor and thus at the mercy of the influence of Belarusians, who came here from Vitebsk governorate and other places [. . .]. The basis for the Belarusification in this region, as anyone will attest to, is laid by the Poles and polonized priests, who started talking to the local Lithuanians exclusively in Polish. Well, they were successful with their heroic deed: No Lithuanian language is being taught on the aforementioned farmsteads, but neither is Polish—everybody is speaking in Belarusian." *Viltis*, January 27, 1913, p. 2.

75. Although "Lithuanian" and "Belarusian" as ethnic/national designations need to be used with care, in general Belarusian speakers were far more numerous than Lithuanian speakers. At the same time, population growth among Belarusian-speaking peasants was higher than among Lithuanian-speaking peasants. Timothy Snyder, *The Reconstruction of Nations: Poland, Ukraine, Lithuania, Belarus, 1569–1999* (New Haven and London: Yale University Press, 2003), 49; Piotr S. Wandycz, *The Lands of Partitioned Poland, 1795–1918* (Seattle and London: University of Washington Press, 1974), 241.

76. Lithuanian politicians rarely ever took their Belarusian counterparts seriously, thus repeatedly causing hard feelings among the latter. *Varpas* 7/8 (1905): 73.

77. In 1909, only 8.2 percent of all those Lithuanian-language newspapers circulating in the seven districts of Kovno governorate were sold in Novoaleksandrovsk district. *Lietuvos žinios*, March 9, 1909, p. 3.

78. *Lietuvos žinios*, March 2, 1913, p. 6.

79. Ibid.

80. *Vilniaus žinios*, September 21, 1906, p. 3.

81. Hubert Gerlich, *Organische Arbeit und nationale Einheit: Polen und Deutschland (1830–1880) aus der Sicht Richard Roepells* (Münster: LIT, 2004); Maciej Janowski, *Polish Liberal Thought before 1918* (Budapest: Central European University Press, 2004), 81 ff.

82. See Klier, *Russians, Jews, and the Pogroms*, 207–233; Jan Kusber, "Zwischen Duldung und Ausgrenzung: Die Politik gegenüber den Juden im ausgehenden Zarenreich," in *Jüdische Welten in Osteuropa*, ed. Annelore Engel-Braunschmidt (Frankfurt am Main: Peter Lang, 2005), 45–64.

83. The creation of consumer cooperatives by peasants became possible only through a 1904 reform, which aimed at facilitating the formation of associations. Klaus Richter, "Anti-Semitism, 'Economic Emancipation' and the Lithuanian Co-operative Movement before World War I," *Quest: Issues in Contemporary Jewish History* 2 (2011), http://www.quest-cdecjournal.it.

84. *Kauno kalendorius 1907 metams* (Kaunas: Š. Kazimiero Draugija, 1906), 77.

85. *Lietuvių laikraštis* 13 (1905): 172.

86. LVIA, f. 378, Bendrasis skyrius, op. 1907, d. 98, S. 1.

87. *Auszra* 7–8 (1885): 233.

88. *Lietuvių laikraštis* 21 (1905): 283–284.

89. Vytautas Petronis, *Constructing Lithuania: Ethnic Mapping in Tsarist Russia, ca. 1800– 1914* (Stockholm: Stockholm University, 2007), 235.

90. *Lietuvių laikraštis* 34 (1905): 485.

91. A consumer cooperative was not founded in Dusetos until 1907. LVIA, f. 378, BS, ap. 1907, b. 98,1. 1. By that time, it was one of only four cooperatives in the entire district of Novoaleksandrovsk. See *Kauno kalendorius 1909 metams*, 43. In comparison to other cooperatives in Lithuania, however, its performance remained below average. *Viltis*, September 4, 1913, p. 2.

92. LVIA, f. 446, op. 7, d. 657a, p. 14.

93. *Lietuvių laikraštis* 34 (1905): 486.

94. Ibid.

95. Ibid.

96. Ibid.

97. LVIA, f. 446, op. 7, d. 657a, 3.

98. *Lietuvių laikraštis* 34 (1905): 486.

99. Ibid., 487.

100. Richter, "Anti-Semitism and 'economic emancipation.'"

101. Agnieszka Friedrich, "Żydzi, Niemcy i Polacy w publicystyce B. Prusa i J. Jelenskiego," in *Żydzi i judaizm we wspolczesnych badaniach polskich*, ed. Krzysztof Pilarczyk (Cracow: Ksiegarnia Akademicka, 2003), 199–213; Theodore R. Weeks, *From Assimilation to Antisemitism: The "Jewish Question" in Poland 1850–1914* (DeKalb, Ill.: Northern Illinois University Press, 2006).

102. Buchen, *Antisemitismus in Galizien*.

103. See Torsten Lorenz, ed., *Cooperatives in Ethnic Conflicts: Eastern Europe in the 19th and Early 20th Century* (Berlin: Berliner Wissenschafts-Verlag, 2006); Kai Struve, *Bauern und Nation in Galizien* (Göttingen: Vandenhoeck & Ruprecht, 2005).

104. Gerhard Bauer and Manfred Klein, *Das alte Litauen: Dörfliches Leben zwischen 1861 und 1914* (Cologne: Böhlau-Verlag, 1998), 172–174.

105. Vladas Sirutavičius, "Nusikaltimai ir visuomenė XIX amžiaus Lietuvoje," *Lietuvių atgimimo istorijos studijos* 12 (1995): 169–172.

106. See, for instance, Leonas Mulevičius, *Kaimas ir dvaras Lietuvoje XIX amžiuje* (Vilnius: Lietuvos Istorijos Instituto Leidykla, 2003), 84.

107. In most other regions of the Empire, where *zemstva* existed, the land captain already had been introduced in 1889. Carsten Goehrke, *Russland: Eine Strukturgeschichte* (Paderborn: F. Schöningh, 2010), 208.

108. *Varpas* 9/10 (1903): 202.

109. *Tėvynės sargas* 8 (1900): 15–16; *Varpas* 12 (1900): 142–143.

110. John D. Klier, "The Pogrom Paradigm in Russian History," in Klier and Lambrosa, *Pogroms*, 23.

111. *Varpas* 2 (1892): 29–30. Jews were the only group in Lithuania that was seen as unfit for assimilation into Lithuanian culture, because "for them it is no bargain (*gešeft*)." See *Varpas* 10 (1890): 151–153.

112. Weiss-Slep, *There Was a Shtetl in Lithuania.*

113. Egidijus Aleksandravičius, *Blaivybė Lietuvoje XIX amžiuje* (Vilnius: Sietynas, 1990), 26; Vytautas Merkys, *Motiejus Valančius: Tarp katalikiškojo universalizmo ir tautiškumo* (Vilnius: Mintis, 1999).

114. Rima Praspaliauskienė, *Nereikalingi ir pavojingi. XVIII a. pabaigos — XIX a. pirmosios pusės elgetos, valkatos ir plėšikai Lietuvoje* (Vilnius: Žara, 2000), S. 160.

115. See, for example, *Vilniaus žinios*, December 19, 1906, p. 2; LVIA, f. 378, PS, ap. 213 (1907), b. 11,1. 26–27; *Viltis*, March 18, 1909, p. 3.

116. LVIA, f. 445, op. 1, d. 3549,1. 4.

117. Ibid.

118. Čepėnas, *Lietuvos istorija*, vol. 1, 357.

119. Kviklys, *Mūsų Lietuva*, vol. 4, 587.

120. LVIA, f. 378, op. 1905, d. 13,1. 37; LVIA, f. 445, op. 1, d. 3549,1. 4.

121. For the case of village constables in, for example, the Lithuanian villages of Vaškiai and Budriai, and — in an extreme case with a total loss of state authority–Alanta, see Ignas Jablonskis, *Budrių kaimas* (Vilnius: Mokslo ir enciklopedijų leidykla, 1993), 23; Algimantas Miškinis, *Istorinė urbanistinė raida iki 1969 m* (Kaunas: Žiemgalos Leidykla, 2005), 36; LVIA, f. 378, PS, ap. 1905, b. 13,1. 142.

122. *Viltis*, September 4, 1913, p. 2.

123. Klier, *Russians, Jews, and the Pogroms*, 30–32.

124. In this sense I strongly disagree with Zalkin's concept of a relatively peaceful and "unique Lithuanian version of pogrom," which appears in his otherwise extremely enlightening article. See Mordechai Zalkin, "Antisemitism in Lithuania," 145.

11. The Russian Army and Pogroms, 1903–1906

1. The manifesto granted an elected state duma and the limited freedoms needed to sustain an electoral regimen. Most power remained in the hands of the autocracy, but the manifesto was greeted by much of the opposition as a great victory against tsarist arbitrariness and oppression.

2. The 1897 national census listed 8,799 Jews in a total population of 27,716 in Chernigov city.

3. Leo Motzkin [A. Linden], ed., *Die Judenpogrome in Russland*, 2 vols. (Cologne: Juedischer Verlag G.M.B.H., 1910), 2: 267–270 (hereafter *Judenpogrome*).

4. The number of pogroms carried out in the weeks following the announcement of the October Manifesto has been estimated at between six hundred and seven hundred by at least two reliable sources and is accepted by most current studies: D. Pasmanik, "Pogromy," *Evreiskaia Entsiklopediia: Svod znanii o evreistve i ego kul'ture v proshlom i nastoiashchem* (Saint Petersburg: Izd-vo Brokgauz-Efron, [1906–1913]): XII, cols. 611–622; and Shlomo Lambroza, "The Pogroms of 1903–1906," in *Pogroms: Anti-Jewish Violence in Modern Russian History*, ed. John D. Klier and Shlomo Lambroza (Cambridge: Cambridge University Press, 1992): 195–247; and Shlomo Lambroza, "The Pogrom Movement in Tsarist Russia, 1903–1906," (Ph.D. dissertation, Rutgers University, 1981). An occasionally cited source gives an even larger number, but its data are not as reliable as those

just mentioned: "From Kishineff to Bialystok: A Table of Pogroms from 1903 to 1906," in *American Jewish Yearbook* 5667 (September 20, 1906 to September 8, 1907) (Philadelphia: The Jewish Publication Society of America, 1906): 38–49, 60–65.

5. Gerald Surh, "The Role of Civil and Military Commanders during the 1905 Pogroms in Odessa and Kiev," *Jewish Social Studies* 15, no. 3 (2009): 39–55. The army's invariable and immediate success at stopping pogroms prompted contemporaries and historians to suggest that the delay was proof of a government conspiracy, the antisemitism of the commanders, or both, though the situations referred to were more complex, as will be shown.

6. One subtext of this chapter is the differences in pogroms occurring in such locales compared to those that occurred in large cities, such as those treated in Surh, "The Role of Civil and Military Commanders."

7. For a brief definition of *pogrom*, see Appendix 1.

8. The term *Russian* will be used in this chapter as a convenient, if not altogether accurate, term to cover all anti-Jewish elements, most frequently, Russians, Ukrainians, and Poles, but also anti-Jewish activists from other ethnic groups, such as Germans, Balts, or Tatars. The exact ethnic makeup of pogrom crowds is rarely identified, but when it is possible to do so, the appropriate terms will be used.

9. Jewish-gentile tensions (like interethnic tensions generally) were more pronounced in urban settings as a result of greater crowding and more tightly drawn identity boundaries. Peasant soldiers would have brought to their military service the mixed experience with Jews of their predominantly village origins, although it is likely that they would have been as susceptible to anti-Jewish agitation from other soldiers and as tempted by opportunities for Jewish plunder as were their village brethren.

10. Among the recent works that attempt to read the 1903–1906 pogroms as part of broader historical developments are Robert Weinberg, *The Revolution of 1905 in Odessa: Blood on the Steps* (Bloomington: Indiana University Press, 1993) and "The Pogrom of 1905 in Odessa: A Case Study," in *Pogroms: Anti-Jewish Violence in Modern Russian History*, ed. John D. Klier and Shlomo Lambroza (Cambridge: Cambridge University Press, 1992): 248–289; Shlomo Lambroza, "The Pogroms of 1903–1906," in *Pogroms: Anti-Jewish Violence in Modern Russian History*, ed. Klier and Lambroza, 195–247; Michael Hamm, *Kiev: A Portrait, 1800–1917* (Princeton: Princeton University Press, 1993), chap. 8; Charters Wynn, *Workers, Strikes and Pogroms: The Donbass-Dnepr Bend in Late Imperial Russia, 1870–1905* (Princeton: Princeton University Press, 1992), chap. 7; Gerald Surh, "Ekaterinoslav City in 1905: Workers, Jews, and Violence," *International Labor and Working Class History*, no. 64 (Fall 2003): 139–166; Faith Hillis, "The Kiev Pogrom of 1905: Community, Street Violence, and the Problem of Mass Violence," working paper, October 2006; and Vladimir Levin, "Preventing Pogroms: Patterns in Jewish Politics in Early Twentieth Century Russia," *Anti-Jewish Violence: Rethinking the Pogroms in East European History*, ed. J. Dekel-Chen et al. (Bloomington: Indiana University Press, 2011).

11. The theory that the pogroms were intentionally, centrally planned by the autocratic government was firmly believed by even the best-informed contemporaries, for example,

the eminent historian Simon Dubnow, and has been accepted until it was decisively discredited by Hans Rogger in essays collected in *Jewish Policies and Right-Wing Politics in Imperial Russia* (Berkeley: University of California Press, 1986), chaps. 2 and 4, and by Heinz-Dietrich Löwe, *Antisemitismus und reaktionäre Utopie. Russ. Konservatismus im Kampf gegen d. Wandel von Staat u. Gesellschaft, 1890–1917* (Hamburg: Hoffmann and Campe, 1978).

12. The absence of central management by the government does not mean that the government bore no responsibility whatsoever for the pogroms. Close study reveals that the chief explanation was not the *central* government's direction and control of the pogroms, but its *lack* of coordination with its *local* representatives and *their* lack of direction and control of the local situation. Not diabolical competence in planning them, but hapless incompetence in allowing them to occur at all accounts for the great bulk of violence visited on Jews and other elements viewed as "unpatriotic." See Surh, "The Role of Civil and Military Commanders."

13. As argued by John Bushnell, *Mutiny amid Repression: Russian Soldiers in the Revolution of 1905–1906* (Bloomington: Indiana University Press, 1985).

14. Tsentral'nyi derzhavnyi istorichnyi arkhiv Ukraiyni, m. Kyiv (TsDIAK), F. 442/op. 855/d. 391, A, ch. 1:11. 5–6.

15. Rossiiskii Gosudarstvennyi Voenno-Istoricheskii Arkhiv (RGVIA), F. 13140/op. 1/d. 780,11. 65–66, "Instruktsiia voiskam, vyzvannym dlia sodeistviia Grazhdanskim vlastiam v preduprezhdenii ili prekrashchenii narodnyx bezporiadkov i volnenii." Undated, though other documents in the same delo are dated 1903 and 1905. Excerpts translated as Appendix 2 appear at the end of this chapter.

16. As stated in an 1877 law that put army troops at the beck and call of a wide variety of civil officials, in accordance with a long list of causes, including and in the first place "the preservation of order and internal security . . ." Officials given this right were headed by governors, governor-generals, city prefects (*gradonachal'niki*), city police chiefs, and *uezd* superintendents (*ispavniki*). *Polnoe sobranie zakonov rossiiskoi imperii, sobranie 2-oe, tom 52, otdelenie 2-oe* (1877) #57748, pp. 160–162.

17. This characterization of the Russian military leadership's attitudes toward domestic police duties is drawn from William C. Fuller, *Civil-Military Conflict in Imperial Russia 1881–1914* (Princeton: Princeton University Press, 1985), chaps. 4 and 5, passim.

18. Although it will not be pursued here, one cannot but add that the reputation of the tsarist officer corps in this period for professionalism and individual initiative was not high. See John Bushnell, "The Tsarist Officer Corps, 1881–1914: Customs, Duties, Inefficiency," *American Historical Review*" 86, no. 4 (1986): 753–780; and Peter Kenez, "Russian Officer Corps Before the Revolution: The Military Mind," *Russian Review* 31, no. 3 (1972): 226–236.

19. RGVIA, F. 13135, op. 1, d. 4,11. 4–40b., 7, 8, 100b.: Doklad o deiatel'nosti voisk Kievskago garnizona za vremia s 13-go po 25-go Oktiabria 1905 g.

20. TsDIAK, F. 442/op. 855/d. 391, A, ch. 1:1. 32. While the authority of Kleigel's extended to only three provinces, the Kiev Military District's jurisdiction included those three (Kiev,

Podolia, and Volhynia) plus four others (Chernigov, Poltava, Khar'kov, and Kursk). Forrest A. Miller, *Dmitri Miliutin and the Reform Era in Russia* (Nashville, Tenn.: Vanderbilt University Press, 1968), 44–45.

21. TsDIAK, F. 442/op. 855/d. 391, A, ch. 1:11. 24–25.

22. TsDIAK, F. 442/op. 855/d. 391, A, ch. 1,1. 19.

23. For example, in Chernigov: *Judenpogrome*, 2: 270; Berezna: Ibid., 271; Kiev: (RGVIA, F. 400, Op. 3, d. 2604,1. 648 ob., 649); Saratov: (*Pravda o evreiskom pogrome v g. Saratove v oktiabr'skie dni 1905 goda* (Saratov: Tip. Soiuza Pechatnago Dela i prodazhi izdanii, 1908): 3; Kerch: *Delo o Kerchenskom pogrome* (St. Petersburg: Tip. Shtaba Otdel'nago Korpusa Pogranichnoi Strazhi, 1907): 17; and Cherkassy: Gosudarstvennyi Arkhiv Rossiiskoi Federatsii (GARF), F. 102, delopro. 3, Op. 103, 1905, 1 ch. 4,1. B, "Svedeniia po Kievskoi gubernii," 11. 20–22ob. Even in Odessa, where the greatest number of Jews were killed in 1905, troops initially were instructed to be willing to shoot at both pogromists and Jews: Robert Weinberg, "The Pogrom of 1905 in Odessa: A Case Study," in Klier and Lambroza, *Pogroms: Anti-Jewish Violence*, 262.

24. Bushnell, *Mutiny*, 11–15.

25. For example, during the March 1905 pogrom in Nikolaev (Kherson Province), a group of drunken soldiers threw stones at a Cossack patrol and then fought with the infantrymen sent to restore discipline. Earlier that day, the same soldiers had stoned a police station, demanding the release of a prisoner. TsDIAK, F. 347, Op. 1, d. 378,11. 3040b.

26. This characterization of rank-and-file Russian soldiers as peasants, and their world as a version of a peasant society, is indebted to John Bushnell's studies: *Mutiny*, passim., and "Peasants in Uniform: The Tsarist Army as a Peasant Society," *Journal of Social History* 13, no. 4 (1980): 565–576.

27. GARF, F. 102, Op. 103, delopro. 3/11., ch. 6 B (1905),11. 7–8.

28. Lambroza, "Pogroms of 1903–1906," 208; M. Fischer, "Homel," *Judenpogrome in Russland*, 2: 37–38.

29. Lambroza, "Pogroms of 1903–1906," 213–216.

30. TsDIAK, F. 442, Op. 855, d. 391, A, ch. II,11. 234–235. "Okhrana" was the generic name for the organs of the state police department charged with security from political oppositionists and revolutionaries.

31. TsDIAK, F. 304, Op. 1, d. 65, "Svedeniia po Mogilevskoi gub." 11. 15–150b.

32. This incident had been reported only a few days earlier (June 15) in Cherkassy: GARF, F. 102, delopro. 3, Op. 103, 1905, 1 ch. 4,1. B, "Svedeniia po Kievskoi gubernii," 1. 19. Whether it was actually acid, as reported by the police, or possibly only lemonade that was thrown may be doubted, though the sting of having been insulted by a Jew must have felt like acid to the policeman and prison chief, whose wife also was doused while sitting with her husband. The attribution of these three reasons for the rioting of drunken recruits may be a less accurate description of the rioters' motives than a post-facto rationalization by the police authors of the report.

33. Ibid., 11. 20–22ob. This detailed report, written by a police official, mentions no misbehavior on the part of the police, yet its conclusion inspires confidence in its overall veracity

by the careful attention to the times, names, circumstances, and the nature and extent of theft and damages on which it was based: "The moment the disorders arose, the police applied all its resources to stopping them, which is why the degree of destruction was not great, and all the important commercial streets and buildings were not touched. Meanwhile, the ranks of the police were exposed to life [threatening] dangers in suppressing the disorders, and stones were twice thrown at the Uezd Superintendent . . ." Ibid., 1. 22.

34. *Materialy k istorii russkoi kontr-revoliutsii. Tom I. Pogromy po offitsial nym 906 dokumentam* (St. Petersburg: Tip. Obshchestv. Pol'za, 1908), App., 182, 189, 190, and Weinberg, *1905 in Odessa*, 128–129; Surh, "Ekaterinoslav City in 1905," 147–149; *Delo o pogrome v Belostoke. 1 v 3 Iiunia 1906 goda. Obvinitel'nyi akt, sudebnoe sledstvie i rechi poverennyx grazhdanskix isttsov, pris. pover. R. L Veismana, G. D. Skariatina i D.I poverennyx grazhdanskix Gillersona*, 2d ed. (St. Petersburg: Tip. A Trud, 1909): 8–11.

35. See, for instance, Erich Haberer, *Jews and Revolution in Nineteenth-Century Russia* (Cambridge: Cambridge University Press, 1995).

36. Surh, "Jewish Self Defense, Revolution, and Pogrom Violence in 1905," in *The Russian Revolution of 1905 in Transcultural Perspective: Identities, Peripheries, and the Flow of Ideas*, ed. Felicitas Fischer von Weikersthal et al. (Bloomington, Ind.: Slavica).

37. 41,903 Jews in a total population of 65,871 in the 1897 national census.

38. Motzkin, *Judenpogrome*, 2:61–63.

39. In addition to the examples of Orsha and Bialystok in 1905 cited above, cases of troops shooting up buildings from which shooting was witnessed, reported, or suspected occurred in Odessa, Kiev, Kerch, and in Bialystok again during its 1906 pogrom. Odessa: *Materialy k istorii russkoi kontr-revoliutsii*, pp. 182, 189, 190; Kiev: *Evreiskaia Entsiklopediia*, 12:621; Kerch: Bobrishchev-Pushkin, A. V., ed., *Delo o Kerchenskom pogrome* (St. Petersburg: Tip. Shtaba Otdel'nago Korpusa Pogranichnoi Strazhi, 1907): 15; Bialystok: *Delo o pogrome v Belostoke*, pp. 9–11.

40. TsDIAK, F. 442, Op. 855, d. 391, ch. 1,11. 256–2570b.

41. Gosudarstvennyi Arkhiv Dnepropetrovskoi Oblasti (GADO), F. 177, Op. 1, d. 2a, 114.

42. Motzkin, *Judenpogrome*, 2: 275–277.

43. Lambroza, "Pogroms of 1903–1906," 204.

44. *Vserossiiskaia Politicheskaia Stachka v Oktiabre*, ed. L. M. Ivanov et al. (Moscow: Izd-vo Akademii Nauk, 1955): 2:50–51; *Delo o pogrome v g. Tomske v 1905 godu* (Otchet o sudebnom zasedanii Tomskogo Okruzhnogo Suda) (Tomsk: Tip. Sibirskago T-va Pechatnago Dela, 1909), pp. 3–15. Although the crowd's anger on October 20 clearly was directed at a broader target, Jews were part of it, and Jewish homes and businesses were attacked the next day.

45. The scene in front of the railroaders' building was top-heavy with authority as the governor, the commander of the city's garrison, and the provincial chief of the gendarmes were all present.

46. During Kiev's October pogrom, a military patrol arrived at one of the markets just as a patrolman drove off a group of looters, then went on his way, thinking the soldiers would guard the market. The looters then returned and resumed their plunder while the soldiers

stood idle. Asked by a passerby why they did not act to prevent the looting, one of the soldiers replied that "we were not ordered [to do that]; we were ordered to see that fights not occur and that Russians not be killed." *Materialy k istorii russkoi kontr-revoliutsii. Tom I, Pogromy po offitsial'nym dokumentam* (St. Peterburg: "Obshchestvennaia pol'za," 1908), 240–241.

47. *Delo o pogrome v Orshe, 21–24 oktiabria 1905 goda. Obvinitel'nyi akt i sudebnboe sledst-vie* (St. Petersburg: Tip. Sh. Busselia, 1908): 7–10.

48. Ibid., 10, 13.

49. The newly mobilized reservists and recruits who attacked Jews in Cherkassy were insubordinate in this sense, but also not yet fully disciplined soldiers.

50. Talimonov was probably an NCO (corporal or sergeant) rather than a full officer, which may help explain his difficulty maintaining order.

51. GARF, F. 102, deloproiz. O.O., 1905/200, ch. 6,11. 103–1040b.

52. Bushnell, *Mutiny.* The Razdel'naia incident may also illustrate the legitimacy of another of the complaints the higher command had against the use of army troops in policing civilian disturbances: that it required the deployment of excessively small units and their dispersal over a wide area, disrupting the unity and continuity of command. Fuller, *Civil-Military Conflict*, 94.

53. TsDIAK, F. 1597, Op. 1, d. 104,1. 11.

54. *Delo o pogrome v Orshe*, 20–21.

55. John D. Klier, *Russians, Jews, and the Pogroms of 1881–1882* (Cambridge: Cambridge University Press, 2011), 115–116, 255, makes clear that Jews did organize self-defense efforts, but that they were sporadic and conditioned on the permission of local authorities.

56. *Der Freynd*, September 20, 1903, p. 4, no. 201, as cited by Lanbroza, "Pogroms of 1903–1906," p. 209; and A. Litvak (Chaim Y. Helfand), "In der yiddisher veltl," *De veker*, January 1/14, 1906, p. 3, as cited by Jonathan Frankel, *Prophecy and Politics: Socialism, Nationalism, and the Russian Jews, 1862–1917* (Cambridge: Cambridge University Press, 1984), 147.

12. Antisemitism in Hungary during the First World War

The author would like to express his gratitude to the archivists in Budapest, Debrecen, and Oradea who greatly aided this research, as well as to Colgate University, which open-handedly funded it.

1. "Hány galíciai család van Nagyvárad?" *Nagyvárad*, August 8, 1918; "Az idegenek eltávolítása: Lakásvita az közgyűlésen," *Nagyvárad*, August 9, 1918; "Hány galíciai van Nagyváradon?" *Nagyváradi Friss Ujság*, August 22, 1918.

2. For the words of the city councilor and mayor: "Izgalmas városi közgyűlés," *Szabadság*, August 9, 1918.

3. For an overview: Peter Gatrell, "Refugees and Forced Migrants During the First World War," *Immigrants and Minorities* 26, nos. 1–2 (2008): 82–110; Peter Gatrell, *A Whole Empire Walking: Refugees in Russia during WW I* (Bloomington: Indiana University Press, 1999). For refugees in Austria-Hungary: Beatrix Hoffmann-Holter, *"Abreisendmachung"*:

Jüdische Kriegsflüchtlinge in Wien, 1914–1923 (Vienna: Böhlau, 1995); Gernot Heiss and Oliver Rathkolb, eds., *Asylland wider Willen: Flüchtlinge in Österrreich im europäischen Kontext seit 1914* (Vienna: Dachs-Verlag, 1995); David Rechter, "Galicia in Vienna: Jewish Refugees in the First World War," *Austrian History Yearbook* 28 (1997): 113–130; Marsha Rozenblit, *Reconstructing a National Identity: The Jews of Habsburg Austria during World War I* (Oxford: Oxford University Press, 2001); Maureen Healy, *Vienna and the Fall of the Habsburg Empire: Total War and Everyday Life in World War I* (Cambridge: Cambridge University Press, 2004).

4. Omer Bartov, "Defining Enemies, Making Victims: Germans, Jews, and the Holocaust," *American Historical Review* 103, no. 3 (1998), 774–776.

5. Péter Bihari, *Lövészárkok a hátországban: Középosztály, zsidókérdés, antiszemitizmus az első világháború Magyarországán* (Budapest: Napvilág, 2008); Paul Hanebrink, *In Defense of Christian Hungary: Religion, Nationalism, and Antisemitism, 1890–1944* (Ithaca, N.Y.: Cornell University Press, 2006), 47–59; Rebekah Klein-Pejšová, *Among the Nationalities: Jewish Refugees, Jewish Nationality, and Czechoslovak Statebuilding* (Ph.D. diss., Columbia University, 2007).

6. Peter Pastor, "The Home Front in Hungary, 1914–18," in *East Central European Society in World War I*, ed. Bela K. Kiraly and Nandor Dreisziger (New York: Social Science Monographs, 1985), 123–134; Gabor Vermes, *István Tisza: The Liberal Vision and Conservative Statecraft of a Magyar Nationalist* (Boulder: East European Monographs, 1985); Dániel Szabó, ed., *Az első világháború* (Budapest: Osiris, 2009).

7. Philip Vilas Bohlman, *The Music of European Nationalism: Cultural Identity and Modern History* (Santa Barbara: ABC-CLIO, 2004), 238.

8. Ady cited in Teréz Mózes, *Váradi zsidók* (Nagyvárad: Literator, 1995), 100.

9. In her memoirs, Margit Imrik Benda described Nagyvárad as "a Jewish city" and estimated that it was "50% Jewish, 30% Romanian, and 20% Hungarian." See Benda, *Egy váradi úrilány: Benda Gyuláné Imrik Margit emlékezése*, ed. Magda Sebős (Budapest: Noran, 2006), 64. Similar figures appear in Dezső Schön, ed., *A tegnap városa: A nagyváradi zsidóság emlékkönyve* (Tel Aviv: A Nagyváradról Elszármazottak Egyesülete, 1981), 90–91. According to the 1910 census, the population was 23 percent Jewish, 31 percent Roman Catholic, and 30 percent Calvinist, with the balance a mix of Lutherans, Greek Catholics, and Eastern Orthodox.

10. On Nagyvárad and its Jewish community: Tamás Csíki, *Városi zsidóság Északkelet- és Kelet-Magyarországon* (Budapest: Osiris, 1999), as well as Liviu Borcea and Gheorghe Gorun, eds., *Istoria orașului Oradea* (Oradea: Cogito, 1995); János Fleiss, *Város, kinek nem látni mását* (Nagyvárad: Charta, 1997); Mircea Moldovan, "Oradea comme une Florence juive au seuil du XXe siècle," in *Permanences et ruptures dans l'histoire des Juifs de Roumanie*, ed. Carol Iancu (Montpellier: Publications Montpellier 3, 2004): 117–126; Mózes, *Váradi zsidók*; Schön, *A tégnap városa*.

11. Mózes, *Váradi zsidók*, 114.

12. Pál Szabó, *Nyugtalan élet*, vol. 1 (Budapest: Szépirodalmi Könyvkiadó, 1971), 434.

13. "A nagyváradi zsidóság jóléti bizottsága," *Egyenlőség*, December 27, 1914.

14. Rozenblit, *Reconstructing a National Identity*, 65–74.

15. Walter Mentzel, "Weltkriegsflüchtlinge in Cisleithanien, 1914–1918," in Heiss and Rathkolb, *Asylland wider Willen*, 25.

16. Emma Iványi, ed., *Magyar Minisztertanácsi jegyzőkönyvek az első világháború korából 1914–1918* (Budapest: Akadémiai Kiadó, 1960), docs. 23, 32, 61.

17. Szabó, *Az első világháború*, 159–162.

18. Klein-Pejšová, *Among the Nationalities*, 17–65.

19. Hajdú-Bihar Megyei Levéltár V. 605/c 3. k. *Bagamér Nagyközség közgyűlési jegyzőkönyve*, November 5, 1915.

20. "Hol volt az intelligencia?" *Szalontai Hirek*, September 28, 1915.

21. "Az ellenséges államok nagyváradi alattvalói," *Nagyvárad*, November 26, 1914.

22. Direcţia Judeţeană Bihor a Arhivelor Naţionale Bihor, fond *Pretura plăsei Tinca*, d. 4.

23. "Ellenőrizzük a menekületeket," *Nagyvárad*, October 3, 1914.

24. Gatrell, *A Whole Empire Walking*, 49–68.

25. It is not clear why Rabbi Hager did not go to Vienna, as did many other Vizhnitz Jews, including the family of the nine-year-old Otto Preminger, the future Hollywood director.

26. Poorer Jews in Nagyvárad were more likely to welcome the Hasidic rabbi. In April 1914, for example, after a local rabbi had turned away their petition to be exempted from the costlier parts of the Passover celebration, a group of poor Nagyvárad Jews appealed to the Hasidic rabbi of Sadigura, also in Bucovina, for guidance. See "A nagyváradi szegény izraeliták levele a csodarabbihoz," in *Boldog Várad*, ed. István János Bálint (Budapest: Héttorony, 1992), 548.

27. Schön, *A tegnap városa*, 96–98.

28. Áharon Kleinmann, ed., *Margitta és vidéke zsidóságának sorsa* (Jerusalem: Chájjim Franck, 1979), 11.

29. "Nagyváradon maradhatnak-e a galíciai iparosok?" *Új Nagyvárad*, September 25, 1915.

30. "A wiznitzi csodarabbi Nagyváradon," *Tiszántúl*, October 10, 1915.

31. "Magyarország több vért áldozott, mint Austria," *Nagyvárad*, December 6, 1917.

32. Healy, *Vienna and the Fall of the Habsburg Empire*, 48–50.

33. Schön, *A tegnap városa*, 94.

34. "A város lisztje. Idegennek nem szabad lisztet adni!" *Nagyvárad*, March 11, 1915.

35. "Megalakul a nagyváradi fogyasztók szövetsége. A Feministák Egyesület akciója a drágaság ellen," *Nagyvárad*, October 3, 1915.

36. D.B.A. "A fölösleges közvetítők," *Tiszántúl*, October 1, 1915.

37. Schön, *A tegnap városa*, 98–99.

38. Poltikatörténeti és Szakszervezeti Levéltár (hereafter PSzL), 689. fond. *Ágoston Péter naplójai*, September 30, 1915, p. 420 and October 14, 1915, p. 430; "Ullmann Rezső hadseregszállitásai," *Tiszántúl*, September 1, 1916.

39. "Erdélyiek — galíciaiak. Hadimunka — uzsora," *Tiszántúl*, September 20, 1916.

40. Direcţia Judeţeană Bihor a Arhivelor Naţionale, fond *Primăria oraşului Salonta*, d. 138. f. 52.

41. See the case of Dezső Tempeleán, a district official in a small town near Nagyvárad, ac-

cused of theft, extortion, and illegal seizures of land. Direcția Județeană Bihor a Arhivelor Naționale, fond *Pretura plăsei Vașcău*, d. 13. f.

42. Péter Ágoston, *A zsidók utja* (Nagyvárad: A Nagyváradi Társadalomtudományi Társaság, 1917); Gyurgyák, *A zsidókérdés Magyarországon*, 479; also see Bihari, *Lövészárkok a hátországban*, 196–201.

43. PSzL, 689. fond. *Ágoston Péter naplójai*, February 7, 1915, p. 19.

44. PSzL, 689. fond. *Ágoston Péter naplójai*, January 29, 1915, p. 10 and October 3, 1915, p. 422.

45. PSzL, 689. fond. *Ágoston Péter naplójai*, November 5, 1915, p. 452.

46. Healy, *Vienna and the Fall of the Habsburg Empire*, 311–12.

47. Antal Sándor, *A magyar zsidóság jövendője. Felelet dr. Ágoston Péter nagyváradi jogtanárnak* (Nagyvárad: Sonnenfeld, 1917), 26, 47.

48. János Székely, *Az eltévedt Ágoston. A magyar fejlődés és a zsidóság* (Nagyvárad: Béres és Held, 1917), 3, 23.

49. "A zsidók utja a városi közgyűlésen," *Nagyvárad*, July 15, 1917; also see "Megmaradhat-e Ágoston Péter a Gyermekbarát alelnöke? Heves vita 'A zsidók utja' miatt a közgyűlésen," *Nagyváradi Napló*, July 15, 1917.

50. "Befejezték a közgyűlést," *Nagyváradi Friss Ujság*, July 15, 1917.

51. By 1918, there were fewer than twenty thousand Galician and Bucovinian refugees in all of Hungary. Klein-Pejšová, *Among the Nationalities*, 49.

52. József Patai, "Az antiszemitizmus Magyarországon, a Galíciaiak és a morál," *Múlt és Jövő* 8, no. 8 (August 1918): 283.

53. Lipót Kecskeméti, "Menekülnek a zsidóságból," in *Az Országos Rabbi-Egyesület negyedszázada 1906–1931*, ed. Arnold Kiss (Budapest: Az Országos Rabbi-Egyesület Kiadása, 1931), 92.

54. Elie Wiesel, *All Rivers Run to the Sea: Memoirs* (New York: Knopf, 1995), 11–13.

55. Bartov, "Defining Enemies, Making Victims," 780.

56. Georg Simmel, "The Stranger," in *On Individuality and Social Forms*, ed. Donald N. Levine (Chicago: University of Chicago Press, 1971), 148.

ABOUT THE CONTRIBUTORS

Vicki Caron is the Diann G. and Thomas A. Mann Professor of History and Modern Jewish Studies at Cornell University. She has published a number of books and articles, including *Between France and Germany: The Jews of Alsace-Lorraine, 1871–1918* (Stanford: Stanford University Press, 1988) and *Uneasy Asylum: France and the Jewish Refugee Crisis, 1933–1942* (Stanford: Stanford University Press, 1999), which has appeared in a French translation as *L'Asile incertain: Les Réfugiés juifs en France, 1933–1942* (Paris: Tallandier, 2008). She also coedited, with Michael Brenner and Uri R. Kaufmann, *Jewish Emancipation Reconsidered: The French and German Models* (Tübingen: Mohr-Siebeck, 2003). She is currently working on a book titled "The Battle for the Republic: Jewish-Catholic Relations in France, 1870–1914" (Harvard University Press, forthcoming), which is envisioned as the first of a two-volume work on Jewish-Catholic relations in France since 1870.

Michal Frankl received his Ph.D. from Charles University in Prague and is currently the head of the Department of Jewish Studies and History of Antisemitism at the Jewish Museum in Prague. His research interests include modern antisemitism, refugee policy, and the Holocaust. He is the coeditor two volumes of the *Theresienstädter Gedenkbücher*, the author of *"Prag ist nunmehr antisemitisch": Tschechischer Antisemitismus am Ende des 19. Jahrhunderts* (Berlin: Metropol, 2011), coauthor with Katerina Čapková of *Unsichere Zuflucht: Die Tschechoslowakei und ihre Flüchtlinge aus NS-Deutschland und Österreich, 1933–1938* (Cologne: Böhlau, 2012), and coeditor with Jindrich Toman of *Jan Neruda a Židé: Texty a kontexty* [Jan Neruda and the Jews: Texts and contexts] (Prague: Akropolis, 2012).

Sam Johnson is a senior lecturer in modern European history at Manchester Metropolitan University (United Kingdom). Her *Pogroms, Peasants, Jews: Britain and Eastern Europe's Jewish Question, 1867–1925* (Houndmills, U.K.: Palgrave Macmillan, 2011) has just been published. Her new project examines the popular media's visualization of Jews in the late Habsburg and Tsarist empires, as well as in France, Britain, and Imperial Germany. She is also the managing editor of the journal *East European Jewish Affairs*.

Hillel J. Kieval is the Gloria M. Goldstein Professor of Jewish History and Thought at Washington University in St. Louis. His many publications on Jewish culture and society from the Enlightenment to World War II include *Languages of Community: The Jewish Experience in the Czech Lands* (Berkeley: University of California Press, 2000) and *The Making of Czech Jewry: National Conflict and Jewish Society in Bohemia, 1870–1918* (New York: Oxford University Press, 1988). He is completing a comparative study of the reappearance of "ritual murder" trials in Europe at the close of the nineteenth century and the beginning of the twentieth century.

Mary Margaroni is a Ph.D. candidate at the Center for Research on Antisemitism at the Technical University of Berlin. Her thesis focuses on antisemitism in Greece across the nineteenth century, from the destruction of Jewish communities in the Peloponnese during the early years of the Greek Revolution (1821–1822) to blood libel in Corfu in 1891, which led to elimination of the Jewish community on that island. The thesis examines the presence of antisemitism in the spheres of folk culture, high politics, intellectual debates, and the Orthodox Church.

Robert Nemes is an associate professor of history at Colgate University. He is the author of *The Once and Future Budapest* (DeKalb: Northern Illinois University Press, 2005), a monograph on nationalism and urbanism in nineteenth-century Hungary. He is currently finishing a book titled "Another Hungary," which uses collective biography to examine the intersection of politics, place, religion, and nationhood in provincial Hungary between 1790 and 1918.

Iulia Onac is pursuing her Ph.D. at the Center for Research on Antisemitism at the Technical University of Berlin. Her dissertation analyzes antisemitism in Romania from the Congress of Berlin in 1878 to the outbreak of World War I in 1914.

Klaus Richter is a lecturer of modern history at the University of Birmingham and the author of *Antisemitismus in Litauen: Juden, Christen und die "Emanzipation" der Bauern, 1889–1914* (Berlin: Metropol, 2013). He received his Ph.D. from the Technical University of Berlin. His research interests also include the history of East Central Europe during World War I and the interwar period, as well as the history of nationalism.

Alison Rose is an adjunct assistant professor of history and gender and women's studies at the University of Rhode Island. She wrote her Ph.D. dissertation at Hebrew University under the supervision of Robert Wistrich. She has published a number of studies on Austrian Jewish history, including *Jewish Women in Fin de Siècle Vienna* (Austin: University of Texas Press, 2008).

Gerald D. Surh is an associate professor of history at North Carolina State University. He has published *1905 in St. Petersburg: Labor, Society, and Revolution* (Stanford: Stanford University Press, 1989), as well as numerous studies on the military, workers, and antisemitic violence in Tsarist Russia.

Daniel Unowsky is a professor of history at the University of Memphis. He is the author of *The Pomp and Politics of Patriotism: Imperial Celebrations in Habsburg Austria, 1848–1916* (W. Lafayette, Ind.: Purdue University Press, 2005) and coeditor (with Laurence Cole) of *The Limits of Loyalty: Imperial Symbolism, Popular Allegiances, and State Patriotism in the Late Habsburg Monarchy* (New York: Berghahn, 2007). He is currently writing a monograph on the 1898 anti-Jewish riots in Habsburg Galicia.

Marija Vulesica is a research assistant at the Center for Research on Antisemitism at the Technical University of Berlin, where she received her Ph.D. in 2011. Her book *Die Formierung des politischen Antisemitismus in den Kronländern Kroatien-Slawonien, 1879–1906* (Berlin: Metropol, 2012), examines antisemitism in Croatia-Slavonia (then part of the Habsburg Monarchy) in the last decades of the nineteenth century. Her work focuses on the history of antisemitism, the Holocaust, and Jewish history in Southeastern Europe.

Ulrich Wyrwa is a professor of history at the University of Potsdam and head of European Research Groups on Antisemitism (1879–1923) at the Center for Research on Antisemitism at the Technical University of Berlin. He has published and edited a number of books on Jewish history, Jewish historiography, and antisemitism, including, most recently (with Werner Bergmann), *Antisemitismus in Zentraleuropa: Deutschland, Österreich und die Schweiz vom 18. Jahrhundert bis zur Gegenwart* (Darmstadt: Wissenschaftliche Buchgesellschaft, 2011).

INDEX

Carpathian Mountains, 82, 241–42

Catholic Center Party, 36, 56

Catholic holidays and celebrations, 20, 50, 72, 83, 105, 119, 185–86, 201, 208, 214, 256, 271n51. *See also* Corpus Christi; Easter; Feast of the Assumption of Mary; Good Friday

Catholic press, 4, 7, 255; Austria, 159; Croatia, 126, 131; Galicia, 17, 20–21, 23, 29, 32; France, 37–38, 41–42, 44, 47, 57, 59; Hungary, 245–47; Italy, 62–66, 68–75; Lithuania, 208, 209. See also *Il Conciliatore: Foglio religioso; Civiltà cattolica; Corriere della Sera; Głos Narodu; Katolički list; Le Monde; Le Pèlerin; Prawda; Tiszántúl*

cemeteries, 252; Jewish, 26–27, 161, 186

charity, 31, 53, 118, 152, 239, 241, 242, 248

Cherkassy, 223–25

Chernigov, 215–16

Chios, 185–89, 194–95, 315n81

Christian People's Party, 18–20, 23, 30–32

Christian Socialism, 2, 17, 21, 23, 31, 36, 69–70, 101, 106, 111, 131, 134, 155, 158

Civiltà cattolica, 39, 61, 68, 72, 73

Claye, Baron A. de, 41

Comămăşteanu, Ghica, 82–83, 86, 88

Conciliatore: Foglio religioso, Il, 63–64

Congress of Berlin (1878), 68, 80, 92

Constant, Julien, 50–52

Constantinople (Istanbul), 183–87, 194

conversion: of Christians to Islam, 186; of Jews to Christianity, 37, 39, 42, 49, 51, 54, 122, 161, 166, 172, 184, 150

cooperative movement, 18, 25, 209–11, 213, 322n83, 323n91

Corfu, 72, 180, 189–96

Corpus Christi, 20, 271n51

Corriere della Sera, 73

Cossacks, 202, 204, 223, 225, 228, 230

Cracow, 17, 18, 23, 26, 28, 29

Croix, La, 37, 56, 57

crowds, 256–58; Austria, 164–65; Croatia,

115–16, 121–22, 127; Galicia, 20–26, 34; Great Britain, 149–52; Greece, 190; Lithuania, 202–204, 213; Moravia, 97–104; Romania, 83, 88; Russia, 219–35, 325n8

Czas, 29

Damascus, 47, 70, 75, 179

Daszyński, Ignacy, 29

Deckert, Josef, 17

Deliyannis, Theodoros, 190–93

Demčinskiy, Nikolay, 205

demography, 16, 80–81, 107, 117–18, 138, 142, 148, 158–60, 182, 238–40, 265n4, 282n106, 314n62, 330n9

Desportes, Henri, 44–48, 49, 55, 56, 261

Di Fant, Annalisa, 71

district captains, 25–27, 33, 98–99, 105, 157, 162–68, 175–76

divorce: Austria, 161–68, 173, 307n40; France, 38, 45, 48, 50

Dobrovšak, Ljiljana, 116, 131

doctors, 47, 66, 80, 97–98, 160, 239

Dominioni, Carlo Caccia, 64–66

Dreyfus, Alfred, 51, 261

Dreyfus affair, 1–4, 261; Austria, 172, 176; France, 37, 48, 51, 57, 282n104; Galicia, 15, 17, 23; Italy, 69

Drumont, Edouard, 36–56, 73, 259, 261, 276n30

du Lac, Father Stanislas, 38–39

Dubnow, Simon, 199–200, 257

duma, 215, 228, 257, 324n1

Dusetos, 199–214, 257

Easter: and blood libel, 72, 105; and violence, 185–86, 201, 214

Eastern Orthodoxy. *See* Orthodox Christianity

economic modernization, 7, 16, 66–67, 80, 109, 133, 183, 209, 214. *See also* capitalism; industrialization education, 3, 251; and antisemitism, 22, 28–29, 92, 109, 195, 208; and Jews, 81, 118, 183; secular, 41, 50

Ekaterinoslav, 223–32

elections, 5, 57; and antisemitism, 9, 18–19, 25, 29–30, 69, 103–12, 155, 190–93

Elisabeth, Empress, 23

emancipation: of Jews, 3–7, 17, 30, 40–44, 52, 67–68, 96, 105–108, 117, 160, 259; of peasants, 214

etrogs, 193–94, 317n120

Evans-Gordon, Major William, 144–46, 150, 154–55, 302n28, 303n31

exclusionary riots, 94–95, 105, 113, 133, 262

fascism: British, 138, 149, Czech, 114

Feast of the Assumption of Mary, 83, 119

featherbeds, 13, 202, 319n27

First Vatican Council, 65

First World War: and antisemitism, 3, 6, 113–14, 236–54; and housing, 236, 238, 241, 248, 251

Fischer brothers, 86–87

flyers and leaflets, antisemitic, 22, 99, 102, 112, 124–25, 129–30, 154

forestry, 24, 82–86, 92

Franz Joseph, Emperor, 106, 159, 163, 176; and "permission" for antisemitic violence, 22–24

French Revolution, 3, 40, 42, 57

Freud, Sigmund, 157, 175

Freze, Aleksandr, 205

Frysztak, 13, 16, 21, 27, 32–33, 270n31

funerals, 100–105, 160–64, 244

Galanté, Abraham, 179–80, 184

Gaster, Moses, 90–91

Geertz, Clifford, 4, 199, 256

gendarmes, 13–14, 20–27, 97–100, 113, 257, 271n58

gender, 157–59, 169–77

Głos Narodu, 17, 27

Good Friday, 41, 186, 194

Graetz, Heinrich, 90

Gramsci, Antonio, 62

Grätzer, Abraham, 99

Graz, 157, 159, 163–64, 168

Greek Catholics, 16, 19, 240, 242

Greek War of Independence, 80, 183–86, 195–96

Gregorig, Josef, 21

Grünberg, David, 82, 86–87

Guérin, Jules, 37, 47

Hagel, Jakób, 26–27, 271n56

Hager, Rabbi Yisroel, 236–37, 244–53, 331n25

Hasidim, 16, 34, 238, 244–46

Heilbronner, Oded, 3

Hervay, Franz von, 157–59, 162–68, 175–76

Hervay, Leontine von, 157–59, 161–78

Hilsner affair, 105–107, 257

Holešov (Holleschau), 97–105, 106–14

Horkheimer, Max, 61

Hrůzová, Anežka, 105

illiteracy, 21, 28, 29, 118–19, 129

Imeretinskii, Adjutant General Prince, 219–21, 234

immigration, Jewish, 2, 6, 8, 33, 80, 107–109, 117–18, 137–40, 143–46, 148–56, 160, 250, 301n4, 303n31

Independent National Party (Croatia), 119–20, 127

industrialization, 5, 6, 80, 158, 161, 199, 214

inns and innkeepers. *See* taverns

intelligentsia, 128, 199, 211–12, 217

Istóczy, Győző, 124, 299n54

Italian Unification, 63–64, 66

Iwkowa, 21

Jasło, 16, 20, 22–23, 25–27, 32

Jelačić, Josip, 116–17

Jesuits, 17, 38–39, 49, 54